Palgrave Series in African Borderlands Studies

Series Editors
Gregor Dobler (Freiburg University)
William Miles (Northeastern University)
Wolfgang Zeller (University of Edinburgh)

Advisory Board
Anthony I. Asiwaju (African Regional Institute)
David Coplan (University of the Witwatersrand)
Alice Bellagamba (University of Milan-Bicocca)
Pierre Englebert (Pomona College)
Jan-Bart Gewald (University of Leiden)
Amanda Hammar (Copenhagen University)
Thomas Hüsken (University of Bayreuth)
Georg Klute (University of Bayreuth)
Baz Lecocq (Ghent University)
Camille Lefebvre (Panthéon-Sorbonne/CNRS)
Kate Meagher (London School of Economics)
Paul Nugent (University of Edinburgh)
Wafula Okumu (African Union Border Programme)
Timothy Raeymaekers (University of Zürich)
Cristina Udelsmann Rodrigues (University Institute of Lisbon)
Holger Weiss (Åbo Akademi University)
Jerzy Zdanowski (Polish Academy of Sciences)
Werner Zips (University of Vienna)

Published in cooperation with the African Borderlands Research Network and the European Science Foundation

African borderlands are among the continent's most creative and most rapidly changing social spaces, acting as theaters of identity formation and cultural exchange, of violent conflict and regional integration, of economic growth and sudden stagnation, of state building and state failure. Because their unique position at the margins of social and legal spaces offers more flexibility to social actors, borderlands reflect changes on the national level more quickly and more radically than most inland regions. They thus become hot spots of social activity and, on an academic level, ideal places to study social, political and economic change. **The Palgrave Series in African Borderlands Studies** is the first series dedicated to the exploration and theoretical interpretation of African borderlands. It contributes to core debates in a number of disciplines—namely political science, geography, economics, anthropology, history, sociology and law—and provides vital insights for practical politics in border-related issues, ranging from migration and regional integration to conflict resolution and peace-building.

The African Borderlands Research Network (ABORNE) is an interdisciplinary network of researchers interested in all aspects of international borders and transboundary phenomena in Africa. The network held its inaugural meeting in Edinburgh in 2007 and has since grown to over 250 members worldwide. ABORNE's core funding is provided by membership fees and the Research Networking Programme of the European Science Foundation.

EUROPEAN
SCIENCE
FOUNDATION

The European Science Foundation (ESF) was established in 1974 to provide a common platform for its Member Organizations to advance European research collaboration and explore new directions for research. It is an independent organization, owned by 78 Member Organizations, which are research funding and research performing organizations, academies and learned societies from 30 countries. ESF promotes collaboration in research itself, in funding of research and in science policy activities at the European level.

Published by Palgrave Macmillan:

Namibia's Red Line: The History of a Veterinary and Settlement Border (2012)
By Giorgio Miescher

Violence on the Margins: States, Conflict, and Borderlands (2013)
Edited by Benedikt Korf and Timothy Raeymaekers

The Borderlands of South Sudan: Authority and Identity in Contemporary and Historical Perspectives (2013)
Edited by Christopher Vaughan, Mareike Schomerus and Lotje de Vries

Violence on the Margins

States, Conflict, and Borderlands

Edited by Benedikt Korf and Timothy Raeymaekers

VIOLENCE ON THE MARGINS
Copyright © Benedikt Korf and Timothy Raeymaekers, 2013.

All rights reserved.

First published in 2013 by
PALGRAVE MACMILLAN®
in the United States—a division of St. Martin's Press LLC,
175 Fifth Avenue, New York, NY 10010.

Where this book is distributed in the UK, Europe and the rest of the World,
this is by Palgrave Macmillan, a division of Macmillan Publishers Limited,
registered in England, company number 785998, of Houndmills,
Basingstoke, Hampshire RG21 6XS.

Palgrave Macmillan is the global academic imprint of the above
companies and has companies and representatives throughout the world.

Palgrave® and Macmillan® are registered trademarks in the United
States, the United Kingdom, Europe and other countries.

ISBN: 978–1–137–33398–8

Library of Congress Cataloging-in-Publication Data

Violence on the margins : states, conflict, and borderlands / edited by
    Benedikt Korf and Timothy Raeymaekers.
        p.   cm. — (Palgrave series in African borderlands studies)
    ISBN 978–1–137–33398–8 (alk. paper)
        1. Borderlands—Africa, Sub-Saharan.   2. Borderlands—Asia.   3. Political
    violence—Africa, Sub-Saharan.   4. Political violence—Asia.   5. Political
    geography—Africa, Sub-Saharan.   6. Political geography—Asia.   I. Korf,
    Benedikt.   II. Raeymaekers, Timothy.   III. Series: Palgrave series in
    African borderlands studies.
    JC323.V56 2013
    320.12096—dc23   2013008610

A catalogue record of the book is available from the British Library.

Design by Integra Software Services

First edition: August 2013

10 9 8 7 6 5 4 3 2 1

Contents

List of Figures

List of Tables

Acknowledgments

This book came about with the support of a great many people. The themes and ideas of this book were first discussed and shared in an international workshop, "Bringing the Margins Back In: War Making and State Making in the Borderlands", held at the University of Ghent, Belgium, February 12–14, 2012. We would like to thank, first of all, the European Science Foundation for its continuous support, in particular for the African Borderlands Research Network (ABORNE), which has been a driving force behind this project. We would also like to express our gratitude to the Universities of Ghent and Zurich for their additional financial contributions toward this workshop and Jonathan Goodhand and Tobias Hagmann for co-organizing the event. Many thanks also to chief editor of History and African Studies at Palgrave, Chris Chappell, for his belief in this project and his support in getting it smoothly through the reviews. A special thanks to Isabelle Thurnherr for being such a great copy editor, having put enormous time and effort in editing the different chapters. In ABORNE, we would like to thank, first of all, the leading editors of this series, Bill Miles, Gregor Dobler and Wolfgang Zeller, as well as our colleague Paul Nugent for their continuous assistance and encouragement. During these last five years, ABORNE has been a fabulous platform of exchange and debate about the increasingly important domain of comparative border studies within Africa and beyond. We truly appreciated the loyal and collegial atmosphere in which all of this could happen and still is taking place. A warm thanks, therefore, to all ABORNE members with whom we have shared much of the lived material, amazement and hard intellectual labor that were crucial to this endeavor. Finally, many thanks to our colleagues at the Conflict Research Group in Ghent and the Department of Geography in Zurich for helping us to stand at the cradle of this comparative study and to the members of the Political Geography group for stimulating our thoughts about the theoretical framings of border, frontier and geography.

PART I

Introducing a Borderland Perspective

CHAPTER 1

Introduction: Border, Frontier and the Geography of Rule at the Margins of the State

Benedikt Korf and Timothy Raeymaekers

Imagine standing somewhere on the Khyber Pass: a rough mountain route harboring the bustling borderline between Afghanistan and Pakistan's Federally Administered Tribal Areas (FATA). In Karkhana bazaar, which straddles the borderline between Afghanistan and Pakistan's Khyber Agency, tourists and UN agents haggle for cheap alcohol and cannabis resin in the market stalls. Bicycle transporters are carrying boxes of smuggled car parts and electric appliances into Peshawar, meeting their counterparts who are carrying drugs and weapons into the Pakistani FATA. Once in a while a U.S. helicopter hovers overhead, determined to seek and destroy fighting Taliban units, which are constantly crossing the border.[1] Imagine now standing on the border in Goma, the Congolese twin town of Rwandan Gisenyi. On the Petite Barriere ("small checkpoint"), a long line of pedestrians crosses this merged city center, like ants on a sugar hill. Women carrying bags of foodstuffs are joined by smugglers transporting minerals from the Congolese mines of North and South Kivu. Their Rwandan counterparts bring petroleum and cement into Congo, along with construction materials and consumer goods from Mombasa and the Far East. Differences in the taxation laws of the two countries lead to widespread smuggling. Some goods are even unofficially reexported into Rwanda to avoid consumer taxes. The military on both sides watches these operations with a lazy eye, taking bribes and occasionally stopping traffic.[2]

Two borders, two similar dynamics. What unites daily border practices in both places are a number of formal and informal checkpoints, which tentatively divide these expanding borderlands and the actions that define them. For many people in Goma and Peshawar, the border has become a resource rather than an obstacle, providing livelihoods and political status and serving as a sanctuary against mutual incursions. These positive experiences have been reciprocally influenced by decades of outright and proxy warfare, allegations of support for militias and rebel groups and hesitant efforts to reach a political rapprochement. The different meanings these borders historically acquired thus appear related to their different configurations across space, which—as Paolo Novak writes—are determined to a large extent by institutional contingencies, social connectivity and the qualities of territory attached to the borders.[3] This volume makes a first attempt to compare a number of Asian and African conflict formations on the basis of people's own experiences on territorial borders and the way these experiences affect the making and unmaking of political configurations. By focusing on such routines and daily performances, the contributors to this volume depict borderland dynamics not just as outcomes of diffusing statehood or globalization, but also as actual political units that generate their own actions and outcomes. Particular attention is paid to the explicit trans-boundary character of conflict and peace, which is presented from political, geographical, historical and ethnographic perspectives. An alternative is sought to the still dominant idea of contemporary state formation as a centrally guided, top-down process, which has led to a deep misunderstanding of borderlands as marginal spaces that are either fraught with avoidance, savagery and rebellion—or lingering in dark oblivion.

Where Does the State End?

This question, asked by the anthropologist and philosopher Talal Asad, is meant to remind us that the state is never a fixed object. Its boundaries change, as does its internal morphology: the different ways of determining exclusion and inclusion, inside and outside, law and exception.[4] In their volume on the margins of the state, Veena Das and Deborah Poole go a long way in deconstructing the fetishism of this fixed unity of the modern nation-state by identifying the different peripheries in which the state has yet to penetrate. They describe margins as sites where law-making and other state performances are not just evaded, but actively transformed and "colonized" by other more or less organized practices, thus generating important political and economic outcomes that may have a decisive impact on state formation in a broader sense (see also Chapter 8). Rather than focusing on the geography of this encounter, they prefer to metaphorically deconstruct the ways in which this myth of the state as the invisible ghostwriter of our lives is reproduced through a continuous *unsettling* of rights, which makes political life both unintelligible and unpredictable. Through embedding itself in such unsettling movements, for example, in the domain of citizenship rights or policing, crisis becomes a powerful technology of state government, which means that margins often become central to the daily reality of state rule.[5]

In this volume, we concentrate directly on the *site* of state marginality: on the particular spaces in which state practices and images are copresent with other systems of rule, and the dynamics this produces between the people, objects and ideas circulating in such spaces. These are questions of geography: of borders, borderlands and boundaries, but also of periphery, center and frontier. Indeed, the unsettling and often violent renegotiation of rights and social conditions that characterizes the margins of state rule has to be imagined in specific sites: be they the human body, a police barrack, or a town on the border. Asking exactly *where* the state ends *geographically* makes it possible to ask, for example, what happens in places, sites and locations where state forms of organization are slowly penetrating other systems of socio-spatial regulation, are competing with other sovereignties, or are even withdrawing from their sovereign right to rule. It also permits us to visualize the often fragmented geographies of sovereignty that characterize state–society encounters at the physical margins of the state, and which often involve important processes of bordering and boundary-drawing between what is categorically termed as distinctions between state and society, formal and informal or public and private systems of rule.[6]

The Border(land) Perspective

The more intriguing question to ask is probably: *what happens* where the state ends. This brings us to the borderland perspective, which is central to this book. Since the mid-1990s, the borderland perspective has challenged the received wisdom about contemporary state formation as a centrally guided, top-down process.[7] Far from being residual spaces, borders are key sites of contestation and negotiation, which, in many ways, are central to state-making processes. Border zones are not just reflective of power relations at the "center", but they are also *constitutive* of them.[8] Because of their frequent tendency toward transgression—either by ignoring, contesting, or subverting state power—border regions also implicitly and explicitly call into question the legitimacy of states and their pretences to control an illusionary cartography of territory and population, and the legitimate use of violence therein. Border practices and interactions tell us that state territoriality can never be a linear process, but people living in border zones—subaltern subjects like cross-border migrants and petty traders but also state officials and members of security agencies—engender their own conventions and regulations that exist parallel, conjointly and in opposition to sovereign state claims on space.

Fundamental to our understanding of state–society relations in border zones in the global South is the acknowledgment that claims to sovereignty are always tentative in the face of fragmented and unpredictable configurations of power. Given their tendency for transgression, borderland practices have a strong potential to recalibrate such state–society boundaries and the often violent relations underpinning them. Despite the default setting of the international system, which in many ways is to respect and preserve inter-state borders, many of today's conflicts emanate from borderland regions and call into question the legitimacy of these borders. Whether on the northeast Indian or Afghan–Pakistani border, or in the Great Lakes region, the Horn of Africa, or the Ferghana Valley in Central Asia, protracted conflicts have fundamentally challenged political forms associated with the (post)modern nation-state and its project of imposing order and authority on dispersed populations. This book, which emerges from a systematic exchange between several research networks on borders and armed conflict, is a first attempt to bring together evidence from diverse conflict sites in Asia and sub-Saharan Africa where state performance has been generally characterized as "weak", "failed" or "collapsed".[9]

The originality of this volume lies in the depiction of contemporary violent conflict and state formation on the basis of people's own experiences at the border, and the way they affect the making and unmaking of political configurations. This includes both descriptions of routinely lived experiences of people inhabiting borderlands and their multiple identifications, spatial logics and relations developed in interaction with diverse political constellations. Contributors to this volume depict such borderland dynamics not just as outcomes of diffusing statehood or globalization, but also as actual political units that generate their own actions and outcomes. Particular attention is paid to the explicit trans-boundary character of conflict and peace presented from a political, geographical, historical, or ethnographic perspective.

The empirical sites of the various borderlands discussed in this volume have in common that they disprove the idea of the unambiguous, unitary sovereignty that a state exclusively holds over a territory: the "modern assumption of 'hard' boundaries within which 100 percent sovereignty prevails and beyond which it [disappears] altogether".[10] Instead of radiating outward from some putative political center,[11] the sovereign power of the state seems to represent not much more than "a diffuse glow",[12] a distant presence[13] that altogether needs to be asserted and legitimated through everyday performance and interaction with the border inhabitants in place. "If the principal fiction of the nation-state is ethnic, racial, linguistic and cultural homogeneity",

Mathew Horsman and Andrew Marshall write, "then borders always give the lie to this construct".[14] And, yet, James Scott reminds us that borderlands are often spaces of multiple sovereignties—spaces where different power holders struggle over control and allegiance of scattered populations. Hegemony has to be worked out, writes Tania Li,[15] and, indeed, the struggle over political power and allegiance has often allowed (forced) people inhabiting these sites to negotiate different loyalties, allegiances and identities between competing norms and regulations (Chapters 5 and 7). Borderlands can become "spaces of refusal",[16] whereby borderlanders do not necessarily exhibit overt political resistance, but refuse to abide by the geographical framings of the nation-state.

The fact that most sites from sub-Saharan Africa and South and Central Asia that are taken as case studies in the various chapters of this book are all somehow situated in borderlands, sitting on the geographical margins of states, does not mean that we fetishize borders. That would also be a wrong starting point, given that the aim is to deconstruct the institutionalization of political power in places where the boundary between state and society has been contested and is taking an indefinite form. Yet a focus on border zones permits us to simultaneously distinguish them from the metaphorical frontiers of identity, nationalism and state power. Following Hastings Donnan and Thomas M. Wilson, we regard border zones as sites where the state's presence has somehow been limited and its monopoly of violence and political authority is finite, unraveling, or subjected to severe contestation. In the vast, loosely populated lowland planes of the Horn of Africa, for example, discussed in Chapters 2 and 3, state borders may be marked on the map, but they do not necessarily materialize as either the "beginning" or "end" of one state vis-à-vis its national neighbor. Rather, this "end" comes in stages, is a fuzzy zone—a reputed "disorderly" or "unruly" frontier.[17] As a result of this undecided *frontier* zone between one political reality and the other (the definition of which we will return to later), the category "unruly" is often a categorical consequence of the type of state penetration one witnesses in such border zones, rather than an objective empirical truth.

Border Polities

Importantly, therefore, the often violent (re)negotiations of political authority in border spaces often involve struggles over geography. As Wilson and Donnan write in their volume on border identities,[18] the realities of everyday life at the border show scant evidence of the fact that borders principally exist to demarcate political space. This complex geography of border areas, which essentially contributes to their political ambiguity as contested but connected places, stands at the center of this present volume. While border encounters are somehow suffused with power and violent contestation in their immediate heartlands, they also *constitute* political systems in a way: first of all, in the wider border areas or intermediate borderlands,[19] as Wolfgang Zeller writes in Chapter 8 on the Uganda–Congo–Sudan triangle—which he renames "Sugango". Second, border polities may also "radiate" outward toward the state territories that surround them and that make their presence felt through various signs and physical performances.[20] Through a discussion of a range of sites across South and Central Asia as well as Africa, the chapters in this volume indicate the varieties of border encounters, which can range from violent contestation to a complete absorption of state regulations by border polities themselves. This resonates with Oscar Martínez's typology of the differing intensities of cross-border interchange (ranging from nonexistent in what he calls "alienated" borderlands to being in full flow in so-called "integrated" borderlands).[21] Our sites represent only a subsection of this typology, mainly that where a significant cross-border flow exists, while the border retains some (at least rudimentary) functions in regulating and controlling flows of goods and people.

As Michiel Baud and Willem van Schendel[22] already observed, one should be extremely aware of the social and political dimensions, not only of such differentiated border interaction, but also of the contested hegemony implied in these interactions and the institutionalization of power in such border places, which involves an implicit or explicit employment of violent means. A peculiarity of the approach pursued in this volume is therefore its strong focus on violence as a means of regulation. This has several reasons, the most important of which involves the intricate and often innovative connections between development and security in such cross-border regions.[23] The recent conflict literature, for example, has noted a growing complexity of political constellations in borderlands touched by protracted warfare, which are shaped among others by new, and often violent, modes of transnational economic accumulation, displacement and identity construction in these cross-border places.[24]

Analytically, borderland practices can generate differing effects on the part of central state administrations. Frequently, they provoke authoritarian reactions, whereby the visibly contested nature of borderland societies becomes conducive for violent and often "exceptional" forms of government. Such has happened for example in the northeast Indian borderlands, where exceptional measures have given sweeping powers to security forces engaged in counterinsurgency operations against the region's "rebellious" populations (Chapter 7). Borderlands can also become cockpits of political creativity, which somehow force state regimes into important concessions. In Africa's Great Lakes region, for example, where the constant movement of people, goods and practices across borders has involved a gradual reinterpretation of institutions of legality, state and territory, practices at the margins have to some extent transformed the state's "center".[25] This volume gathers in-depth knowledge of the technologies of rule in such border areas and the way they are legitimized by conglomerations of social forces, rather than contests between "states" and "societies": all authors of this volume prefer a microanalysis of such border arrangements as they evolve through time and space, particularly zooming in on the ways these border arrangements have become productive of exceptional measures and political outcomes.

Borders and Frontiers

Another peculiarity of this volume is that it finally tries to reconcile two vocabularies on the margins of the state that have often been used in opposition to each other: those of borderlands and frontiers. The vocabulary of the *borderland* is often characterized by an analytical focus on subversion and transgression: on daily practices of cross-border smuggling, corruption, bootleg and contraband operations and the "business" of the border way of life.[26] Borders are there "where the action is",[27] it is said, because of the pivotal position they fulfill in connecting local and global scales of economic exchange and political interaction. As many of the contributions to this volume suggest, borderlands are by no means the anachronistic backwaters that the state-fed elites in faraway capital cities see in them. Borders are often the "real" centers (see Chapter 3). Daily life at the border makes it clear that "states" and "citizens" somehow continue to depend on and reproduce each other, as the regulations emerging in border spaces often mirror or at least pay allegiance to state frameworks *at both sides* of the territorial boundary. Even in sites where the state's presence at the border is unraveling, regulative frameworks provide a particular space for border dwellers to make use of opportunities that customs regulations (and their "illegal" bypassing), price differentials and supply and demand patterns across the border offer.[28]

Borderlands generate important resources that have a decisive impact on state- and peace-building outside their immediate surroundings.[29] Even as they are situated far away from capital cities, border areas play an essential role in calibrating power relations between the state and its citizens. That is exactly why border territories continue to remain inherently "central" to the dominance of state administrations over their mythical domains of economic redistribution—the flows of peoples, goods and capital—as well as the legitimate means of force over distinct geographic terrains: because they continue to function to a large extent as frontiers of the state's spatial and civilizational project and, consequently, of its "rightful" and sovereign rule over a territorially fixed population.

Notwithstanding these metaphorical proximities, the *frontier* is something different than a border.[30] Frontiers are not necessarily boundaries, but rather political spaces with distinct spatialities of rule and sovereign power. For Africanists, the term "frontier" for a long time has been linked to the seminal work of Igor Kopytoff. His *The African Frontier* (1987) represents a historical account of the processes of pacification and inculturation of precolonial African peripheries. For Kopytoff, the frontier is "above all a political fact, a matter of political definition of geographical space".[31] But the term "frontier" has been used more widely to describe " . . . [a zone] of cultural overlap, characterized by a mixing of cultural styles. They are liminal spaces, simultaneously dangerous and sites of creative cultural production open to cultural play and experimentation as well as domination and control".[32] Often, the frontier becomes "a fault line and [. . .] a contested zone [. . .] a zone of conflict and competition".[33] Frontier dynamics have occurred along state borders, but also along larger civilizational divides, delineating different geographies of settlement patterns, political organization and economic surplus generation—from spatially denser to looser and less intensive modes of production and settlement, for example, along highland–lowland, or sedentary–mobile (pastoralist) divides. From the point of view of political centers, the frontier usually signals the civilizational *carte blanche,* the empty space, the *"herrenloses Land"* (land without a master, literally),[34] which awaits civilization and intrusion from the political center. The frontier is usually the space where territorial and institutional penetration of the modern state has (not yet) been completed. The teleological rationale of modernity, of globalization, sees these spaces as leftovers from a premodern past, destined to become modernized.

The work of territorialization and the frontier dynamics it produces are mostly state supported or state facilitated, although the state often is not directly involved in it as a key actor, but works through proxy (non-state) agents.[35] These can be settlers who claim and appropriate land in a seemingly empty space or traders who control commerce and businesses in the local trade hubs. More outspokenly than borderlands, therefore, frontier zones also represent an openly visible *ideological* project of civilizing the not-yet-civilized or reputedly "barbarian" populations inhabiting such contested regions. Furthermore, frontiers are also distinct geographical spaces where state power is actively *territorialized* through material and symbolic means. James Scott, for example, describes frontiers as "shatter zones", or "zones of refuge" inhabited by "peoples [. . .] who have [. . .] been fleeing the oppressions of state-making projects".[36] These sites do generate a number of challenging effects of polytaxis and institutional mixture.

In the literature so far, "borderland" and "frontier" have rather been used as two separate vocabularies. We suggest that these two vocabularies describe different spatialities and temporalities of struggles over geography that have to be situated in specific empirical sites (table1.1). Because of their joint attention to the "friction of terrain"[37] between the state's civilizing and territorializing projects and people that somehow continue to dwell in the interstices of such state control, both vocabularies have been analytically useful, because they both direct us to specific social, economic and spatial dynamics of rule, authority, appropriation and dispossession. In this volume, we are interested in theorizing the institutionalization of political power in these border areas by describing the intricate dynamics of territorializing and legitimizing rule—"the (re)writing of space and civilization"—in zones situated on the geographical edges of several political systems (see Chapter 2). In such overlapping or interstitial zones, elements of "borderland" and elements of "frontier" dynamics might and will in fact be present in different and sometimes contrasting configurations. The question then is what are the specific configurations and the wider geographies of rule in a specific site.

Although Benedikt Korf, Tobias Hagmann and Martin Doevenspeck (Chapter 2) suggest that frontier dynamics develop diverse spatialities, these different frontiers nevertheless have in common that they are spatially dynamic: frontiers do not denote static zones or spaces, but they move spatially in a certain direction in a teleological sense of territorializing space—what Schmitt calls *Landnahme*. This distinguishes the frontier dynamic from the borderland dynamic: in the latter, the borderline acquires a defining

Table 1.1 The "borderland" and "frontier" perspectives

	"Borderlands"	*"Frontier"*
Spatial metaphor Center–periphery relation	Line (with space surrounding it) "Borderlands are where the action is" = borders as centers, central margins, borders as resources	Zone Civilizational overlapping zones at the margins of the sovereign state
Spaces of . . .	Borderlands as space on both sides of the territorial boundary with different regulative frameworks	Space of encounter and overlap between different geographies of settlement, social organization and economic surplus generation (highland–lowland, core–periphery, etc.)
Territorialization	Border towns as nodes of connections, flows, circulation	Empty space, wilderness, un-civilization ("*herrenloses Land*")
Spatialities at work	Flows, networks; transgression	Territorialization ("*Landnahme*"), settlement, pacification

feature of the spatialities of flows and circulation *across* borders. These flows are bound to the specific spatialities of the borderland vis-à-vis the political center. The civilizational encounter that drives a frontier dynamic is spatially more diffuse than simply a line on the map. The frontier dynamic also emerges from the difference between center and periphery (of metropoles and marginal spaces), while the borderland is characterized by two types of hinterland "behind" the borders that often share similar characteristics in terms of livelihoods and mutually depend on each other. Analytically, the difference between "border" and "frontier" seems to be that (state) borders are clear lines on the map, but separate things that are often not too dissimilar, while a frontier characterizes a diffuse zone of transition from one set of social, political and economic geography to a different set of geography (figure 1.1).

Frontiers are not borders, but frontier logics often appear in borderlands. State borders are often the vanishing points of frontier spaces. In those political spaces where nation-state borders are porous rather than impermeable, where the state sovereignty is experienced as a "distant glow" rather than a permanent presence, borderlands as sites of flows and transgression often assume powers as central margins. Those border spaces only assume these powers to the extent that they are also *frontiers* of the state government and its

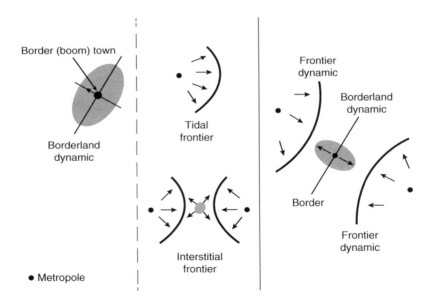

Figure 1.1   Spatialities of frontier and borderland.

sovereign pretences to territory as well as the flows of people, goods and ideas that traverse the borderlines cutting through these spaces: political power in the borderland is constituted to an important extent through its relationship, both practically and ideologically, with the state. In that sense, borders should be analyzed in terms of relational spaces: borders are as per definition part of the global regulative frame of nation-state sovereignty—the vocabulary of state and global actors in their relation to the flow of goods, people and ideas these regimes pretend to capture and control in borderlands. This distinctive character of borders give borderlanders the possibility to appropriate or "bend" these regimes for their specific political or economic projects. In this perspective, borderland dynamics in many of the empirical sites that the chapters in this book compile are sub-geographies *in* the frontier, with the frontier encompassing a larger spatial extent, within which borders emerge and borderland dynamics play out.

All borderland sites discussed in this book implicitly or explicitly contain elements of frontier. For example, Aboubakr Tandia describes the Senegalese government's talk of "retarded" mentality of the forest people in the Casamance (Chapter 9); Zeller writes about the forced corporal discipline and confinement found in the borderlands in northern Uganda (Chapter 8); Korf et al. write about highland versus lowland 'clash of civilizations' in Ethiopia's pastoralist frontiers (Chapter 2); Christine Bichsel describes the politics of land occupation as a strategy to claim territory along a disputed state border (Chapter 6)—and we could enumerate many more examples from the case studies in this book. What is it, then, that makes borderlands "frontiers of state, nation and identity"?[38] From the perspective of the state, both frontiers and borderlands are unruly spaces, and, yet, both enact the state from its peripheral spaces and thereby produce a certain kind of state effect, albeit through non-state and often "illegal" actions. The specific configurations of power in such spaces produce a very specific geography of rule and social order, which are both part of the process of state-making and its continuous transgression.

Chapter Outline: Multiple Sites of Rule and Contestation

The various chapters in this book study geographies of rule, power and authority in different borderland configurations that manifest different frontier dynamics (table 1.1). Similarly to the more generic discussion on sovereignty in the post-colony by Thomas Blom Hansen and Finn Stepputat,[39] the discussion between these chapters should be interpreted as a "fruitful tension" between more Gramscian approaches to the social construction of borderlands and their immediate governmental effects, and more Foucauldian/Agambenesque expressions of sovereignty in the territorial margins of state law (although only few authors in our compilation engage explicitly with these theoretical implications). The book is divided into four sections. In the first section, we put forward a theoretical comparison, which tries to capture the particular spatial logics that turn borderlands in Africa and Asia often into violent frontiers of state and other foundations of rule. These comparisons are given more substance in the following two sections of the book, which concentrate subsequently on the multiple sovereignties that characterize these borderlands and make them become contentious spaces of social and political change. Finally, the last section more explicitly connects these dimensions of multiple sovereignty and spatial friction to armed conflict in borderlands, which is a present theme in the entire book but only there is brought to its theoretical apex. In a final conclusion, Jonathan Goodhand links these different issues again to the ongoing theoretical and policy debates and tries to set out some lines for future research.

What makes a border a "frontier" of political and economic development? In their joint chapter, Korf, Hagmann and Doevenspeck try to formulate an answer to this question by elaborating a proper typology of contemporary frontier zones in Africa. They do so by clarifying, first, that frontier zones are not the empty spaces characterized by violent social disorder as many protagonists of (state) government and territorial expansion tend to depict them. Rather, they are examples of what Carl Schmitt calls *Landnahme:* the "civilizing" mission of expanding sovereign power, which accompanies processes of land appropriation in what by the expanding power is considered as "unowned" territory (*herrenloses Land*), or empty space. This process of *Landnahme* is illustrated in the contemporary land frontiers of north Benin and eastern Ethiopia, which are discussed in the second part of Chapter 2. Both frontiers in fact signal spaces of encounter, of mutual penetration and interference between different settlement patterns, modes of political organization and economic surplus generation—for example, between pastoralist and farmland institutions. Not surprisingly, they are both situated on important social boundaries (respectively of the Yorubaphone/migrant populations of central Benin and of the Oromo/Somali populations of highland/lowland Ethiopia). In different ways, such encounters also accompany the meeting point of clashing ideological projects, through which metropolises and indigenous populations legitimize their claims to political space. These often contrasting territorialities, which also frequently change over time, lead to challenging political dynamics in these frontier zones (Chapter 2).

In the third chapter, Markus Virgil Hoehne and Dereje Feyissa take up the question of political scales and recall that borders have largely been conceptualized as constraints, as spatial barriers. Similarly to Korf et al., their intention is to look into the productive aspect of borders and borderland dynamics. They directly connect to the, now returning, viewpoint that borders indeed have retained their importance as imagined "lines in the sand"[40] as well as concrete barriers that separate lands and peoples. Borders, they suggest, offer multiple resources, economic and political ones, which often reconstitute the state at its margins. In this process, borderlands are securitized and developed. Their double case study from the Ethio-Sudanese and the Somaliland–Puntland borders, which are both situated in the Horn of Africa, give more flesh to this argument and simultaneously offer potential routes toward regional integration in this part of sub-Saharan Africa through either "soft" or "hard" border practices and developments.

In the second section of the book, authors Sylvia Brown as well as Karen Büscher and Gillian Mathys provide further details about the ways borders simultaneously function as resources and problematic sites of mutual penetration. For example, the Karen people, who inhabit the border region between Burma and Thailand, have strategically used the in-betweenness of their contested territory as a critical resource, foremost to exploit the "rough terrain"[41] of the border and recalibrate an unfavorable balance of power. The area occupied by the Karen National Union (KNU), a rebel movement that has been fighting the Burmese government from its stronghold in Thailand for six decades, thus constitutes an important "laboratory of social change" (Chapter 4), locked in a dialectical relationship between the Thai and Burmese governments and the "liberated" Karen people that belong to neither. But whereas their intermediary position on the neuralgia points of the international black market (in rice, gems, textile, teak, cattle and manufactured goods) has generated legitimacy for the KNU in these "liberated zones", its wealth and legitimacy declined drastically from the 1990s onward as a result of changing geopolitical relations in the region. Particularly the development of regional infrastructure—itself a result of improving Thai–Burmese relations—has diminished what Scott calls the "friction of terrain",[42] making it easier for expanding (developmental) states to "pacify" border populations. Somewhat ironically, it also radically inverted the border advantage of the KNU's leadership as a "quasi-state" in favor of a more ethno-nationalist agenda under the name of ethnic kin groups. In that sense, the Karen appear to provide an important counterargument for the perceived "statelessness" of South Asian borderland populations as they combine such immediate ethnic claims with a more long-term agenda of federal democracy.

In a contrasting case study, Büscher and Mathys' chapter zooms in on the seemingly permanent regional standoff in the border region of Rwanda and the Democratic Republic of Congo (DRC). Avoiding a macro-level analysis, they particularly look into the flows of people and goods in a historical "no-man's-land" on the border between these two countries, a territory that is disputed until this day. Similarly to Brown as well as Hoehne and Feyissa, they emphasize the "in-betweenness" of the border, which produces ambivalent opportunities—or resources—for people who are able to somehow employ the border to generate or sustain livelihoods. However, Hoehne and Feyissa mainly emphasize the border as a political resource—thus how it can be mobilized to induce the political center to engage in the periphery, in terms of both security and economic development—whereas Büscher and Mathys mainly emphasize the economic livelihood resources that the border(land) offers. They provide multiple examples of local arbitrage economies,[43] a concept reiterated by Hoehne and Feyissa, which defines economic activities for which the border has become the exact *raison d'être*. The coexistence of different regulatory regimes on either side of the border reportedly generates an opportunity structure, which invites smuggling, unofficial exchange rates and illegal crossings of goods and people. Büscher and Mathys concentrate their attention on what they call the "navigation" of these borderlands by subaltern subjects—national minorities excluded from full citizenship in either state outside the immediate borderland, and petty traders and hustlers who somehow come to the borderland to gain a living. The informal settlement, or "no-man's-land", located in the border space between these two separate countries thus generates a kind of exceptional situation in which people constantly have to shift and renegotiate their identities in "ever-increasing maneuvers of power and submission" (Chapter 5), while at the same time remaining central to the urban economy as well as national claims to territorial sovereignty.

The third section of the book specifically discusses the struggle for space in the borderland with regard to the political *frontier*—the way in which the human territoriality of the border is integrated into legitimized claims on geographical space. In her ethnographic study of development aid in the Central Asian Ferghana Valley (which simultaneously bridges and divides the countries Kyrgyzstan, Tajikistan and Uzbekistan), Bichsel illustrates very succinctly that territorial development is in essence always an ideological project by describing how strategies of peace-building (in this case by the Swiss Agency for Development Cooperation) indirectly reconfigure human territoriality in this disputed border region. By reducing, first, social conflicts in the area to a competition over economic resources, and, second, locating these conflicts primarily at international borders, development agencies interested in peace unwillingly underwrite competing state assertions to such contested territories, which transforms border communities into "frontier" populations. In the absence of other means, Bichsel writes, Kyrgyzstani and Tajikistani state authorities increasingly instrumentalize citizens to "defend" the border on their behalf and make claims to the disputed land. Very similarly to Ethiopia's Somali region (Chapter 2), therefore, the inflicted violence and tensions over this land produce property relations that consolidate state territory as "national" territory. As such, the politics of "actual land use", it is suggested, serves to produce a specific attachment to land by claiming and capturing plots in previously unclaimed spaces.

In his chapter on India's northeastern borderland, Bert Suykens provides more analytical complexity to this exceptional situation of disputed border areas with reference to the Disputed Area Belt (DAB) between Assam and Nagaland. Although this region has a much more different history than the previously discussed Central African case study, the situation in northeast India is actually characterized by a very similar fragile peace, an interim situation that has resulted in the permanent suspension of "normal" law and that produces a very similar political ambivalence. On the one hand, Suykens writes, every border region somehow represents the heart of political allegiance to the nation-state, because it is here where one can effectively claim the "meaning of the nation" (Chapter 7). This centrality of the border enables border dwellers to successfully claim certain "public" goods (like land property) and compel competing authorities into important concessions. On the other hand, though, borderlands are also zones of massive encroachment by these competing regimes, which symbolically transform inhabitants to instruments for claiming territory.

Suykens suggests that the imagination of a historical antagonism between the plains people of Assam and the hill tribes of Nagaland is indeed central to understand the difficulties in negotiating a political solution for the border dispute that characterizes this permanent state of exception in the DAB. In fact, he makes clear how the conscious un-regulation of rights to property and wealth in this "unowned" territory has become part and parcel of an active policy of legalized encroachment, whereby settler communities continuously have to buy protection from competing public authorities. This situation is illustrated quite visibly by the statement of an Assam police officer, who calls the practice of legalizing forest encroachment "an official system of bribes" (Chapter 7). This example, which somehow recalls the patronage relations on the central Benin and Ivorian land frontiers discussed in Chapter 2 and by Paul Richards and Jean-Pierre Chauveau,[44] reminds us of the fact that the endorsement of indeed any right in such disputed territories remains inherent to a fundamental *social* relationship: a social construct that is not carried forward by the law as such but by the successful location of this right in a structure of codes and normative registers that make such rights appear legitimate and sovereign. In the empirical sites discussed in this volume, such rights frequently remain open to permanent negotiation, which is part of the reason why the active denial of populations of their citizenship rights and livelihoods remains central to the contest over sovereign rule.

While armed violence is mostly implicitly present in the first three sections of this book (luring in the background in Sudan, Ethiopia and Somaliland, and more closely present in DRC and northeast India), the fourth section of this book offers the reader a more explicit focus on the relationship between sovereignty and violent conflict across borders. With case studies from Eastern and Western Africa (north Uganda and Casamance), Chapters 8 and 9 provide a detailed political economy of these regional conflicts but add an important geographical dimension. Using an explicitly topographical approach, Zeller connects various nodes in the northern Ugandan border economy by traveling with the reader from the seaport of Mombasa (Kenya), where many of the goods to north Uganda and South Sudan are imported, to the "boomtown" of Bibia, near the Sudanese border. Along the journey, he notices a particular kind of "borderland governance", which has established itself as a result of "being on the edge of state territory and the verge of warfare". The "get it while you can" mentality that characterizes this border town "reeking of dust, diesel and beer" appears to be maintained by a rather exceptional situation that connects the border to Uganda's war economy, and substantially informs the political implication of state representatives in this contested border space.

Zeller adds another important aspect to his analysis when he writes that the *expectation* of border dwellers to operate under exceptional conditions has produced several levels of "borderland governance": in unstable border areas like northern Uganda, the direct outsourcing of political authority to non-state actors (like vigilante groups or private businesses) might in fact provide a "local" solution to a "global" problem, as these forces become essential to the functioning of contested states.[45] While such political reconfigurations are by no means only peaceful, the ambivalence of (returning) state presence through top-down reconstruction and technological development can become quite harmful because it might choke off conditions that provide an impetus to such informal equilibria.

Writing from Senegal, Tandia takes a similar starting point as Zeller by questioning the extent to which the Casamance borderland has become the backyard of a particular kind of "wariness": a complex intermingling of armed actors with local borderland politics through the margins of the cross-border economy in cash crops, cattle and drugs (marijuana and cocaine), which in many ways sustains the "civil" war—in the sense that actors not living in this border area continue to instrumentalize and exploit its political, social and territorial marginalization for geopolitical and economic purposes. In this context of conscious un-regulation, the continued marginality and uprooting of local borderland people has become at once an instrument of extraversion, as Jean-François Bayart, Stephen Ellis and Béatrice Hibou put it,[46] but even more so a structural condition, which continues to reproduce local "surplus populations"[47] that keep this economy going. Tandia's case also exhibits borderlands as "trans-local scales of multilevel and multi-actor spaces", where a kind of "transnationalism from below" has emerged in the domain of border vigilante movements: conflict management is a pattern of transnational politics involving balances as well as asymmetries in relationships, which can be collaborative as well as confrontational.

Coda

In this volume, we have looked into borderland sites in Africa as well as South and Central Asia, albeit not in a strictly comparative way. Already Baud and van Schendel[48] have expressed doubts about the possibility of comparing borderlands along their temporal (and thus teleological) evolution or their spatial distinctiveness according to world regions, normally labeled as "Africa", "Asia" or "Europe". In this volume, we therefore refrain from a strictly comparative analytical frame, but rather look at the various forms of spatial b/ordering that takes place in different sites. Our cases indicate that similar, but also diverse and shifting geographies of rule involving border(ing) and frontier dynamics can be found in these various sites and that it is not possible to detect specific dynamics in African versus Asian types of borderlands. A key factor in defining the complex geographies of rule that we find at different borderlands seems to be the extent to which the state has accomplished the task of territorializing the margins, namely that it is about the spatial outreach of the state and the resultant geographies of sovereignty. These relational geographies between metropolises and margins define space for transgression or subversion, but also dynamics of territorialization or spaces of flows.

Grosso modo, the analyses in this book support the following three propositions: *first*, the cultural study of borderland communities teaches us that political borders and social boundaries often do not correspond.[49] In order to claim sovereignty, an important challenge for political actors in border areas is not only to make these two matching, but also to make this overlap appear legitimate—acceptable to its inhabitants and the broader societies of which they allegedly form part. Following Robert Latham, we might distinguish here between borderland authority and what he calls "social sovereignty" over border subjects: whereas authority can be defined as the ability to place action and practices into a meaningful social frame or context, sovereignty is rather a feature of structures—it involves the broader *body* of codes and rules that are the locus of preeminent power in this social field.[50] An important feature of borderland polities and their multiple coexisting sovereignties in fact is that they do not necessarily entail the formation of an integrated social order or hegemony—to use Gramsci's terms—over a configuration of people and places. On the contrary, the domain of social sovereignty can actually be quite narrow, as the case of Sugango demonstrates (Chapter 8). In line with Hansen and Stepputat, however, we contend that it is important to understand how such *de facto* configurations of sovereignty develop also through a formal language of law, which since the mid-twentieth century has become the dominant horizon for political authority and imagination across the developing world.[51] In fact, many authors actively refer to this language to indicate how claims to sovereign power in the world's borderlands are always intimately connected to the declaration of an unruly outside or downside of society: of "bandits", "criminals", "smugglers", "youth gangs", "drug lords", "warlords", "mafiosi", "traitors" and "terrorists"—*en fin* of outlaws and liminal figures" that cannot be understood without reference to their specific relations to states and hegemonic discourses of social order.[52]

Our *second* proposition is that this permanent copresence of multiple bodies of regulations in the borderlands epistemologically gives the border a central place in the configuration of political order: in fact they have to be seen as shadows of the dominant sovereign power. In part to deconstruct this hegemonic image of the indivisible sovereign state, and in part also to give flesh to the everyday realities of rule in postcolonial societies, it has become more and more useful to describe what Smart calls the "continuum of persistence" between legality and illegality, which can range from ignored coexistence to open challenges of state sovereignty.[53] While effectively challenging the state's monopoly of violence, the multiple organizations, constellations and political networks that convey power in the borderlands are engaging in sovereign practices themselves. Therefore, to understand this association between the multiple sovereignties and the consolidation of political order in the borderlands, one needs to look at the ways this association is constituted in everyday practice—at the "methods of organization, spatial arrangement and formal representation"[54] of actions attempting to organize life in such contested and instable areas—which make these places into state frontiers.

Finally, it is important to remember that this method of writing space in the borderland is never complete, but continues to involve important struggles over geography, authority and political legitimacy. Rather than a physical given, it is our contention that the diverging levels of penetrability of the border spaces discussed in this volume (which range from impenetrable fortresses to porous web-like spaces) should be interpreted as the temporary *effects*, the historical outcome of patterns of circulation, diffusion and interdependence

that connect border areas not only to state governments, but also to other nodes of political power from the local to the global level. Lying at the edges of various forms of public authority, borders potentially form gates or bridges, rupture or connection points that make them either "divisive" or "permeable" (Chapter 3), depending on the particular constellations of identity, power and economic accumulation that characterize their wider political geographies. To this end, it becomes necessary to merge analytically two kinds of vocabularies, which place these border constellations in a wider geographic context of contentions over sovereign rule: border and frontier.

Notes

1. P. Novak, "The flexible territoriality of borders," *Geopolitics* 16, no. 4 (2011): 754.
2. M. Doevenspeck, "Constructing the border from below: Narratives from the Congolese–Rwandan state boundary," *Political Geography* 30, no. 3 (2011): 133.
3. P. Novak, "The flexible territoriality of borders," *Geopolitics* 16, no. 4 (2011): 755.
4. T. Asad, "Where are the margins of the state?" in *Anthropology in the margins of the state,* ed. V. Das and D. Poole (Santa Fe, NM: School of American Research Press, 2004), 279–288.
5. A. Horstmann and R. K. Wadley, *Centering the margin: Agency and narrative in Southeast Asian borderlands* (Oxford: Berghahn, 2006); T. Raeymaekers, "The silent encroachment of the frontier: A politics of transborder trade in the Semliki Valley (Congo–Uganda)," *Political Geography* 28 (2009): 55–65.
6. T. Mitchell, "Society, economy and the state effect," in *The anthropology of the state: A reader,* ed. A. Sharma and A. Gupta (Oxford: Blackwell, 2006); H. van Houtum and T. van Naerssen, "Bordering, ordering and othering," *Tijdschrift voor Economische en Sociale Geografie* 93 (2001): 125–136.
7. D. Newman and A. Paasi, "Fences and neighbours in the post modern world: Boundary narratives in political geography," *Progress in Human Geography* 22, no. 2 (1998): 186–207; H. Donnan and T. M. Wilson, *Borders: Frontiers of identity, nation and state* (Oxford & New York: Berg, 1999); D. Newman, "The lines that continue to separate us: Borders in our 'borderless' world," *Progress in Human Geography* 22, no. 2 (2006): 186–207; V. Pavlakovich-Kochi, B. Morehouse and D. Wastl-Walter, *Challenged borderlands: Transcending political and cultural boundaries* (Aldershot: Ashgate, 2004); V. Kolossov, "Border studies: Changing perspectives and theoretical approaches," *Geopolitics* 10, no. 4 (2005): 606–632; H. Donnan and T. M. Wilson, *A companion to border studies* (Malden, MA: Wiley, 2012).
8. M. Baud and W. Van Schendel, "Toward a comparative history of borderlands," *Journal of World History* 8, no. 2 (1997): 211–242.
9. The initiative for this volume emerged from a joint workshop of the ESF-funded African Borderlands Research Network (ABORNE), the Asia

JAMES EARL CARTER LIBRARY
GA. SOUTHWESTERN UNIVERSITY
AMERICUS GA 31709

Border Research Network (ABRN), the Conflict Research Group at the University of Ghent and the political geography unit based at the University of Zurich. The aim of this workshop was to take stock of existing knowledge of regional conflict analysis from a border perspective based on critical and longitudinal fieldwork in sub-Saharan Africa and South Asia. We thank both universities as well as ESF-ABORNE for kindly supporting this initiative.

10. J. Scott, *The art of not being governed: An anarchist history of upland Southeast Asia* (New Haven, CT: Yale University Press, 2009), 59.

11. M. Mann, "The autonomous power of the state: Its origins, mechanisms and the results," *European Journal of Sociology* XXV, 1984: 185–213 (reproduced in Brenner et al. *State/space. A reader*, Malden, MA: Blackwell, 2003).

12. J. Scott, *The Art of not being governed: An anarchist history of upland Southeast Asia* (New Haven, CT: Yale University Press, 2009), 59.

13. N. Rose, *The powers of freedom. Reframing political thought* (Cambridge: Cambridge University Press, 1990).

14. M. Horsman and A. Marshall, *After the nation-state: citizens, tribalism and the new world disorder* (London: HarperCollins, 1994), 45.

15. T. M. Li, *The will to improve: Governmentality, development and the practice of politics* (Durham, NC: Duke University Press, 2007).

16. R. Jones, "Spaces of Refusal: Rethinking sovereign power and resistance at the border," *Annals of the Association of American Geographers* 102, no. 3 (2012) 685–699.

17. M. Baud and W. Van Schendel, "Toward a comparative history of borderlands," *Journal of World History* 8, no. 2 (1997): 227–228.

18. T. M. Wilson and H. Donnan, *Border identities. Nation and state at international frontiers* (Cambridge: Cambridge University Press, 1998).

19. M. Baud and W. Van Schendel, "Toward a comparative history of borderlands," *Journal of World History* 8, no. 2 (1997): 221–222.

20. T. Callaghy, R. Kassimir and R. Latham, *Intervention and transnationalism in Africa. global–local networks of power* (Cambridge: Cambridge University Press, 2001).

21. O. Martínez, *Border people: Life and society in the U.S.–Mexico borderlands* (Tucson, AZ: University of Arizona Press, 1994), 5–10.

22. M. Baud and W. Van Schendel, "Toward a comparative history of borderlands," *Journal of World History* 8, no. 2 (1997): 220.

23. M. Duffield, "War as network enterprise. The new security terrain and its implications," *Cultural Values* 6, no. 1-2 (2002) 153–165; Janet Roitman, *Fiscal disobedience. An anthropology of economic regulation in Central Africa* (Princeton, NJ: Princeton University Press, 2005).

24. M. Pugh, N. Cooper and J. Goodhand, *War economies in a regional context: Challenges of transformation* (Boulder: Lynne Rienner, 2004); J. Goodhand, "Frontiers and wars: The opium economy in Afghanistan," *Journal of Agrarian Change* 5, no. 2 (2005): 191–216; S. Jackson, "Borderlands and the transformation of war economies: Lessons from the DR Congo," *Conflict, Security and Development*

JAMES EARL CARTER LIBRARY
GA. SOUTHWESTERN UNIVERSITY
AMERICAS, GA.

6, no. 3 (2006) 425–447; T. Raeymaekers, "Protection for sale? War and the transformation of regulation on the Congo - Ugandan border," *Development and Change* 44, no. 4 (2010): 563–587.

25. S. Jackson, "Borderlands and the transformation of war economies: Lessons from the DR Congo," *Conflict, Security and Development* 6, no. 3 (2006): 425–447; T. Raeymaekers, "The silent encroachment of the frontier: A politics of transborder trade in the Semliki Valley (Congo–Uganda)," *Political Geography* 28 (2009): 55–65.

26. D. B. Coplan, "A river runs through it: The meaning of the Lesotho-free state border," *African Affairs* 100, no. 398 (2001): 90; see also Chapter 3.

27. S. Jackson, "Borderlands and the transformation of war economies: Lessons from the DR Congo," *Conflict, Security and Development* 6, no. 3 (2006): 426.

28. K. Meagher, "A back door to globalisation? Structural adjustment, globalisation & transborder trade in West Africa," *Review of African Political Economy*, no. 95 (2003): 57–75.

29. M. Pugh and N. Cooper, *Whose peace? Critical perspectives on the political economy of peacebuilding* (Basingstoke: Palgrave Macmillan, 2008); see also Chapter 3.

30. D. Gerhard, "The frontier in comparative view," *Comparative Studies in Society and History* 1, no. 2 (1959): 205–229; J. Anderson and L. O'Dowd, "Border, border regions and territoriality: Contradictory meanings, changing significance," *Regional Studies* 33, no. 7 (1999): 593–604; D. Newman and A. Paasi, "Fences and neighbours in the post modern world: Boundary narratives in political geography," *Progress in Human Geography* 22, no. 2 (1998): 186–207.

31. I. Kopytoff, "The internal African frontier—The making of African political culture," in *The African frontier—The reproduction of traditional African societies*, ed. I. Kopytoff (Bloomington, IN: Indiana University Press, 1987), 11.

32. H. Donnan, "Anthropology of borders," in *International encyclopedia of the social & behavioral sciences*, ed. Neil J. Smelser and Paul B. Baltes (Amsterdam: Elsevier, 2001), 1290.

33. R. J. Reid, *Frontiers of violence in north-east Africa* (Oxford: Oxford University Press, 2011).

34. C. Schmitt, *Der Nomos der Erde im Völkerrecht des Jus Publicum Europaeum* (Berlin: Duncker & Humblot 1997 [1950]); see also B. Korf and C. Schetter, "Räume des Ausnahmezustands. Carl Schmitts Raumphilosophie, Frontiers und Ungoverned Territories," *Peripherie* 126–127, 147–170. 2012 (in print); Chapter 2.

35. D. Geiger, *Frontier encounters—Indigenous communities and settlers in Asia and Latin America* (Copenhagen: International Work Group for Indigenous Affairs, 2008).

36. J. Scott, *The art of not being governed: An anarchist history of upland Southeast Asia* (New Haven, CT: Yale University Press, 2009), 7.

37. J. Scott, *The art of not being governed: An anarchist history of upland Southeast Asia* (New Haven, CT: Yale University Press, 2009), xi.

38. T. M. Wilson and Hastings Donnan, *Border identities. Nation and state at international frontiers* (Cambridge: Cambridge University Press, 1998).

39. T. B. Hansen and F. Stepputat, "Introduction: States of imagination," in *States of imagination: Ethnographic explorations of the postcolonial state*, ed. Thomas B. Hansen and Finn Stepputat (Durham, NC: Duke University Press, 2001), 1–40.

40. J. Williams, *The ethics of territorial borders: Drawing lines in the shifting sand* (Basingstoke: Palgrave Macmillan, 2006).

41. J. Fearon and D. Laitin, "Ethnicity, insurgency, and civil war," *American Political Science Review* 97, no. 1 (2003), 75–90.

42. Scott, J. The art of not being governed. An anarchist history of upland Southeast Asia. New Haven, CT: Yale University Press, 2009, p. 40.

43. J. Anderson and L. O'Dowd, "Border, border regions and territoriality: Contradictory meanings, changing significance," *Regional Studies* 33, no. 7 (1999): 597.

44. P. Richards and J.-P. Chauveau, "Land, agricultural change and conflict in West Africa: Regional issues from Sierra Leone, Liberia and Cote d'Ivoire," *CSAO/SWAC*, Issy-les-Moulineaux, 2007.

45. K. Titeca, "The 'Masai' and 'miraa': Public authority, vigilance and criminality in a Ugandan border town," *Journal of Modern African Studies* 47, no. 2 (2009): 291–317; B. Chalfin, *Neoliberal frontiers. An ethnography of sovereignty in West Africa* (Chicago, IL: The University of Chicago Press, 2010).

46. J.-F. Bayart, Stephen Ellis and Béatrice Hibou, *The criminalization of the state in Africa* (Oxford: James Currey, 1999).

47. J. Scott, *The art of not being governed: An anarchist history of upland Southeast Asia* (New Haven, CT: Yale University Press, 2009), 9.

48. M. Baud and W. Van Schendel, "Toward a comparative history of borderlands," *Journal of World History* 8, no. 2 (1997): 236ff.

49. F. Barth, *Group and boundaries* (London: Allen and Unwin, 1969).

50. R. Latham, "Social sovereignty," *Theory, Culture and Society* 17, no. 4 (2000): 3.

51. T. B. Hansen and F. Stepputat, "Introduction: States of imagination," in *States of imagination: Ethnographic explorations of the postcolonial state*, ed. T. B. Hansen and F. Stepputat (Durham, NC: Duke University Press, 2001), 301.

52. T. B. Hansen and F. Stepputat, "Introduction: States of imagination," in *States of imagination: Ethnographic explorations of the postcolonial state*, ed. T. B. Hansen and F. Stepputat (Durham, NC: Duke University Press, 2001), 305.

53. A. Smart, "Predatory rule and illegal economic practices," in *States and illegal practices*, ed. J. Heyman (Oxford: Berg, 1999), 99–128.

54. T. Mitchell, "Society, economy and the state effect," in *The anthropology of the state: A reader*, ed. A. Sharma and A. Gupta (Oxford: Blackwell, 2006), 70.

References

Anderson, J. and L. O'Dowd. "Border, border regions and territoriality: Contradictory meanings, changing significance." *Regional Studies* 33, no. 7 (1999): 593–604.

Asad, T. "Where are the margins of the state?" In *Anthropology in the margins of the state*, edited by V. Das and D. Poole. Santa Fe, NM: School of American Research Press, 2004: 279–288.

Barth, F. *Ethnic group and boundaries*. London: Allen and Unwin, 1969.

Baud, M. and W. Van Schendel. "Toward a comparative history of borderlands." *Journal of World History* 8, no. 2 (1997): 211–242.

Bayart, J.-F., S. Ellis and B. Hibou. *The criminalization of the state in Africa*. Oxford and Bloomington, IN: James Currey and Indiana University Press, 1999.

Callaghy, T., R. Kassimir and R. Latham. *Intervention and transnationalism in Africa. Global–local networks of power*. Cambridge: Cambridge University Press, 2001.

Chalfin, B. *Neoliberal frontiers. An ethnography of sovereignty in West Africa*. Chicago, IL: The University of Chicago Press, 2010.

Coplan, D. B. "A river runs through it: The meaning of the Lesotho-free state border." *African Affairs* 100, no. 398 (2001): 81–116.

Das, V. and D. Poole, eds. *Anthropology in the margins of the state*. Santa Fe, NM: School of American Research Press, 2004.

Doevenspeck, M. "Constructing the border from below: Narratives from the Congolese–Rwandan state boundary." *Political Geography* 30, no. 3 (2011): 129–142.

Donnan, H. "Anthropology of borders." *International encyclopedia of the social & behavioral sciences*, edited by N. J. Smelser and P. Baltes. Amsterdam: Elsevier, 2001.

Donnan, H. and T. M. Wilson. *Borders: Frontiers of identity, nation and state*. Oxford: Berg, 1999.

Donnan, H. and T. M. Wilson. *A companion to border studies*. Malden, MA: Wiley, 2012.

Duffield, M. "War as network enterprise. The new security terrain and its implications." *Cultural Values* 6, no. 1-2 (2002): 153–165.

Fearon, J. and D. Laitin. "Ethnicity, insurgency, and civil war." *American Political Science Review* 97, no. 1 (2003): 75–90.

Geiger, D. *Frontier encounters—Indigenous communities and settlers in Asia and Latin America*. Copenhagen: International Work Group for Indigenous Affairs, 2008.

Gerhard, D. "The frontier in comparative view." *Comparative Studies in Society and History* 1, no. 2 (1959): 205–229.

Goodhand, J. "Frontiers and wars: The opium economy in Afghanistan." *Journal of Agrarian Change* 5, no. 2 (2005): 191–216.

Hansen, T. B. and F. Stepputat, eds. "Introduction: States of imagination." In *States of imagination: Ethnographic explorations of the postcolonial state*, Durham, NC: Duke University Press, 2001: 1–40.

Horsman, M. and A. Marshall. *After the nation-state: Citizens, tribalism and the new world disorder*. London: HarperCollins, 1994.

Horstmann, A. and R. K. Wadley. *Centering the margin: Agency and narrative in Southeast Asian borderlands*. Oxford: Berghahn, 2006.

Jackson, S. "Borderlands and the transformation of war economies: Lessons from the DR Congo." *Conflict, Security and Development* 6, no. 3 (2006): 425–447.

Jones, R. "Spaces of refusal: Rethinking sovereign power and resistance at the border." *Annals of the Association of American Geographers* 102, no. 3 (2012): 685–699.

Kolossov, V. "Border studies: Changing perspectives and theoretical approaches." *Geopolitics* 10, no. 4 (2005): 606–632.

Kopytoff, I., ed. "The internal African frontier—The making of African political culture." In *The African frontier—The reproduction of traditional African societies,* Bloomington, IN: Indiana University Press, 1987: 3–84.

Korf, B. and C. Schetter. "Räume des Ausnahmezustands. Carl Schmitts Raumphilosophie, Frontiers und Ungoverned Territories." *Peripherie* 126–127, 147–170. 2012 (in print).

Latham, R. "Social sovereignty." *Theory, culture and society* 17, no. 4 (2000): 1–18.

Li, T. M. *The will to improve: Governmentality, development and the practice of politics.* Durham, NC: Duke University Press, 2007.

Mann, M. "The autonomous power of the state: Its origins, mechanisms and the results." *European Journal of Sociology* XXV (1984): 185–213 (reproduced in Brenner et al. *State/space. A reader.* Malden, MA: Blackwell, 2003).

Martínez, O. *Border people: Life and society in the U.S.–Mexico borderlands.* Tucson, AZ: University of Arizona Press, 1994.

Meagher, K. "A back door to globalisation? Structural adjustment, globalisation and transborder trade in West Africa." *Review of African Political Economy,* no. 95 (2003): 57–75.

Mitchell, T. "Society, economy and the state effect." In *The anthropology of the state: A reader,* edited by A. Sharma and A. Gupta. Oxford, Malden, MA; and Carlton: Blackwell, 2006: 169–186.

Newman, D. "The lines that continue to separate us: Borders in our 'borderless' world." *Progress in Human Geography* 22, no. 2 (2006): 186–207.

Newman, D. and A. Paasi. "Fences and neighbours in the post modern world: Boundary narratives in political geography." *Progress in Human Geography* 22, no. 2 (1998): 186–207.

Novak, P. "The flexible territoriality of borders." *Geopolitics* 16, no. 4 (2011): 741–767.

Pavlakovich-Kochi, V., B. Morehouse and D. Wastl-Walter. *Challenged borderlands: Transcending political and cultural boundaries.* Aldershot: Ashgate, 2004.

Pugh, M., N. Cooper and J. Goodhand. *War economies in a regional context: Challenges of transformation.* Boulder, CO: Lynne Rienner, 2004.

Pugh, M. and N. Cooper: *Whose peace? Critical perspectives on the political economy of peacebuilding.* Basingstoke: Palgrave Macmillan, 2008.

Raeymaekers, T. "The silent encroachment of the frontier: A politics of transborder trade in the Semliki Valley (Congo–Uganda)." *Political Geography* 28, 2009: 55–65.

Raeymaekers, T. "Protection for sale? War and the transformation of regulation on the Congo–Ugandan border." *Development and Change* 44, no. 4 (2010): 563–587.

Reid, R. J. *Frontiers of violence in north-east Africa.* Oxford: Oxford University Press, 2011.

Richards, P. and J.-P. Chauveau. "Land, agricultural change and conflict in West Africa: Regional issues from Sierra Leone, Liberia and Cote d'Ivoire." *CSAO/SWAC*, Issy-les-Moulineaux, 2007.

Roitman, J. *Fiscal disobedience. An anthropology of economic regulation in Central Africa.* Princeton, NJ: Princeton University Press, 2005.

Rose, N. *The powers of freedom. Reframing political thought.* Cambridge: Cambridge University Press, 1990.

Schmitt, C. *Der Nomos der Erde im Völkerrecht des Jus Publicum Europaeum.* Berlin: Duncker & Humblot, 1997 [1950].

Scott, J. *The art of not being governed: An anarchist history of upland Southeast Asia.* New Haven, CT: Yale University Press, 2009.

Smart, A. "Predatory rule and illegal economic practices." In *States and illegal practices*, edited by Josiah Heyman. Oxford: Berg, 1999: 99–128.

Titeca, K. "The 'Masai' and 'Miraa': Public authority, vigilance and criminality in a Ugandan border town." *Journal of Modern African Studies* 47, no. 2 (2009): 291–317.

Van Houtum, H. and T. van Naerssen. "Bordering, ordering and othering." *Tijdschrift voor Economische en Sociale Geografie* 93 (2002): 125–136.

Williams, J. *The ethics of territorial borders: Drawing lines in the shifting sand.* Basingstoke: Palgrave Macmillan, 2006.

Wilson, T. M. and H. Donnan. *Border identities. Nation and state at international frontiers.* Cambridge: Cambridge University Press, 1998.

CHAPTER 2

Geographies of Violence and Sovereignty: The African Frontier Revisited

Benedikt Korf, Tobias Hagmann
and Martin Doevenspeck

Kopytoff Revisited

In his classic *The African Frontier*,[1] Igor Kopytoff provided a powerful explanation of the processes of pacification and inculturation of precolonial African peripheries. For Kopytoff, the frontier was "an area over which political control by the regional metropoles is absent or uncertain".[2] Kopytoff's understanding of frontier is essentially one of a politically constructed space: "The frontier is above all a political fact, a matter of political definition of geographical space".[3] His work is primarily motivated by this distinctive understanding of peripheral African spaces and places. In this chapter, we draw attention to the analytics that can be garnered from Kopytoff's work on the frontier, which allows understanding contemporary political dynamics in some parts of the African continent. We are primarily interested in a discussion of the logic or rationale of governing that shapes present-day African frontiers. In other words, we propose using Kopytoff's heuristics of the African frontier, but apply them in empirical contexts different to those where Kopytoff did in his original work: *postcolonial*, not precolonial, Africa is our empirical site. In order to achieve this, we first develop a typology of the political frontier and illustrate it with two case studies from eastern Ethiopia and northern Benin.

In *The Frontier in Comparative View*, Dietrich Gerhard articulates the point that the frontier "is something entirely different from a border between states, or even from a border region between organized civilizations".[4] Frontiers are not boundaries or borderlands *per se*, but the frontier logic often appears in borderlands. Surprisingly, Kopytoff's frontier concept has not drawn much attention in the study of contemporary African peripheries and borderlands. In their review of the literature, Wendl and Rösler[5] come to the conclusion that debates on peripheries have shifted from the study of frontiers to the study of borders and borderlands. Border studies have mostly been concerned with the flow of goods and people, cross-border transactions and cooperation as well as more ethnographic, people-centered approaches that emphasize the social construction and reproduction of borders through daily practices and imaginations.[6] Often considered an obstacle to Africa's economic, political and social ambitions, a recent collection of articles has underlined how borders serve divided ethnic communities as economic, political, identity, status and rights resources,[7] thereby emphasizing the productive aspect of borders, borderlands and border peoples. Hence, a border is not so much a line that divides, but a dynamic relation and social practice.

The erection of territorial borders has often been a measure by the metropolitan core to map out sovereign power at the frontier. But what kind of order emerges at the border? Is the border the end of one and the beginning of another political order? Joel Migdal, for example, writes that boundaries "signify the point at which something becomes something else, at which the way things are done changes".[8] Or does the border as a space develop its own order? At the same time, "border" can have several meanings, referring to not only the territorial state border, but also a social boundary, for example, between different "civilizations" or ethnic groups.[9] Boundaries entail a spatial and a relational component; they include symbolic and social dimensions that are marked in maps, but may also signify other dividing lines, which cannot be found on maps. Border, then, is not so much a line, but signifies a relation—a relation between core and periphery, which is marked by a distinct logic of rule.

Frontiers also signify a geographical imagination of a boundary dividing civilization from the "not yet" civilized (unoccupied, "empty") territory. This geographical imagination has material effects: Frontiers are mostly located at the peripheries of modern states and they are characterized by violent patterns of social and political (dis)order, or a fractured geography of violence and multiple sovereignties. Although imagined as an empty space, the frontier is *not* an "ungoverned" space; it is *not* a space of disorderly violence and social anomy. Rather, the frontier is a project of what Carl Schmitt refers to as land appropriation or *Landnahme*. The geographical imagination of empty space is crucial for this state project: "*Der landnehmende Staat kann das genommene koloniale Land hinsichtlich des Privateigentums...als herrenlos behandeln*",writes Schmitt in *Nomos* ("The land-appropriating state can treat the acquired colonial land with regard to private property rights as unowned," our translation from German original).[10] Similar to the frontier logic, Schmitt's argument is based on a theory of civilizations: More civilized groups gain the right to appropriate land in territories occupied by less civilized societies, which are made objects of becoming more organized by more civilized peoples. In other words, *Landnahme* is part and parcel of a civilizing mission, and the frontier is the space where it is accomplished through land appropriation. This civilizing mission is accompanied by struggle, resistance, subordination and oppression. At the same time, the frontier molds a zone of encounter,[11] of mutual penetration and interference:[12] a territorial space with specific characteristics of order, and a specific geography of sovereign power and rule.

Pierre-Yves Le Meur[13] coined the term "political frontier", which we use in this chapter to understand different *longue durée* processes of land appropriation in contemporary African peripheries and the encounters these produce. Our conceptualization of the political frontier goes beyond Kopytoff's original model, which emphasizes processes of ethnogenesis, by revisiting his reading and remolding of Frederick Jackson Turner's[14] original frontier thesis. Two types of political frontiers and associated spatial dynamics and social, economic and political rationales can thus be distinguished: Kopytoff's interstitial frontier and Turner's tidal frontier. Here, our use of the frontier concept differs from Chalfin, Brenda remarkable work on neoliberal frontiers in West Africa.[15] Chalfin takes the state border as a place where global neoliberalism flourishes, where the frontier of global neoliberalism sets in. Her concept of border and borderland is different from the frontier concept, which we discuss, following Turner and Kopytoff, in this chapter. In the following sections, we elaborate our concept of "political frontier" by distinguishing two ideal types with specific geographies of violence and sovereignty and apply them as a heuristic framework in an empirical analysis of two contemporary frontiers in Ethiopia and Benin.

The Frontier as Rationale of Rule

Historically, frontiers have emerged in different settings, times and places. The historian Alfred J. Rieber distinguishes three basic types of frontiers: consolidated state frontiers as observed in Western Europe's transition from feudalism to centralized monarchies; dynamic frontiers of advancing settlements such as the American, British, Imperial Russian and Chinese frontiers; and symbolic frontiers corresponding to popular imaginings of the geographic confines of different civilizations, cultures and religions.[16]

Hastings Donnan defines "frontier" as a " ... [zone] of cultural overlap, characterized by a mixing of cultural styles. They [frontiers] are liminal spaces, simultaneously dangerous and sites of creative cultural production open to cultural play and experimentation as well as domination and control".[17] But most often, the frontier is "a fault line and ... a contested zone ... a zone of conflict and competition".[18] Often, but not always, frontiers emerge along state borders or larger civilizational divides, for example, between sedentary farmlands and pastoralist rangeland livelihoods or between lowland wetland civilizations and upcountry people. The frontier signals the space of encounter and transition between different geographies of settlement, political organization and economic surplus generation—from more spatially dense to looser and less intensive modes of livelihoods. From the viewpoint of the metropolitan core, the former tend to be labeled as "civilization" while the latter are considered a civilizational *carte blanche*—an empty space or unruly hinterland, where a state of nature prevails that pits barbarians against each other. The teleological rationale of modern statehood and sovereign power has it, of course, that the latter spaces are remnants from a premodern past, destined to become extinct as modern statehood expands to the margins.

The Political Frontier

What is then the frontier, or, in other words, what makes the frontier an interesting concept for the analysis of current African peripheries? We suggest that there are three, partly complementary, partly distinctive, dimensions that distinguish the frontier from the viewpoint of political geography. By identifying these three dimensions of the frontier we seek to contribute to a theory of the frontier, which builds upon the existing, disparate body of works on the frontier, but is not limited to the latter/or goes beyond individual contributions.

First, the frontier can be apprehended as *an ideological project* or as the imagination of those who claim political space at the margins of the metropolis. The idea that frontiers are an institutional vacuum or no-man's-land that needs to be claimed and occupied by outsiders is essential. Kopytoff talks about the frontier as "an institutional vacuum" because "the metropole defined an area in its periphery as open to legitimate intrusion".[19] This leads us to an examination of the discursive and symbolic strategies with which metropolises and political centers, both national and international, legitimize their claims on a particular frontier zone. While frontiers are often claimed by outsiders for economic interests, political motifs are equally important. This is demonstrated by the current discourse on state-building and reconstruction, which portrays African peripheries as essentially "blank slates" in need of international intervention and order.[20]

Second, the frontier is a geographical space where state power is *territorialized* both materially and symbolically. This occurs in a process in which the state divides peripheral territories into "complex and overlapping political and economic zones and rearranges people and resources within these units, and create[s] regulations delineating how and by whom these areas can be used".[21] The metropolis, or, in this particular context, the political center of the nation state, does not live up to the proclaimed ideal of the state as the guarantor of welfare and political stability in the frontier. Yet, interpretations that stress the absence or weakness of the state in the frontier are often misleading.[22] Through population displacement, public policies, property rights and variegated center–periphery relations—often of a patrimonial character—political centers govern the frontier from afar. It is by this process of territorialization, both through population movements (both voluntary and forced ones)[23] and policies, that the metropolis is both absent and forcefully present in its frontier.

Third, the frontier is a space with *specific characteristics of disorder and violence*. Particular configurations of order and disorder, often of a violent nature, manifest themselves in the frontier. The encounter between settler and indigenous populations, the overlap of different cultural styles, the transition between different production systems, the meeting of nationally defined territories, the territorial strategies by which metropolises regulate their hinterlands and the resistance of local populations to these and other trends reproduce violence and "political disorder"[24] as ways of doing politics that are recurrently practiced in the frontier. What is often perceived as an unruly behavior by frontier inhabitants is often tolerated, if not initiated, by metropolises, who comply with different political norms and levels of violence in their frontier areas as compared to the political center.

A Typology of Frontiers as Geographies of Rule

Kopytoff developed his work on the African frontier by engaging with Turner's seminal contribution *The Significance of the Frontier in American History*. Turner defined the frontier as the line of most rapid and most effective Americanization. In his interpretation, the frontier moved westward, and the successive battles between colonists and Native American meant a gradual move away from civilized Europe. According to Turner, frontier colonization took place in several settlement waves, which gradually occupied the "empty" space of the Wild West and "civilized" it. Turner's model is teleological as he describes a linear, singular frontier that emerges out of a historical necessity of civilization. He described the expansion of the settlement frontier in the American West as a tidal encroachment of European settlers into an area of "free land". The settler transforms spaces of wilderness into spaces of civilization through successive forms of frontiers: traders and trappers are followed by ranchers and miners. The latter are followed by farmers, and finally townsmen. Turner's settlement frontier advances on a linear, one-directional path toward enculturation, pacification and civilization. The frontier, therefore, is a short-lived form of territorial expansion from the metropolises into the peripheries of empires or states. The metropolis gradually consumes the untamed periphery and transforms it into a part of the metropolis, thereby pacifying the periphery. Turner's argument emphasized that the frontier experience of encountering wilderness and civilizing it had significant impacts on the institutional values of what became American society more broadly (or what he termed the national character). In other words, the frontier experience was formative for metropolitan society.

Turner's frontier is one of a constant territorial penetration, which civilizes previously untamed spaces. Danilo Geiger[25] summarizes the operating logic of this Turner frontier with four recurrent processes. *First*, the state shows only sporadic (i.e., unsubstantial) territorial presence. *Second*, the state purports the idea of "freely available" land and natural resources (waiting to be brought into proper use). *Third*, indigenous people are considered as standing outside of the moral universe; they represent a kind of untamed nature, a savage people. *Fourth*, the frontier is characterized by a system of predatory economic relations, based on unequal exchange. This economy is dominated by "intruders" (e.g., settlers) and not by indigenous inhabitants. Geiger summarizes this frontier as a space where "the state does not fully assert its claim to the monopoly of violence, in the sense that it considers violence by settlers and other private actors to some degree necessary and justified".[26] Geiger[27] also determined three frequently overlapping types of frontiers, namely frontiers of settlement, frontiers of extraction and frontiers of control.

Kopytoff referred to Turner's frontier as the "tidal" frontier and distinguished it from the "internal" frontier that he observed in precolonial Africa. Kopytoff's internal frontier emerged at the interstitial spaces of different kingdoms and princely polities. Settlers, herdsmen, farmers and runaway slaves split off from existing metropolises (dominant societies, political orders, petty kingdoms) and started occupying "open spaces" at the territorial margins of – the "spaces-in-between" – other dominant societies, political orders and kingdoms. Both types of frontier, Turner's settlement or tidal frontier and Kopytoff's interstitial or internal frontier, therefore share the founding myth of frontiersmen who conquer a no-man's-land, free land or open space. But the frontier dynamics differ. Turner's frontier described the expansion of metropolises into the periphery, whereas Kopytoff's interstitial frontier suggested the emergence of new social and political formations, the ethnogenesis of peripheral groups, which, if successful, would themselves

Turner   **Kopytoff**

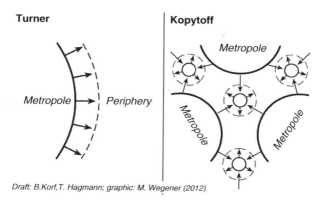

Draft: B.Korf,T. Hagmann; graphic: M. Wegener (2012)

Figure 2.1 Different interactions between metropolis and periphery in the Turner and Kopytoff frontiers.

become dominant and lose a part of their population as it ventures to establish new frontiers. At the periphery, the nucleus of new metropolises and kingdoms emerged. Whereas Turner described the frontier in, linear and irreversible fashion, Kopytoff's interstitial frontier is cyclical, dynamic and reversible.

We want to suggest that the Turner and Kopytoff frontiers represent two distinct and ideal-typical logics of territorialization, which continue to be relevant today and help us understand and describe contemporary political dynamics of African statehood and political (dis)order both at the center and in the margins (figure 2.1 and table 2.1). In the following two sections, we will illustrate these types of frontier with two summary case studies: the Ethiopian–Somali frontier, which serves as an example of Turner's settlement or tidal frontier, and the northern Benin frontier, which is a reminder of Kopytoff's interstitial or internal frontier. Of course, hybrids of the two types may also exist.

The "Turner" Frontier in Ethiopia's Somali Lowlands

The subtle, but crucial difference between borderland and frontier as geographical versus relational spaces becomes apparent when considering the political geography of Ethiopia's eastern lowlands. Several dynamics of the political frontier can be observed in Ethiopia's Somali region, which is also called the Ogaden.[28] This region is inhabited by ethnic Somalis, whose livelihood depends on agropastoralism and transhumant livestock herding. In this section, we will outline that its geographies of rule follow the Turner frontier logic. These dynamics date back to the forced incorporation of the

Table 2.1 The geographies of rule of the Turner and Kopytoff frontiers

	Turner	*Kopytoff*
Frontier logic	Settlement or tidal frontier: expansion of the metropolitan center	Interstitial or internal frontier: emergence of new social formations (ethnogenesis)
Original empirical context within which the concept was developed	American "Wild West" and European colonial expansion	Precolonial African frontier
Frontier spaces	Wilderness at the periphery of metropolises, states and empires	Institutional vacuum at the spaces in between of different empires and kingdoms
	Frontier space as "no-man's-land" (from the intruder's perspective)	
Temporal dynamics	Linear, irreversible (transformative), short-lived	Cyclical, dynamic, reversible
Spatial dynamics	Metropolis (center) consumes the periphery	Peripheries generate new metropolises (centers)

Somali lowlands into the Ethiopian (formerly Abyssinian) imperial state, which began in the mid-nineteenth century. Before 1977, the region's political geography was marked by center–periphery relations evolving from a "fiscal-military mode" characterized by predatory taxation and military expeditions (1850–1920) to a period of "imperial tutelage", which combined increased bureaucratic control, patrimonial relations and continued violence (1920–1977).[29] After the Ethiopian–Somali or Ogaden War of 1977/1978, during which the Somali Democratic Republic unsuccessfully attempted to annex Ethiopia's Somali region, approximately 800,000 Somalis fled Ethiopia to escape repression by its security forces.[30] Both the imperial government and the socialist regime of the Derg sought to "civilize" and "pacify" the Somali periphery into the Ethiopian nation-state. Small groups of highland settlers and soldiers based in the region's various military camps constituted the Ethiopian state's expanding frontier. The key elements of this frontier strategy were an Amharization policy, the settlement of pastoral groups and coercive measures against Somalis opposing the expansion of Ethiopian state sovereignty.

Ethiopian and European colonization of the Ogaden sparked repeated bouts of armed resistance by Somalis in the nineteenth and twentieth centuries.[31] Although Ethiopian armies were able to subdue the local insurgents, the Ethiopian state failed to integrate Somalis into the national body politic, making the Ogaden a site of protracted militarized encounters between Christian Ethiopian highlanders and Muslim Somali lowlanders. Center–periphery relations changed when the Ethiopian Peoples' Revolutionary Democratic Front (EPRDF) toppled the Derg in 1991. Ethiopia was decentralized on the basis of ethnolinguistic groups, granting the country's ethnic groups or "nations, nationalities and peoples" the right to self-determination.[32] As a result, Somalis in eastern Ethiopia for the first time obtained the right to self-administration, and the Somali language, rather than Amharic, became the language of instruction. EPRDF's "ethnic federalism" aimed to correct the historic marginalization of those groups subjugated by imperial and socialist Ethiopia such as the Somalis. By recognizing Somalis as a constituency within a multiethnic democratic state, the tidal wave of conquest and forced—but rarely successful—assimilation came to a temporary halt in 1991.[33] In spite of promises of democratization and decentralized decision-making, the federal government partly revived some of the historic tactics of governing the Somali periphery, which are a reminder of, but not identical to, the Turner frontier. The autonomy of the regional administration was strongly eroded by its continued reliance on instructions by federal bureaucrats and politicians. Commanders of the Ethiopian National Defense Forces (ENDF) troops stationed in the region became influential local decision-makers as the government's counterinsurgency agenda against the rebel Ogaden National Liberation Front (ONLF) rose to prominence after 2007 (figure 2.2).

The frontier experience of Ethiopia's Somali region is compounded by multiple and overlapping boundaries. The region is a border zone between Ethiopia and Somalia; more specifically, to the northeast is the *de facto* state of Somaliland, to the east are the autonomous republic of Puntland as well as south-central Somalia and to the southeast are the remains of the Somali Democratic Republic. While an internationally recognized border between Ethiopia and Somalia exists, it does not take into account the existence of these nonrecognized state entities. Similarly, the local production system, livelihoods and pastoral trading routes transcend state borders, both officially and unofficially.[34] If we look at the flows of goods and services that transit the region, we find vibrant trade corridors, with livestock and charcoal going from Ethiopia's Somali region through Somaliland up to the Middle East and, further south, to central Somalia up to Mogadishu. A reverse flow of "contraband" goods, mostly consumer goods originating in Asia, is imported through Djibouti, Berbera, Boosaaso and the southern ports. Ethiopia's Somali frontier is also a constantly shifting dividing line between Ethiopian highlands and Somali lowlands, separating what is perceived as two different "civilizations": the Christian-dominated, sedentary highlands, and the Muslim pastoralist lowlands. From the perspective of the "highlanders", who have historically controlled state power in Ethiopia, Ethiopian Somalis are "citizens of doubt",

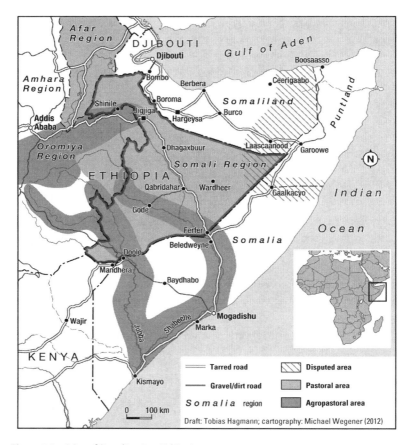

Figure 2.2 Map of Somali region, Ethiopia.

who might side with neighboring Somalia. Conversely, Ethiopian Somalis' experience of oppression and displacement at the hands of the Ethiopian state reproduces negative stereotypes about Ethiopian highlanders or *habesha*.

Despite differences among successive regimes in Ethiopia, the Somali lowlands continue to be perceived in the imagination of the Ethiopian elite as a frontier space in need of state intervention. *First*, pastoralist rangelands, in particular common-pool grazing reserves at the periphery of the Ethiopian state, are seen as a "no-man's-land", as freely available land resources that need to be put to use by adopting agriculture.[35] *Second*, although pastoralism gained some recognition after 1991, previous governments have considered it as an archaic, outdated, premodern lifestyle, which needs to be overcome by settling herders.[36] *Third*, this imagination reflects a teleological model of progress, modernity and civilization, which progresses from pastoralism through agropastoralism to sedentary cultures—with an urban lifestyle at its peak. *Fourth*, the Ethiopian state responds to its inherent geographical imagination with a project of taming the frontier: penetrating empty spaces through settlements along the Shabelle, Genale (Juba) and other river basins. This policy was initially pursued by the Derg, for example, in the large-scale Gode irrigation scheme, attempting to sedentarize pastoralists and encouraging highland settlers to out-migrate to the Somali lowlands. While the EPRDF government abandoned its predecessor's forced settlement policy, it continues to advocate for the "voluntary settlement" of pastoralists.[37] *Fifth*, the Somali region and war-torn Somalia are perceived as unruly territory, which threatens Ethiopia and thus requires a sustained Ethiopian military presence in order to secure the metropolis.

Historically and today, the expansion of the metropolitan core in the name of, successively, imperialism, socialism and, most recently, democracy has marked the Ethiopian–Somali frontier. Over time, the Ethiopian state's agenda in the Ogaden has shifted between conquering the Somali frontier, capturing its natural resources, controlling population movement and defending the home country. Hence, the expansion of the Ethiopian–Somali frontier was not tidal, but is rather ongoing. One observes a historic continuity in the way in which the Ethiopian state furthers the administrative control of people and territory in its Somali hinterland, a process that Christopher Clapham, referring to the Derg, described as "*encadrement*".[38] Donor countries have often supported government intervention in the Ogaden, in the name of enabling both development and security. For instance, the European Union has recently underlined the allegedly aggressive character of Somalis in Ethiopia, who "tend to solve their differences through confrontation",[39] thereby reproducing a violent imaginary of the Somali region as uncivilized space that needs to be tamed by planned, bureaucratic measures. Finally, Ethiopia's military intervention in Somalia (2006–2008), which led to the downfall of the Islamic Courts Union (ICU),[40] was a reminder of the fluidity of the Ethiopian–Somali frontier, whose contours may reach up to Mogadishu in times of heightened political conflict. Less known is the military intervention and state of exception that the Ethiopian rulers have brought to Somalis inside Ethiopia, in particular to the Ogaadeen clan and its home territories.[41]

What role does the Somali frontier play at the margins of the Ethiopian state? For the Ethiopian highland elite, the Somali borderland is a largely empty space, devoid of civilization, waiting to become pacified. It is the periphery to the core of the Ethiopian state. But we want to argue here that although the Somali region appears to be at the periphery, it is nevertheless central to the constitution of the Ethiopian nation-state. While ENDF troops and local militia composed of ethnic Somalis have attempted to instill tight military control in the Ogaadeen heartland following the escalation of the ONLF insurgency in 2007, both in the Ogaden and during its intervention in Somalia, Ethiopia has been challenged to bring those zones of wilderness under control.[42] This signals again a crucial difference in the ever-evolving highland–lowland interactions: the increasingly authoritarian government by Prime Minister Meles Zenawi has detained, silenced and intimidated opposition parties and critics in the metropolis following the 2005 elections, which were heavily contested,[43] yet the Somali lowlands have remained a much less controlled frontier space.

Frontier, then, becomes part of the logic of governing, the zone of indistinction between those who are included as excluded (namely the Somali inside Ethiopia, but not really Ethiopians) and those who are excluded as included. In this sense, the frontier is not an institutional vacuum as Kopytoff's model suggested, but it is included as exception to the sovereign body of the Ethiopian space—and the Somalis become a kind of *homine sacri*: they are included as excluded, as pure bodies without citizenship rights.[44] The Somali frontier, seen as a zone of indistinction where the state of nature—the violent, untamed pastoralist societies still in existence—comes into contact with the state of law of the Ethiopian sovereign, is therefore a central tenet for the constitution of the Ethiopian state; it is more that that—it is a frontier in the global war against terror. In this frontier, exception and rule, Hobbes' state of nature[45]—the lawless rule of violence—and the state of law, civilization and modernity are becoming indistinguishable.[46]

To some extent, the irritation that pastoralist mobility—a society in motion—poses to highlanders is the paradigmatic idea that, to paraphrase James Scott,[47] sedentary agriculture seems to be seen as a necessary condition for state-making and state control. Non-sedentary livelihoods then appear as incompatible with and an irritant to state-making ambitions. This peculiar situation begs a question once asked by Talal Asad:[48] where does the (Ethiopian) state "end"? This "end" does not refer to only the territorial confinement of the state's territorial boundaries (the state borders), but rather the state's presence, control and rule of law. In those vast, loosely populated lowland plains, a state border may be marked on maps, but does not necessarily materialize as the "end" of one state vis-à-vis its neighbor. Rather, this "end" comes in stages; it is a fuzzy zone of a disorderly frontier space.

Benin: A "Kopytoff Frontier" in the Making

The political geography of agricultural colonization in north-central Benin is characterized by the simultaneous perpetuation and retranslation of models of social and political organization in settlement processes driven by dynamics of social fission. This dynamic was also described as the central characteristic of the model of the internal African frontier by Kopytoff.[49]

While historical patterns of social and political or military organization have been studied in detail for southern Benin[50] and northern Benin,[51] there is comparatively little information available for the region between Parakou and Bassila (figure 2.3). According to Y. Person,[52] this area was settled as long ago as the fifteenth century by Yorubaphone groups from the Yoruba core areas around Oyo and the sacred city of Ile-Ife in present-day Nigeria. According to John Igué, during one of the migration phases, they founded the settlement axis of Manigri, Igbere, Dogue, Igbomakro and Wari Maro, which today marks the northern linguistic frontier of the Yoruba in Benin.[53] Remnants of abandoned villages are found everywhere, which are explained in oral traditions as the result of fission of the aforementioned villages (figure 2.3). This can be seen as evidence of historical frontier processes, and, at the same

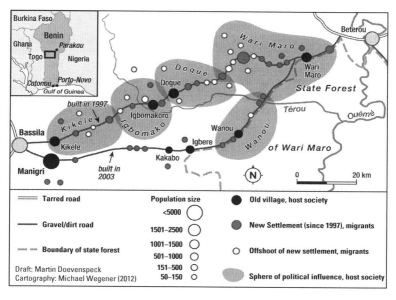

Figure 2.3 Map of north-central Benin.

time, in view of the great number of these old places of settlement, as an indicator that the region was once much more densely settled than at the beginning of agricultural colonization in the late 1990s.

Historically, there are three different bordering processes that contributed to the peripheral position of the region before the formation of the current frontier: precolonial instability due to slave raids and wars, selective economic development and forest protection measures during the colonial period and forced resettlement following independence. For a long time, the area was part of a buffer zone between the Baatombu aristocracies of precolonial Borgou in the north, the Dahomey systems of rule in the south and Oyo in the east, and during the eighteenth and nineteenth centuries it was the target of all kinds of slave raids. While slave hunts by the kings of Dahomey were carried out within the framework of the transatlantic slave trade and the expansion of royal palm oil plantations, raids by the Baatombu were also aimed at seizing foodstuffs and cattle. In the colonial period, economic exploitation was at first limited to the export of palm oil from the plantations in the south, which led to a general separation of the south from the remaining parts of the country. A reorganization of the colonial transport infrastructure became necessary when agricultural export strategies were diversified, with the forced expansion of cotton and groundnut cultivation in the north. In addition, three big forest reserves were created after the Second World War. As a result, the region became cut off from all important transport routes. As part of the government's modernization policy following independence, the people disadvantaged by their peripheral situation were forcibly resettled along the main transport route, where agricultural extension services, clinics and schools were located. Villages that resisted were penalized in a military manner, lost all administrative functions and found themselves trapped in one of the politically and economically most isolated rural areas of Benin.

A more recent frontier process started with the construction of a new east–west rural road. Since 1997, an increasing number of migrants have been attracted by the availability of land with a high agricultural potential and founded a large number of new settlements with a fast-growing multi-ethnic population. As a result of immigration, the established local political power structures within the host societies have become more dynamic. Much as in central Benin, the formation of new patron–client relationships has reinforced the existing multiplicity of political authorities, the negotiability of their spheres of responsibility and the rivalry between traditional, neo-traditional and new political institutions, which compete in shaping political and economic relations with the immigrants.[54] At the same time, there is a conflicting constitution of new political entities in the immigrant societies, where local power is legitimized by a person's status as a firstcomer. In other words, the chief of a new settlement is its founder. However, this principle of anteriority is very flexible, and chiefs claiming firstcomer status do not lack rivals who challenge their position. In a situation of institutional instability, the immigrants reinterpret the established rules of political interaction, and decision-making structures are continuously renegotiated. In these negotiations, models and ideas about political order established in different home areas interfere with those of previous places of residence of the immigrants, who additionally take over and translate elements from the host society, and thus produce locally modified models of political organization. The emergence of these models therefore takes place in a semiautonomous arena that is continuously influenced by factions of the host society.[55] The latter is shaped in its turn by a multiplex-institutional structure, in which many contrasting historical and social elements are embedded. In this respect, political systems in the settlers' milieu are partly a result of different local conflicts and negotiations between competing immigrant fractions, and partly an effect of the polycephalism, the multiplicity of sources of social order and political authority, of the host societies.

These dynamics are characterized by three central features of the internal African frontier or Kopytoff frontier: (1) the institutional vacuum, (2) the structural drift of society and (3) the firstcomer principle.

In contrast to Turner, who largely ignores the population encountered by the frontier migrants, or anonymizes it as wilderness, Kopytoff takes into account the presence of a host society, because the margins of the metropolis to which groups migrate due to fission dynamics are not necessarily uninhabited. "These are the easiest frontiers but they are not the only ones".[56] Like the institutional vacuum highlighted by Kopytoff, which arises due to the encounter of groups at the margins, the idea of the frontier as an uninhabited space is a subjective and politically motivated interpretation by the new settlers: "The definition of the frontier as 'empty' is political and made from the intruders' perspective. . . . In this sense, they saw it as an institutional vacuum in which they could consider themselves not to be morally bound by institutional constraints".[57]

The Benin frontier described here is not characterized by a void, but by a maneuvering room that is exploited flexibly by both migrants and parts of the host society. This flexibility arises from the fact that the range or effectiveness of the established political authorities in the host society is decreasing due to internal conflicts and the multiplicity of competing claims in respect to decision-making competences. The frontier is not an "institutional no-man's-land" and is not constructed as such by the settlers. Rather, there is an institutional opulence, which leads to regulatory pluralism as a result of the negotiability of competences. Actors in both the immigrant and host societies strive for the (re)institutionalization of their own political and social models under conditions of all-round competition and mutual influence.

Kopytoff recognizes the transformation potential of frontier processes.[58] Social models can develop local and regional variants, and the regulatory models of new political entities do not have to be exact replicates of existing ones. "This kind of structural drift might indeed have been one of the mechanisms by which such segmentary systems produced variations within the overall pattern".[59] In this case study, structural drift can be regarded as a product of strategies of reinstitutionalization of political and social models implemented by different groups at the same time and in competition with each other. Here we see a conservative effect of the African frontier, to the extent that some principles of political culture that bind the groups together are reproduced: regulatory pluralism, despotic power structures, clientelism, venality and the links between politics and kin, ethnicity and region. The new settlements thus remain liable to fission, which means that the frontier process is perpetuated culturally, socially and politically.

Kopytoff emphasizes the advantages of being first in a new settlement area. He argues that, even more than the position of first son, first wife or first one in the age hierarchy, the position of being the first settler and founder of a community enables one to gain and to keep various privileges.[60] This first-comer principle, which Kopytoff finds so important, is also significant for political and social conditions at the northern frontier in Benin. Being recognized as the firstcomer means that one's authority is accepted, and to this day oral traditions of the founding of settlements are a reflection of interests of the different parties concerned. But even when there is no doubt about who is the founder of a new settlement, rivals seeking power in the village will still challenge him. The principle of anteriority can relate to different contexts and spatial scales: first immigrant in the region, first ethnic group, first of an ethnolinguistic group, first in the hamlet, et cetera. Taking into account the relationship between firstcomer and latecomer can help us to understand the new settlement structure of the study area, for in this case the motive of *chercher la chefferie*, or looking for the chief (or chieftaincy), has led to the founding of smaller and smaller settlements as offshoots of new immigrant villages, and thus to the establishment of new local frontiers within the frontier.

Kopytoff described the model of the internal African frontier as a primarily local phenomenon, as a process characterized by multiple factors, within which elements of political culture in Africa are perpetuated and existing models of order are retranslated. The agricultural colonization process in northern Benin has followed most of these patterns. If we assume a flexible concept of the metropolis, which includes the regions of origin of the migrants, the places they have stopped at during their travels and the host society and its social and political models, the constitution of settler societies and new political entities in the transitional space between central and northern Benin can be understood as a current frontier process. If, as Kopytoff assumes, social processes in Africa should be understood in the frontier context, this agricultural colonization offers one of the rare opportunities to study a frontier process from the beginning: "The early stages of small incipient polities, however, have been seldom available to direct observation".[61] In contrast to the Turner frontier, which is characterized by a succession of connected unidirectional waves of settlement, the political frontier in this case study is primarily a local phenomenon. Multiple and multidirectional processes create local structures, within which elements of political culture are perpetuated and existing models of governance are retranslated.

The Political Frontier: Violence, Sovereignty and the Geography of Rule

Kopytoff wrote *The African Frontier* as a historical analysis of precolonial African political geography. In this chapter, we have tested the usefulness of the frontier terminology for the analysis of those *postcolonial* African political spaces where the ambivalent relations between metropoles and peripheries are currently renegotiated. Our analytical interest was to understand the frontier as a rationale of rule with specific inherent spatialities of political (re)order(ing). We have distinguished two different ideal types of political frontier: the Turner frontier and the Kopytoff frontier. While the Turner frontier, originally developed in the study of the American "Wild West", is driven by a constant push to integrate wild zones into the metropolises, Kopytoff's frontier model applied to a context of institutional vacuum at interstitial spaces in between different kingdoms. Both models of frontier describe different and distinct logics of territorialization, which we have applied to an analysis of the postcolonial political spaces of the Ethiopian–Somali frontier (Turner) and the northern Benin frontier (Kopytoff).

The Turner frontier subsumes the inherent rationale of unoccupied, empty spaces waiting to become civilized. The frontier is the territorial container within which a Hobbesian state of nature is still in place. It complies with Schmitt's notion of "*herrenloses Land*". Both, the image of state of nature and that of "*herrenloses Land*" imply the geographical imagination of savage or empty territories, of disorderly places devoid of rule. At the Ethiopian–Somali frontier, this state of nature (as untamed society) merges with the everyday image of the conflict-prone pastoralist areas, which is contrasted to the ideal of a highland "culture"—a sedentary culture, which is a requirement for proper state-making. While we tend to define the frontier territorially—and Schmitt's dictum of *Landnahme* would suggest just that—the frontier is then a spatially and temporally discrete entity where a state of exception is in place; Agamben would probably suggest that, while we can locate the frontier as a territorial space (the Somali region, for example), the crux of the matter is that the governing logic of the state of exception pervades, and goes beyond the territorial confines of the Somali container space.[62]

The Kopytoff frontier is characterized by more subtle spatializations of metropolises and peripheries and "no-man's-land". The institutional vacuum that characterizes those territories makes them appear to the metropolises as "open to legitimate intrusion".[63] However, Kopytoff also suggests that the incomers and the host societies both are entangled in the emergence of a bricolage of different social orders, resulting in polycephalic local authority structures with constant (re)negotiations of political authority and its sources of legitimacy. The northern frontier in Benin illustrates this process well, where claims to rights and authority, in particular those relating to land property rights, are in flux, and even the "firstcomer principle" is subject to interpretation and negotiation. In Benin, such negotiations and political conflicts have been confined largely to the local political arena.

There is, clearly, a politics of scale to the geographies of rule inherent in different frontier spaces. At the northern frontier of Benin, we analyzed the micro-politics of localized processes of inculturation between the incomers and host societies, while for the Ethiopian–Somali frontier, we described the macro-geographies of a kind of civilizational clash between highland and lowland, sedentary and pastoralist societies and the quest of the political center to colonize and transform the pastoral frontier into "fully governed, fiscally fertile zones".[64] The state's ambition to tame the pastoral frontier turned out more violent than the polycephalism of the Kopytoff frontier in Benin. But, as the case of the Ivory Coast illustrates, this does not need to be so.[65] At the northern frontier of the Ivory Coast, political struggle over who has legitimate claims to territories has turned into an important driver for the violent struggle over political control at the center of the nation-state. The politics of scale at the political frontier also suggests that we find overlapping and multiple dynamics in a particular political space with macro-geographies of the Turner frontier meeting a more polycephalic or hybrid negotiation of political orders in specific localities.

Scott[66] has reminded us that peripheries are often spaces of multiple sovereignty where different—mostly distant—power holders struggle over control and allegiance of its often scattered populations. This situation has frequently allowed those who inhabit peripheries to juggle between different loyalties, allegiances and alliances. Our suggestion is that the terminology of (political) "frontier" provides a useful framing to grasp these fluid and fragile geographies of violence and sovereignty, although those struggles take different spatial forms and dynamics.

Notes

1. I. Kopytoff, ed. "The internal African frontier—The making of African political culture," in *The African frontier—The reproduction of traditional African societies*, (Bloomington & Indianapolis: Indiana Indiana University Press, 1987a), 3–84.
2. I. Kopytoff, "Frontiers and frontier societies," in *Encyclopedia of Africa south of the Sahara*, ed. J. Middleton (New York: Charles Scribner's Sons, 1987b), 170.
3. I. Kopytoff, ed. "The internal African frontier—The making of African political culture," in *The African frontier—The reproduction of traditional African societies*, (Bloomington, IN: Indiana University Press, 1987a), 11.
4. D. Gerhard, "The frontier in comparative view," *Comparative Studies in Society and History* 1, no. 2 (1959): 206.
5. T. Wendl and M. Rösler, eds. "Frontiers and borderlands. The rise and relevance of an Anthropological research genre," in *Frontiers and borderlands. Anthropological perspectives*, (Frankfurt: Peter Lang, 1999), 1–27.
6. Copland 2010, Dobler 2010, Nugent 2002, Raeymaekers 2009, Doevenspeck 2011a.
7. F. Dereje and M. V. Hoehne, "Resourcing state borders and borderlands in the Horn of Africa," Working Paper No. 107 (Halle: Max Planck Institute for Social Anthropology, 2008).
8. J. Migdal, ed. "Mental maps and virtual checkpoints: Struggles to construct and maintain state and social boundaries," in *Boundaries and belonging: States and societies in the struggle to shape identities and local practices*, (Cambridge: Cambridge University Press, 2004), 5.
9. F. Barth, "Boundaries and connections," in *Signifying identities: Anthropological perspectives on boundaries and contested values*, ed. A. P. Cohen (London: Routledge, 2000), 17–36; F. Barth, ed. "Introduction," in *Ethnic groups and boundaries: The social organization of culture difference*, (London: George Allen and Unwin, 1969).
10. C. Schmitt, *Der Nomos der Erde im Völkerrecht des Jus Publicum Europaeum* (Berlin: Duncker & Humblot, 1950), 171.
11. D. Geiger, *Frontier encounters—Indigenous communities and settlers in Asia and Latin America* (Copenhagen: International Work Group for Indigenous Affairs, 2008).
12. M. Doevenspeck, "Migration im ländlichen Benin. Sozialgeographische Untersuchungen an einer afrikanischen Frontier," in *Studien zur Geographischen Entwicklungsforschung* 30 (Saarbrücken: Verlag für Entwicklungspolitik, 2005).
13. P. Y. Le Meur, "State making and the politics of the frontier in central Benin." *Development and Change* 37, no. 4 (2006): 871–900.
14. F. J. Turner, "The significance of the frontier in American history," in *Annual report of the American Historical Association*, 1893: 199–207.
15. B. Chalfin, *Neoliberal frontiers: An ethnography of sovereignty in West Africa* (Chicago, IL: Chicago University Press, 2010).

16. A. J. Rieber, "Frontiers in history," in *International encyclopedia of the social & behavioral sciences*, ed. N. J. Smelser and P. B. Baltes (Amsterdam: Elsevier, 2001), 5813.

17. H. Donnan, "Anthropology of borders," in *International Encyclopedia of the Social & Behavioral Sciences*, ed. N. J. Smelser and P. B. Baltes (Amsterdam: Elsevier, 2001), 1290.

18. Reid (2011: 22) describes the frontier as "highly militarized societies—especially when we recognize the frontier . . . as a fault line and . . . a contested zone . . . a zone of conflict and competition".

19. I. Kopytoff, ed. "The internal African frontier—The making of African political culture," in *The African frontier—The reproduction of traditional African societies*, (Bloomington, IN: Indiana University Press, 1987a), 9, 16.

20. C. Cramer, *Civil war is not a stupid thing: Accounting for violence in developing countries* (London: Hurst and Company, 2006), 255.

21. P. Vandergeest and N. L. Peluso, "Territorialization and state power in Thailand," *Theory and Society* 24, no. 2 (1995): 387.

22. T. Hagmann and B. Korf, "Agamben in the Ogaden: Violence and sovereignty in the Ethiopian–Somali frontier," *Political Geography*, no. 4 [in press], 2012: 205–214.

23. M. Doevenspeck, "The thin line between choice and flight: Environment and migration in rural Benin," *International Migration* 49, no. 1 (2011b): 50–68.

24. P. Chabal and J. P. Daloz, *Africa works: Disorder as political instrument* (Bloomington, IN: Indiana University Press, 1999).

25. D. Geiger, "Turner in the Tropics: The 'frontier' concept revisited." Paper presented to the Inter-Disciplinary Workshop "Dimensions, Dynamics and Transformation of Resource Conflicts between Indigenous Peoples and Settlers in Frontier Regions of South and Southeast Asia," Mont-Soleil/St. Imier, September 25–29, 2002; D. Geiger, *Frontier encounters—Indigenous communities and settlers in Asia and Latin America.* (Copenhagen: International Work Group for Indigenous Affairs, 2008).

26. D. Geiger, "Turner in the Tropics: The 'frontier' concept revisited." (Paper presented to the Inter-Disciplinary Workshop "Dimensions, Dynamics and Transformation of Resource Conflicts between Indigenous Peoples and Settlers in Frontier Regions of South and Southeast Asia," Mont-Soleil/St. Imier, September 25–29, 2002), 7.

27. D. Geiger, *Frontier encounters—Indigenous communities and settlers in Asia and Latin America.* (Copenhagen: International Work Group for Indigenous Affairs, 2008).

28. Eastern Ethiopia is also known as Ogaden, which refers to the region's predominant clan family, the Ogaadeen. Known as Ogaden province during the imperial period and the reign of the socialist-military Derg dictatorship, with the federalization of the country, the region was renamed as the Somali regional state of Ethiopia.

29. C. Barnes, *The Ethiopian state and its Somali periphery, circa 1888–1948,* PhD thesis (Cambridge: University of Cambridge, 2000).

30. M. Brons, M. Doornbos and M. A. Mohamed Salih, "The Somali–Ethiopians: The quest for alternative futures," *Eastern Africa Social Science Research Review* 11, no. 2 (1995): 45–70; G. Tareke, "The Ethiopia–Somalia War of 1977 revisited," *International Journal of African Historical Studies* 33, no. 3 (2000): 635–667.

31. C. L. Geshekter, "Anti-colonialism and class formation: The eastern Horn of Africa before 1950," *International Affairs* 18, no. 1 (1985): 1–32.

32. FDRE (Federal Democratic Republic of Ethiopia), *Constitution of the Federal Democratic Republic of Ethiopia proclamation* (1. Addis Ababa: Federal Democratic Republic of Ethiopia, 1995).

33. T. Hagmann, "Beyond clannishness and colonialism: Understanding political disorder in Ethiopia's Somali region, 1991–2004," *Journal of Modern African Studies* 43, no. 4 (2005): 509–536; T. Hagmann and M. H. Khalif, "State and politics in Ethiopia's Somali region since 1991," *Bildhaan: An International Journal of Somali Studies* 6 (2006): 25–49.

34. S. Devereux, *Vulnerable livelihoods in Somali region, Ethiopia* (Brighton: Institute of Development Studies, 2006).

35. See, for example, the 2005 Federal Land Use Proclamation, which states that "Government, being the owner of rural land, communal rural land holdings can be changed to private holdings as may be necessary" (Federal Democratic Republic of Ethiopia Rural Land Administration and Use Proclamation (No. 456/2005, para 5,3)).

36. G. Kassa, "An overview of government policy interventions in pastoral areas: Achievements, constraints and prospects," Paper presented to the "National Conference on Pastoral Development in Ethiopia" (Pastoralist Forum Ethiopia, Wabi Shebelle Hotel, Addis Ababa, February 2, 2000).

37. FDRE (Federal Democratic Republic of Ethiopia), *Constitution of the Federal Democratic Republic of Ethiopia proclamation* (1. Addis Ababa: Federal Democratic Republic of Ethiopia, 1995).

38. C. Clapham, "Controlling space in Ethiopia," in *Remapping Ethiopia: Socialism and after*, ed. W. James *et al.* (Oxford: James Currey, 2002), 14.

39. European Union, *Preliminary statement on the election appeals' process, the rerun of elections and the Somali region elections* (Addis Ababa: European Union, 2005), 8.

40. K. Menkhaus, "The crisis in Somalia: Tragedy in five acts," *African Affairs* 106, no. 204 (2007): 357–390.

41. T. Hagmann and B. Korf, "Agamben in the Ogaden: Violence and sovereignty in the Ethiopian–Somali frontier," *Political Geography* 31, no. 4 (2012): 205–214.

42. T. Hagmann and B. Korf, "Agamben in the Ogaden: Violence and sovereignty in the Ethiopian–Somali frontier," *Political Geography* 31, no. 4 (2012): 205–214.

43. J. Abbink, "Discomfiture of democracy? The 2005 election crisis in Ethiopia and its aftermath," *African Affairs* 105, no. 419 (2006): 173–199.

44. G. Agamben, *Homo sacer. Sovereign power and bare life* (Stanford, CA: Stanford University Press, 1998).

45. T. Hobbes, *Leviathan.* Edited with an introduction by J. C. A. Gaskin, (Oxford: Oxford University Press, [1651] 1996).

46. This argument is fully developed in T. Hagmann and B. Korf, "Agamben in the Ogaden: Violence and sovereignty in the Ethiopian–Somali frontier," *Political Geography* 31, no. 4 (2012): 205–214.
47. J. Scott, *The art of not being governed. An anarchist history of upland Southeast Asia*, (New Haven, CT: Yale University Press, 2009).
48. T. Asad, "Where are the margins of the state?," in *Anthropology in the margins of the state*, eds. V. Das and D. Poole, (Santa Fe: School of American Research Press, 2004), 279–288.
49. I. Kopytoff, ed. "The internal African frontier—The making of African political culture," in *The African frontier—The reproduction of traditional African societies*, (Bloomington & Indianapolis: Indiana University Press, 1987a), 3–84.
50. G. Elwert, *Wirtschaft und Herrschaft von "Daxome" (Dahomey) im 18. Jahrhundert. Ökonomie des Sklavenraubs und Gesellschaftsstruktur 1724–1818* (München: Renner, 1971).
51. J. Lombard, *Structures de type "féodal" en Afrique noire: Études des dynamismes internes et des relations sociales chez les Bariba du Dahomey* (Paris: Mouton, 1965).
52. Y. Person, "Notes sur les Baseda (Bassila-Cercle de Djougou)." *Études dahoméennes* 15 (1956): 35–68.
53. J. Igué, "La civilisation agraire des populations Yoruba du Dahomey et du Moyen Togo," Thèse de Doctorat de 3è cycle (Paris: Université Paris Ouest Nanterre La Défense, 1970), 62.
54. P. Y. Le Meur, "State making and the politics of the frontier in central Benin," *Development and Change* 37, no. 4 (2006): 871–900.
55. M. Doevenspeck, "Migration im ländlichen Benin. Sozialgeographische Untersuchungen an einer afrikanischen Frontier," *Studien zur Geographischen Entwicklungsforschung* 30 (Saarbrücken: Verlag für Entwicklungspolitik, 2005).
56. I. Kopytoff, ed. "The internal African frontier—The making of African political culture," in *The African frontier—The reproduction of traditional African societies*, (Bloomington, IN: Indiana University Press, 1987a), 11.
57. I. Kopytoff, ed. "The internal African frontier—The making of African political culture," in *The African frontier—The reproduction of traditional African societies*, (Bloomington, IN: Indiana University Press, 1987a), 25.
58. Despite certain tendencies toward homogenization reflected in the "pan-African models" postulated by him.
59. I. Kopytoff, ed. "The internal African frontier—The making of African political culture," in *The African frontier—The reproduction of traditional African societies*, (Bloomington, IN: Indiana University Press, 1987a), 27.
60. I. Kopytoff, "The internal African frontier—The making of African political culture," in *The African frontier—The reproduction of traditional African societies*, ed. I. Kopytoff (Bloomington, IN: Indiana University Press, 1987a), 53.
61. I. Kopytoff, "The internal African frontier—The making of African political culture," in *The African frontier—The reproduction of traditional African societies*, ed. I. Kopytoff (Bloomington, IN: Indiana University Press, 1987a), 78.

62. T. Hagmann and B. Korf, "Agamben in the Ogaden: Violence and sovereignty in the Ethiopian–Somali frontier," *Political Geography* 31, no. 4 (2012): 205–214.
63. I. Kopytoff, "The internal African frontier—The making of African political culture," in *The African frontier—The reproduction of traditional African societies*, ed. I. Kopytoff (Bloomington, IN: Indiana University Press, 1987a), 16.
64. J. Scott, *The art of not being governed. An anarchist history of upland Southeast Asia* (New Haven, CT: Yale University Press, 2009), 10.
65. T. Förster, "Maintenant, on sait qui est qui: Statehood and political reconfiguration in northern Côte d'Ivoire," *Development and Change* 41, no. 4, 2010: 699–722.
66. J. Scott, *The art of not being governed. An anarchist history of upland Southeast Asia*, (New Haven, CT: Yale University Press, 2009).

References

Abbink, J. "Discomfiture of democracy? The 2005 election crisis in Ethiopia and its aftermath." *African Affairs* 105, no. 419 (2006): 173–199.

Agamben, G. *Homo sacer. Sovereign power and bare life.* Stanford, CA: Stanford University Press, 1998.

Asad, T. "Where are the margins of the state?" In *Anthropology in the margins of the state*, edited by V. Das and D. Poole. Santa Fe: School of American Research Press, 2004: 279–288.

Barnes, C. *The Ethiopian state and its Somali periphery, circa 1888–1948.* PhD thesis, Cambridge, University of Cambridge, 2000.

Barth, F. "Boundaries and connections." In *Signifying identities: Anthropological perspectives on boundaries and contested values*, edited by A. P. Cohen. London: Routledge, 2000: 17–36.

Barth, F., ed. "Introduction." In *Ethnic groups and boundaries: The social organization of culture difference*, London: George Allen and Unwin, 1969.

Brons, M., M. Doornbos, and M. A. Mohamed Salih. "The Somali–Ethiopians: The quest for alternative futures." *Eastern Africa Social Science Research Review* 11, no. 2 (1995): 45–70.

Chabal, P. and J. P. Daloz. *Africa works: Disorder as political instrument.* Bloomington, IN: Indiana University Press, 1999.

Chalfin, B. *Neoliberal frontiers: An ethnography of sovereignty in West Africa.* Chicago, IL: Chicago University Press, 2010.

Clapham, C. "Controlling space in Ethiopia." In *Remapping Ethiopia: Socialism and after*, edited by W. James, D. L. Donham, E. Kurimoto and A. Triulzi. Oxford: James Currey, 2002: 9–30.

Coplan, D. "African borderlands." *Journal of Borderland Studies* 25, no. 2 (2010): Special issue.

Cramer, C. *Civil war is not a stupid thing: Accounting for violence in developing countries.* London: Hurst and Company, 2006.

Dereje, F. and M. V. Hoehne. "Resourcing state borders and borderlands in the Horn of Africa." Working Paper No. 107. Halle: Max Planck Institute for Social Anthropology, 2008.

Devereux, S. *Vulnerable livelihoods in Somali region, Ethiopia.* Brighton: Institute of Development Studies, 2006.

Dobler, G. "On the border to chaos: Identity formation on the Angolan–Namibian border, 1927–2008." *Journal of Borderland Studies* 25, no. 2 (2010): 22–35.

Doevenspeck, M. Migration im ländlichen Benin. Sozialgeographische Untersuchungen an einer afrikanischen Frontier." *Studien zur Geographischen Entwicklungsforschung* 30, Saarbrücken: Verlag für Entwicklungspolitik, 2005.

Doevenspeck, M. "Constructing the border from below: Narratives from the Congolese–Rwandan state boundary." *Political Geography* March 30 (2011a): 129–142.

Doevenspeck, M. "The thin line between choice and flight: Environment and migration in rural Benin." *International Migration* 49, no. 1 (2011b): 50–68.

Donnan, H. "Anthropology of borders." In *International encyclopedia of the social & behavioral sciences,* edited by N. J. Smelser and P. B. Baltes. Amsterdam: Elsevier, 2001: 1290–1293.

Elwert, G. *Wirtschaft und Herrschaft von "Daxome" (Dahomey) im 18. Jahrhundert. Ökonomie des Sklavenraubs und Gesellschaftsstruktur 1724–1818.* Münich: Renner, 1971.

European Union. *Preliminary statement on the election appeals' process, the re-run of elections and the Somali region elections.* Addis Ababa: European Union, 2005.

FDRE (Federal Democratic Republic of Ethiopia). *Constitution of the Federal Democratic Republic of Ethiopia proclamation* 1. Addis Ababa: Federal Democratic Republic of Ethiopia, 1995.

Förster, T. "Maintenant, on sait qui est qui: Statehood and political reconfiguration in Northern Côte d'Ivoire." *Development and Change* 41, no. 4 (2010): 699–722.

Geiger, D. *Frontier encounters—Indigenous communities and settlers in Asia and Latin America.* Copenhagen: International Work Group for Indigenous Affairs, 2008.

Geiger, D. "Turner in the Tropics: The 'frontier' concept revisited." Paper presented to the Inter-Disciplinary Workshop "Dimensions, Dynamics and Transformation of Resource Conflicts between Indigenous Peoples and Settlers in Frontier Regions of South and Southeast Asia," Mont-Soleil/St. Imier, September 25–29, 2002.

Gerhard, D. "The Frontier in comparative view." *Comparative Studies in Society and History* 1, no. 2 (1959): 205–229.

Geshekter, C. L. Anti-colonialism and class formation: The eastern Horn of Africa before 1950. *International Affairs* 18, no. 1 (1985): 1–32.

Hagmann, T. "Beyond clannishness and colonialism: Understanding political disorder in Ethiopia's Somali region, 1991–2004." *Journal of Modern African Studies* 43, no. 4 (2005): 509–536.

Hagmann, T. and M. H. Khalif. "State and politics in Ethiopia's Somali region since 1991." *An International Journal of Somali Studies* 6 (2006): 25–49.

T. Hagmann and B. Korf. "Agamben in the Ogaden: Violence and sovereignty in the Ethiopian–Somali frontier." *Political Geography* 31, no. 4 (2012): 205–214.

Hobbes, T. *Leviathan.* Edited with an introduction by J. C. A. Gaskin. Oxford: Oxford University Press, [1651] 1996.

Igué, J. "La civilisation agraire des populations Yoruba du Dahomey et du Moyen Togo." Thèse de Doctorat de 3è cycle. Paris: Université Paris Ouest Nanterre La Défense, 1970.

Kassa, G. "An overview of government policy interventions in pastoral areas: Achievements, constraints and prospects." Paper presented to the "National Conference on Pastoral Development in Ethiopia," Pastoralist Forum Ethiopia, Wabi Shebelle Hotel, Addis Ababa, February 2, 2000.

Kopytoff, I., ed. "The internal African frontier—The making of African political culture." In *The African frontier—The reproduction of traditional African societies*, Bloomington & Indianapolis: Indiana University Press, 1987a: 3–84.

Kopytoff, I. "Frontiers and frontier societies." In *Encyclopedia of Africa south of the Sahara*, edited by J. Middleton. New York: Charles Scribner's Sons, 1987b: 70–171.

Le Meur, P. Y. "State making and the politics of the frontier in central Benin." *Development and Change* 37, no. 4 (2006): 871–900.

Lombard, J. *Structures de type "féodal" en Afrique noire: Études des dynamismes internes et des relations sociales chez les Bariba du Dahomey.* Paris: Mouton, 1965.

Menkhaus, K. "The crisis in Somalia: Tragedy in five acts." *African Affairs* 106, no. 204 (2007): 357–390.

Migdal, J. "Mental maps and virtual checkpoints: Struggles to construct and maintain state and social boundaries." In *Boundaries and belonging: States and societies in the struggle to shape identities and local practices*, edited by J. Migdal. Cambridge: Cambridge University Press, 2004: 3–26.

Nugent, P. *Smugglers, secessionists and loyal citizens on the Ghana–Togo frontier: The lie of the borderlands since 1914.* Oxford: James Currey, 2002.

Person, Y. "Notes sur les Baseda (Bassila-Cercle de Djougou)." *Études dahoméennes* 15 (1956): 35–68.

Raeymaekers, T. "The silent encroachment of the frontier: A politics of transborder trade in the Semliki Valley (Congo–Uganda)." *Political Geography* 28 (2009): 55–65.

Reid, R. J. *Frontiers of violence in north-east Africa.* Oxford: Oxford University Press, 2011.

Rieber, A. J. "Frontiers in history." In *International encyclopedia of the social & behavioral sciences*, edited by N. J. Smelser and P. B. Baltes. Amsterdam: Elsevier, 2001: 5812–5818.

Schmitt, C. *Der Nomos der Erde im Völkerrecht des Jus Publicum Europaeum.* Berlin: Duncker & Humblot, 1950.

Scott, J. *The art of not being governed. An anarchist history of upland Southeast Asia.* New Haven, CT: Yale University Press, 2009, p. 40.

Tareke, G. "The Ethiopia–Somalia war of 1977 revisited." *International Journal of African Historical Studies* 33, no. 3 (2000): 635–667.

Turner, F. J. "The significance of the frontier in American history." In *Annual report of the American Historical Association*, 1893: 199–207.

Vandergeest, P. and N. L. Peluso. "Territorialization and state power in Thailand." *Theory and Society* 24, no. 2 (1995): 385–426.

Wendl, T. and M. Rösler, eds. "Frontiers and borderlands. The rise and relevance of an Anthropological research genre." In *Frontiers and borderlands. Anthropological perspectives*, Frankfurt: Peter Lang, 1999: 1–27.

CHAPTER 3

Centering Borders and Borderlands: The Evidence from Africa

Markus Virgil Hoehne and Dereje Feyissa

Introduction

Borders in Africa have generally been conceived as barriers, but they also provide what Nugent and Asiwaju (1996) call "conduits and opportunities". The academic discourse on state borders in the continent is largely focused on the constraints side. The main topics of the literature on African borders and borderlands are conflicts over borders, marginalization of the people living along the borders, informal cross-border economies such as smuggling and the disregard of the local population for the "artificial" and often ill-administered borders.[1] A second body of (not necessarily Africa-related) literature perceives borders as limiting economic and other exchanges, or, to the contrary, argues that borders are frequently irrelevant when looking at transnational and global processes of exchange and identity formation.[2] Studies of transnationalism and globalization emphasize the diminishing importance of territoriality and, consequently, posit the detachment of culture, politics and economy from any fixed borders.[3] Borders and borderlands feature, if at all, as zones of displacement and deterritorialization.[4] Achille Mbembe[5] drew attention to recent dynamics in contemporary Africa related to conflicts within and between states and/or the exploitation of natural resources such as oil and diamonds through external actors, which transcend the focus on the state as clear-cut unit, defined by its borders.

Nonetheless, there are voices that argue convincingly that borders in their various capacities as concrete barriers, as imagined lines separating lands and people and as structures related to borderlands are still extremely important.[6] We think it is worth taking state borders and borderlands as given because, first, in Africa state borders have been more stable than elsewhere in the world since the early twentieth century.[7] Second, state borders obviously have "border effects". They shape political, economic and social structures, and also create a new kind of agency that is at the disposal of those living in the borderlands and/or belonging to the borderland communities. This latter aspect has, with a few exceptions, attracted little systematic attention in the Africa-centered literature.

We ask how people who live along state borders in Africa have adjusted to the borderland situation, and what strategies they use to extract different types of resources from borders and borderlands. By resources we refer to immaterial resources such as social relations (across the border), placement within the territorial, political or social landscape and any kind of claim that can be made with regard to state borders and/or borderlands in order to attain social, economic or political benefits. We distinguish between borders and borderlands on the following grounds: by borders we mean the institution of interstate division according to international law or the invocation thereof (as in the case of Somaliland). Borderlands, on the other hand, are territorially defined as the physical space along the border—on both sides of it.[8] We specifically engage with borders as institutions that can be made use of or appropriated,[9] and borderlands as fields of opportunities for the people inhabiting them.

In the following, we discuss the literature on state borders as constraints. Subsequently, we briefly touch on important insights from the anthropology of borders and borderlands, before we provide examples from various African contexts (from secondary literature on Africa as a whole and from our own research, which is centered on the Horn of Africa) that underpin the relevance of our perspective.

Borders as Constraints

The borders-as-constraints literature proposes that borders are arbitrary, are irrelevant and/or generate conflict. While these positions are not always related and cannot be located at the same level of analysis (some are based on ethnographic or historical research, while others are informed by globalization theory), the borders-as-constraints literature has one thing in common: it stresses the problematic sides of borders.

Arbitrary Borders

About 42 percent of the total length of land boundaries in Africa is drawn by "parallels, meridians and equidistant lines without any consideration of social realities".[10,11] At first glance, this underlines the arbitrary nature of state borders on the continent. Already some decades ago, in 1972, Saadia Touval refuted the perspective of Africans as pure victims, however. He emphasized that in a number of cases African rulers actively engaged with European colonizers. In some cases, local strongmen were able to influence the demarcation of the colonial boundaries and profit from their external contacts, which helped to stabilize their authority. Other authors have also highlighted the precolonial roots of borders and re-bordering processes, and the involvement of Africans (albeit predominantly the ruling elite) in the colonial partition of the continent.[12] A. I. Asiwaju[13] argued that boundaries have separated people connected through lines of communication, traditions, shared sociopolitical institutions and economic resources and, sometimes, common systems of rule. He found that the borders dividing African states were not absolute. Cross-border integration took place every day, and many clandestine cross-border activities such as smuggling challenged the authority of the state. Borders were therefore understood as essentially legal limits, which distinguish the jurisdiction of different political regimes and their respective administrations. But borderlanders frequently ignored the arbitrary colonial lines, and "the partition can hardly be said to have taken place".[14] In the same vein, Günther Schlee[15] characterized the district boundaries in Kenya as "colonial constructs" that ignored local realities beyond the immediate interests of the colonizers. This led to cognitive discrepancies: "The result is that people inhabiting the same country have quite different views of the legitimacy and usefulness or even the existence of boundaries".[16]

This part of the borders-as-constraints literature therefore emphasizes that state (or administrative) borders in Africa frequently cut through areas of shared culture and dense social, economic and political relationships. The borders are arbitrary and often not accepted by the population. The local reaction to the borders is disregard to the degree possible. Consequently, borderlands are zones of sociopolitical ambivalence. Since clearly demarcated borders are a necessary condition for modern statehood, tensions between borderlanders and the state, and between states, are inevitable.

Conflict-prone Borders

From a contemporary perspective, it is a bitter irony that Asiwaju in the mid-1980s advised politicians in postcolonial Africa to follow the Somali lead. He referred to the Somali (back then) as the "only partitioned groups in Africa among whom reactions have taken the form of an active nationalist movement".[17] Somali nationalism is indeed intimately related to the problem of arbitrary colonial borders in the Horn of Africa.[18] In colonial time, the Somali peninsula was divided between France, Italy, Great Britain, and Ethiopia.

After the independence of the Somali Republic in 1960, Somalis lived in Somalia, Ethiopia, and colonies that later became Kenya (1963) and Djibouti (1977). Somali nationalists advocated the unity of all Somali territories and claimed the right to self-determination for Somalis who remained outside the Somali state.[19] Already in the 1960s, the so-called "Greater Somalia" policy led to major conflicts of Somalia with Kenya and Ethiopia.[20] The weakness of Ethiopia after the fall of Emperor Haileselassie in 1974 prompted Somalia's attack on its neighbor in pursuit of its irredentist dream, resulting in one of Africa's bloodiest interstate wars, popularly known as the Ogaden War (1977–78). The devastating defeat of the Somali national army weakened the regime of President Mohamed Siyad Barre. Mounting militant opposition during the 1980s culminated in the fall of the government and the collapse of the state, which was followed by internal territorial reorganization. In 1991, Somaliland in the northwest seceded unilaterally from the rest of Somalia. Puntland in the northeast was declared an autonomous region in 1998. In 2006, Islamists in the south started fighting for power and Somali unity. One of their strategies for mobilizing followers was to vow to attack Ethiopia in order to free the Somalis there. Subsequently, Ethiopian and Kenyan forces, among others, intervened in southern Somalia. Many Somalis are worried that these interventions lead to territorial control within Somalia by neighboring countries. Borders are again questioned and reshaped.

The conflict between Eritrea and Ethiopia that came to a head in the devastating 1998–2000 war is intrinsically related to colonial partition and border politics. It has its prehistory in decades of guerrilla war against the Ethiopian governments before 1991, and continued in the form of a proxy war in collapsed Somalia throughout the 2000s.[21] Similarly, current uncertainties over the political future of Southern Sudan in the context of its July 2011 declaration of independence have been followed by new military clashes between the south and the north in 2012. Taken together, these constellations, make the Horn of Africa a "prime theater" for ongoing violent conflicts related to state borders. Moreover, the people residing in borderlands are often treated with suspicion by the governments in the region. They are economically and culturally marginalized[22] or suffer from outright oppression.[23]

Other regions of sub-Saharan Africa have also had their share of border-related conflicts. Secessionist movements in Katanga and Biafra in the 1960s and continuing conflicts in the Casamance (Senegal), the Anglophone provinces of Cameroon, Cabinda in Angola, the Caprivi Strip (Namibia) and, recently, northern Mali point to the violent potential of colonial borders that were sanctioned by the Organization of African Unity (OAU) in the 1960s.[24] In their study of the Mano River region of West Africa, which comprises

Liberia, Guinea, Sierra Leone, and the Ivory Coast, Marilyn Silberfein and Al Hassan Conteh (2006) argued that "the porous and contestable features of African boundaries are two interacting themes that are closely linked to the emergence and spread of conflict in Africa".[25] The porosity of the border in the Mano River region has facilitated the movement of weapons, the transnational mobilization of fighters including child soldiers, the proliferation of contraband, the prevalence of refugees and the illicit exploitation of strategic resources. The artificiality of the border and its contestation by competing states has resulted in irredentist projects such as the aspiration of recreating "Greater Liberia". According to Silberfein and Conteh, the interplay between the porous and contested nature of the state borders along the Mano River region has created an explosive interstate conflict situation that has increasingly erupted into intrastate and interstate violence in West Africa.

Against the background of the contested nature of the (post)colonial borders and the frequent marginalization of the borderlanders, it comes as no surprise that many guerrilla movements in Africa, including the Revolutionary United Front (RUF) in Sierra Leone, the União Nacional para a Independência Total de Angola (UNITA) in Angola, the Lord's Resistance Army (LRA) in Uganda, the Oromo Liberation Front (OLF), the Ogaden National Liberation Front (ONLF) in Ethiopia and the Tuareg in northern Mali, have emanated from border zones.

Irrelevant Borders

A very different but related view is advanced in transnational and globalization theories, which see state borders as inconsequential and undesirable.[26] The advocates of these theories posit

> a new borderless world, in which the barrier impact of borders became insignificant [. . .]. Faced with the onslaught of cyber and satellite technology, as well as the free unimpeded flow of global capital, borders would—so the globalization purists argued—gradually open until they disappeared altogether.[27]

This perspective partly corresponds to what Vladimir Kolossov called the "global paradigm", according to which "state boundaries are being gradually transformed into virtual lines and are being replaced by economic, cultural and other boundaries".[28] The scale of interconnectedness engendered by globalization is expressed in quantitative and qualitative terms, such as money flows across the world's foreign exchange markets, the speed of travel of goods and people and the connections forged and possibilities opened through the Internet.[29] The downside is that global interconnectedness refers to global warming, massive deforestation and depletion of other natural resources and networks of crime and terror. In view of these dynamics, "the territorial referents of civic loyalty are increasingly divided for many persons along different spatial horizons [. . .] that may create disjunct registers of affiliation".[30] Commenting on the shrinking sovereignty of African states, Arjun Appadurai stressed that these states "care less about policing borders but focus their energies on policing and sanctifying important cities, monuments, and resources at the urban centers of the regime".[31] It seems that globally, and particularly in Africa, state borders are increasingly irrelevant for defining political, economic and social action.[32]

Beyond Borders as Constraints and Irrelevant Borders

Despite the obviousness of border-related conflicts and the arbitrariness of many borders in Africa, we take issue with the argument that the artificiality of the continent's colonial borders explains their problematic nature in postcolonial times. All borders in general and state borders in particular are artificial in the sense that they are the products of human imagination put into practice.[33] Moreover, borders were often drawn in the context of wars and conflicts. In Europe, many of the current state borders go back to changes related to either World War I or World War II.[34]

We also refute the vision of a borderless world, as it fails to capture the reality on the ground in at least two important respects. For one, globalization is not only about flows and connections but also about "systematic processes of closure and containment".[35] Borders have become more salient, given the continued relevance of mechanisms of inclusion into a privileged collective self and the exclusion of "others". This certainly concerns the relationship between Africa and Europe. Second, closure has attained a new lease on life in the post-9/11 world and the advent of what Newman (2006) called the "securitization discourse". In the wake of the terror attacks on the United States, "governments have begun to reassess their border-opening policies. The securitization discourse has, once again, become prominent as governments move towards re-closing their borders and making them more difficult to cross in the face of perceived security threat".[36] New immigration and deportation regimes,[37] as well as growing camp systems, from Dadaab (one of the world's largest refugee camps in northern Kenya) to Guantanamo, are part of contemporary re-bordering processes. These are certainly relevant arguments against the irrelevance of borders. It has to be noted, though, that the securitization discourse stresses the agency of state institutions along borders. The (re-)bordering and border-crossing processes within which the agency of the borderlanders is situated remain opaque.

Generally, it seems to us that the borders-as-constraints literature is largely normative. It argues against the "bad" (arbitrary, conflict-prone and hindering) or for the "good" (secured and surveyed) border. In contrast, we propose a nonjudgmental perspective focusing on peoples' agency and creativity with regard to state borders and borderlands, turning what appears to be a liability into an asset. This perspective was pioneered long ago by a human geographer named Eric Fischer. Other researchers (often anthropologists) working along borders and in borderlands have followed suit more recently.

A Differentiated Approach to Borders and Borderlands

Based on the study of southern Tyrol, Fischer (1949) developed his perspective on the imprint of boundaries upon social life. He posed the pertinent question of why the international border should matter

> The longer a boundary functions, especially an international boundary, the harder it becomes to alter it. The transportation net gets adjusted to the boundary, market towns take their specific importance from it, habits of the local population are shaped by it, ideas are moulded under the impact of different educational systems. Once established, boundaries tend to persist through their impact upon the human landscape.[38]

Fischer's description of the state border between Austria and Italy aptly captures political developments in Europe in the twentieth century, where, particularly after the World Wars, governments embarked on intensive projects of nationalizing their borders. African borders and borderlanders, however, have followed different trajectories. Border regions were often neglected by the political centers. Yet marginalization is only one side of the "border coin". The other is a huge potential for local agency as we outline below. In contrast to Fischer's study, in which the center developed an interest in the border, in many African cases it is the borderlanders taking a decisive stance regarding the border that influences the political centers.[39] Thus, like Baud and Van Schendel,[40] we argue for a view from the "periphery", which sometimes is not peripheral at all. Nonetheless, Fischer's position is helpful when it comes to the issue of borders gaining social and economic validity over time.

The contemporary anthropology of state borders and borderlands gained momentum with Wilson and Donnan (1998), who focused on politics of representation, redefinition and resistance in border zones. Following this approach, Michael Rösler and Tobias Wendl argued that "located at the fringes of nation-states, borderlands usually lack precise boundaries and are more exposed to foreign, trans-border influences and cross-border movements than are the heartlands".[41] In our view, it is exactly this lack of precise boundaries that creates opportunities for the borderlanders. While they might be physically detached from the political center, borderlanders are partly in control of what happens at the borders, which is again vital for the polity as a whole.[42] State borders are similar to social borders in the sense that both mark off collective identities. Where they differ is in the degree of rigidity. Within state borders, national identities are fortified by citizenship, economic regimes and international legal agreements that particularly in Africa contribute to the postcolonial sanctification of state borders,[43] whereas social borders usually exhibit more fluidity. Still, ultimately, state borders, despite their "natural appearance" on maps, are socially and politically constructed.[44]

The constructedness or arbitrary nature of state borders does not mean that they are inconsequential. With regard to state regimes and legal arrangements, borders set in motion new economic and sociopolitical processes that are as much enabling as they are constraining. Furthermore, state borders have unintended as well as intended consequences. They demarcate and separate, but also encourage people to explore new connections as well as cross-border opportunities and incentives that come along with residing in borderlands. These are sometimes in line with and sometimes against state policies and interests. Timothy Raeymaekers, whose empirical material comes from the Congolese–Ugandan borderlands, added that "recent analysis in African borderlands points at the high level of overlap and complicity that often exists between different systems of survival and regulation [including state regulation]".[45]

The aspect of border as political resource has been mentioned by Lentz (2003), who analyzed dynamics between ignorance and invocation of the border in resource conflicts in the borderlands between Ghana and Burkina Faso. At a more generic level, Fredrik Barth argued that

> Throughout history political boundaries have been rich in affordances, offering opportunities for army careers, customs-duty collecting agencies, defence construction contracts and all manners of work and enterprise. They have provided a facility of retreat and escape for bandits and freedom fighters eluding the control of states on both sides; and they are a constant field of opportunities for mediators, traders and middlepersons of all kinds.[46]

According to Barth, the opportunities of borders derive from their setting the scene for social activities as well as their establishing connections through separating political and economic spaces. In order to profit from borders, people have to become active and spin connections. The boundary thereby becomes shaped by social and material processes.[47] We wish to add here that the opportunities that borders provide are not ready-made. Their realization requires effort and varies depending on the particular border sites that people occupy.

Paul Nugent (2002) explored the opportunities provided by the Ghana–Togo border. These were related particularly to the formation of national and "informal" economies in which the opportunities are embedded. Nugent criticized the conventional wisdom about African boundaries, which focuses solely on the constraints side of state borders.[48] Once in place, he maintained, the state border creates strong local interests whose proponents seek to preserve the status quo. Nugent noted that for the most part, at least in western Africa, national identification proved far more valuable than cross-border ethnic identifications. Rather than disengaging from the state, as many would have predicted, border communities such as those along the Ghana–Togo border have actively sought to shape and utilize the state and its borders. Similarly, Hüsken (2009), who has worked along the border between Egypt and Libya, stressed that the integrity of the different nation-states is not questioned by the cross-border actors, who often belong to the same tribal group, but live on opposite sides of the border. Rather, cross-border actors consciously adhere to and use their different national identities. With regard to this "state shaping" from below, Nugent (2002) showed the relevance and limits of James Scott's (1990) model of the hidden transcript of power relations. Many scholars working within the borders-as-constraints paradigm use Scott's model implicitly or explicitly as an analytical frame, in which contraband trade, for instance, is viewed as an act of resistance. Instead, Nugent proposed analyzing the dynamic interplay among various actors in the construction, maintenance and consolidation of borders. Smuggling, in his perspective, is not an act of resistance to state borders, nor is it just the continuation of older trade relations "by other means". "Apart from opening up new trade routes, the smuggling complex also summons forth a new breed of entrepreneurs whose very livelihoods depended upon the perpetuation of the international boundary".[49] Nugent's focus on the changes that borders introduce, and from which certain opportunities for borderlanders possibly arise, resonates very well with Fischer's (1949) observation about the impact of boundaries on human geography.

A concept that is very close to Nugent's argument (which he however does not mention in his work) is that of "arbitrage economies". James Anderson and Liam O'Dowd defined arbitrage economies as "economic activities for which the border is the *raison d'etre* [. . .] The co-existence of different regulatory regimes on either side of the border generates a form of opportunity structure which invites smuggling, unofficial exchange rates and illegal immigration" (italics in the original).[50] In their perspective, border-dependent activities "may be seen in terms of 'arbitrage' or the exploitation of differentials in prices, interest rates, exchange rates and share prices over time and space".[51]

Horstmann and Wadley (2006) likewise approached borders as opportunity structures. They emphasized how people are not merely constrained by borders but that border crossing also opens up new options for local agency. They noted that

> borderlands are unique forms of peripheries as zones between often competing or unequal states. This international character increases the peripherality and ambiguity of the borderlands as inhabitants seek benefits from both sides of the border, and as the states try to control their activities.[52]

The latter point about state control was underlined by Mathijs Pelkmans, who did research along the Georgia–Turkey border. He argued that

> [a]lthough the strategic power of citizens may be higher at the margins, and border dwellers may display more conspicuously ambiguous loyalties, these characteristics may be the precise reason for intensified state regulation, as the history of Soviet borders amply demonstrates.[53]

Drawing on these works outlining the complexities of and the opportunities provided by state borders and the human actions across them and within the borderlands, we continue to challenge the conventional focus on state borders in Africa as constraints or as irrelevant. Without denying that borders also put limitations on people's lives, and that borderlands are in some regards marginal zones, we propose that borders offer manifold resources. The opportunities of borders can be seized in the borderlands, but also beyond them. The resourcing of borderlands is, as we argued elsewhere,[54] dependent on intervening variables, some of which are structural, while others are related to the individual capacities of the actors involved.[55]

Case studies from the Horn of Africa

We offer here additional ethnographic evidence from the Horn of Africa to demonstrate not only that borders are centers in their own right but also how borderland communities actively shape and transform state-making processes through local practices. The examples focus on the political and social processes of the Ethio-Sudanese and the Somaliland–Puntland borders.

Case Study 1: The Ethio-Sudanese Border

The first case deals with the contrasting modes of signification of the Ethio-Sudanese border by the Anywaa and the Nuer. It presents the situation in the Gambella region of western Ethiopia, bordering Sudan. Except for a tiny section that lives in Southern Sudan, the majority of the Anywaa live in the Gambella region. The opposite is true for the Nuer. The majority of the Nuer live in Southern Sudan, though a section of the Nuer, the Jikany, live in the Gambella region. According to the 2007 census, the Jikany Nuer are a demographic majority, constituting 47 percent of Gambella's population. The Anywaa, though "firstcomers" in the region's settlement history, currently constitute only 24 percent of Gambella's population. The current demographic structure of the Gambella region is a result of the historic expansion of the Nuer from Southern Sudan to the east (into today's Ethiopia) since the second half of the nineteenth century. This expansion has continued to these days. The Anywaa have been at the receiving end, losing a substantial chunk of their territories to the Nuer. The founding of the Ethiopian state in the early twentieth century has offered a political opportunity for the Anywaa in their struggle for survival. Drawing on their settlement pattern and their greater competence in Ethiopian mainstream culture, they have sought to construct the Nuer as Sudanese citizens and therefore as foreigners who trouble Ethiopian citizens. They utilize the international border as a discursive resource, inasmuch as the majority of the Nuer have migrated to Gambella after the demarcation of the international border in 1902. In fact, the Anywaa invoke this border in the regional power game more than the Ethiopian governments do. This is a discursive practice that gives the impression that the Anywaa are more state than the state.[56] In their call for the fortification of the border, the Anywaa have found themselves in the forefront of championing a state project, though their main concern is defending an ethnic interest, namely containing Nuer expansion that resulted in occupation of their territories. Nevertheless, the Anywaa's mode of signification of the border has the effect of reproducing state ideology—sovereignty over a bounded territory—at a local level. In fact, they have actively assisted the process of state-building in Ethiopia in one of its historic peripheries. Such local participation in state-building is crucial, because the Ethiopian state has, by and large, a legitimacy deficit in peripheral areas such as Gambella. This and other regions, however, need to be controlled, since they contain strategic resources that the state wishes to exploit, such as riverine lands, gold and petroleum.

The Anywaa's neighbors, the Nuer, pursue a different strategy regarding the international border, though their actions, too, shape state-building in Ethiopia in a different way. The Nuer are border-crossers par excellence both at the local and national levels. As mobile pastoralists, they have a flexible concept of social and political borders. They have built an identity system with a very assimilationist motif. E. E. Evans-Pritchard's Nuer of the 1930s and the contemporary Nuer have something basic in common, though the sociopolitical conditions of their existence have gone through radical transformations,[57] namely the ease at which they assimilate outsiders at various levels of identification. Border crossing is a norm and immigration is considered not as a threat but something to be celebrated. The Nuer invoke the same imagery of the flexible social borders to justify national border crossings. While pursuing fluctuating opportunity structures in the Sudan and in Ethiopia, the Nuer have practiced an alternative citizenship, which is equivalent to a "dual citizenship" in a language of the state. The current Ethiopian government, led by the Ethiopian People's Revolutionary Democratic Front (EPRDF), has embarked on a novel state-building approach since 1991, which puts an accent on ethnic belonging and territoriality, a political order widely known as ethnic federalism.[58] Accordingly, ethnicity is the official state ideology and the main unit of political action. Ethnicity is territorialized in the form of ethnically carved out regional states or subregional governments that constitute the Ethiopian federation. Thus, in the Gambella regional state, both the Anywaa and the Nuer have their respective zonal governments.

Nuer border crossing, which is also applicable to other mobile pastoralist groups, has directly collided with Ethiopia's ethnic federalism. Many Nuer from Southern Sudan have continued to cross the border and settle inside and outside the Nuer zone in the Gambella regional state, redefined as "foreign" ethnic territory within ethnic federalism. One recent example is the settlement of a Nuer community known as the Cieng Reng, who have been settling in traditionally Anywaa territories since the outbreak of the Sudanese civil war in 1983. The Cieng Reng settlement in Gambella has been politicized by the Anywaa particularly after the 1994 census, which has ensconced Anywaa ethnic sensibilities by suddenly turning the Nuer from an insecure ethnic minority into an ethnic majority.[59] The Cieng Reng have contested their definition as foreigners by the Anywaa. In doing so, they have drawn on a cultural repertoire that not only accepts but encourages immigration. When their identity politics failed to bear fruit at the regional level, the Cieng Reng went to Addis Ababa, the national capital, in 2000 and directly challenged the EPRDF government to grant them citizenship. To make their demand more compelling, their leader, Kong Diw, framed the issue in the language of the state, which means becoming citizens through participation in a national war. This was a reference to the Ethio-Eritrean border war of 1998–2000, in which many Nuer from Gambella fought. Confronted by a morally and politically loaded demand, the EPRDF agreed to a compromise. It granted the Cieng Reng a residence and permitted them to settle the issue the "Nuer way" by allowing the Sudanese Nuer to integrate into the Nuer local communities in the Gambella region. Though this was a significant concession, the Cieng Reng have continued their quest for full recognition. Supported by their local Nuer neighbors, the Cieng Reng have ultimately attained full Ethiopian citizenship in 2008, with kebeles of their own. Kebeles are the lowest level of local government in Ethiopia.

While the Nuer turned their engagement in Ethiopia and particularly with the government into a success, the Anywaa seemed to lose out. The Anywaa's disappointment with the center grew sharply since 2002, when they failed to get the support they anticipated from the EPRDF during a deadly power struggle with the Nuer in parts of Gambella region between June 2002 and January 2003 that cost the lives of many people from both sides. Upon the occurrence of this conflict, the government introduced a new power-sharing arrangement ostensibly to balance the Anywaa historical and the Nuer demographic arguments for political entitlement. This greatly alienated the Anywaa, who once again felt abandoned by the Ethiopian state. As a result, there has been a discursive convergence among the various Anywaa political actors, who earlier followed divergent strategies of containment. Disgruntled groups of Anywaa expressed their anger by attacking government establishments and ambushing civilian highlanders (who were perceived as representing the government and were not part of the original population of the region). In reaction, a mob of highlanders went on the rampage, indiscriminately killing Anywaa males with rocks and machetes. Some members of the federal army deployed in the region, who were exclusively highlanders, also participated in the killing using automatic weapons. The Anywaa increasingly felt that they were cornered not only by the Nuer but also by the EPRDF. More recently, Anywaa elites in Gambella and in the diaspora turned their local resistance into a global struggle for human rights, claiming that the government of Ethiopia committed or at least tolerated genocide in the Gambella region.

The contemporary engagement of the Nuer in Gambella does not entail, in the perspective of the Cieng Reng and the Nuer in general, a lifelong commitment to the Ethiopian national identity. In fact, many Cieng Reng have gone back to Southern Sudan since the 2005 Sudanese Comprehensive Peace Agreement (CPA) brought about a relative peace and stability in their former homeland. The opportunistic political behavior of the Cieng Reng reflects the Nuer conception of borders of all kinds as permeable and offering multiple resources. The main resources on the Ethiopian side in the 1980s and 1990s were relative peace, humanitarian aid, education and career opportunities.

In reference to this conception of borders, the educated section of the Nuer on both sides of the Ethio-Sudanese border sees dual citizenship as a win-win formula for their borderland community. This approach is spearheaded by the Gaat-Jak Nuer, the largest Nuer community divided by the border, who explicitly formulate the benefits of division by the border. Interestingly, none of them is secessionist or advances the creation of a cross-border "Greater Nuer" political community. Instead, they advocate for political representation in both the countries. The "rationality" of the partition is well articulated in one of the Gaat-Jak Nuer media outlets called Maiwut and Gambella Educational Research Foundation (MGERF). In its 2005 issue, MGERF featured an article with the title "The Gaat-Jak Nuer: One Nation, Two States", which articulates their double bind to the Ethiopian and south Sudanese states.

How this will be acted out in the newly independent Southern Sudan remains to be seen. The extent to which the EPRDF has tolerated Nuer border crossing, albeit in the form of rigidly formulated ethnic federalism, is, at least, an instance of how statehood can be negotiated through local practices. Responding to greater contestation over territoriality among the pastoralists' communities, the EPRDF has, in recent times, sought to tone down ethnicity in political practice toward a pragmatic and flexible understanding of social identities. There are some indications that show the Ethiopian government's desire to use the double bind of the Nuer to forge stronger economic ties with the new, oil-rich state of Southern Sudan. In a speech by the late Prime Minister Meles Zenawi delivered to the parliament in February 2011, he used the language of "kinship" as a kind of social capital, in reference to the cross-border settlement and to justify the need for a stronger regional economic integration. This shows how the Ethio-Sudanese border over time has changed its significance also for the center. Over the past decades, it has transformed from being a border between hostile states on different sides during the Cold War in the 1980s to a "line in the sand" across which regional integration was envisioned by Addis Ababa in 2011.[60] The border-related practices of the Nuer between Sudan and Ethiopia arguably have contributed to this transformation of a hard to a soft border.

Case Study 2: The Somaliland–Puntland Border

The second case focuses on the border of Somaliland and Puntland, two state-like entities in northern Somalia. This border and the borderlands along it, which are inhabited by two clans called Dhulbahante and Warsangeli, are contested between the government of Somaliland in Hargeysa and the government of Puntland in Garowe. The conflict provides the local borderlanders the opportunity to gain some resources by switching allegiances between the two centers. It is the borderlanders who tip the balance of power between Somaliland and Puntland. However, since 2004, the conflict between both sides has increasingly played out militarily. This transformed the borderlands into militarized zones and led to new fighting, from which mostly the local population suffered. The case shows that the borderlands between Somaliland and Puntland are where (national) identities and politics are questioned, negotiated and reinforced, with important implications for both the peripheries and the centers of the two state-like entities.[61]

When Somaliland was founded in northwestern Somalia in May 1991 against the background of collapsing Somalia, it was declared independent within the borders of the former British Protectorate.[62] While Somaliland did not receive international recognition, it since then steadily developed as a viable *de facto* state. Its existence is based on the consensus of the majority of the population, which belongs to the Isaaq clan family residing in central Somaliland, to stay independent from the rest of Somalia, which is characterized by civil war, warlordism, external interventionism and, more recently, piracy and Islamic extremism. In eastern Somaliland, however, where roughly one-quarter of the population lives, the support for Somaliland's independence was always extremely limited. People there, who belong to the Dhulbahante and Warsangeli clans, were Somali nationalists and adhered to the vision of a united Somalia. They only agreed to secession due to the military dominance of the Isaaq in 1991 and due to the hopeless chaos in the south at that time. Their support for Somaliland decreased over the past two decades, fueled by what they perceived as deliberate marginalization of their clan homelands by the government in Hargeysa.

Puntland was established in August 1998 in northeastern Somalia. It is, according to its constitution, part of Somalia and aims at the establishment of a united but federal Somali state. Its population is defined genealogically. Puntland is essentially a regional state for all Harti, which is a clan federation comprising Majeerteen, Dhulbahante, Warsangeli and some smaller groups. Harti belongs to the larger Darood clan family, which also has a strong presence in southern Somalia (and in eastern Ethiopia and northern Kenya). The people of Puntland do not recognize the independence of Somaliland. Many Dhulbahante and Warsangeli residing in the regions of Sool, eastern Sanaag and southern Togdheer, who politically are Somali nationalists, supported the foundation of Puntland while still being to some degree involved in Somaliland. Therefore, their territories became contested between Somaliland and Puntland. Due to the economic and military weakness of both the centers, the borderland communities were left on their own by both sides until the early 2000s. Locals realized that remaining in between politically comes with certain advantages. Some Dhulbahante and Warsangeli elites held positions in the governments of Somaliland and Puntland and tried to attract resources for themselves and their local constituencies. But no state presence was established in the contested borderlands. Traditional authorities were the real rulers in the area. Some of them cleverly used their representative capital to align their people with either Somaliland or Puntland; some of them were awarded "gifts" by the governments for these (often temporarily limited) services.

The situation began to change around 2001, when both centers started encroaching into their respectively eastern or western peripheries by establishing rump administrations and police and military forces in key towns and villages. Still, the staff of these local administrations and forces consisted of members of the local borderland communities, who saw this as an opportunity to gain salaries and other support from Hargeysa or Garowe. It was not uncommon to find brothers or first cousins serving on opposed sides, which in fact meant simply that the income of the (extended) family was increased. Another form of encroachment into the contested borderlands was the establishment of new regions on the Puntland side in the Dhulbahante and Warsangeli territories. Garowe created the region Heylaan with the capital Badhan in, what is for the Somaliland government, eastern Sanaag. It also founded the region Ayn (Somali: Cayn) with the capital Buuhoodle in what, according to Hargeysa, is southern Togdheer. The local population mostly endorsed the foundation of new administrative structures; it seemed to increase their political weight (at least in Puntland).

The competition of Somaliland and Puntland for the local borderland constituencies therefore provided local political and military elites, traditional authorities and some "ordinary" people with political and financial resources. The negative side of staying in between Somaliland and Puntland was that the local politics in Sool, eastern Sanaag/Heylaan and southern Togdheer/Ayn was increasingly influenced by the conflict between the two centers. Local traditional authorities and political elites lost some of their followers when too strongly leaning on one side or switching between both sides too often. From end of 2002 onward, Hargeysa and Garowe pursued their opposed claims increasingly by taking military steps into the contested borderlands. This triggered new political dynamics. The arrival of nonlocal (Isaaq or Majeerteen) troops in the Dhulbahante and Warsangeli territories caused considerable unrest. First, military clashes happened when President Dahir Rayale Kahin of Somaliland arrived with an entourage of about 200 soldiers on a visit in Lasanod, the capital of Sool region mostly inhabited by Dhulbahante, in December 2002. Puntland sent some troops to counter Somaliland's "intrusion" and fighting broke out in Lasanod, killing a number of soldiers and civilians. A year later, Puntland sent police forces to Lasanod to stop fighting between two Dhulbahante lineages. The police was followed by military troops that occupied Lasanod and established a new administration in town. Hargeysa reacted by sending its army to the Sool region. A front line was established running some 30 kilometers west of Lasanod through the Sool region. Fighting between both armies erupted in October 2004, leaving dozens of soldiers—most of whom were locals—dead or wounded. Tensions also increased in the parts of Sanaag region where the Warsangeli lived and some fighting happened there in 2006. Somaliland finally succeeded in taking over Lasanod in October 2007. Tens of thousands of Dhulbahante fled and for one month pro- and anti-Somaliland militias fought in Lasanod. Since the end of 2007, the town is in the hands of Somaliland. While some locals appreciate the peace and stability Somaliland brought, most complain that the military conflict in the area had a negative effect on the already weak local economy, which depended on livestock export, transit trade and small businesses.

New problems arose since 2009, when diaspora actors, traditional authorities and others belonging to the Dhulbahante clan residing in Sool and southern Togdheer/Ayn founded a new movement called Sool, Sanaag and Ayn (SSC).[63] Its aims were to end the occupation of Lasanod by Somaliland forces, to stabilize security in the SSC regions, to work for the development of these regions and to secure direct access to international aid. The motivation to establish this kind of administration derived from Hargeysa's and Garowe's monopolization of aid and economic development in the centers of the respective state-like entities over the past years. Moreover, the distance of the SSC from Garowe was caused by the lack of will of the Puntland government to recapture Lasanod. Some fighting escalated between SSC forces and clan militias from Buuhoodle on the one side, and Somaliland troops on the other in late 2010 and early 2011. After internal splits, the SSC lost support among the Dhulbahante. It was succeeded by the administration of the Khaatumo State of Somalia, which was declared at a clan conference in Taleh in Sool region in January 2012. The Khaatumo administration declared its subjection under the federal constitution of Somalia. Thereby it hoped to gain support of the Transitional Federal Government (TFG), which had been created by the international community at conferences for Somalia in Kenya and Djibouti, 2004 and 2009.

Fighting escalated also in northwestern Puntland from 2006 onward, where the Warsangeli fiercely resisted what they considered the "illegal" exploitation of mineral and other natural resources in the Galgala Mountains by the Puntland administration. In this context, some religious militants took advantage of the situation. Their leader, Sheikh Mohamed Said Atom, a local Warsangeli figure and religious scholar, combined the agenda of his patrilineal relatives with Wahabist religious ideology and soon challenged the "apostate" government in Garowe. The local religious extremists received support from the southern Somali Islamist group Al Shabaab.

The main danger for the governments in Hargeysa and Garowe was that the establishment of autonomous or splinter administrations in the contested borderlands undermined their self-definition as independent state in its colonial borders (Somaliland) and Harti administration (Puntland). But these new developments also substantially changed the room for maneuver for the concerned borderlanders. Many of them stopped looking to Hargeysa or Garowe to gain something. They oriented themselves toward the south, where either the TFG or Al Shabaab were perceived as allies. The level of political negotiations therefore changed from regional to national, at least in some regards. Simultaneously, at least Hargeysa complemented its military strategy against the "borderland rebels" by supporting moderate development projects, particularly in the Dhulbahante territories. For instance, it provided funds for building a new campus for the university in Lasanod. Some people in the center realized that besides the claim to the colonial borders, what was at stake in Somaliland's east was the peace on which the success of the polity hinged.

Discussing Both Cases and Their Implications for Borders as Centers in Africa

The dynamics along the Ethio-Sudanese as well as along the Somaliland–Puntland border show that borders can simultaneously pose problems and provide opportunities for the borderland communities. The Anywaa perceive the border, at least since the coming to power of the EPRDF and the territorial reordering of Ethiopia within the framework of ethnic federalism, as a means to protect them against Nuer invasion. They become even more state than the state by invoking a strict citizenship regime where Addis Ababa tolerates what seems to be the "natural state of porosity" along its western border. The Nuer, on the other hand, similarly to the Dhulbahante and Warsangeli between Somaliland and Puntland, profit from their possibility of flexible national alignment. These latter groups are borderlanders as described by Asiwau,[64] whose loyalty to either of the states they can belong to is not very strong. Nonetheless, our cases also show that the flexible behavior of borderlanders can have unforeseen consequences for the centers and for the borderlanders themselves. The Anywaa–Nuer competition in the Gambella region forced the government of Ethiopia to clarify its stance. It had to grant residence to the Nuer coming over from Sudan and settling with their relatives in western Ethiopia. In this process, Addis Ababa, however, came dangerously close to losing the support of the Anywaa, who felt that the government had undermined its own principles of territorial sovereignty. The situation in the contested borderlands between Somaliland and Puntland, where the borderland elites openly played their double game, required both the governments in Hargeysa and in Garowe to take increasingly serious steps to fortify their opposed claims. From being neglected peripheries, the Dhulbahante and, to a lesser degree, the Warsangeli regions turned into hot spots of conflict and political crisis. This had the negative consequence that the local population, particularly in the Sool and southern Togdheer regions, suffered from the militarization of their homelands. On the other hand, it had the positive effect that particularly Hargeysa realized that without the borderlanders Somaliland risks loosing its most precious asset—its peace. Many external observers see Somaliland's peace (compared to the ongoing warring in the south) as the best reason why this *de facto* state indeed deserves international recognition. Similarly, the unrest in the Gambella region since the early 2000s and particularly the "global" agitation of some Anywaa elites against the policy of Addis Ababa put the western periphery on the agenda of the Ethiopian government. The strategy of the Warsangeli in the Galgala Mountains was somewhat different. To sustain their war against a Puntland administration that was perceived as predatory, the newly emerging leader Sheikh Atom aligned himself with the Islamists in the south. While this was not welcomed by most Warsangeli outside the mountains, many locals accepted this as a measure to put Garowe under pressure. The peripheral borderland mountains were thereby transformed into a political arena that now merited attention not only by Garowe but also by national and even international political actors in Somalia.

These dynamics, enhancing the peripheries' presence on government agendas, are fully in line with Nugent's observation that the "un-statish" practices at the margins of states can shape states probably even more than state practices in the center.[65] The flexible attitude of the Nuer regarding borders and the playing of double games by the Dhulbahante and Warsangeli challenged the states to take a stance regarding their concept of territoriality and citizenship. In the case of Ethiopia, it led to the tolerance of border crossing and a more flexible attitude to ethnic identity as the defining characteristic of its citizens. However, it also led to the eruption of "ethnic" conflict in the Gambella region. In the case of Somaliland, the unruly Dhulbahante forced Hargeysa to underpin its territorial claims to the contested borderlands between Somaliland and Puntland with military and, more recently, some development-oriented engagement. In the face of the Warsangeli resistance in the Galgala Mountains, Garowe has favored a military solution. This further weakens the Harti alliance, which is the basis of Puntland's existence and, together with the infiltration of the area by Islamist fighters from the south, continues to undermine the stability of the whole polity.

The case studies above also underline Raeymaekers' point that "an interesting aspect of the borderland perspective is that it questions the idea that state-making necessarily involves the gradual diffusion of power outwards, i.e. from the 'centre' towards the periphery".[66] The Anywaa and Nuer are not only competing for access to resources and power in the Gambella region. They also try to induce their visions of how the Ethiopian state ought to be functioning in the center. Regarding state formation in northern Somalia, it can be argued that it was only the challenge that the contested borderlands between Somaliland and Puntland posed to the centers that made Hargeysa and Garowe engage seriously in state-building beyond their respective core territories.

Conclusion

The dominant focus on state borders in Africa is on borders as constraints. Most writers until the end of the twentieth century perceived the artificial colonial borders on the continent as the barriers responsible for social, political and economic crises. Borderlands were understood as peripheral spaces inhabited by marginalized people excluded from state, social and other services, and suffering from interstate conflict. Alternatively, particularly since 1990, borders represent untimely constructs that have to be overcome in an age of transnational flows and globalization. Only recently, ethnographic accounts of border life have begun to stress the opportunities provided by state borders. In this chapter, we set out to systematize these newer approaches and to center borders and borderlands in Africa. By looking at various cross-border dynamics involving presumably marginalized and divided people, we shed light on the sometimes counterintuitive complexities brought about by border divisions. This does not mean that some 125 years after the infamous Berlin conference in 1884, the so-called "Congo conference", which—contrary to popular opinion—had only a limited impact on the process of partitioning Africa,[67] we wish to rehabilitate colonial partition. Still, we advocate for a more "sober" and empirically grounded perspective focusing on the lived realities of colonial and postcolonial partition. The normative perspective on the "bad" borders in Africa ignores the opportunities they provide to the partitioned people and other border constituencies. These opportunities are brought about by the "border effects" in the social, political and economic landscape along and related to the border. Certainly, these border effects change over time, as our case studies from the Horn of Africa have shown. Whether they outweigh the obstacles for the communities divided by the borders or not is an empirical question. For sure, however, borders are much more central and provide more opportunities for many Africans than the literature on borders as constraints or on irrelevant borders summarized in this text would have it. Borders and borderlands are the sites of global, national, and local dynamics and regimes of power that converge at the borders and charge them with a potentiality that can be grasped in relation to them in the borderlands and beyond.

Acknowledgments

Both authors wish to thank the Max Planck Institute for Social Anthropology in Halle/Saale, Germany, for financial, institutional and intellectual support during the long gestation process of their perspective on borders and borderlands. An earlier version of this paper has been presented at the workshop "Bringing the Margins Back In: War Making and State Making in the Borderlands" in Ghent, Belgium, February 12–14, 2010. We thank the participants there for encouraging comments and Timothy Raeymaekers for additional review comments.

Notes

1. Matthies 1977; Asiwaju 1985; Miles 1994; Clapham 1996a: 237–241; Nugent and Asiwaju 1996; Nugent 2002; Schlee 2003; Vorrath 2010.
2. A. Appadurai, "Sovereignty without territoriality: Notes for a postnational geography." in *The anthropology of space and place: locating culture*, ed. S. Low and D. Zuniga (Malden, MA: Blackwell, 2003), 337–349; J. Ferguson, "Transnational topographies of power: Beyond 'the state' and 'civil society' in the study of African politics," in *Accelerating possession: Global futures of property and personhood,* edited by B. Maurer and G. Schwab (New York: Columbia University Press, 2006), 76–98.
3. M. Kearney, "The local and the global: The anthropology of globalization and transnationalism." *Annual Review of Anthropology* 24 (1995): 547–565.
4. A. Gupta and J. Ferguson, "Beyond 'culture': Space, identity, and the politics of difference." *Cultural Anthropology* 7, no. 1 (1992): 18.
5. A. Mbembe, "At the edge of the world: Boundaries, territoriality, and sovereignty in Africa." in *Globalization and Violence, vol. 2: Colonial and postcolonial globalizations*, ed. P. James and P. Darby (London: Sage, 2006), 160–168.
6. M. Acuto, "Edges of the conflict: A three-fold conceptualization of national borders." *Borderlands e-Journal* 7, no. 1 (2008). <http://www.borderlands.net.au/vol7no1_2008/acuto_edges.htm> (May 11, 2011).
7. C. Clapham, "Rethinking African states". *African Security Review* 10, no. 3 (2001): n.p.

8. M. Baud and W. Van Schendel, "Toward a comparative history of borderlands." *Journal of World History* 8, no. 2 (1997): 216.

9. C. Lentz, "'This is Ghanaian territory!': Land conflicts on a West African border." *American Ethnologist* 30, no. 2 (2003): 274.

10. V. Kolossov, "Border studies: Changing perspectives and theoretical approaches." *Geopolitics* 10 (2005): 628–629.

11. This is a feature that distinguishes borders in Africa from borders elsewhere in the world. Baud and Van Schendel (1997: 235–240) suggested convincingly that the circumstances of "border formation" had an impact on the way how borders and borderlands have been studied in different parts of the world in the twentieth century.

12. C. Lentz, "'This is Ghanaian territory!': Land conflicts on a West African border." *American Ethnologist* 30, no. 2 (2003): 273–289; A. Mbembe, "At the edge of the world: Boundaries, territoriality, and sovereignty in Africa." in *Globalization and violence, vol. 2: Colonial and postcolonial globalizations*, ed. P. James and P. Darby (London: Sage, 2006), 148–171.

13. A. I. Asiwaju, "The conceptual framework." in *Partitioned Africans: ethnic relations across Africa's international boundaries, 1884–1984*, ed. A. I Asiwaju (London: C. Hurst, 1985), 2.

14. A. I. Asiwaju, "The conceptual framework." In *Partitioned Africans: Ethnic relations across Africa's international boundaries, 1884–1984*, ed. A. I Asiwaju (London: C. Hurst, 1985), 4.

15. G. Schlee, "Some effects on a district boundary in Kenya." in *The politics of age and gerontocracy in Africa*, ed. M. Aguilar (Trenton, NJ: Africa World Press, 1998), 232.

16. G. Schlee, "Some effects on a district boundary in Kenya." in *The politics of age and gerontocracy in Africa*, ed. M. Aguilar (Trenton, NJ: Africa World Press, 1998), 229.

17. A. I. Asiwaju, "The conceptual framework." in *Partitioned Africans: Ethnic relations across Africa's international boundaries, 1884–1984*, ed. A. I Asiwaju (London: C. Hurst, 1985), 14.

18. J. Drysdale, *The Somali dispute* (London: Pall Mall Press, 1964); C. L. Geshekter, "Anti-colonialism and class formation: The eastern Horn of Africa before 1950," *International Journal for African Historical Studies* 18, no. 1 (1985): 1–32.

19. Information Service of the Somali Government, *The Somali Peninsula: a new light on imperial motives* (Mogadishu: Information Service of the Somali Government, 1962); I. M. Lewis, "Introduction." in *Nationalism and self-determination in the Horn of Africa*, ed. I. M. Lewis (London: Ithaca Press, 1983), 13.

20. V. Matthies, *Der Grenzkonflikt Somalias mit Äthiopien und Kenya. Analyse eines zwischenstaatlichen Konflikts in der Dritten Welt* (Hamburg: Institut für Afrikakunde, 1977).

21. ICG. "Ethiopia and Eritrea: Preventing war." *Africa Report*, No. 101, 2005; M. Abdul, "Ethiopia's strategic dilemma in the Horn of Africa." *Social Science Research Council* (2007). <http://hornofafrica.ssrc.org/Abdul_Mohammed/>.

22. J. Markakis, "Borders and borderland communities in the Horn: the failure of integration." Paper presented at the conference "Divided they stand: The affordances of state borders in the Horn of Africa" (Max Planck Institute for Social Anthropology, Halle/Saale, September 7–8, 2006).

23. H. A. Mahmoud, "Seeking citizenship on the border: Kenya Somalis, the uncertainty of belonging, and public sphere interactions." Paper presented at the 12th CORDESIA General Assembly (Yaoundé, Cameroon, December 7–11, 2008).

24. A. Mbembe, "At the edge of the world: Boundaries, territoriality, and sovereignty in Africa." in *Globalization and violence, vol. 2: Colonial and postcolonial globalizations*, ed. P. James and P. Darby (London: Sage, 2006), 158.

25. M. Silberfein and Al Hassan Conteh, "Boundaries and conflict in the Mano River region of West Africa." *Conflict Management and Peace Science* 23, no. 4 (2006), 343.

26. Appadurai 1991, 2003; Glick Schiller, Basch and Blanc-Szanton 1992; Ferguson 2006.

27. D. Newman, "Borders and bordering: Towards an interdisciplinary dialogue." *European Journal of Social Theory* 9, no. 2 (2006): 172.

28. V. Kolossov, "Border studies: Changing perspectives and theoretical approaches." *Geopolitics* 10, 2005: 612.

29. Held et al. 2001; A. McGrew, *The transformation of democracy? Globalization and territorial democracy* (Cambridge: Polity Press, 1997), 6–7.

30. A. Appadurai, "Sovereignty without territoriality: Notes for a postnational geography." in *The anthropology of space and place: Locating culture*, ed. S. Low and D. Zuniga (Malden, MA: Blackwell, 2003), 341.

31. A. Appadurai, "Sovereignty without territoriality: Notes for a postnational geography." in *The anthropology of space and place: Locating culture*, ed. S. Low and D. Zuniga (Malden, MA: Blackwell, 2003), 341.

32. A similar point was made by Wimmer and Glick Schiller (2002), albeit on a higher level of abstraction. They criticize the "bounded thinking" dominant in western academia for much of the nineteenth and twentieth centuries, which took the nation state and its borders for granted. Cross-border movements were perceived as deviation. Against this backdrop, the authors argue for analyses (of social, economic and other dynamics, particularly related to migration) beyond the national container.

33. E. R. Leach, "The frontiers of 'Burma'." *Comparative Studies in Society and History* 3, no. 1 (1960): 49–68; F. Barth, ed. "Introduction." in *Ethnic group and boundaries: The social organization of culture difference*, (Boston, MA: Little Brown, 1969).

34. E. Fischer, "On boundaries." *World Politics* 1, no. 2 (1949): 196–222; V. Kolossov, "Border studies: Changing perspectives and theoretical approaches." *Geopolitics* 10 (2005): 607.

35. R. Shamir, "Without borders? Notes on globalization as a mobility regime." *Sociological Theory* 23, no. 2 (2005): 197.

36. D. Newman "Borders and bordering: Towards an interdisciplinary dialogue." *European Journal of Social Theory* 9, no. 2 (2006): 182; see also J. Anderson, "Borders after 11 September 2001." *Space and Polity* 6, no. 2 (2002): 227–232.
37. N. De Genova and N. Peutz. *The deportation regime: Sovereignty, space and freedom of movement* (Duke: Duke University Press, 2010).
38. E. Fischer, "On boundaries." *World Politics* 1, no. 2 (1949): 197–198.
39. C. Lentz, " 'This is Ghanaian territory!': Land conflicts on a West African border." *American Ethnologist* 30, no. 2 (2003): 282–284; F. Dereje, "More state than the state? The Anywaa's call for the rigidification of the Ethio-Sudanese border," in *Borders and borderlands as resources in the Horn of Africa,* ed. F. Dereje and M. V. Hoehne (London: James Currey, 2010), 27–44.
40. M. Baud and W. Van Schendel, "Toward a comparative history of borderlands." *Journal of World History* 8, no. 2 (1997): 212.
41. M. Rösler and T. Wendl, eds. "Introduction." in *Frontiers and borderlands: Anthropological perspectives*, (Frankfurt: Peter Lang 1999), 8.
42. J. Roitman, "The productivity of the margins. The reconstitution of state power in the Chad Basin." in *Anthropology in the margins of the state*, ed. V. Das and D. Poole (Oxford: Oxford University Press 2004), 192–193; G. Dobler, "Oshikango: The dynamics of growth and regulation in a Namibian boom town." *Journal of Southern African Studies* 35, no. 1 (2009): 115–131.
43. J. Herbst, "The creation and maintenance of national boundaries in Africa." *International Organisation* 43, no. 4 (1989): 673–692; J. Herbst, *States and power in Africa: Comparative lessons in authority and control* (Princeton, NJ: Princeton University Press, 2000); C. Clapham, *Africa and the international system. The politics of state survival* (Cambridge: Cambridge University Press, 1996b).
44. R. H. Jackson, *Quasi-states. Sovereignty, international relations, and the Third World* (Cambridge: Cambridge University Press, 1990), 7; M. Baud and W. Van Schendel, "Toward a comparative history of borderlands." *Journal of World History* 8, no. 2 (1997): 211–212; V. Kolossov, "Border studies: Changing perspectives and theoretical approaches." *Geopolitics* 10 (2005): 612; Held *et al.*, *Global transformations. Politics, economics and culture* (Cambridge: Polity Press, 2001); A. McGrew, *The transformation of democracy? Globalization and territorial democracy* (Cambridge: Polity Press, 1997), 606.
45. T. Raeymaekers, "The silent encroachment of the frontier: A politics of transborder trade in the Semliki Valley (Congo–Uganda)." *Political Geography* 28, no. 1 (2009): 55.
46. F. Barth, "Boundaries and connections." in *Signifying identities: anthropological perspectives on boundaries and contested values*, ed. A. Cohen (London: Rutledge 2000), 17.
47. F. Barth, "Boundaries and connections." In *Signifying identities: Anthropological perspectives on boundaries and contested values*, ed. A. Cohen (London: Rutledge 2000), 18.
48. P. Nugent, *Smugglers, secessionists and loyal citizens on the Ghana–Togo frontier* (Athens, OH: Ohio University Press, 2002), 5–8.

49. P. Nugent, *Smugglers, secessionists and loyal citizens on the Ghana–Togo frontier* (Athens, OH: Ohio University Press, 2002), 12.

50. J. Anderson and L. O'Dowd, "Borders, border regions and territoriality: Contradictory meanings, changing significance." *Regional Studies* 33, no. 7 (1999): 597.

51. J. Anderson and L. O'Dowd, "Borders, border regions and territoriality: Contradictory meanings, changing significance." *Regional Studies* 33, no. 7 (1999): 597.

52. A. Horstmann and R. Wadley. "Centering the margins in Southeast Asia: Introduction." In *Centering the margin: Agency and narrative in Southeast Asian borderlands*, ed. A. Horstmann and R. Wadley (Oxford: Berghahn Press, 2006), 2.

53. M. Pelkmans, *Defending the border: Identity, religion, and modernity in the Republic of Georgia* (Ithaca, NY: Cornell University Press, 2006), 13.

54. F. Dereje and M. V. Hoehne, eds. "State borders and borderlands as resources: An analytical framework." in *Borders and borderlands as resources in the Horn of Africa*, (London: James Currey 2010), 18–20.

55. Zartman (2010: 6) also mentions two major variables that characterize a border and, related to that, define what kind of opportunities a border offers. His variables are the "political nature" and "depth". The first comprises the relation of the border to the center (and vice versa) as well as the degree of enforcement of the border. The second refers to the political, social and/or other differences marked by the border. The question is whether the border divides unrelated groups or enemies, or runs between closely related groups and/or states.

56. For a fuller exposition of the Anywaa mode of signification of the international border, see Dereje (2010).

57. S. Hutchinson, *Nuer dilemmas: Coping with money, war and the state* (Berkeley , CA: University of California Press, 1996).

58. D. Turton, *Ethnic federalism: The Ethiopian experience in comparative perspective* (Oxford: James Currey, 2006).

59. The census found that 46 percent of the regional population are Nuer, and 21.1percent are Anywaa.

60. F. Dereje, "More state than the state? The Anywaa's call for the rigidification of the Ethio-Sudanese Border." in *Borders and borderlands as resources in the Horn of Africa*, ed. F. Dereje and M. V. Hoehne (London: James Currey, 2010), 31.

61. The processes outlined here have been discussed in great detail in Hoehne (2010, 2011).

62. Between the late 1880s and 1960, the northwest of the Somali peninsula had been British administered. The Italians controlled the area from the northeast to the south. On June 26, the British Protectorate became independent. The Italian colony (which by then was officially a UN trusteeship administered by the Italians) followed on July 1, 1960. On the same day, both territories united to form the Somali Republic.

63. The movement is abbreviated SSC because "Ayn" is correctly written "Cayn" in Somali; the "c" stands for a sound close to the Arabic "?" (ayn). For the reader's convenience, an anglicized transcription of Somali personal and place names has been used in this text.

64. A. I. Asiwaju, ed. "The conceptual framework." in *Partitioned Africans: Ethnic relations across Africa's international boundaries, 1884–1984*, (London: C. Hurst, 1985), 12.
65. P. Nugent, "Border anomalies: The role of local actors in shaping spaces along the Gambia–Senegal and Ghana–Togo borders." in *Beside the state: Emergent powers in contemporary Africa*. ed. A. Bellagamaba and G. Klute (Cologne: Rudiger Koppe, 2008), 121.
66. T. Raeymaekers, "The silent encroachment of the frontier: A politics of transborder trade in the Semliki Valley (Congo–Uganda)." *Political Geography* 28, no. 1 (2009): 18.
67. S. Katzenellenbogen, "It didn't happen in Berlin: Politics, economics and ignorance in the setting of Africa's colonial boundaries." in *African boundaries: Barriers, conduits and opportunities,* ed. A. I. Asiwaju and P. Nugent (London: Pinter, 1996), 21–34; A. Mbembe, "At the edge of the world: Boundaries, territoriality, and sovereignty in Africa." in *Globalization and violence, vol. 2: Colonial and postcolonial globalizations*, ed. P. James and P. Darby (London: Sage, 2006), 152.

References

Abdul, M. "Ethiopia's strategic dilemma in the horn of Africa." *Social science research council* (2007). <http://hornofafrica.ssrc.org/Abdul_Mohammed/> (date of access) (Jun 10, 2012).
Acuto, M. "Edges of the conflict: A three-fold conceptualization of national borders." *Borderlands e-Journal* 7, no. 1 (2008). <http://www.borderlands.net.au/vol7no1_2008/acuto_edges.htm> (May 11, 2011).
Anderson, J. "Borders after 11 September 2001." *Space and Polity* 6, no. 2 (2002): 227–232.
Anderson, J. and L. O'Dowd. "Borders, border regions and territoriality: Contradictory meanings, changing significance." *Regional Studies* 33, no. 7 (1999): 593–604.
Appadurai, A. "Global ethnoscapes: Notes and queries for a transnational anthropology." In *Recapturing anthropology*, edited by R. Fox. Santa Fe, NM: School of American Research Press, 1991: 191–210. <http://vzopc4.gbv.de:8080/DB=6/SET=187/TTL=3/MAT=/NOMAT=T/CLK?IKT=1008&TRM=%3C&cvtourl%3E>.
Appadurai, A. "Sovereignty without territoriality: Notes for a postnational geography." In *The anthropology of space and place: Locating culture*, edited by S. Low and D. Zuniga, Malden, MA: Blackwell, 2003: 337–349.
Asiwaju, A. I., ed. "The conceptual framework." In *Partitioned Africans: Ethnic relations across Africa's international boundaries, 1884–1984,* London: C. Hurst, 1985: 1–18.
Barth, F., ed. "Introduction." In *Ethnic group and boundaries: The social organization of culture difference*, Boston, MA: Little Brown and Company; London: Allen and Unwin, 1969.

Barth, F. "Boundaries and connections." In *Signifying identities: Anthropological perspectives on boundaries and contested values,* edited by A. Cohen, London: Routledge, 2000: 17–36.

Baud, M. and W. Van Schendel. "Toward a comparative history of borderlands." *Journal of World History* 8, no. 2 (1997): 211–242.

Clapham, C. "Boundary and territory in the Horn of Africa." In *African boundaries: Barriers, conduits and opportunities,* edited by P. Nugent and A. I. Asiwaju, London: Pinter, 1996a: 237–250.

Clapham, C. *Africa and the international system. The politics of state survival.* Cambridge: Cambridge University Press, 1996b.

Clapham, C. "Rethinking African states". *African Security Review* 10, no. 3 (2001): n.p.

De Genova, N. and N. Peutz. *The deportation regime: Sovereignty, space and freedom of movement.* Duke, NC: Duke University Press, 2010.

Dereje, F. and M. V. Hoehne, eds. "More state than the state? The Anywaa's call for the rigidification of the Ethio-Sudanese border." In *Borders and borderlands as resources in the Horn of Africa,* London: James Currey, 2010: 27–44.

Dereje, F. and M. V. Hoehne, eds. "State borders and borderlands as resources: An analytical framework." In *Borders and borderlands as resources in the Horn of Africa,* London: James Currey, 2010: 1–25.

Dobler, G. "Oshikango: The dynamics of growth and regulation in a Namibian boom town." *Journal of Southern African Studies* 35, no. 1 (2009): 115–131.

Dobler, G. "On the border to chaos: Identity formation on the Angolan–Namibian border, 1927–2008." *Journal of Borderland Studies* 25, no. 2 (2010): 22–35.

Drysdale, J. *The Somali dispute.* London: Pall Mall Press, 1964.

Ferguson, J. "Transnational topographies of power: Beyond 'the state' and 'civil society' in the study of African politics." In *Accelerating possession: Global futures of property and personhood,* edited by B. Maurer and G. Schwab, New York: Columbia University Press, 2006: 76–98.

Fischer, E. "On boundaries." *World Politics* 1, no. 2 (1949): 196–222.

Geshekter, C. L. "Anti-colonialism and class formation: The eastern Horn of Africa before 1950." *International Journal for African Historical Studies* 18, no. 1 (1985): 1–32.

Glick Schiller, N., L. Basch, and C. Blanc-Szanton, eds. "Transnationalism: A new analytic framework for understanding migration." In *Towards a transnational perspective on migration: race, class, ethnicity, and nationalism reconsidered,* New York: New York Academy of Sciences, 1992: 1–24.

Gupta, A. and J. Ferguson. "Beyond 'Culture': Space, identity, and the politics of difference." *Cultural Anthropology* 7, no. 1 (1992): 6–23.

Held, D., A. Grew, D. Goldblatt and J. Perraton. *Global transformations. Politics, economics and culture.* Cambridge: Polity Press, 2001.

Herbst, J. "The creation and maintenance of national boundaries in Africa." *International Organisation* 43, no. 4 (1989): 673–692.

Herbst, J. *States and power in Africa: Comparative lessons in authority and control.* Princeton, NJ: Princeton University Press, 2000.

Hoehne, M. V. "People and politics along and across the Somaliland–Puntland border." In *Borders and borderlands as resources in the Horn of Africa*, edited by F. Dereje and M. V. Hoehne, London: James Currey, 2010: 97–121.

Hoehne, M. V. "Political orientations and repertoires of identification: State and identity formation in northern Somalia." PhD dissertation, Martin Luther University of Halle-Wittenberg, 2011.

Horstmann, A. and R. Wadley, eds. "Centering the margins in Southeast Asia: Introduction." In *Centering the margin: Agency and narrative in Southeast Asian borderlands,* Oxford: Berghahn Press, 2006: 1–26.

Hüsken, T. "The neo-tribal competitive order in the borderland of Egypt and Libya." In *Respacing Africa,* edited by U. Engel and P. Nugent, Amsterdam: Brill, 2009: 170–205.

Hutchinson, S. *Nuer dilemmas: Coping with money, war and the state.* Berkeley, CA: University of California Press, 1996.

ICG. "Ethiopia and Eritrea: Preventing war." *Africa Report*, No. 101, 2005.

Jackson, R.H. *Quasi-states. Sovereignty, international relations, and the Third World.* Cambridge: Cambridge University Press, 1990.

Information Service of the Somali Government. *The Somali Peninsula: A new light on imperial motives.* Mogadishu: Information Service of the Somali Government, 1962.

Katzenellenbogen, S. "It didn't happen in Berlin: Politics, economics and ignorance in the setting of Africa's colonial boundaries." In *African boundaries: Barriers, conduits and opportunities,* edited by A. I. Asiwaju and P. Nugent, London: Pinter, 1996: 21–34.

Kearney, M. "The local and the global: The anthropology of globalization and transnationalism." *Annual Review of Anthropology* 24 (1995): 547–565.

Kolossov, V. "Border studies: Changing perspectives and theoretical approaches." *Geopolitics* 10 (2005): 606–632.

Leach, E. R. "The frontiers of 'Burma'." *Comparative Studies in Society and History* 3, no. 1 (1960): 49–68.

Lentz, C. " 'This is Ghanaian territory!': Land conflicts on a West African border." *American Ethnologist* 30, no. 2 (2003): 273–289.

Lewis, I. M., ed. "Introduction." In *Nationalism and self-determination in the Horn of Africa,* London: Ithaca Press, 1983: 1–22.

Mahmoud, H. A. "Seeking citizenship on the border: Kenya Somalis, the uncertainty of belonging, and public sphere interactions." Paper presented at the 12th CORDESIA General Assembly, Yaoundé, Cameroon, December 7–11, 2008.

Markakis, J. "Borders and borderland communities in the Horn: The failure of integration." Paper presented at the conference 'Divided they stand: The affordances of state borders in the Horn of Africa'. Max Planck Institute for Social Anthropology, Halle, September 7–8, 2006.

Matthies, V. *Der Grenzkonflikt Somalias mit Äthiopien und Kenya. Analyse eines zwischenstaatlichen Konflikts in der Dritten Welt.* Hamburg: Institut für Afrikakunde, 1977.

Mbembe, A. "At the edge of the world: Boundaries, territoriality, and sovereignty in Africa." In *Globalization and violence, Vol. 2: Colonial and postcolonial globalizations*, edited by P. James and P. Darby, London: Sage, 2006: 148–171.

McGrew, A. *The transformation of democracy?: Globalization and territorial democracy.* Cambridge: Polity Press, 1997.

Miles, W. F. S. *Hausaland divided. Colonialism and independence in Nigeria and Niger.* Ithaca, NY: Cornell University Press, 1994.

Newman, D. "Borders and bordering: Towards an interdisciplinary dialogue." *European Journal of Social Theory* 9, no. 2 (2006): 171–186.

Nugent and Asiwaju, eds. "Introduction: The paradox of African boundaries" In *African boundaries: Barriers, conduits and opportunities,* London: Pinter, 1996: 1–17.

Nugent, P. *Smugglers, secessionists and loyal citizens on the Ghana–Togo Frontier.* Athens, OH: Ohio University Press, 2002.

Nugent, P. "Border anomalies: The role of local actors in shaping spaces along the Gambia–Senegal and Ghana–Togo borders." In *Beside the state: Emergent powers in contemporary Africa.* edited by A. Bellagamaba and G. Klute, Cologne: Rudiger Koppe, 2008

Pelkmans, M. *Defending the border: Identity, religion, and modernity in the Republic of Georgia.* Ithaca, NY: Cornell University Press, 2006.

Raeymaekers, T. "The silent encroachment of the frontier: A politics of transborder trade in the Semliki Valley (Congo–Uganda)." *Political Geography* 28, no. 1 (2009): 55–65.

Rösler, M and T. Wendl, eds. "Introduction." In *Frontiers and borderlands: Anthropological perspectives,* Frankfurt: Peter Lang, 1999: 1–27.

Roitman, J. "The productivity of the margins. The reconstitution of state power in the Chad Basin." In *Anthropology in the margins of the state,* edited by V. Das and D. Poole, Oxford: Oxford University Press, 2004: 191–224.

Schlee, G. "Some effects on a district boundary in Kenya." In *The politics of age and gerontocracy in Africa,* edited by M. Aguilar, Trenton, NJ: Africa World Press, 1998: 225–265.

Schlee, G. "Redrawing the map of the Horn: The politics of difference." *Africa* 73, no. 3 (2003): 343–368.

Scott, J. *Domination and the arts of resistance: Hidden transcripts.* New Haven, CT: Yale University Press, 1990.

Shamir, R. "Without borders? Notes on globalization as a mobility regime." *Sociological Theory* 23, no. 2 (2005): 197–217.

Silberfein, M. and Al Hassan Conteh. "Boundaries and conflict in the Mano River region of West Africa." *Conflict Management and Peace Science* 23, no. 4 (2006): 343–361.

Touval, S. *The boundary politics of independent Africa.* Cambridge, MA: Harvard University Press, 1972.

Turton, D. *Ethnic federalism: The Ethiopian experience in comparative perspective.* Oxford: James Currey, 2006.

Vorrath, J. "On the margin of statehood? State–society relations in African borderlands." In *Understanding life in the borderlands: Boundaries in depth and in motion*, edited by I. W. Zartman, Athens: University of Georgia Press, 2010: 85–104.

Wilson, T and H. Donnan, eds. "Nation, state and identity at international borders." In *Borders: Frontiers of identity, nation and state,* Oxford: Berg, 1998: 1–30.

Wimmer, A. and N. Glick Schiller. 2002. "Methodological nationalism and beyond. Nation-state building, migration and the social sciences." *Global Networks* 2, no. 4 (2002): 301–334.

Zartman, I. W. "Introduction: Identity, movement and response." In *Understanding life in the borderlands: Boundaries in depth and in motion*, edited by I. W. Zartman, Athens: University of Georgia Press, 2010: 1–18.

PART II

The Border's Rough Terrain: Violence, Security and the Border

CHAPTER 4

Treading a Fine Line: State-Making and Conflict within Eastern Burma

Sylvia Brown

Introduction

Burma's eastern borderlands have long been of concern to the lowland state for a number of reasons. In the premodern, colonial and postcolonial periods, the people located between rival Burmese and Thai kingdoms have tended to shift allegiance at will; they have produced their own political authorities rivaling the Burmese state, and the land on which they live contains important natural and strategic resources. These characteristics have resulted in intense interest from a Burmese state intent on penetrating the borderlands and controlling both the people and territory located within. However, they are not the only group with political and economic interests in the area; organized forms of political authority operating above the village level also include multiple armed opposition groups. A significant non-state political authority is the Karen National Union (KNU), an armed opposition group that provides certain governance services in the eastern borderlands of Burma in direct competition with the Burmese state.

This chapter argues that the KNU's claim to parts of eastern Burma encompasses changing political and economic "neuralgia points" for the Burmese state. Since the KNU has not been decisively co-opted or crushed like many of the other armed opposition groups in Burma, it remains in conflict with the Burma Army in an "equilibrium of instability", which allows the Burmese military to justify high levels of militarization in the country.[1] The nature of the conflict and the KNU's modes of contestation have changed over time, though, in a dialectical relationship with the Burmese state.

Discussion then turns to how the KNU in its sixth decade of armed conflict now mediates its legitimacy with both international and local stakeholders. It argues that key staff within the KNU's welfare departments adopt a strategic stance of independence and humanitarianism toward international donors, while they are positioned as technocratic civil servants in dealings with the KNU and local populations. They therefore wear multiple hats and must make coherent projects out of different stakeholder priorities. It is argued here that in this case, "brokers" are needed to negotiate between foreign funders and the KNU, as well as between the KNU and local communities. In practice this means that a non-state public authority such as the KNU, and particularly the brokers within it, have to tread a fine line while navigating local and international conceptions of legitimate political authority.

Research Methodology

The research behind this analysis was conducted as part of recent PhD fieldwork, which studied the activities of youths working in nonmilitary roles in the KNU along the Burmese–Thai border.[2] The research used an ethnographic approach[3] and examined the internal structure of the movement, the individual motivations of participants, the movement's history and Burmese politics. To mitigate the problem of difference between what people say they do and what they actually do, the research was triangulated using observation of the actual activities and discussions with KNU staff as well as analysis of internal documents and news sources. Information was also verified for authenticity with a number of key informants within the movement, with a number of informed outsiders and at later dates with the same source.

One of the problems of researching sociopolitical conflict is that vested interests, personal histories, ideological loyalties, propaganda and a dearth of firsthand information can lead to wildly different testimonies.[4] In this case, the adoption of a methodologically composite approach, as Barakat *et al.* (2002) suggest, the investment of a significant amount of time in building trust with research participants, the encouragement of actor participation in the research and the adoption of a flexible approach and attitude to results during the research process resulted in coherent findings.[5]

Peripheral Conflicts in the Southeast Asian Borderlands

This chapter is concerned with a particular type of "peripheral conflict"[6] between the state and armed opposition groups that is especially prevalent in the borderlands of Southeast Asian states, as a result of a long history of conflict over territorial control and sovereignty. Before the idea that the state should control all of the territory to fixed borders became hegemonic with postcolonial conceptions of statehood, precolonial texts show that state power in Southeast Asia revolved around economic centers and rarely reached the hinterlands.[7] However, in Southeast Asia's more recent history, James Scott (2009) argues that many of the same processes of land enclosure and pacification of the local population found in Tilly's (1992) and Thomas Gallant's (1999) studies of European state formation are evident, prompting clashes with local populations who have historically avoided subjugation under a centralized state.

Resistance to state-making among borderland people continued through the colonial period, with colonial rulers finding that borderland societies demonstrated a much greater capacity for opposition to foreign rule than centralized, lowland kingdoms did.[8] Although colonial rule forcefully curbed the powers of customary chieftaincies and precolonial political forms,[9] it did not always entirely eliminate them, and indirect rule was common.

In the postcolonial period, territorial control and the development of the state's coercive power became more important as national boundaries were demarcated in independence transitions. Postcolonial state elites then overwhelmingly adopted the Westphalian idea of absolute state sovereignty to the edges of state borders and utilized the colonial structures of coercion to pursue a changed emphasis on penetration of the periphery, rather than radiance of power.[10] As a result, absolute rather than multiple and overlapping national sovereignty, control of civil society, the constitutive monopoly of legitimate violence and the right to expropriate economic resources formed the objectives of postcolonial regimes.[11] However, the claims of the central state to absolute sovereignty over the borderlands, although recognized in the international state system, have often not been an empirical reality on the ground and have been violently contested.[12]

From the perspective of the civilian population in the periphery, James Scott (2009) and Christian Scherrer[13] argue that the imposition of direct rule in the postcolonial period met with opposition from local populations who preferred to maintain their status as "acephalous" or self-rule societies without centralized forms of governance. At this point, the desires of unarmed civilians in the borderlands intersected with those of military entrepreneurs operating without the sanction of the law. Gallant (1999) argues that as the state expands its reach and coercive power, armed non-state actors are drawn and pushed into remote, inaccessible areas, where the difficult terrain and their links to the rural population protect and shelter them from their state pursuers.

In semi-peripheral areas, Gallant[14] argues that armed groups or individuals outside the state had less freedom due to the more restrictive physical geography and had to rely to a greater extent on the cooperation and compliance of the local population: "social geography, as it were, had to take the place of the cover provided by the physical environment in the periphery". In this situation, armed groups operated less as predators and engaged in alliances with local populations wishing to retain or regain local sovereignty.[15] As a result, the rise in power of armed non-state actors in the periphery and semi-periphery of states magnifies the state's interest in penetrating and consolidating its power in the borderlands.[16] Through a process of either co-opting or crushing locally powerful individuals or armed groups, states experience a "border effect" that strengthens their capacities and establishes the "writ of the state" as "the law of the land" in peripheral areas.[17]

Peripheral conflicts in Southeast Asia are fundamentally about sovereignty and the spatialization of power, but frequently they have taken on an ethnonationalist character due to the nature of state-making and the particular logic of conflict employed by the state and armed opposition groups. Southeast Asian states have attempted to co-opt or crush locally powerful individuals or armed groups; however, this has created highly fragmented patterns of sovereignty, legitimacy and coercive power as locally powerful leaders establish variegated relationships with the state.

International borders are often argued to be a critical resource for groups contesting the state, providing both economic opportunities and protection. For example, Blanchard (2005) argues that control of economically strategic borders is a central pursuit of states and rebels wishing to boost their coffers, while Salehyan (2007) argues that the use of external sanctuaries is one of the most common strategies employed by armed opposition groups. A whole body of literature on "refugee warriors" explores the ways in which rebel groups exploit sanctuary and an international border to recalibrate an unfavorable balance of power.[18] Internal borderlands can also be useful since the state may be unable to control impenetrable terrain within its national borders. James D. Fearon and David D. Laitin (2003), for instance, find that rough terrain is positively correlated with the prevalence of civil war.

This chapter examines how a changing political and geographical landscape impacts upon the KNU as an armed opposition group and how it responds to these challenges. Focusing the analytical gaze on an area within the extensively politically and militarily contested Southeast Asian borderlands takes advantage of a particular moment in history and geography described by Horstmann (2002) as a "laboratory of social change".

A borderland perspective is useful for understanding the KNU and the Burmese state, because it challenges the idea that state-making necessarily involves the gradual diffusion of power outward, from the center to the periphery; instead, it puts the spotlight on the ways in which borderland practices constitute and reform the state.[19] In this light, the state in developing countries is more accurately viewed as the product of complex processes of often conflictive negotiations that occur at the interface between the public and the private, the informal and the formal, the illegal and the legal.[20] These processes may include negotiations with alternative forms of public authority outside the state. Where these forms of public authority are armed groups, it is more accurate to see states as being "deeply involved in the emergence and logic of armed groups".[21]

The chapter proceeds in the next section with an examination of the neuralgia points for the Burmese state over KNU sovereignty in the eastern borderlands of the country. The third section then considers how the KNU has responded to changes in its territorial control and the regional political environment by transforming its income streams. The fourth section concludes by discussing the implications this case has for theoretical understandings of governance provision by armed opposition groups in borderland areas.

Building Karen State in the Borderlands: Rise and Decline of the KNU

The KNU's conflict with the Burmese state emerged in the country's transition to independence after colonial rule. Unhappy with the political form of the new state and with Burman–Karen ethnic tensions running high, a growing Karen pan-ethnic consciousness evolved into a full rebellion as educated Karen elites articulated their grievances against the central state and were mobilized into the KNU. They took up arms against the state in 1949 with the intention of shaking off the vestiges of a culture of political dependency and developing their own strategy of national liberation.[22] Since then, conflict has become entrenched and, with the exception of a few short-lived ceasefire agreements, has continued ever since, until the current ceasefire agreement was signed in 2012.

The KNU lost its territory in the delta and areas surrounding Rangoon early on in the war and has retreated eastward ever since to fortified "liberated zones" in the remote borderlands,[23] eventually ending up with its headquarters over the border in Thailand in the border trading town of Mae Sot. Nowadays, the "liberated zones" are conflict zones, as the Burma Army attempts to wrest control of the KNU's last remaining territory and exert its power. However, the KNU continues to contest sovereignty and provide governance services alongside or in the place of the state in large parts of eastern Burma, with some novel and interesting changes in its operations, as this chapter goes on to examine.

For the majority of its operational life, the KNU has been supported primarily by the Karen peasantry in the eastern areas of Burma,[24] but its fortunes are locked in a dialectical relationship with the Burmese state. While the Burmese state collapsed after independence, the KNU rose in power, but when the Burmese military finally managed to consolidate its hold over key economic and strategic spaces, the KNU declined in power. The rise and decline of the KNU are briefly outlined here before the chapter turns to examine how a greatly weakened KNU has transformed its income streams and delivery of governance services in eastern Burma.

1949–1989: KNU State-Making in Eastern Burma

By 1949, the KNU had articulated a vision of Karen nationalism and independence around which it sought to mobilize diverse Karen communities. The goal was secession for a large part of eastern Burma (the Salween Hill Tracts, Tenasserim Division and the eastern part of Pegu District).[25] In the years immediately following independence, the Burmese state was weak and controlled little territory, with the KNU occupying territory just 9 miles from the capital in Rangoon.[26] By contrast, the KNU controlled large parts of the delta and eastern Burma. However, the Burma Army quickly regained control of the delta areas of Burma, and from the 1960s and 1970s, as the Burma Army has gained in strength, the KNU has retreated ever eastward into its "liberated zones" in the borderland mountains and jungle, taking with it migrant Karen communities from around the delta, Yangon and Insein.[27]

During 1962–1988, Burma underwent a disastrous period of socialism under military rule in the guise of the Burmese Socialist Programme Party. Termed "the Burmese way to socialism" and marked by extreme isolation and nationalization of industry, the government's introspective policies destroyed the official economy, and the black market flourished.[28] The KNU capitalized on the Burmese state's economic mismanagement by controlling and taxing the increasing black market border trade with Thailand. It established its first customs gate at Phalu, south of the Myawaddy–Mae Sot border crossing, in 1964, soon after the start of socialism, quickly followed by another at Kawmoorah–Wangkha. By the peak of trade in 1983, there were a further ten gates, each with a garrison of up to 200 troops.[29]

The KNU levied a five to ten percent tax on all of the black market commerce (rice, gems, tin ore, textiles, teak, gems, cattle and manufactured goods) crossing through these customs gates.[30] Each gate remitted 40 percent of its revenue to KNU headquarters and used the remainder to maintain the army units in its sector.[31] At its height, the black market cross-border trade was estimated to be providing over 80 percent of Burma's consumer goods[32] and was worth between 1 and 2 million baht (US$40,000–80,000) per day.[33]

The most important part of this income, until a mid-1990s' Burma Army offensive, was the teak trade, including a tax on sawmills.[34] Burma contains 70 percent of the world's teak forests, which are rapidly depleting, but for many years this trade helped to finance the arms needed to defend the Kawthoolei state (the name chosen for the KNU's liberated areas).[35] Though their strict morals meant that the KNU were never involved in the large drugs-trafficking operations in the region, the border trade remained highly lucrative as the black market flourished.[36]

Exploitation of the border trade and resources transformed Burma's eastern borderlands into a central economic space on the margins of the country and facilitated processes of capitalism in the borderlands, provoking intense speculation by the Burmese and Thai states.[37] The Burmese economy during this time was thus characterized as a "poor center and rich periphery".[38]

The Burmese black market border trade and the KNU's control of territorial resources in the borderlands became neuralgia points for the Burmese state, because it undermined the policy of socialism as well as the state's imagined projection of power to the edges of its national boundaries. Instead of customs revenue accruing to the Burmese state, it accrued to the KNU and went for defending the civilian population, maintaining the Karen National Liberation Army (KNLA) and their dependents, developing political and support wings and funding numerous clinics and schools in the "liberated zones".

Zachariah Mampilly (2007: 244) argues that rebel groups, which rely on a specific ethnic, regional or national population, face pressure from civilians to provide governance. Armed opposition groups that control significant territory are then more likely to provide governance services to the local population specifically to buttress their claims to represent a targeted population and indicate their strength to the central state.[39] The KNU is a prominent example of this. Within their extensive "liberated zones", the KNU built up a "pseudo-government" with a bureaucratic apparatus including ministries, taxation and revenue systems, education, health and relief services and a "national" language.[40] Effectively, it established itself as a government within a *de facto* state, declaring its independence in a letter to the Secretary-General of the United Nations in 1953 and seeking external recognition as the "Kawthoolei Free State" (the name chosen for the new Karen State).[41]

From the perspectives of the Karen's Thai neighbors and western (primarily American) interests in the region, the staunchly anticommunist KNU served an important geopolitical "buffer" function in preventing the communist parties of Thailand, Burma, China and Malaya from linking up.[42] Until the fall of the Soviet Union, the KNU was treated as a quasi-state and used as a proxy for Thai power, enjoying military, financial and moral support as well as a safe haven in Thailand.[43]

The KNU's control of the borderland shadow economy granted it a degree of external legitimacy, while concurrently undermining central state economic policies in the Burmese heartland, the state's socialist ideology and, therefore, its state-making program. However, it also created a "border effect",[44] which magnified the state's interest in its borderlands.

1990–2012: Decline of the KNU

After the end of the Cold War and the dissolution of the Communist Party of Burma, the Burmese military embarked upon a changed state-making strategy in which the newly capitalist regime pursued military-economic ceasefire agreements with the ethnic armed opposition groups and used these to establish territorial control and recalibrate the political economy of the borderlands.[45] The Burmese regime confiscated land and natural resources in the borderlands to limit access to valuable natural resources such as mines, prime agricultural land and strategic sites for hydropower and gas pipeline construction projects in order to generate rents. It then distributed these rents to powerful individuals, groups and neighboring governments willing to enter into an alliance with the Burmese military and solve the problem of violent resistance to its rule in the borderlands.[46]

With the elimination of the communist threat in the region, the KNU were no longer needed as a proxy force for Thailand, and throughout the late 1980s and 1990s "Bangkok and Rangoon collaborated to end support for the borderland power-holders in the 'buffer zone'".[47] In a new Thai government policy to transform battlegrounds along its borders into marketplaces, the Thai government under General Chaovolit broke the international boycott of Burma (formed after the Burmese military reasserted power in 1988) and recognized the Burmese regime's legitimacy in exchange for logging and fishing rights.[48] Its trans-boundary resource access deals with the Burmese state fundamentally changed the control of the borderland economy.[49] Trade became legitimized (and taxed by both the Thai and Burmese governments), roads were built and Thailand gradually became Burma's biggest foreign investor and trading partner, with official bilateral trade valued at US$3.577 billion for fiscal year 2009–2010, most of it due to gas exports, which are the primary "rent" for Burmese rulers.[50] In this way, powerful Thai military and business leaders have engaged in patrimonial politics with the Burmese regime.

In return for access to rents, they have come under pressure from the Burmese regime to limit Burmese exiles' political activism and the activities of the KNU on Thai soil.

The decline in the KNU's revenues is directly related to the Burma Army's seizure of border trade and establishment of bilateral economic agreements with Thailand.[51] Furthermore, with new logging roads and tacit Thai support, the Burma Army was able to launch a series of large-scale attacks on KNU military strongholds and customs gates, leading to the loss of significant KNU territory, including the lucrative border customs gates.[52] Thus, as the Burma Army has become stronger and established greater control over the eastern borderlands, the KNU has become correspondingly weaker. By 2010, the KNU's central treasury budget had declined to a mere US$133,300.[53] Each of the KNLA's seven brigades continued to be responsible for raising their own income from local businesses, tax, some border trade and the sale of natural resources such as gold, zinc and hardwood to Thailand,[54] but the amount raised is reportedly too little to support even a small guerrilla force, and a news interview with a KNU leader in 2009 revealed that the KNU was facing financial difficulties.[55] For example, the KNU's fourth brigade income was only around US$40,000 in 2009.[56]

Facing vastly superior military strength, the KNU cannot possibly hope to gain a military victory, and its significance as a military actor in Burma has greatly declined. However, armed opposition groups primarily seek to maintain the conflict over a long period of time rather than decisively overthrow the state government, in order to force the government to the negotiating table by either military might or inflicting high costs.[57] Thus, as a Karen National Defense Organization (KNDO) soldier interviewed in this study stated when asked about the KNU's military goals: "We are fighting to gain time not to occupy the space".[58] One of the problems with the maintenance of the armed struggle is that improving Thai–Burmese relations since the 1990s have resulted in Thailand putting increasing pressure on the KNU and, since 2009, have led to a ban on the KNU commanding their troops from Thai soil or bringing weapons across the border.[59]

As the KNU loses its revenue streams and territory, its bureaucratic apparatus has shrunk. Moreover, the KNU faces problems conducting public meetings and communicating with villagers inside Burma, due to the lack of territorial control, and has financial and recruitment difficulties.[60] However, some of its bureaucratic departments have managed to transform their modes of operation and re-emerge as significant humanitarian aid and development actors in eastern Burma. Provision of health, education and humanitarian relief services to the civilian population in the KNU's former "liberated zones" has been reinvigorated with new, external revenue streams through international nongovernmental organization (INGO) humanitarian aid, as the following section elaborates.

Changing Modes of Contestation over Sovereignty in Eastern Burma

While the KNU controlled large areas of eastern Burma, it effectively operated as a *de facto* state and provided a variety of governance services to the civilian population in its areas. As Mampilly argues, it is important for armed opposition groups to ensure that the passive majority of the civilian population do not turn against them; therefore, they may seek to provide collective goods and better governance conditions than their rivals to generate broad support and legitimacy beyond individual participants.[61] However, as the KNU has lost territory and revenues since the 1990s, its budget for governance services has greatly decreased.

Zahar argues that armed opposition groups like the KNU, which have a limited resource base, have a strong incentive to develop relations with transnational actors in order to generate revenues and build their external legitimacy by association.[62] In this case, the KNU's welfare wings have managed to develop relations with INGOs in the refugee camps in Thailand and use these to generate funding for the provision of governance services to populations in the Karen State. This does not appear to have been a purposely crafted strategy; rather, it emerged as a result of a constellation of factors: the KNU's decline in territorial control, the increase in conflict in its former "liberated zones", an escalating humanitarian crisis as a result of internal displacement and attacks on villagers' livelihoods, a lack of KNU resources to respond to the need for humanitarian aid, an increase in INGOs bearing witness to the humanitarian crisis and political lobbying by diaspora and western pressure groups of western governments.

In 2010, the KNU's education department received the entirety of its US$365,000 annual budget from external INGO funding.[63] The KNU's assistance organization for internally displaced persons (Committee for Internally Displaced Karen People, CIDKP) also received its approximately US$25,000 annual budget from external funding, as did the KNU's health department's approximately US$230,000 health budget.[64] All of these organizations have separated their operational work from the KNU in order to qualify for donor funding. Compared to the US$6.7 million cross-border aid delivered by TBBC (a consortium of international donors involved in refugee aid in Thailand), Free Burma Rangers and Mae Tao clinic (a Burmese-run clinic based in Thailand) in 2010[65] and the US$371 million in Official Development Assistance delivered through central Burma, the approximately

US$620,000 total funding to the KNU's welfare wings is a very small amount, representing less than 10 percent of the cross-border aid delivered by the three main INGOs. However, it dwarfs the KNU's approximately US$133,300 central treasury income from natural resource rents, small businesses and household tax.

The transformed revenue stream for the KNU's education service enables it to deliver possibly the largest education service in a conflict zone in the world, covering 1,041 schools (96 percent of the total schools in Karen State) and 93,842 students in Karen State, some of which are mobile village schools in hiding.[66] All school supplies (140,000 kg worth in 2010) are distributed from Thailand, some by road under cover of other Thai imports, but most by a large network of community volunteers who carry the supplies on their backs through the jungle.[67]

The KNU's health department is also entirely funded by INGOs and reaches around 110,000 internally displaced villagers in Karen State through 37 semipermanent health clinics, each staffed by approximately ten local health workers. It also coordinates its work with an indigenous NGO, the Backpack Health Worker Team, who provide mobile health services with over 70 health work teams.[68] Mobile humanitarian relief is also delivered by the relief wings of the KNU in Karen State with armed protection of aid delivery provided by the KNU's armed wing.

Contesting State-Making by "Out-Governing" the State

The KNU's provision of governance services is argued here to be a nonmilitary method of contesting Burmese state-making practices. This is because the messages transmitted through the provision of welfare services, especially education, undermine the messages transmitted by the Burmese state and allow the KNU to provide alternative information, ideas and identities to the Karen population. Given the Burmese regime's strict access to information, especially to students, the provision of alternative information can be considered as political opposition or contestation. As Beatty argues, educating ordinary citizens about politics is an important way for political activists to build a sympathetic public.[69] However, it is not just political information that undermines the Burmese state's attempts to prevent political opposition to its rule; the articulation of alternative identities, cultures and histories also undermines its attempts to build a Burman-dominated nationalism. Thus, the Burmese state's attempts to generate a degree of consent from the civilian population are undermined, which may then facilitate the civilian population's attempts to resist more coercive methods of Burmese state-making. Furthermore, the provision of a KNU education curriculum allows the KNU to build support for its political ideology, recreates its political culture and signals sovereignty internally, which can then be used to build external legitimacy.[70]

Giving material support (such as humanitarian aid) to populations attempting to remain outside state control also undermines Burmese state-making practices in areas it has yet to establish control, in particular its attempts to starve the villagers out of the hills and into relocation sites.[71] The Burma Army's attacks on aid workers in this function suggest that it perceives aid workers operating outside its control as a threat. The distribution of aid also serves to build the KNU's legitimacy among the local population, even where aid is provided by other organizations, because civilians view the KNU positively by comparison with the Burma Army for even allowing aid to be delivered in the area, rather than attacking it. As the KNU's General Secretary stated:

> The people see if the KNU does not allow them [NGOs] they cannot go inside.
> [Karen State][72]

More directly, material support provided by organizations affiliated to the KNU can build the KNU's internal legitimacy among the civilian population as part of the social compact, even if it has not funded or provided the aid itself.[73] As Mampilly argues, governance provision by armed groups serves to convince their target population that they offer a better alternative than the state and buttresses their claims to represent the population.[74] A Karen Youth Organization (KYO) leader involved in the delivery of humanitarian aid to IDPs inside Karen State, who was interviewed as part of this study, reported that donors insist he always explain where the aid is coming from and that it is not from the KNU, but, despite this, the aid still legitimizes the KNU in the recipients' eyes because the KNU has facilitated its delivery.[75]

> FBR [Free Burma Rangers] and other relief work is taken advantage of by the KNU to show they work for the Karen people.[76]

This last point has long been a politically sensitive issue for the KNU's welfare wings and the international donors who fund them. It originated as an issue in the Karen refugee camps in the 1990s, when the KNU was argued to be controlling the distribution of aid and using it to build its own legitimacy.[77] Some commentators also argued that the refugee camps in Thailand were KNU villages transplanted onto Thai soil, constituting a non-territorial basis of power for the organization.[78] Likewise, the provision of cross-border aid from Thailand by organizations affiliated to the KNU has been argued to provide material support and legitimization to the KNU, although there has been very little actual "aid leakage".[79] However, external aid is also just another form of "rent", which has the potential to undermine legitimacy in the same way.[80]

How Has the KNU Managed to Transform Its Revenue Streams?

The KNU has managed to secure INGO funding for its welfare services by capitalizing on its preexisting relationships with INGOs serving the refugee community in Thailand. As a result, this study found that an important role for staff within the KNU's welfare wings is brokering the policies of the KNU and the local needs of the recipient population inside Burma with international donors. Figure 4.1 indicates how KNU brokers are strategically positioned. The term "brokers" is used by David Mosse and David Lewis to refer to people in the context of development programs, usually situated between the state and the community, who read the meaning in a project into the different institutional languages of its stakeholder supporters.[81]

As a young leader within the KNU's CIDKP explained:

> Funding comes from outside donations, like NGOs and a small amount from individuals like the Karen community abroad, not from the KNU. We operate as a humanitarian CBO [community-based organization] even though we are linked to KNU. We have to sign agreements that aid will not be made conditional upon support for anyone and we will not be biased in our delivery. We also have to explain that we are not KNU and we wear our hats or T-shirts with our logo to show we are CIDKP.[82]

This brokerage role has long been in operation among the KNU organizations working on governance services in the refugee camps, but it also became important to the KNU's welfare wings working outside the refugee camps and across the border as INGO funding expanded to include cross-border aid for displaced civilians in eastern Burma. However, the KNU's welfare wings operating inside Karen State struggle to build their external legitimacy among external funders as a result of their political ties to the KNU. As a result, the KNU's welfare wings have largely been reformulated as local NGOs in order to qualify for INGO funding.

Key staff responsible for brokering their organization's relationship with external funders report that they tend to adopt a stance of humanitarianism toward international donors, while continuing to be positioned as civil servants in their relationship with the KNU. Thus, these "brokers" wear multiple hats, negotiate different stakeholder policies and priorities and attempt to build coherent projects out of this complexity.

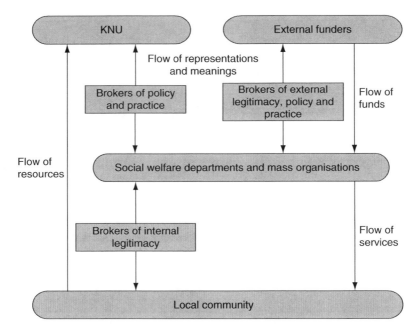

Figure 4.1 Strategic positions of KNU brokers.

Delivering the KNU's Education Service in Burma with INGO Funding: Case Study of Saw T.

Saw T. is an animist believer, aged 34, who works in the education department of the KNU. He comes from an area in which multiple armed groups are active and joined the education department as an intern. He has worked his way up the organization to become the education officer of internally displaced persons (IDP's) in the new consortium (Karen State Educational Assistance Group, KSEAG) that links the KNU's education department and local INGOs.

Saw T. manages KSEAG's relationship with schools in Karen State including registering new schools, managing the distribution of stipends and resources and reporting upward. He speaks excellent English and is adept at the technocratic project management necessary for working with INGOs, easily managing complicated spreadsheets, proposals and reports. He is also familiar with the politics of the KNU's education department and the political sensitivities involved in delivering the KNU curriculum in partially securitized or government-controlled areas of Karen State.

Crucially, Saw T. is able to interpret schooling situations to donors, funding realities to local schools and KNU education policies to both groups of stakeholders. He also negotiates the distribution of school materials with other armed groups in the local area. To do this, he adopts a strategic stance of independence and humanitarianism toward international donors, while being positioned as a KNU civil servant in his relationship with the KNU and the local population.

Saw T. explained that the education department of the KNU struggled to source INGO funding because UNICEF and USAID did not want to support an organization with links to an armed group. To mitigate this issue, two separate organizations were created to present themselves as operationally distinct from the KNU and its armed activities inside Karen State. The Karen Refugee Committee Education Entity (KRCEE) was created for education services in the refugee camps, while the education department joined together with an independent NGO, the Karen Teacher Working Group (KTWG) and an international funder (Partners Relief and Development) to create the KSEAG for an education service inside Karen State.

Factors Enabling the KNU's Changed Modes of Contesting Burmese State-Making

This study found at least five important factors enabling the KNU's changed modes of contesting Burmese state-making in Karen State discussed in this chapter. First, the KNU's externally funded organizations are reliant upon continued sanctuary in Thailand. As several scholars identify, where a neighboring state is sympathetic, or unable to secure its borders, the presence of an international border can be crucial for an armed opposition group by providing a sanctuary space, enabling the group to develop and grow.[83] It also alters the balance of power, as armed opposition groups unconstrained by boundaries gain an advantage over government troops who must usually respect boundaries.[84]

Sanctuary in Thailand has been key to the longevity of the KNU, because it offers organizing space and facilities for the headquarters of the KNU's constituent organizations. Operationally, Thailand has long provided a safe place for the KNU leadership to travel, conduct meetings and bank its income, but Thailand's excellent communication facilities (mobile phone coverage, inexpensive IT hardware and cheap broadband networks) also make sanctuary in Thailand especially important for contact with international organizations, which is impossible for the KNU in Burma. However, this case shows that sanctuary is only advantageous to the nonmilitary side of the KNU's operations, as it is no longer allowed to bring weapons across the border or command its troops from Thai soil.

Second, mobile providers of governance services and mobile community-mobilizing teams are dependent upon local support for hosting, feeding and managing the security of their staff, as well as facilitating the delivery of governance services through areas the KNU does not control. As a result, although the KNU is less reliant upon local taxation for its changed revenue streams, it remains reliant on nonmaterial local support in the form of intelligence, recruits and legitimacy. This may explain why the KNU does not appear to be transforming into a more predatory group (judging by human rights reports from the region), despite its material reliance on external "rents" for income.

Third, they are reliant upon the sanctuary granted by the difficult terrain of the borderlands for covert travel around Karen State. Fourth, they are reliant upon transnational funding and nonmaterial organizational assistance (e.g., computer training). Fifth, they appear to benefit from a relative lack of appropriate governance services provided by either the Burmese State or other groups claiming political authority in Karen State.

Factors Constraining the KNU's Changed Modes of Contesting Burmese State-Making

There are at least four factors constraining the transformed modes of contesting Burmese state-making by KNU-affiliated organizations. First, increasing pressure on the KNU by their Thai host is starting to affect the KNU's non-military activities as well as its military operations. Externally funded KNU organizations depend on their Thai base for communicating with funders, banking revenues and purchasing supplies, but increasing restrictions on the mobility and activities of the KNU on Thai soil by Thai authorities are causing increasing difficulties.

Since Thailand reengaged economically with the Burmese state after the communist threat in the region disappeared after the end of the Cold War, Thai policies toward Burmese opposition groups based in its territory have been based more on Thai business interests than geopolitical concerns, leading to increased pressure on the KNU by its Thai host.[85] Thus, as Salehyan's (2010) study of rebels and sanctuaries aptly describes, sanctuaries come with strings attached and can be a mixed blessing. The Thai government has an incentive to allow cross-border aid to continue from its territory in order to prevent more people migrating across its border, but it has also come under pressure from the Burmese regime to suppress the activities of the opposition groups on its soil.[86]

KNU-affiliated organizations are not registered in Thailand as charities, and around 95 percent of staff based in KNU-affiliated offices on the Thai side of the border had no form of identification other than a KNU membership card at the time of research. Holding a KNU membership card used to prevent arrest while traveling around the border areas of Thailand, but since the Thai authorities have been placing more pressure on the KNU, the card has become almost worthless. As a result, staff are dependent upon the changing whims of local Thai officials for security and permission to travel and conduct meetings. Thus, as the following young leader explained, for young brokers there are significant difficulties as well as advantages to sanctuary in Thailand:

> Working in Thailand you can talk with visitors and journalists easier. You cannot bring foreigners inside Karen State. It's easier to do networking and communicate with other CBOs and NGOs. We don't work in the (Burmese) military-controlled area because we cannot do anything. Also along the border is territory that is not completely controlled by the KNU so you cannot keep a stable office and it's difficult to move lots of equipment. Working in Thailand has a security problem, you cannot move. Most of our friends do not have a legal document so face some problems some times and it costs money [in bribes to Thai officials] for that.[87]

KNU organizations in Thailand therefore tread a fine line trying to retain their sanctuary space in order to secure external funding and build legitimacy among international donors, while delivering services inside eastern Burma and trying not to lose touch with their core polity.

Second, declining territorial control and increasing poverty and displacement have resulted in a lack of educated youths joining the KNU, which makes the organization and management of its nonmilitary activities more difficult. At the time of research, many youths worked in several nonmilitary roles concurrently with different organizations due to the lack of appropriately skilled recruits. Third, refugee resettlement from the camps in Thailand has taken away the best source of the most highly educated recruits, who usually also have the highest level of English language skills, resulting in very little recruitment of youths from the refugee camps. Moreover, the resettlement program has taken away a large chunk of the KNU's most skilled staff, who tended to be based at the organization's headquarters in Thailand while also maintaining a resident's card in one of the refugee camps.

Fourth, the KNU's transformed modes of contesting Burmese state-making remain constrained by state bias by INGO donors. Non-state organizations that use force against a state government are criminalized in the Westphalian state system, and by extension the administrative structures of such groups may also be criminalized and undermined by interventions with a state-centric view of authority in developing countries. This is a frustrating situation for the KNU, as the General Secretary at the time of research (Zipporah Sein) explained in an open letter to the US House of Representatives, Committee of Foreign Affairs, Hearing on Burma:

> The KNU controls and operates in significant territory in Karen State. We operate local services, including schools and clinics. We provide safety and security to people fleeing attacks by the Burmese Army. However, the United Nations and governments refuse to work with us in delivering humanitarian assistance, providing education and other assistance to the population, most of whom live in poverty. One reason given for this is that we are an armed group. However, the largest armed group in Burma is the dictatorship, and the United Nations and governments work with them, despite the fact that they are illegitimate and break international law. Our Army is to defend civilians, not attack them as the Burmese Army does. In addition, we respect human rights and support democracy, and are a democratic organization. We have also offered to abide by monitoring rules and requirements set by the UN or other donors, and unlike the dictatorship, place no restrictions on the delivery of aid. It does not, therefore, seem logical to refuse to work with the KNU.[88]

State governments and business people do in fact work with armed opposition groups on occasion, since those with strong local links and coercive power may offer viable alternatives in states where officials are unable or unwilling to maintain territorial control, security or oversight of cross-border transactions.[89] In the KNU's case, Geneva Call and the International Committee of the Red Cross maintain a relationship with the group;[90] however, the UN and, to a lesser extent, INGOs do not, despite the increase in humanitarian access agreements with armed opposition groups elsewhere. To mitigate this issue, the KNU has been compelled to distance its welfare wings supported by donor funding from the parent party and, in some cases, set up parallel organizations for refugee camp education and education inside eastern Burma.

Conclusion

Since the end of the Cold War, there has been a decline in territorially based insurgencies.[91] Mampilly argues that this is because the cost of holding territory outweighs the value it provides today.[92] However, as Stathis Kalyvas and Laia Balcells (2010) suggest, this may mean that the "technology of rebellion" has changed, rather than an overall decline in rebellion itself. This case illustrates how the KNU's technology of rebellion is changing in the post–Cold War geopolitical environment and in a context of increasing involvement by humanitarian actors. It also provides an example of how armed opposition groups may more broadly transform their strategies of conflict and contestation over central state-making in peripheral areas.

Philip Bobbit suggests that if the state system is superseded by alternative orders, such as the globalized market, then insurgent groups may also reflect this shift by developing decentralized, non-national and non-territorial structures (like Al-Qaeda, for example).[93] Kalyvas and Balcells (2010) similarly suggest that with the reduction of outside funding for conflict actors after the end of the Cold War, rebel groups have increasingly turned to criminal activities to compensate their reduced revenues, assisted by globalization and transnational criminal networks. However, as this case demonstrates, criminal activities are not the only source of revenue for armed opposition groups; they may also or instead turn to INGOs for funding of their governance services.

The KNU's education service inside Karen State, funded by INGOs, is now almost 3 times the value of its estimated central treasury income. Collectively, the funding given to its welfare wings and mass organizations will easily outweigh the KNU's traditional revenue from the sale of natural resources and tax. Since there are no indications that the KNU has either managed to increase its sales of natural resources on the black market or shift to narcotics-based revenue streams (a common source of funding for many other armed groups in Burma), this suggests that INGO funding forms the majority of its revenue streams.

However, while transnational formations can sustain armed opposition groups, they can also shape forms of social order and authority.[94] Chandler (2009) has argued that changing theoretical approaches to state sovereignty as state capacity to meet the human needs of its population, rather than political independence, may reframe external interventions, but they may also shape the strategies of armed opposition groups. As external interventions are reframed as meeting the sovereign obligations of a state to its civilian population in the state's absence or neglect, so armed opposition groups may lay claim to a degree of sovereignty or at least political legitimacy by virtue of their presence as humanitarian aid providers. Thus, as the sovereign state system becomes less hegemonic and other frames of sovereignty take its place, armed opposition groups may seek to mimic alternative frames of sovereignty instead of mimicking states.

Kriger argues that "controlling territory allows insurgents to offer utilitarian benefits to civilians in ways that groups without territory could never do",[95] and Mampilly (2007) agrees that territorial control is a precondition to the delivery of governance services. However, this case shows that despite a great decline in KNU-controlled territory, with transformed revenue streams, the KNU's welfare wings manage to provide extensive welfare services to the civilian population in Karen State, including in partially securitized and government-controlled areas. What is particularly interesting about this is the way they have adopted the key advantages of guerrilla warfare used by the KNU's military wing: mobility, favorable terrain, relationships with the local population, support from international allies and safe base areas, or sanctuary,[96] and applied them to the delivery of governance services. These strategies are also long familiar to villagers in hiding in Karen State, where mobile livelihoods are adopted to evade state authority.[97] Mobility, familiarity with the terrain and local support are essential to the provision of a variety of governance services by the KNU and the NGOs from across the border in order to evade Burma Army troops who attack services and staff provided outside its own structures.[98] Like guerrilla soldiers, mobile health service providers avoid using roads and bridges that are patrolled by the Burma Army and move through jungle paths instead.[99]

Given the absence of appropriate state services or international responses to the humanitarian crisis in eastern Burma, this assistance is very valuable and often the only viable way of reaching vulnerable people in the borderlands.[100] However, it also enables the KNU to continue contesting Burmese state-making. The fungibility of external revenue sources enables the KNU's welfare departments to remit back to the KNU's central treasury the 5 percent of the budget they are each officially granted, enabling a greater proportion of income to be spent on the army, who continue to contest Burmese state-making practices through guerrilla warfare.[101] As this chapter argued, the aim is not to defeat the Burma Army militarily, but to put pressure on it to negotiate with the KNU, which it started to do after the national elections and formation of a new government in 2011.

Notes

1. C. Christie, "A modern history of Southeast Asia: Decolonization, nationalism and separatism," *Tauris Academic Studies* (London: Institute of Southeast Asian Studies, 1996), 78; T. Kramer, "Burma's cease-fires at risk: Consequences of the Kokang crisis for peace and democracy," *Peace & Security Briefing* 1 (2009): 5.
2. I spent 10 months living at the headquarters of the Karen Youth Organization (KYO) during 2008 and 2009, having previously worked as a volunteer in the same organization for 2 years and for a local human rights group for 1 year.
3. During the 10-month fieldwork period in 2008–2009, 35 life histories, 144 structured and semi-structured interviews and numerous informal discussions were conducted, supplementing the understanding I had previously gained through work with local Karen organizations since 2003.

4. C. Nordstrom and A. Robben, eds. "The anthropology and ethnography of violence and sociopolitical conflict," in *Fieldwork under fire: Contemporary studies of violence and survival,* (Berkeley, CA: University of California Press, 1995).

5. S. Barakat *et al.,* "The composite approach: Research design in the context of war and armed conflict," *Third World Quarterly* 23, no. 5 (2002): 992.

6. Fearon (2004: 277) uses the term "peripheral insurgencies" to describe "civil wars involving rural guerrilla bands operating typically near the state's borders". I prefer the word "conflict" instead of "insurgency" since it is less normatively loaded with assumptions about the legitimacy of borders, armed groups and state governments.

7. A. Walker, *The legend of the golden boat: Regulation, trade and traders in the borderlands of Laos, China, Thailand, Burma and China* (Honolulu: University of Hawai'i Press, 1999), 7.

8. C. Scherrer, *Ethnicity, nationalism and violence: Conflict management, human rights, and multilateral regimes* (Aldershot and Burlington: Ashgate, 2003), 12.

9. P. Englebert, *State legitimacy and development in Africa* (Colorado: Lynne Rienner, 2002), 78.

10. A. Walker, *The legend of the golden boat: Regulation, trade and traders in the borderlands of Laos, China, Thailand, Burma and China* (Honolulu: University of Hawai'i Press, 1999).

11. C. Scherrer, *Ethnicity, nationalism and violence: Conflict management, human rights, and multilateral regimes* (Aldershot: Ashgate, 2003).

12. R. Jackson, *Quasi-states: Sovereignty, international relations and the Third World* (Cambridge: Cambridge University Press, 1990); J. Herbst, *States and power in Africa: Comparative lessons in authority and control* (Princeton, NJ: Princeton University Press, 2000).

13. C. Scherrer, *Ethnicity, nationalism and violence: Conflict management, human rights, and multilateral regimes* (Aldershot: Ashgate, 2003), 12.

14. T. Gallant, "Brigandage, piracy, capitalism, and state-formation: Transnational crime from a historical world-systems perspective," in *States and illegal practices,* ed. J. Heyman (Oxford: Berg, 1999), 33–34.

15. T. Gallant, "Brigandage, piracy, capitalism, and state-formation: Transnational crime from a historical world-systems perspective," in *States and illegal practices,* ed. J. Heyman (Oxford: Berg, 1999), 25–61.

16. T. Gallant, "Brigandage, piracy, capitalism, and state-formation: Transnational crime from a historical world-systems perspective," in *States and illegal practices,* ed. J. Heyman (Oxford: Berg, 1999), 25–61; A. McCoy, "Requiem for a drug lord: State and commodity in the career of Khun Sa," in *States and illegal practices,* ed. J. Heyman (Oxford: Berg, 1999), 129–167.

17. T. Gallant, "Brigandage, piracy, capitalism, and state-formation: Transnational crime from a historical world-systems perspective," in *States and illegal practices,* ed. J. Heyman (Oxford: Berg, 1999), 51–52.

18. For example, G. Loescher *et al.,* "Protracted refugee situations and the regional dynamics of peacebuilding," *Conflict, Security and Development* 7, no. 3 (2007):

491–501; S. Lischer, *Dangerous sanctuaries: Refugee camps, civil war, and the dilemmas of humanitarian aid* (New York: Cornell University Press, 2005).

19. T. Raeymakers, *The central margins: Congo's transborder economy and state-making in the borderlands*, DIIS Working Paper 2009:25 (Copenhagen: Danish Institute for International Studies, 2009).

20. T. Hagmann and D. Péclard, "Negotiating statehood: Dynamics of power and domination in Africa," *Development and Change* 41, no. 4 (2010): 552.

21. K. Schlichte, "With the state against the state? The formation of armed groups," *Contemporary Security Policy* 30, no. 2 (2009): 248.

22. C. Christie, "A modern history of Southeast Asia: Decolonization, nationalism and separatism," *Tauris academic studies* (London: Institute of Southeast Asian Studies, 1996), 78; T. Kramer, "Burma's cease-fires at risk: Consequences of the Kokang crisis for peace and democracy," *Peace & Security Briefing* 1 (2009): 76.

23. M. Smith, *Burma: Insurgency and the politics of ethnicity* (London and New York: Zed Books, 2nd Revised Ed., 1999).

24. D. Brown, *The state and ethnic politics in South-East Asia* (London and New York: Routledge, 1994), 54.

25. A. M. Thawnghmung, "The Karen revolution in Burma: Diverse voices, uncertain ends," *Policy Studies* 45: 2008.

26. A. M. Thawnghmung, "The Karen revolution in Burma: Diverse voices, uncertain ends," *Policy Studies* 45: 2008.

27. Cusano, in A. South, "Burma's longest war: Anatomy of the Karen conflict," Amsterdam: Transnational Institute, <http://www.tni.org/sites/www.tni.org/files/download/Burma%27s%20Longest%20War.pdf>, 14, (November 5, 2011).

28. C. Grundy-Warr *et al.*, "Power, territoriality and cross-border insecurity: Regime security as an aspect of Burma's refugee crisis," *Geopolitics* 2, no. 2 (1997): 85; J. Harriden, "Making a name for themselves: Karen identity and the politicization of ethnicity in Burma," *Journal of Burma Studies* 7 (2002): 119.

29. Boucand and Boucand 1992, in C. Chen Wei Ching, "Karen Power domains and networks: The political geography of exile," Bachelor Thesis (National University of Singapore, 1998).

30. C. Grundy-Warr *et al.*, "Power, territoriality and cross-border insecurity: Regime security as an aspect of Burma's refugee crisis," *Geopolitics* 2, no. 2 (1997): 84; R. T. Naylor, *Wages of crime: Black markets, illegal finance, and the underworld economy* (New York: Cornell University, 2004), 68.

31. Boucand and Boucand 1992, in C. Chen Wei Ching, "Karen power domains and networks: The political geography of exile," Bachelor Thesis (National University of Singapore, 1998).

32. R. Renard, "The Karen rebellion in Burma," in *Secessionist movements in comparative perspective*, ed. R. Premdas (New York: Macmillan St. Martin's Press, 1990).

33. Global Witness, "A conflict of interest—The uncertain future of Burma's forests," *Global Witness*, 2003, http://www.globalwitness.org/library/conflict-interest-english, 71 (November 3, 2011).

34. R. T. Naylor, *Wages of crime: Black markets, illegal finance, and the underworld economy* (New York: Cornell University, 2004), 68.

35. R. T. Naylor, *Wages of crime: Black markets, illegal finance, and the underworld economy* (New York: Cornell University, 2004), 68.

36. C. Grundy-Warr *et al.*, "Power, territoriality and cross-border insecurity: Regime security as an aspect of Burma's refugee crisis," *Geopolitics* 2, no. 2 (1997): 85; J. Harriden, "Making a name for themselves: Karen identity and the politicization of ethnicity in Burma," *Journal of Burma Studies* 7 (2002): 119.

37. P. Meehan, "Drugs, insurgency and state-building in Burma: Why the drugs trade is central to Burma's changing political order," *Journal of Southeast Asian Studies* 42, no. 3 (2011): 385.

38. T. Kudo, "Border industry in Myanmar: Turning the periphery into the center of growth," *IDE Discussion Paper* 122, Institute of Developing Economies (2007): 14.

39. Z. Mampilly, "Stationary bandits: Understanding Rebel Governance," PhD Thesis, University of California, Los Angeles (2007): 244.

40. C. Grundy-Warr and K. Dean, "Not peace, not war: The myriad spaces of sovereignty, peace and conflict in Myanmar/Burma," in *Reconstructing conflict: Integrating war and post-war geographies*, ed. S. Kirsch and C. Flint (Farnham: Ashgate, 2011), 98.

41. C. Grundy-Warr *et al.*, "Power, territoriality and cross-border insecurity: Regime security as an aspect of Burma's refugee crisis," *Geopolitics* 2, no. 2 (1997): 84.

42. Smith, in C. Grundy-Warr *et al.*, "Power, territoriality and cross-border insecurity: Regime security as an aspect of Burma's refugee crisis," *Geopolitics* 2, no. 2 (1997): 84.

43. C. Grundy-Warr *et al.*, "Power, territoriality and cross-border insecurity: Regime security as an aspect of Burma's refugee crisis," *Geopolitics* 2, no. 2 (1997): 70–115.

44. T. Gallant, "Brigandage, piracy, capitalism, and state-formation: Transnational crime from a historical world-systems perspective," in *States and illegal practices*, ed. J. Heyman (Oxford: Berg, 1999).

45. K. Woods, "Ceasefire capitalism: Military–private partnerships, resource concessions and military state-building in the Burma–China borderlands," *Journal of Peasant Studies* 38, no. 4 (2011): 751.

46. A. McCoy, "Requiem for a drug lord: State and commodity in the career of Khun Sa," in *States and illegal practices,* ed. J. Heyman (Oxford: Berg, 1999), 129–167.

47. A. McCoy, "Requiem for a drug lord: State and commodity in the career of Khun Sa," in *States and illegal practices,* ed. J. Heyman (Oxford: Berg, 1999), 146–147.

48. M. Smith, *Burma: Insurgency and the politics of ethnicity* (London and New Jersey: Zed Books, 1991), 408.

49. From December 1988 to May 1989, the Burmese regime granted 42 logging concessions to 36 Thai companies, many of them linked to Thai military

interests rather than specialist forestry firms (Brunner *et al.* 1998). The concessions doubled the area being exploited and gave the Burmese regime 20,000 baht per ton of teak extracted, although the Thai companies were also forced to pay the KNU 5,000 baht per ton in compensation (Smith 1991: 393).

50. R. Renard, "The Burmese connection: Illegal drugs and the making of the golden triangle," *Studies on the Impact of the Illegal Drug Trade* 6 (1996): 108; Xinhua (2010) "Myanmar–Thai bilateral trade doubled in five years," *Xinhua News*, July 7, 2010, http://news.xinhuanet.com/english2010/business/2010-09/07/c_13482884.htm, (December 3, 2010); S. Turnell, "Burma's economy 2008: Current situation and prospects for reform," *Burma Economic Watch*, 2008, http://www.econ.mq.edu.au/Econ_docs/bew/BurmaEconomy2008.pdf, (June 4, 2012); C. Grundy-Warr *et al.*, "Power, territoriality and cross-border insecurity: Regime security as an aspect of Burma's refugee crisis," *Geopolitics* 2, no. 2 (1997): 87.

51. Global Witness, "A conflict of interest—The uncertain future of Burma's forests," *Global Witness*, 2003, <http://www.globalwitness.org/library/conflict-interest-english>, (November 3, 2011).

52. C. Grundy-Warr and K. Dean, "Not peace, not war: The myriad spaces of sovereignty, peace and conflict in Myanmar/Burma," in *Reconstructing conflict: Integrating war and post-war geographies*, ed. S. Kirsch and C. Flint (Farnham : Ashgate, 2011), 98.

53. Although the KNU does not reveal its financial situation, the 5 percent of the KNU's annual budget allocated to the education department was reported to be 200,000 Thai baht in an interview with a Karen State Educational Assistance Group (KSEAG) coordinator on November 19, 2010, indicating that the KNU's central budget is around 4 million Thai baht, or US$133,300 as in December 2010.

54. N. Yan, "KNU struggles to acquire arms," *Irrawaddy*, published August 24, 2009, <http://www.irrawaddy.org/article.php?art_id=16629>, (October 10, 2010).

55. Irrawaddy, "KNU in serious crisis," March 24, 2009, <http://www.irrawaddy.org/article.php?art_id=15357>, (October 10, 2010).

56. Interview with a KNU Fourth Brigade township officer on November 10, 2010, Suan Pueng.

57. J. Fearon, "Why do some civil wars last so much longer than others?" *Journal of Peace Research* 41, no. 3 (2004): 289.

58. Interview with Saw V. (Male, 32), a KNDO Officer, district KYO leader, KSCB staff member and KSCDC officer, July 11, 2009, Mae Sot.

59. Irrawaddy, "KNU in serious crisis," March 24, 2009, http://www.irrawaddy.org/article.php?art_id=15357, (October 10, 2010).

60. Irrawaddy, "KNU in serious crisis," March 24, 2009, http://www.irrawaddy.org/article.php?art_id=15357, (October 10, 2010).

61. Z. Mampilly, *Rebel rulers: Insurgent governance and civilian life during war* (Ithaca, NY: Cornell University Press, 2011), 54.

62. Zahar 2001 in Z. Mampilly, *Rebel rulers: Insurgent governance and civilian life during war* (Ithaca, NY: Cornell University Press, 2011), 89.

63. KSEAG, *KSEAG final narrative report 2011*, 2011, <http://ktwg.org/Library/ KSEAG%20Annual%20Report%202010%20full%20Version.pdf>, (November 30, 2011).

64. Interview with Saw A. G., (male) a young CIDKP leader, Mae Sot, May 27, 2009.

65. TBBC, *Program report, January to June 2011* (2011): 82, <http://www. tbbc.org/resources/resources.htm#reports>, (November 30, 2011); Backpack Health Worker Team, "Provision of primary healthcare among internally displaced persons and vulnerable populations of Burma," 2011 funding proposal, http://www.backpackteam.org/wp-content/uploads/ 2011/01/2011%20BPHWT%20%20Proposal%20231110.pdf, (December 5, 2011); Backpack Health Worker Team, "Provision of primary healthcare among internally displaced persons and vulnerable populations of Burma," 2010 annual report, <http://www.backpackteam.org/wpcontent/uploads/2011/11/ BPHWT%202010%20Annual%20report.pdf, (December 6, 2011).

66. KSEAG, *KSEAG final narrative report 2011* (2011): 11–12, <http:// ktwg.org/Library/KSEAG%20Annual%20Report%202010%20full%20 Version.pdf>, (November 30, 2011).

67. KSEAG, *KSEAG final narrative report 2011* (2011): <http://ktwg.org/Library/ KSEAG%20Annual%20Report%202010%20full%20Version.pdf>, (November 30, 2011).

68. T. J. Lee *et al.*, "The impact of human rights violations on health among internally displaced persons in conflict zones: Burma," in *Public health and human rights: Evidence-based approaches,* ed. C. Beyrer and H. F. Pizer (Baltimore, MD: Johns Hopkins University Press, 2007), 3.

69. L. Beatty, "Challenge and survival: Political resistance in authoritarian Burma," PhD Thesis, George Washington University (2011): 255.

70. A. Horstmann, "Incorporation and resistance: Borderlands, transnational communities and social change in Southeast Asia," Oxford: ESRC Transnational Communities Program Working Paper WPTC-02-04, 2002; Z. Mampilly, *Rebel rulers: Insurgent governance and civilian life during war* (Ithaca, NY: Cornell University Press, 2011), 56.

71. KHRG, *Bullets and bulldozers: The SPDC offensive continues in Toungoo District,* Field report dated February 19, 2007, <http://www.khrg.org/khrg2007/ khrg07f1.html>, (December 9, 2011).

72. Interview with Naw Zipporah Sein, KNU General Secretary, Mae Sot, December 11, 2010.

73. A. South, *Burma's longest war: Anatomy of the Karen conflict,* Amsterdam: Transnational Institute (2011): 35, http://www.tni.org/sites/www.tni.org/files/ download/Burma%27s%20Longest%20War.pdf, (November 5, 2011).

74. Z. Mampilly, "Stationary bandits: Understanding rebel governance," PhD Thesis, University of California, Los Angeles (2007): 31.

75. Interview with a KYO leader, Mae Sot, June 3, 2009.
76. Interview with an NGO leader/KNU official/KYO leader, Mae Sot, June 23, 2009.
77. Christopher 1998 and Lee 2001, in A. M. Thawnghmung, "The Karen revolution in Burma: Diverse voices uncertain ends," *Policy Studies* 45 (2008): 22; M. Callahan, "Political authority in Burma's ethnic minority states: Devolution, occupation, and coexistence," *Policy Studies* 31 (2007): 37.
78. Christopher 1998 and Lee 2001, in A. M. Thawnghmung, "The Karen revolution in Burma: Diverse voices, uncertain ends," *Policy Studies* 45 (2008): 22.
79. A. South, *Burma's longest war: Anatomy of the Karen conflict*, Amsterdam: Transnational Institute, 2011: 41, <http://www.tni.org/sites/www.tni.org/files/download/Burma%27s%20Longest%20War.pdf>, (November 5, 2011).
80. J. Svensson, "Foreign aid and rent-seeking," *Journal of International Economics* 51 (2000): 437–461.
81. D. Mosse and D. Lewis, *Development brokers and translators: The ethnography of aid and agencies* (Bloomfield, CT: Kumarian Press, 2006), 16.
82. Interview with Saw A. G., (male) a young CIDKP leader, Mae Sot, May 27, 2009.
83. S. Gates, "Recruitment and allegiance: The microfoundations of rebellion," *Journal of Conflict Resolution* 46 (2002).
84. I. Salehyan, "Transnational rebels: Neighbouring states as sanctuary for rebel groups," *World Politics* 59 (2007).
85. Irrawaddy, "KNU in serious crisis," March 24, 2009, <http://www.irrawaddy.org/article.php?art_id=15357>, (October 10, 2010).
86. A. South, *Burma's longest war: Anatomy of the Karen conflict*, Amsterdam: Transnational Institute, 2011: 35, <http://www.tni.org/sites/www.tni.org/files/download/Burma%27s%20Longest%20War.pdf>, (November 5, 2011); C. Fink, "Militarization in Burma's ethnic states: Causes and consequences," *Contemporary Politics* 14, no. 4 (2008): 460.
87. Interview with Saw C., (male, aged 29) a Burma Issues co-ordinator, Mae Sot, January 28, 2009.
88. KNU, *KNU submission to US House of Representatives,* (Office of the Supreme Headquarters, Karen National Union, Kawthoolei, 2009), <http://www.facebook.com/note.php?note_id=217527345864>, (September 20, 2010).
89. W. Reno, "Sovereign predators and non-state armed group protectors" (Paper presented at "Curbing Human Rights Violations of Armed Groups conference," UBC Centre of International Relations, Vancouver, November 13–15, 2003), 21.
90. Interview with Naw Zipporah Sein, KNU General Secretary, December 2, 2010, Mae Sot.
91. S. Kalyvas and L. Balcells, "International system and technologies of rebellion: How the end of the Cold War shaped internal conflict," *American Political Science Review* 104 (2010).

92. Z. Mampilly, *Rebel rulers: Insurgent governance and civilian life during war* (Ithaca, NY: Cornell University Press, 2011), 253.

93. Bobbit 2008: 98, in Z. Mampilly, *Rebel rulers: Insurgent governance and civilian life during war* (Ithaca, NY: Cornell University Press, 2011), 253.

94. Z. Mampilly, *Rebel rulers: Insurgent governance and civilian life during war* (Ithaca, NY: Cornell University Press, 2011), 83.

95. Kriger 1992: 169, in Z. Mampilly, *Rebel rulers: Insurgent governance and civilian life during war* (Ithaca, NY: Cornell University Press, 2011), 54.

96. C. Guevara, *Guerrilla warfare* (Wilmington, DE: Scholarly Resources, 2001), 58; B. Loveman and T. Davies, "Introduction: Guerrilla warfare, revolutionary theory, and revolutionary movements in Latin America," in *Guerrilla warfare*, ed. C. Guevara (Wilmington, DE: Scholarly Resources, 2001), 4.

97. K. Malseed, "Where there is no movement: Local resistance and the potential for solidarity," *Journal of Agrarian Change* 8, no. 2-3 (2008): 496.

98. Backpack Health Worker Team, *Chronic emergency: Health and human rights in eastern Burma*, 2006. <http://www.burmacampaign.org.uk/reports/ChronicEmergency.pdf> (December 3, 2010); T. J. Lee *et al.*, "The impact of human rights violations on health among internally displaced persons in conflict zones: Burma," in *Public health and human rights: Evidence-based approaches*, ed. C. Beyrer and H. F. Pizer (Baltimore, MD: Johns Hopkins University Press, 2007), 3; KHRG, *Civilians as targets*, Commentary, KHRG #2006-C1, May 19, 2006, <http://www.khrg.org/khrg2006/khrg06c1.pdf>, (August 18, 2010); KHRG. *Development by decree: The politics of poverty and control in Karen State*, 2007, <http://www.khrg.org/khrg2007/khrg0701.html> (December 3, 2010); K. Malseed, "Where there is no movement: Local resistance and the potential for solidarity," *Journal of Agrarian Change* 8, no. 2-3 (2008): 499.

99. T. J. Lee *et al.*, "The impact of human rights violations on health among internally displaced persons in conflict zones: Burma," in *Public health and human rights: Evidence-based approaches*, ed. C. Beyrer and H. F. Pizer. (Baltimore, MD: Johns Hopkins University Press, 2007), 40.

100. A. South, *Burma's longest war: Anatomy of the Karen conflict*, Amsterdam: Transnational Institute, 2011: 40, <http://www.tni.org/sites/www.tni.org/files/download/Burma%27s%20Longest%20War.pdf>, (November 5, 2011).

101. Interviews with education, health and IDP relief department leaders between October 2008 and August 2009.

References

Backpack Health Worker Team. *Chronic emergency: Health and human rights in eastern Burma*, 2006. <http://www.burmacampaign.org.uk/reports/ChronicEmergency.pdf> (December 3, 2010).

Barakat, S., M. Chard, T. Jacoby and W. Lume. "The composite approach: Research design in the context of war and armed conflict." *Third World Quarterly* 23, no. 5 (2002): 991–1003.

Beatty, L. "Challenge and survival: Political resistance in authoritarian Burma." PhD Thesis, George Washington University, 2011.

Blanchard, J-M. "Linking border disputes and war: An institutional-statist theory." *Geopolitics* 10, no. 4 (2005): 688–711.

Brown, D. *The state and ethnic politics in South-East Asia.* London and New York: Routledge, 1994.

Brunner, J., K. Talbot and C. Elkin. *Logging Burma's frontier forests: Resources and the regime.* Washington, DC: World Resources Institute, 1998.

Callahan, M. "Political authority in Burma's ethnic minority states: Devolution, occupation, and coexistence." *Policy Studies* 31 (2007).

Cederman, L-E., A. Wimmer and B. Min. "Why do ethnic groups rebel? New data and analysis." *World Politics* 62, no. 1 (2010): 87–119.

Chandler, D., "Unraveling the paradox of the 'responsibility to protect'" *Irish Studies in International Affairs*, 20 no. 20, pp. 27–39.

Chen Wei Ching, C. "Karen power domains and networks: The political geography of exile." Bachelor Thesis, National University of Singapore, 1998.

Christie, C. "A modern history of Southeast Asia: Decolonization, nationalism and separatism." *Tauris academic studies.* London: Institute of Southeast Asian Studies, 1996.

DfID. *Review of aid to refugees and internally displaced people on the Thailand–Burma border,* 2008. <http://www.refugees.org/uploadedFiles/Investigate/Anti-Warehousing/Countries/DFID%20080700%20Review%20of%20Aid%20to%20Refs%20%20IDPs%20on%20the%20border%282%29.pdf> (August 27, 2010).

Eldon, J., C. Waddington, and Y. Hadi. "Health system reconstruction: Can it contribute to state-building?" Study commissioned by the Health & Fragile States Network, London: HLSP Institute, 2008.

Englebert, P. *State legitimacy and development in Africa.* Colorado and London: Lynne Rienner, 2002.

Fearon, J. and D. Laitin. "Ethnicity, insurgency, and civil war." *American Political Science Review* 97, no. 1 (2003): 75–90.

Fearon, J. "Why do some civil wars last so much longer than others?" *Journal of Peace Research* 41, no. 3 (2004): 275–301.

Fink, C. "Militarization in Burma's ethnic states: Causes and consequences." *Contemporary Politics* 14, no. 4 (2008): 447–462.

Gallant, T. "Brigandage, piracy, capitalism, and state-formation: Transnational crime from a historical world-systems perspective." In *States and illegal practices*, edited by J. Heyman. Oxford: Berg, 1999: 25–61.

Gates, S. "Recruitment and allegiance: The microfoundations of rebellion." *Journal of Conflict Resolution* 46 (2002): 111–130.

Global Witness. "A conflict of interest—The uncertain future of Burma's forests." *Global Witness* 2003, http://www.globalwitness.org/library/conflict-interest-english, 71, (November 3, 2011).

Grundy-Warr, C., A. Rajah, W. Elaine and Z. Ali. "Power, territoriality and cross-border insecurity: Regime security as an aspect of Burma's refugee crisis." *Geopolitics* 2, no. 2 (1997): 70–115.

Grundy-Warr, C. and K. Dean. "Not peace, not war: The myriad spaces of sovereignty, peace and conflict in Myanmar/Burma." In *Reconstructing conflict: Integrating war and post-war geographies*, edited by S. Kirsch and C. Flint. Farnham and Burlington: Ashgate, 2011: 91–114.

Guevara, C. *Guerrilla warfare*. 3rd Ed. Wilmington, DE: Scholarly Resources, 2001.

Hagmann, T. and Péclard, D. "Negotiating statehood: Dynamics of power and domination in Africa." *Development and Change* 41, no. 4 (2010): 539–562.

Harriden, J. "Making a name for themselves: Karen identity and the politicization of ethnicity in Burma." *Journal of Burma Studies* 7 (2002): 84–144.

Herbst, J. *States and power in Africa: Comparative lessons in authority and control.* Princeton, NJ: Princeton University Press, 2000.

High, H. "Dreaming beyond borders: The Thai/Lao borderlands and the mobility of the marginal." In *On the borders of state power*, edited by M. Gainsborough. New York: Taylor & Francis, 2009.

Horstmann, A. "Incorporation and resistance: Borderlands, transnational communities and social change in Southeast Asia." Working Paper WPTC-02-04, Oxford: ESRC Transnational Communities Program, 2002.

Irrawaddy. "KNU in serious crisis." *Irrawaddy*, published on March 24, 2009a. <http://www.irrawaddy.org/article.php?art_id=15357> (October 10, 2010).

Irrawaddy. "Sleepless in Mae Sot." *Irrawaddy*, published on March 6, 2009b. <http://www.irrawaddy.org/article.php?art_id=15255> (October 10, 2010).

Jackson, R. *Quasi-states: Sovereignty, international relations and the Third World.* Cambridge: Cambridge University Press, 1990.

Kalyvas, S. and L. Balcells. "International system and technologies of rebellion: How the end of the Cold War shaped internal conflict." *American Political Science Review* 104 (2010): 415–429.

KHRG. *Development by decree: The politics of poverty and control in Karen State*, 2007. <http://www.khrg.org/khrg2007/khrg0701.html> (December 3, 2010).

KNU. *KNU submission to US House of Representatives.* Office of the Supreme Headquarters, Karen National Union, Kawthoolei, 2009. <http://www.facebook.com/note.php?note_id=217527345864> (20 September 2010).

Kramer, T. "Burma's cease-fires at risk: Consequences of the Kokang crisis for peace and democracy." *Peace & Security Briefing* 1 (2009): 1–8.

KSEAG. "KSEAG final narrative report 2011." 2011, <http://ktwg.org/Library/KSEAG%20Annual%20Report%202010%20full%20Version.pdf>, (November 30, 2011).

Kudo, T. "Border industry in Myanmar: Turning the periphery into the center of growth." *IDE Discussion Paper* 122, Institute of Developing Economies, 2007.

Lawi W. "Burmese block imports at three Thai border crossings." *Irrawaddy*, 2010. <http://www.irrawaddy.org/article.php?art_id=18986> (December 3, 2010).

Lawi W. "Crackdown threats remain." *Irrawaddy*, 2009. <http://www.irrawaddymedia.com/article.php?art_id=16826> (December 3, 2010).

Lee, T. J., *et al.* "The impact of human rights violations on health among internally displaced persons in conflict zones: Burma." In *Public health and human rights:*

Evidence-based approaches, edited by C. Beyrer and H. F. Pizer. Baltimore, MD: Johns Hopkins University Press, 2007, 33–64.

Lischer, S. *Dangerous sanctuaries: Refugee camps, civil war, and the dilemmas of humanitarian aid.* New York: Cornell University Press, 2005.

Loescher, G., J. Milner, E. Newman and G. Troeller. "Protracted refugee situations and the regional dynamics of peacebuilding." *Conflict, security and development* 7, no. 3 (2007): 491–501.

Malseed, K. "Where there is no movement: Local resistance and the potential for solidarity." *Journal of Agrarian Change* 8, no. 2-3 (2008): 489–514.

Mampilly, Z. "Stationary bandits: Understanding rebel governance," PhD Thesis, University of California, Los Angeles, 2007.

Mampilly, Z. *Rebel rulers: Insurgent governance and civilian life during war.* Ithaca, NY: Cornell University Press, 2011.

McCartan, B. "Secret UN deals may entice Myanmar." *Asia Times*, January 30, 2009. <http://www.atimes.com/atimes/Southeast_Asia/KA30Ae01.html> (August 27, 2010).

McCoy, A. "Requiem for a drug lord: State and commodity in the career of Khun Sa." In *States and illegal practices*, edited by J. Heyman. Oxford: Berg, 1999: 129–167.

Meehan, P. "Drugs, insurgency and state-building in Burma: Why the drugs trade is central to Burma's changing political order." *Journal of Southeast Asian Studies* 42, no. 3 (2011): 376–404.

Moore, M. "Revenues, state formation and the quality of governance in developing countries." *International Political Science Review* 25, no. 3 (2004): 297–319.

Moss, T., G. Pettersson and N. van de Walle. "An aid-institutions paradox? A review essay on aid dependency and state building in sub-Saharan Africa." Working Paper No. 74, Washington, DC: Center for Global Development, 2006.

Mosse, D and D. Lewis. *Development brokers and translators: The ethnography of aid and agencies.* Bloomfield, CT: Kumarian Press, 2006.

Naylor, R. T. *Wages of crime: Black markets, illegal finance, and the underworld economy.* New York: Cornell University, 2004.

Nordstrom, C. and A. Robben, eds "The anthropology and ethnography of violence and sociopolitical conflict." In *Fieldwork under fire: Contemporary studies of violence and survival*, Berkeley, CA: University of California Press, 1995.

Raeymakers, T. *The central margins: Congo's transborder economy and state-making in the borderlands.* DIIS Working Paper 2009:25, Copenhagen: Danish Institute for International Studies, 2009.

Renard, R. "The Karen rebellion in Burma." In *Secessionist movements in comparative perspective*, edited by R. Premdas. New York: Macmillan St. Martin's Press, 1990.

Renard, R. "The Burmese connection: Illegal drugs and the making of the golden triangle." *Studies on the impact of the illegal drug trade* 6: 1996.

Reno, W. "Sovereign predators and non-state armed group protectors." Paper presented at "Curbing Human Rights Violations of Armed Groups conference," UBC Centre of International Relations, Vancouver, November 13–15, 2003.

Salehyan, I. "The delegation of war to rebel organisations." *Journal of Conflict Resolution* 54, no. 3 (2010): 493–515.

Salehyan, I. "Transnational rebels: Neighbouring states as sanctuary for rebel groups." *World Politics* 59 (2007): 217–242.

Scherrer, C. *Ethnicity, nationalism and violence: Conflict management, human rights, and multilateral regimes.* Burlington: Ashgate, 2003.

Schlichte, K. "With the state against the state? The formation of armed groups." *Contemporary security policy* 30, no. 2 (2009): 246–264.

Scott, J. *The art of not being governed: An anarchist history of upland Southeast Asia.* New Haven and London: Yale University Press, 2009.

Scott, Z. "Literature review on state-building" Review article prepared for DfID, 2007.

Smith, M. *Burma: Insurgency and the politics of ethnicity.* London: Zed Books, 2nd Revised Ed., 1999.

Smith, M. *Burma: Insurgency and the politics of ethnicity.* London: Zed Books, 1991.

South, A. "The quest for Karen unity." *The Irrawaddy*, published October 9, 2006.

South, A. "Humanitarian aid to IDPs in Burma: Activities and debates." *Forced Migration Review* 30 (2008): 17–18.

South, A. "Burma's longest war: Anatomy of the Karen conflict." 2011. Amsterdam: Transnational Institute. <http://www.tni.org/sites/www.tni.org/files/download/Burma%27s%20Longest%20War.pdf>, 14 (November 5, 2011).

Svensson, J. "Foreign aid and rent-seeking," *Journal of International Economics* 51 (2000): 437–461.

Thawnghmung, A. M. "The Karen revolution in Burma: Diverse voices, uncertain ends." *Policy Studies* 45, 2008.

Tilly, C. "Coercion, capital, and European States." *AD 1990–1992.* Cambridge: Blackwell, 1992.

Turnell, S. "Burma's economy 2008: Current situation and prospects for reform." Burma Economic Watch, 2008, <http://www.econ.mq.edu.au/Econ_docs/bew/BurmaEconomy2008.pdf>, (June 4, 2012).

Walker, A. *The legend of the golden boat: Regulation, trade and traders in the borderlands of Laos, China, Thailand, Burma and China.* Honolulu: University of Hawai'i Press, 1999.

Woods, K. "Ceasefire capitalism: Military–private partnerships, resource concessions and military state-building in the Burma–China borderlands." *Journal of Peasant Studies* 38, no. 4 (2011): 747–770.

Xinhua. "Myanmar–Thai bilateral trade doubled in five years." *Xinhua News,* July 7, 2010, <http://news.xinhuanet.com/english2010/business/2010-09/07/c_13482884.htm> (December 3, 2010).

Yan N. "KNU struggles to acquire arms." *Irrawaddy*, published August 24, 2009. <http://www.irrawaddy.org/article.php?art_id=16629> (October 10, 2010).

CHAPTER 5

Navigating the Urban "In-Between Space": Local Livelihood and Identity Strategies in Exploiting the Goma/Gisenyi Border

Karen Büscher and Gillian Mathys

Just like the bodies that are buried in the neutral zone, with their head in Congo and their feet in Rwanda. Somehow that is the reality of the inhabitants of Birere.[1]

Introduction

This chapter starts from an ethnographic study of the urban borderland of Goma (Democratic Republic of the Congo)–Gisenyi (Rwanda), and more specifically the border district Birere. This Congolese urban district is situated right upon the border with Rwanda, and it partly occupies the *zone neutre* or *zone tampon*, the natural buffer strip that runs along the border separating the Democratic Republic of the Congo (DRC) from Rwanda. In Birere, the geographic space connecting Goma to Gisenyi, two distinct political, economic and cultural worlds come together. Although they were created almost at the same moment, the evolution of these two cities (and two nations) has followed a different path.

Since the mid-1990s, the DRC and Rwanda have taken diverging roads of political and economic development, making this border a border between two very diverse political orders and societal projects. Consequently, the relation between Congo and Rwanda, Goma and Gisenyi is one of asymmetries and inequalities.[2] According to Paul Nugent, border towns often impersonate different kinds of unequal relationships.[3] Whilst the asymmetries of power and wealth may not be as extreme as in the case of Mexico–US border towns, the regional inequalities are more striking in Africa.[4]

For the case of Goma–Gisenyi, these inequalities are characterized in the different political regimes and regulatory systems, and in different levels of state capacity and security on both the national and regional level. Furthermore, these two cities have different dimensions, functions as well as a profoundly different political and economic significance on the national and regional level. Gisenyi is a small, clean, well-organized and safe town of approximately 70,000 inhabitants, well equipped with infrastructure[5] and where the state is strongly and visibly present on all levels. Goma is a fast expanding city of nearly 700,000[6] inhabitants, characterized by a weak state, an anarchic, informal urbanization, the presence of a huge international peacekeeping force, yet also very high crime levels.

According to Martin Doevenspeck, due to these inequalities, the border between the DRC and Rwanda is a "distinct cut-off point" and cannot be perceived as a borderland in the sense of a transborder transition zone of cultural and social overlap. Faced with such asymmetries and inequalities, he argues that the notion "fragmented borderland" is more apt.[7]

However, starting from an ethnographic study of daily actions, interactions and discourses of local actors in the Birere district, in this chapter we argue against this observation by perceiving Birere as a space of "in-betweenness".[8] This does not mean that we ignore or negate the inequalities between the DRC and Rwanda, or the exclusionary narratives that can sometimes be heard with regard to this border.[9] We will however argue that it is precisely this *difference* and the existence of *two separated* sets of regulations and political and economic organizations that has created possibilities and opportunities bridging the two cities in a joined dependence on transborder exchange. Border cities thrive on these differences and on the necessity and possibility of linking it.[10] As transit points between two different business spheres, two different regimes of control and taxation, border cities become places of multiple opportunities, which, for the case of Goma–Gisenyi, are to be largely situated in the informal sphere.

In Birere, the district that literally bridges these two different spheres, daily actions and interactions of local actors are characterized by a constant negotiation and navigation between these spheres. This navigation has to be perceived in the context of the historical open character of the border. There is a constant coming and going of goods and people between the two cities, through the two official border posts as well as through the unofficial openings along the informal settlements of Birere.

The socioeconomic reality of this urban *in-between zone* is emerging from a strong interaction, where local borderlanders of both sides engage in an intense exchange and where border crossing is perceived by them as a permanent condition. The *in-betweenness* of this urban space is clearly embodied in the occupation of the neutral buffer strip and its transformation into a zone of transborder smuggling. In Birere, it is clear how the two towns have "practically merged into a single urban agglomeration, with houses in some places built right up the border and private doors in garden walls constituting entry and exit post beyond public control".[11]

People living and working in Birere largely depend on the exceptional status of this *in-between zone*, as it generates economic opportunities. Navigating between two mingled yet different socioeconomic spaces has become an important feature of urban border culture and livelihood strategies. Living at the intersection of different worlds and cultures, the merchants and inhabitants of Birere are constantly shifting and renegotiating identities in ever-increasing maneuvers of power and submission, and often they adopt multiple realities.[12] Different kinds of actors (formal and informal, state and non-state) are directly or indirectly involved in the exploitation of the border as a source of income opportunities.

The skillful exploitation of the border through everyday survival strategies on the Goma–Gisenyi border will be the main focus of this chapter. We will analyze how borderlanders of Birere have developed strategies of exploitation or instrumentalization of this *in-betweenness*, by strategically combining opportunities on both sides. They do so by navigating between different spaces, economic regimes as well as identities. With one foot in Rwanda and the other in Congo, the borderlanders of Birere live and act in two intertwined economic, social, political and cultural worlds.

This chapter is based on ethnographic data collected during 11 months of fieldwork by Karen Büscher conducted in the city of Goma in the context of a PhD thesis. Most of the research in the Birere district was carried out between 2007 and 2009. Interviews were conducted with local administrative authorities, traders, shop owners and transporters.

Goma–Gisenyi: A Border Runs through It

Buursink argues that to speak of a border city, it should not only be located physically in the proximity of a border, but it should also be dependent on the border for its existence.[13] For our case, this is true in a very literal sense. Goma's history of urbanization is inextricably bound up with its "twin city"[14] Gisenyi at the Rwandan side of the border.

Between the relatively late *discovery* of Lake Kivu by Count von Götzen in 1894 and 1910/1911,[15] Lake Kivu and its eastern and western shores were the subject of much debates and discussions between Germany and the Congo

Free State (Belgium from 1908). The region that was contested was called *zone contesté* or *streitiges Gebiet*. The borders in the *zone contesté* were mapped during the 1884–1885 Berlin conferences, thus before any European had ever seen Lake Kivu. As such, the conflict was the result of the truly arbitrarily mapping of political boundaries in unexplored territory.[16] The conflict over the mapping of the region had direct ramifications for the way colonial space was appropriated. In the *zone contesté*, the relationship between territory and power was pretty straightforward: occupation was linked directly to control over territory. This resulted in a jostle for posts: both German and Congolese troops tried to establish a post in the area where the boundary was disputed. As there could be no real solution to the boundary dispute between Germany and the Congo Free State as long as the region was not mapped scientifically, Hecq (official of the Congo Free State) and Bethe (German commander) drew an agreement stipulating the terms of behavior in this disputed region. German and Congolese authorities had the right to create posts of equal numbers and force.[17]

However, the authorities of the Congo Free State were not allowed to interfere in political questions and the foundation of a post did not imply a formal occupation, but rather an attestation of rights over territory. It was agreed upon by the metropolitan governments that this agreement was accepted until the exact position of the border could be decided.[18]

The determination of the exact location of the border was to be the task of several border commissions. The occupation of the Kivu region proceeding, Gisenyi was founded in 1905. The Hecq–Bethe agreement explains why posts often mirrored each other. When one post was established, the other colonizing power had to establish a post on the other side of the border, with an equal military force, in order to secure claims. Consequently, Goma (1906) was erected as a reaction to the foundation of the German post of Gisenyi.

In 1910 (1911), the border that still is in place nowadays was delineated in an agreement between the Belgian, German and British colonizing powers. The physical trace of the border has changed very little since then, except that from 1916 onward Rwanda was *de facto* no longer governed by the Germans, but ruled by Belgium as part of a mandated territory (Ruanda-Urundi), relegating the once *national* border to an internal one. Belgium and Ruanda-Urundi formed a customary unit and shared the same currency. That the border was *internal* to Belgian colonial space meant that the border remained relatively *open*.

Nevertheless, even if the border was internal to the Belgian colonial sphere, this did not imply that it was irrelevant, as it created political and economic spaces.[19]

Congo gained its independence before Rwanda, creating tensions along the border. Belgians in Rwanda feared that anti-European sentiments in Congo might spill over into Rwanda, which was at that time under rule of exception.[20] The developments in Goma were closely monitored by the intelligence forces. Small fights did take place between Goma and Gisenyi, for example, between January 12 and 14, 1961. *"Le jeudi 12, dans la milieu de l'après-midi, éclata une bagarre le long de la frontière; les protagonistes étaient des policiers ruandais, des policiers et soldats congolais et divers civils [...]"* ("Thursday 12 [January] in the afternoon, a fight broke out along the border; the protagonists were Rwandan police officers, Congolese police and soldiers as well as numerous civilians").[21]

Until the 1990s, economic and political transborder relations between Congo and Rwanda were stable. The close relationship between Zaire's long-time dictator, Mobutu, and the Rwandan president, Habyarimana, was reflected in lax border controls.[22] The porous character of the border generated an intense economic exchange, largely to be situated in the informal sphere. The historical informal long-distance trade between Congo and Eastern Africa became more pronounced during Mobutu's Second Republic.[23] Mukohya Vwakyanakazi attributes the expansion of the informal economy between the 1970s and 1980s to the proximity of the border. According to him, the amount of smuggled goods was considerable: for example up to 60 percent of coffee produced in 1985–1986 would have been marketed outside of the formal economy.[24] These trading networks were controlled by some of Kivu's politicians and Rwandan immigrant elites,[25] with the complicity of customs officials and police at several—including Goma's—border posts.[26]

The first important rupture in the border regime occurred in 1994 during the Rwandan genocide,[27] when more than 1 million Hutu refugees fled into the city of Goma, causing a major humanitarian crisis and the start of a long history of violent conflict in the DRC. When the Mobutu regime proved to be unwilling to secure the border, the Rwandan army invaded and started the first Congolese war. During the second Congolese war, Goma became the seat of the Rwandan-backed rebel movement Rally for Congolese Democracy-Goma (RCD-Goma). During the *de facto* occupation of eastern Congo by Rwanda from 1998 to 2003, there were virtually no border controls.[28] Transborder trade flourished in the light of the expanding market of coltan and cassiterite, connecting Kivu's artisanal mining centers to the international resource market, via Kigali.

Being the siege of the rebel movement, the city of Goma was disconnected administratively and territorially from the Congolese capital of Kinshasa. This disconnection reinforced the city's historic position in transborder trade

networks and its economic outward orientation toward markets in Eastern
Africa, the Middle East and Asia.

With the political decline of the RCD-Goma and the Congolese elections
of 2006, the degree of Congolese state control over the Congolese–Rwandan
border increased.[29] From August 2007 until the end of 2008, the insurgency
of Laurent Nkunda meant a new period of tension on the Goma–Gisenyi
border. With Nkunda threatening to take over the city of Goma and with
rumors circulating of Rwandan involvement, a general atmosphere of distrust
and fear strongly influenced transborder interaction in this urban borderland.

The situation stabilized after Nkunda's arrest in 2009 and the political
rapprochement between the Kinshasa and Kigali regimes. An important result
was the *ouverture 24/24*, or the day-and-night opening of the main border
post between Goma and Gisenyi.

Regardless of the tense episodes in transborder relations, the border
between the two *twin* cities has always remained a zone of intense contact and
interaction between Congo and Rwanda. Today, between Goma and Gisenyi
there is a constant mobility in two directions for very different reasons.
Congolese teachers go to Rwanda because of higher salaries, while Rwandan
students often go to Congolese schools because of lower costs. Even for ordinary activities such as checking one's bank account or searching for a good
Internet connection or even a good party, crossing the border is engrained
in daily life. Many Congolese Goméens have moved to Gisenyi in the last 3
years, because of inflation of house prices as a result of the increasing presence of humanitarian organizations and UN staff in Goma.[30] For Rwandans,
Goma (where taxes are lower) offers other economic opportunities than in
Rwanda, and attracts many of them to daily transit to the city in search for a
job or to do business.[31]

Economic differences stimulate transborder trade, making it the key
source of income for thousands of Congolese and Rwandans. Besides these
economic differences, the higher degree of state control in Rwanda is also
key. Ambulant vending, for example, often performed by female vendors, is
forbidden in Rwanda, pushing them across the border to gain a living.[32]

A very particular element in the history of this urban borderland is the
occupation of the *zone neutre* or *zone tampon*, in theory an unoccupied stretch
of no-man's-land dividing Congo from Rwanda in the absence of a natural boundary. Illegal settlement in the neutral zone between the two official
border checkpoints, Petite Barrière and Grande Barrière, already took place
in the early 1960s. Official documents mention Congolese, who had settled
beyond the line of border pillars, *de facto* on Rwanda territory. According to
these documents, the *zone neutre* became a "place where fraudulent and even
subversive activities increased which were difficult to control".[33]

Constructing activities in the neutral zone intensified from the 1980s onward, when border control was rather lax.[34] During the RCD period, occupation of the neutral zone from both Congolese as well as Rwandan side increased, as at that time there were virtually no border controls.[35] Nevertheless, during certain moments, the Congolese state attempted to gain control over this borderland. Probably from the 1970s onward, attempts were undertaken to "normalize" the neutral zone. In collaboration with the Rwandan authorities, mixed border commissions had to map the problem and rematerialize the border. However, not even the very institutions safeguarding the border were sacrosanct: in 1993 it was established that the extension of the Congolese customs post of *Poid Lourds* (Birere) was situated on Rwandan territory.[36] Nowadays, illegal settlements at the Rwandan side have been removed, but on the Congolese side illegal houses and shacks are still littering the neutral zone.

Birere: A Place *in Between*

Birere is a very crowded, lively and chaotic district on the Congolese side of the border, and the center of informal economic activities. It stretches along the border from the airport to the city center (see map annex 1). Birere contains three administrative districts: Kahembe, Mapendo and Mikeno. Because of their shared economic, demographic and morphologic characteristics, they are often treated as one district. Ethnologically, Birere means "dried banana leaves" in Kinande,[37] referring to the original roof covering of the first settlements in this district. Birere is among the oldest occupations of Goma. The first Belgian settlement later evolved in what was called the *quartier indigène* according to the colonial urban morphology.[38]

Today, with an estimated number of 130,000 inhabitants,[39] Birere is the most densely populated neighborhood in Goma, with the smallest plots (with an average of 20 m^2) and the highest concentration of households in one plot (with an average of five).[40] The most represented ethnic groups among its inhabitants are Hutu, Hunde, Havu, Nande and Shi.[41]

Although Birere houses a very poor population and it is marked by a fast demographic expansion, it is also the most attractive place in the city to engage in informal activities.

Because rent prices are high, many newcomers start occupying or constructing illegally. As is the case for the whole of the city of Goma, the fast demographic expansion did not go hand in hand with an adequate urban planning. Today, Birere is the most explicit example of what is locally called a 'spontaneous district' (*quartier spontané*) or 'anarchic settlement' (*occupation anarchique*).

Compared to other urban districts in Goma, Birere is relatively well provided with water and electricity, because its infrastructure dates back to colonial times. However, the existing infrastructure is oversaturated and run-down, and there is an enormous lack of basic education and health services.[42]

Most of the people doing business in Birere live in other districts. Besides poverty, this district is also characterized by insecurity and high crime rates. Inhabitants of Goma and Gisenyi often perceive Birere as a "red zone", a filthy, risky place, where going from the city center to Birere is like "going down from the US to Mexico".[43] Also referred to as Tchetcheni, Birere is a "quartier des bandits, prostituées, soulards, vagabonds, brigands".[44]

At the same time, Birere is unarguably a zone of opportunities and the heart of economic activity, housing numerous stores, warehouses, restaurants and popular clubs or *ngandas*. With regard to these commercial activities, its location is ideal, along the border, near the international airport and close to the administrative center.

Thousands of people walk long distances every day from the peripheral districts to this popular center to do some *affaires* and to buy or sell goods for the best price. In Birere, people from all kinds of directions, statuses and ethnic origins come together and interact in all kinds of moneymaking activities. It is in this part of the city that important business deals are being concluded, yet at the same time where people balance all sorts of survival strategies in order to have something to eat at the end of the day.[45]

It is the proximity of the border with Rwanda that makes this district the perfect site for *affaires*. One of the two official crossing points is located in Birere: the *Petite Barrière* is the border opening for pedestrians, linking Birere with the Gisenyi market. All day long, until the closure of the barrier at 6 o'clock in the evening, this crossing point is crowded with Congolese and Rwandese vendors, traders, laborers and students, crossing in both directions. Together with the *Grande Barrière* (located further down south from Birere), about 15,000 people cross these two posts officially everyday.[46] While over the *Grande Barrière* minerals, petrol, cars and constructing materials are imported or exported, the *Petite Barrière* is the gate for portable goods. From the Congolese side, over the small barrier, foodstuff, alcohol and other consumption products are sold in Rwandan markets. From the Rwandan side, meat, bread and milk are brought to Goma.[47]

As has been shown above, the evolution of the Birere district is inextricably bound up with the border. The social, economic and spatial development of this district has evolved around the central position and significance of the border. In the next part, we will show that Birere *can* be perceived as a borderland in the sense that it is a distinct socioeconomic space where particular border activities, livelihoods and identities are articulated.

We will argue that in the context of intense transborder mobility, Birere is a space *in between*, where borderlanders have developed an everyday culture, inducing cross-border socioeconomic and cultural patterns that significantly differ from the two parent societies.[48] Its position as a space *in between* is impersonated in its relationship to the *zone neutre*, which is partly incorporated into Birere's vibrant commercial center and plays an important role in informal commerce.

The *in-betweenness* of Birere develops itself through the constant and in many cases illegal coming and going, and through the failure of official or formalized attempts to reorder this borderland. The failure of these formalized attempts to regulate both the mobility and urbanization in this district is not surprising given the dependency of many people—even state actors—on the exceptional status of this *in-between* zone. The navigation in this zone, between mingled yet different socioeconomic spaces, has become an important feature of urban livelihoods.

Makoro: *Navigating along Different Geographic and Economic Spaces*

As James Anderson and Liam O'Dowd have observed, the coexistence of different regulatory regimes on either side of a border generates an opportunity structure that invites smuggling, unofficial exchange rates and illegal immigration. They perceive the exploitation of these differences (prices, interest rates, exchange rates, etc.) in terms of *arbitrage economies*, or economic activities for which the border is the *raison d'être*.[49] These cross-border economic relationships generated by *arbitrage* tend to be "limited, sometimes short term and unstable, informal and perhaps illegal".[50]

The proximity of the border in Birere has generated such an *arbitrage economy*. Differences in tax and customs services between Rwanda and Congo engender a fruitful environment for fraudulent traffic of various small goods. Many consumer goods such as electrical appliances, alcohol or construction materials are cheaper in the DRC, and are unofficially reexported to Rwanda, from where they came.[51]

As a result of the particular nature of the *zone neutre*—controlled on paper, but leaving loopholes to circumvent this control—it is a fruitful environment for smugglers, for which the aforementioned traffic is a highly lucrative business. As one Birere trader explained: "When you want to make money, you come here, to Birere, you build a house with two entries: one that opens on the Congolese side, the other on the Rwandan side".[52]

Consequently, the ambiguous nature of the border and the uncontrolled housing creates a context in which "members of an ethnic group, or even a single family, may choose to live on either side of a border line in order to exploit the benefits of both spheres".[53] Apparently, in Birere living literally *on* the border provides the most possibilities to benefit from these spheres.

The fraudulent traffic of various small goods is facilitated by the porous nature of the border. Transborder traffic takes place via the *Petite Barrière*, but also along hidden openings (through private houses and gardens), and through the labyrinth of small pathways in the neutral zone crossing private yards, locally referred to as the *makoro*. These loopholes are used by many smugglers to get their merchandise to the other side of the border without paying the multiple and costly taxes collected at the barriers. Congolese and Rwandan Birere smugglers have developed trading networks appropriating these little tracks, in informal agreements with local inhabitants and border patrols.

These smuggling networks along the *makoro* are in a way embodying the central significance of transborder mobility in the daily practices of Birere. Surviving and making money out of the border is all about the capacity and knowledge of navigating between different countries, cities, tax systems, currencies, languages and identities. These navigation skills are clearly integrated in the livelihood strategies of Birere's borderlanders.

One example of how local actors exploit the border in their urban livelihoods is the phenomenon of *chora chora*. This concept refers to various forms of small-scale smuggling between Goma and Gisenyi.[54] On a more specific level, it refers to Rwandan (most often female) smugglers who illegally transport small goods (such as sugar, rice and cosmetic products) across the border. They have become specialists in smuggling their products in sometimes very inventive ways, using the official border post, the *makoro* and even Lake Kivu. If possible, they hide the goods in their clothes, or in the schoolbags of their children. If not, they will enter in negotiation with the patrols or they can stock their goods in a friend's house somewhere at the *zone neutre* and wait until night to smuggle it to the other side.[55] Through their experience, these women have established a well-developed system of connections and collaborations on both sides of the border.[56]

Another particular example are the numerous disabled traders who are active across the Goma–Gisenyi border. This remarkable group of local traders earn their daily income by the transportation of small commodities (such as flower, charcoal, cloths or soap) from one town to the other. On both sides, they work for different *commerçants*, for whom they deliver goods to depots indicated by the traders. The disabled have, according to Congolese law, the right to import goods with reduced taxes. Congolese as well as Rwandese businessmen use these traders for the undeclared traffic of their goods. Some of these *handicapés de Birere* have become themselves well-known businessmen and respected agents in the district. United through some sort of syndicate, they operate in a well-organized manner and form an important economic pressure group in case of, for example, contested intervention on transborder activities.[57] In a way, *les handicapés de Birere* are borderlanders that "realize that their very marginality—their borderland advantage in the interstice—gives them the opportunity to exploit the ambiguous values of powerful crossborder movements".[58]

The strategies of urban borderlanders such as the *chora chora* and the disabled traders are examples of the active resourcing of borders by local inhabitants, as described by Markus Virgil Hoehne and Dereje Feyissa in Chapter 3. By navigating the borderland, opportunities from both sides are exploited. Acting in this *in-between space* offers multiple opportunities, for multiple kinds of actors. Where for the *chora chora* the *zone neutre* is exploited as a gateway for illegal smuggling, for others it is just used as a field to cultivate small crops for private consumption. Logically, for state agents also, operating in this borderland offers benefits, as they engage in resourcing the border by their involvement in fraud. For migration and customs officers that operate at the crossing post and for the soldiers patrolling the borderline, complicity in fraudulent transborder trade is the main source of their daily income. That the number of these state officials who are actually involved in, or turn a blind eye to the illicit activities at the border, might be quite high is suggested by the number of agencies represented at the border. According to Aloys Tegera and Dominic Johnson, 30 different agencies were involved in tax control on the Goma–Gisenyi border in 2007.[59] Whereas Congolese border officials seem to be easy to bribe, the Rwandan border guards seem to be generally open for negotiations but much more aware of observation by their superiors.[60]

In this section, we have demonstrated how the exploitation of the borderland of Birere as an *in-between space* is reflected in border livelihoods as described above. However, the strategic combining of benefits from both sides is not only a matter of navigating between geographic places and different tax systems. It is at the same time also a matter of navigating between two cultural worlds, languages and identities.

Enfants de Birere: *Navigating Different Identities*

Within the anthropology of frontiers and borders, there has been a growing interest in processes of identity formation.[61] These studies consider the borderland as a social construction, engendering it through daily experiences, activities and discourses. An anthropology of borders focuses on the negotiation of identities where it is expected that identity is problematic.[62]

The geographic dimension of identity plays an important role in a context where mobility across a national border is high. Navigating between different geographies, borderlanders are related in a very specific way to place(s). In borderlands, place and identity are made and unmade across a multiplicity of geographical scales.[63]

Some anthropologists have argued that in a context of intense mobility, crossing and overlap, there is a general dislocation of people, no longer fixed in specific places. This dislocated experience leads to a "deterritorialization" of identities.[64]

In the urban borderland of Birere, although it is an ambiguous space where it is not always clear what is Congolese or Rwandan territory, this deterritorialization of space seems to play out in a different manner. The experience of mobility and crossing leads to a connection with *several* spaces, in which the place plays an important role. In Birere there is a continuing significance of place and space in practices, and a strong "emplacement"[65] of people's actions and activities.

Identity is an important element in this emplacement, and identity strategies ramify the capability of people developing transborder livelihoods.

For Birere traders, vendors, et cetera, identity is an important asset in their daily livelihoods and survival strategies. In the first place, identity is socially constructed through actions and practices, of which language is a key feature. The *lingua franca* in Birere is Kiswahili, although many Congolese and Rwandans in Birere are fluent in both Kiswahili and Kinyarwanda. In a context of intense contact and overlap, in Birere it is very difficult to distinguish if one has Rwandan or Congolese origins. Through a long history of precolonial mobility, and colonial and postcolonial transborder migration, many families in both Goma and Gisenyi have mixed Congolese–Rwandan ancestries.

However, language is not the only marker of identity. Although prohibited by Congolese law, some of the Birere transborder traders have double nationalities.[66] In Birere, double nationality is managed in a strategic way. Identifying yourself as being Congolese or Rwandan and as such being connected or placed at both sides of the border, Birere's actors acquire a privileged position in different ways. For example, to avoid heavy taxes, Birere traders show their Congolese national election card while discussing with municipal tax collectors. It is locally believed that these state agents especially target Rwandan traders or shop owners, distrusting them because of their so-called "dubious loyalty" (for exploiting benefits on both sides of the border, but only investing on their own side). On other occasions, while for example negotiating agreements with the *chora chora* or shop suppliers from Gisenyi, it will be more advantageous to identify yourself as a Rwandan citizen.[67]

Identities thus function as a resource, an asset in the exploitation of the border by combining benefits from both sides. The link between identities and economic strategies in the borderland has also been analyzed by Victor Muzvidziwa,[68] who studied the pragmatic use of multiple identities by female traders on the Zimbabwe–South African border. He describes how their *identity strategies* enable them to survive and to cope with the difficult economic and political local conditions of this borderland. In Birere, a similar dynamic can be observed, and the capacity to navigate different geographical and identity scales determines inhabitants' level of transborder mobility and access to economic opportunities. Just as Muzvidziwa observed in his case, borderlanders in Birere "developed a capacity to make strategic decisions and to deploy their identities in an advantageous manner".[69]

In navigating the borderland as an in-between place, the connection to both sides of the border is crucial. But there is another level of emplacement that is of importance—also directly linked to processes of identification—namely people's connection and identification with the border and the borderland itself. In her analysis of identity processes in the Shabe borderland between Benin and Nigeria, Donna K. Flynn[70] describes how border residents of both sides have forged a strong sense of a shared *border identity*, based on perceived rights to border crossing (and the benefits of transborder trade). This collective transnational border identity reflects a strong territorial claim to the border; by explaining that "they *are* the border", border people of Shabe are *embodying* the border. For Birere, we can partly observe a similar reality.

A remarkable way to identify with the border and transborder reality is the identification as children of Birere (*enfants de Birere*). Local traders, vendors and shop owners in Birere are labeling themselves this way. To be a child of Birere means different things. First of all, it implies a certain spatial or geographic connection to the Birere district, for example, by renting a small shop in one of the malls. At the same time, it implies a connection to the border by the engagement in mobile economic and social transborder networks. Being *enfant de Birere* means being active in exploiting the opportunities that lie within the proximity of the border and border crossing itself.

But calling oneself an *enfant de Birere* is also a clear matter of self-perception (*image de soi*) of being able to navigate the border. As a Birere merchant explains:

> Me, I can manage things well here. To do some business here [Birere], it is like a play, you see. You just have to know the rules, the *système*. We are real children of Birere. We know how to make some money here and on the other side [Rwanda]. And the events [fighting, war] don't frighten us, we are used to all conditions.[71]

Thus, being a child of Birere means being part of a border life and using the border as a resource. It also requires spatial knowledge and social cross-border contacts. Local traders will stress the fact that only the "real" children of Birere know how to use the *makoro* by navigating through the labyrinth of informal cross-border pathways and by arranging agreements with local inhabitants and border patrols to get their goods cheaply to the other side of the border. As such, in line with Flynn's argument, the common border experience results in a sense of "deep placement" in the border[72] and in Birere as an *in-between space* of opportunity. Children of Birere can have both Congolese and Rwandan origins, and this common border identity is expressed through their shared dependence on the border and their claims on the border for maximum profit.

However, it is important here to remark that the negotiation of identity is not unproblematic in this borderland. Where the shared border experience of the *enfants de Birere* seems to suggest that the geographical and social border becomes irrelevant, this is not the case. Regional dynamics of exclusionary politics and violent conflict have partly interrupted the emergence of a veritable *transnational* identity to which Flynn refers.

In the DRC in general, and in Kivu in particular, debates over nationality and citizenship, framed in terms of who is "autochthonous" and who is not, are sensitive issues.[73]

The legal definition of national identity has been problematic since early independence and remains until today a source of confusion and conflict. That the search for a definition of national citizenship occurred through the exclusion of specific ethnicities is particularly obvious in North Kivu.[74] Although scholars agree that "Rwandophones" or Kinyarwanda speakers (both Hutu and Tutsi) have settled in this region since precolonial times, they have increasingly been perceived as foreigners.[75] In opposition to the original or autochthonous inhabitants of this area, Rwandophones in Goma are identified as *non-originaires*.

Discrimination of and violence against Rwandopohones in North (as well as South) Kivu increased at moments of intensified political competition, such as the democratization process of the early 1990s. The Rwandan refugee crisis since the second half of the twentieth century with its climax in 1994 and the two Congolese wars further sharpened discourses of autochthony.[76]

Birere could not escape these tensions; on the contrary, discourses on autochthony have proved to be easily manipulated and mobilized in this district. During moments of increased political or military tension in the region, to be identified in Birere as Rwandan or "from the other side" can have serious consequences. In such a situation, national identity is a means for the emplacement of the "other" on the other side of the border.

This can be illustrated by the tense situation that emerged in Birere as a result of Nkunda's rebellion[77] in 2007 and 2008. Rumors of direct and indirect involvement of Rwanda in Nkunda's rebellion circulated rapidly in Birere and resulted in anti-Rwandan aggression, where vendors or traders identified as Rwandophones were mocked and jeered in the streets.

In this instance, Birere as an *in-between* place and the shared experiences of emplacement are replaced by feelings of insecurity linked to the perception of illusory aggressors on the other side of the border in the *in-between* zone; "the *zone tampon* is an ideal spot for spies to meet. We saw them coming to talk to each other, those from the CNDP, the businessmen and the Rwandans".[78] These feelings of "otherness" were capitalized upon by local power brokers. During this time, the local district chiefs of Birere organized several surveys in their districts, in order to identify *infiltrés* (non-Congolese with no valid residence permit).

These surveys were conducted in a very efficient manner in collaboration with other local urban authorities. These initiatives, although supported by at least part of the inhabitants, nevertheless created considerable tensions in the district. Many Rwandans working and residing for years in Birere suddenly decided to spend the night on the other side of the border in Gisenyi, for security reasons.

Concluding Remarks

We have seen that in a sense the Goma/Gisenyi border could be seen as a clear cut-off line between Rwanda, with its well-organized administrative structure and state apparatus and a fully functional army, and the DRC, marked by a dysfunctional state and loose military apparatus. The debate about citizenship and belonging also seems to point at a "fragmented" borderland.[79] Especially—but not solely—at times of increased military and political tension, the border emerges as an excuse for xenophobic discourses.

However, that is only part of the story. The *in-between* place that is Birere thrives on "bridging" the differences that exist between the two states. The analysis of everyday border livelihoods and identities demonstrated how border life in Birere evolved around the exploitation of these differences.[80] In that sense, we could interpret this border agency in the way Anderson and O'Dowd interpreted *arbitrage economies*, emerging from the border and the exploitation of its ambiguities and asymmetries. As such, in the everyday exploitation of the border as a "lucrative field",[81] this urban borderland becomes a social laboratory, "creatively exploited by situational shifts and innovative combinations, putting its resources together in new ways, experimenting".[82]

The emplacement of the *enfants de Birere* on the border points at the strategic use of identity in order to be able to gain from this ambiguous *in-between* space. The statement that identity can be used as a strategy is not new, nor is it unique for this concrete case. Achille Mbembe, for example, has pointed at the mobilization of identities by the "postcolonial subject" in order to achieve maximum instrumentality and efficacy,[83] and Theodore Trefon has described the opportunistic use of identity in Kinshasa to gain a broader access to social networks.[84]

However, these dynamics are given a very particular interpretation in the concrete context of this transborder setting. Here, they have become part of the strategic use of the border and the exploitation of its ambiguity, similar to processes on the Zimbabwean/South African and Nigerian/Benin border.[85]

In order to fully exploit the benefits and border opportunities of both sides, flexible navigation between different places, languages and identities became a key feature of the socioeconomic strategies of borderlanders. In this chapter, we have demonstrated how, through this navigation, the *enfants de Birere* have developed the skills and knowledge to use their marginal border position in daily surviving strategies.

As such, the inhabitants and merchants of Birere, straddled in between Rwanda and Congo, are indeed like the bodies buried in the neutral zone: they are *in-between spaces*. This position enables them to profit from both spaces, but at times it can also put them at risk when identified as belonging to the other side of the border.

Notes

1. Interview local observer (Goma, December 2009).
2. M. Doevenspeck, "Constructing the border from below: Narratives from the Congolese–Rwandan state boundary," *Political Geography* 30, no. 3 (2011): 129–142.
3. P. Nugent, "Border towns and cities in comparative perspective: Barriers, flows and governance," in *A companion to border studies*, ed. T. Wilson and H. Donnan (Oxford: Blackwell, 2012).
4. P. Nugent, "Sizing up asymmetry: State logics and power dynamics in the Senegambian and Ghana–Togo borderlands," forthcoming.
5. M. Doevenspeck, "Constructing the border from below: Narratives from the Congolese–Rwandan state boundary," *Political Geography* 30, no. 3 (2011): 129–142.
6. République Démocratique du Congo, *Rapport Annuelle 2009* (Goma: Mairie de Goma).
7. M. Doevenspeck, "Constructing the border from below: Narratives from the Congolese–Rwandan state boundary," *Political Geography* 30, no. 3 (2011):134.

8. J. Dürrschmidt, "So near yet so far: Blocked networks, global links and multiple exclusion in the German–Polish borderlands," *Global Networks* 6 (2006): 245–263.

9. M. Doevenspeck, "Constructing the border from below: Narratives from the Congolese–Rwandan state boundary," *Political Geography* 30, no. 3 (2011): 129–142.

10. G. Dobler, "Oshikango: The dynamics of growth and regulation in a Namibian boom town," *Journal of Southern African Studies* 35 (2009): 115–131.

11. A. Tegera and D. Johnson, "Rules for sale: Formal and informal cross-border trade in eastern DRC," *Regards Croisés,* no. 19bis (2007): 19.

12. J. Dürrschmidt, "So near yet so far: Blocked networks, global links and multiple exclusion in the German–Polish borderlands," *Global Networks* 6 (2006): 246.

13. J. Buursink, "The binational reality of crossborder cities," *GeoJournal* 54 (2001): 7–19.

14. Term used in the social and geographic urban literature to point at particular relationships between two cities merely separated by an international border that has largely lost its "barrier" function. See O. Heddebaut, "The binational cities of Dover and Calais and their region," *GeoJournal* 54 (2001): 61–71; J. B. Pick, N. Viswanathan and J. Hettrick, "The U.S.–Mexican borderlands region: A binational spatial analysis," *Social Science Journal* 38 (2001). However separated by a border and different state systems, regulations and laws, these twin cities form a shared social and economic space.

15. In 1910, the border was demarcated formally and on paper. In 1911, the "contested zones" were transferred to either the Germans or the Belgians, according to the 1910 protocol.

16. Most complete overview of diplomatic discussions: W. M. Roger Louis, *Ruanda-Urundi. 1884–1919* (Oxford: Clarendon Press, 1963).

17. A. M. Delathuy, [J. Marchal], *L'histoire du Congo 1900–1910. E.D. Morel contre Léopold II* (Paris: L'Harmattan, 1996), 53.

18. Delathuy, *L'histoire du Congo 1900–1910. E.D. Morel contre Léopold II* (Paris: L'Harmattan, 1996).

19. D. Newbury, "From 'frontier' to 'boundary': Some historical roots of peasant strategies of survival in Zaire," in *The crisis in Zaire: Myths and realities,* ed. G. Nzongola-Ntalaja (Trenton, NJ: Africa World Press, 1986), 87–97.

20. P. Lefèvre and J.-N. Lefèvre, *Les Militaires Belges et le Rwanda* (Bruxelles: Racine, 2006).

21. AAB, RWA 97, Rapport à monsieur le Résident général sur les incidents de frontières à Kissenyi–Goma, January 12–14.

22. M. Doevenspeck, "Constructing the border from below: Narratives from the Congolese–Rwandan state boundary," *Political Geography* 30, no. 3 (2011): 133.

23. D. M. Tull, *The reconfiguration of political order in Africa. A case study of North Kivu (DR Congo)* (Hamburg: Institut für Afrikakunde, 2005), 88.

24. M. Vwakyanakazi, "Import and export in the second economy in North Kivu," in *The real economy of Zaïre. The contribution of smuggling and other*

unofficial activities to national wealth, ed. J. MacGaffey (Oxford: James Currey, 1991), 50.

25. D. M. Tull, *The reconfiguration of political order in Africa. A case study of North Kivu (DR Congo)* (Hamburg: Institut für Afrikakunde, 2005), 88.

26. M. Vwakyanakazi, "Import and export in the second economy in North Kivu," in *The real economy of Zaïre. The contribution of smuggling and other unofficial activities to national wealth*, ed. J. MacGaffey (Oxford: James Currey, 1991).

27. M. Doevenspeck, "Constructing the border from below: Narratives from the Congolese–Rwandan state boundary," *Political Geography* 30, no. 3 (2011): 129–142.

28. M. Doevenspeck, "Constructing the border from below: Narratives from the Congolese–Rwandan state boundary," *Political Geography* 30, no. 3 (2011): 134.

29. M. Doevenspeck, "Constructing the border from below: Narratives from the Congolese–Rwandan state boundary," *Political Geography* 30, no. 3 (2011): 129–142.

30. K. Büscher and K. Vlassenroot, "Humanitarian presence and urban development: New opportunities and contrasts in Goma, DRC," *Disasters* 34 (2010): 256–273.

31. Sematumba, O. *et al.* "Les frontières: Lieux de division où passerelles d'echange?" *Fissures* 005 (2007).

32. Interview ambulant vendor (Goma, May 2010).

33. Division Provinciale de l'Urbanisme et Habitat du Nord-Kivu, "Proces-Verbal de la réunion de la sous-commission technique mixte chargée de la matérialisation de la ligne frontières des bornes entres le Zaire et le Rwanda tenue à Gisenyi du 24 au 25 janvier 1994," referring to "Convention Goma–Kisenyi du 25 Mars 1961 par les autorités Civiles et Militaires des Villes de Goma et Kisenyi sous la supervision de l'ONU."

34. Interview Chef de Division d'Urbanisme (Goma, November 2009).

35. Interview Chef de Division de l'Urbanisme (Goma, November 2009); Interview local observer (Goma, December 2009).

36. Division Provinciale de l'Urbanisme et Habitat du Nord-Kivu, "Mémorandum préparé par le conseil préfectoral de sécurité de Gisenyi en vue de sa rencontre avec le comité de sécurité de Goma prévue le 23 décembre 1993 à Gisenyi".

37. C. M. Kasereka, "Problème de gestion administrative des quartiers urbains spontanes. Cas de Birere à Goma, 2000–2005" (M.A. thesis, UNIGOM, 2006).

38. E. R. Barigora, "La croissance Spatiale et Demographique de la ville de Goma" (M.A. thesis, ISP Rutshuru, 2008).

39. République Démocratique du Congo, *Rapport Annuel 2008 Quartier Kahembe* (Goma: Mairie de Goma, 2009); République Démocratique du Congo, *Rapport Annuel 2008 Quartier MAPENDO* (Goma: Mairie de Goma, 2009); République Démocratique du Congo, *Rapport Annuel 2008 Quartier MIKENO* (Goma: Mairie de Goma, 2009).

40. C. M. Kasereka, "Problème de Gestion Administrative des Quartiers Urbains Spontanes. Cas de Birere à Goma, 2000–2005" (M.A. thesis, UNIGOM, 2006);

République Démocratique du Congo, *Etude globale sur la situation des ménages dans la ville de Goma après l'éruption du volcan Nyiragongo le 17 janvier 2002. Rapport d'analyse* (Goma: JSIG-Goma & Ministère de la Région Wallone, 2003).

41. République Démocratique du Congo, *Rapport Annuel 2008 Quartier Kahembe* (Goma: Mairie de Goma, 2009); République Démocratique du Congo, *Rapport Annuel 2008 Quartier Mapendo* (Goma: Mairie de Goma, 2009); République Démocratique du Congo, *Rapport Annuel 2008 Quartier Mikeno* (Goma: Mairie de Goma, 2009); Interview chefs du Quartier Kahembe, Mikeno, Mapendo (Goma, October 2008).

42. République Démocratique du Congo, *Etude globale sur la situation des ménages* (Goma: Mairie de Goma, 2009).

43. Informal talks local observer (Goma, February 2008).

44. C. M. Kasereka, "Problème de Gestion Administrative des Quartiers Urbains Spontanes. Cas de Birere à Goma, 2000–2005" (M.A. thesis, UNIGOM, 2006).

45. K. Vlassenroot and K. Büscher "The city as a frontier: Urban development and identity processes in Goma." *Working paper 61. Cities and fragile states* (2009): 9. <http://eprints.lse.ac.uk/28479/1/WP61.2.pdf.

46. INICA 2006, in M. Doevenspeck, "Constructing the border from below: Narratives from the Congolese–Rwandan state boundary," *Political Geography* 30, no. 3 (2011): 136.

47. Own observations.

48. J. Dürrschmidt, "So near yet so far: Blocked networks, global links and multiple exclusion in the German–Polish borderlands," *Global Networks* 6 (2006): 246.

49. J. Anderson and Liam O'Dowd, "Borders, border regions and territoriality: Contradictory meanings, changing significance," *Regional Studies* 33 (1999): 593–604.

50. J. Anderson and Liam O'Dowd, "Borders, border regions and territoriality: Contradictory meanings, changing significance," *Regional Studies* 33 (1999): 597.

51. M. Doevenspeck, "Constructing the border from below: Narratives from the Congolese–Rwandan state boundary," *Political Geography* 30, no. 3 (2011): 136.

52. Interview Birere commerçant (Goma, October 2009).

53. A. I. Asiwayu and P. Nugent, *African boundaries. Barriers, conduits and opportunities* (London: Printer, 1996).

54. M. Doevenspeck and N. M. Morisho, "Navigating uncertainty: Observations from the Congo–Rwanda border," in *Borders as resources*, ed. B. Bruns and J. Miggelbrink (Wiesbaden: VS-Verlag, 2011).

55. Interviews with different *chora chora*.

56. For a more detailed description of other groups of smugglers engaged in these practices, see M. Doevenspeck and N. M. Morisho, "Navigating uncertainty: Observations from the Congo–Rwanda border," in *Borders as resources*, ed. B. Bruns and J. Miggelbrink (Wiesbaden: VS-Verlag, 2011).

57. This phenomenon is not unique for Goma; at other border locations in the DRC as well, one observes similar situations. See, for example, T. Raeymaekers, "The

silent encroachment of the frontier: A politics of transborder trade in the Semliki Valley (Congo–Uganda)," *Political Geography* 28 (2009): 55–65.

58. D. K. Flynn, "'We are the border': Identity, exchange, and the state along the Bénin–Nigeria border," *American Ethnologist* 24, no. 2 (1997): 35.

59. A. Tegera and D. Johnson, "Rules for sale: Formal and informal cross-border trade in eastern DRC," *Regards Croisés,* no. 19bis (2007).

60. M. Doevenspeck, "Constructing the border from below: Narratives from the Congolese–Rwandan state boundary," *Political Geography* 30, no. 3 (2011): 142.

61. See, for example, R. R. Alvarez, Jr., "Towards anthropology of the borderlands: The Mexican–US border and the crossing of the 21st century," in *Frontiers and borderlands: Anthropological perspective,* ed. T. Wendl and M. Röser (Frankfurt: Peter Lang, 1999); H. Donnan and T. M. Wilson, *Border approaches: Anthropological perspectives on frontiers* (Lanham, MD: University Press of America, 1994); H. Donnan and T. M. Wilson, *Border identities. Nation and state at international frontiers* (Cambridge: Cambridge University Press, 1998); D. K. Flynn, "'We are the border': Identity, exchange, and the state along the Bénin–Nigeria border," *American Ethnologist* 24, no. 2 (1997): 311–330; V. Muzvidziwa, "Zimbabwe's cross-border women traders: Multiple identities and responses to new challenges," *Journal of Contemporary African Studies* 19 (2001): 67–79; R. Kaiser and E. Nikiforova, "Borderland spaces of identification and dis/location: Multiscalar narratives and enactments of Seto identity and place in the Estonian–Russian borderlands," *Ethnic and Racial Studies* 29 (2006): 928–958; D. Newman and A. Paasi, "Fences and neighbours in the postmodern world: Boundary narratives in political geography," *Progress in Human Geography* 22 (1998).

62. H. Donnan and T. M. Wilson, *Borders: Frontiers of identity, nation and state* (Oxford: Berg, 1999), 11.

63. Balibar 1998, cited in R. Kaiser and E. Nikiforova, "Borderland spaces of identification and dis/location: Multiscalar narratives and enactments of Seto identity and place in the Estonian–Russian borderlands," *Ethnic and Racial Studies* 29 (2006): 928–958.

64. See, for example, Akhil Gupta and James Ferguson, "Beyond 'culture': Space, identity and the politics of difference," *Cultural Anthropology* 6 (1992).

65. H. Englund, "Ethnography after globalism: Migration and emplacement in Malawi," *American Ethnologist* 29 (2002): 261–286.

66. Own observations. How many is impossible to say, as Congolese law precludes it. Nevertheless, precaution is necessary. That some people have two passports is often hailed as the "prove" of a "Janus-faced" Rwandaphone population. Pointing at the double nationality of some Birere traders does not imply an endorsement of these xenophobic discourses by the authors.

67. Own observations.

68. V. Muzvidziwa, "Zimbabwe's cross-border women traders: Multiple identities and responses to new challenges," *Journal of Contemporary African Studies* 19 (2001): 67–79.

69. V. Muzvidziwa, "Zimbabwe's cross-border women traders: Multiple identities and responses to new challenges," *Journal of Contemporary African Studies* 19 (2001): 74.
70. D. K. Flynn, "'We are the border': Identity, exchange, and the state along the Bénin–Nigeria border," *American Ethnologist* 24, no. 2 (1997): 311–330.
71. Interview local trader Birere (Goma, October 2008).
72. D. K. Flynn, "'We are the border': Identity, exchange, and the state along the Bénin–Nigeria border," *American Ethnologist* 24, no. 2 (1997): 312.
73. S. Jackson, "Sons of which soil? The language and politics of autochtony in eastern D.R. Congo," *African Studies Review* 49 (2006): 95–123; R. Doom and J. Gorus, *Politics of identity and economics of conflict in the Great Lakes region* (Brussels: VUBPRESS, 2000); T. Turner, *The Congo wars: Conflict, myth and reality* (New York: Zed Books, 2007), 113.
74. T. Turner, *The Congo wars: Conflict, myth and reality* (New York: Zed Books, 2007).
75. See D. Newbury, "Returning refugees: Four historical patterns of 'coming home' to Rwanda," *Comparative Studies in Society and History* 47 (2005): 252–285 for a discussion of mobility patterns in the Lake Kivu region from a historical perspective, and S. Jackson, "Sons of which soil? The language and politics of autochtony in eastern D.R. Congo," *African Studies Review* 49 (2006): 95–123 for a discussion of exclusive discourses.
76. T. Turner, *The Congo wars: Conflict, myth and reality* (New York: Zed Books, 2007); R. Doom and J. Gorus, *Politics of identity and economics of conflict in the Great Lakes region* (Brussels: VUBPRESS, 2000).
77. In 2004, a former RCD commander, Laurent Nkunda, created his CNDP movement (Congrès National pour la Défense du Peuple), with the aim of protecting the Congolese Tutsi population. Until the end of 2008, the CNDP regularly clashed with Mayi-Mayi, FDLR (Forces Démocratiques de Libération du Rwanda) and the Congolese army and succeeded in gaining control over large parts of Masisi and Rutshuru.
78. Informal talk focus group Birere traders (Goma, October 2008).
79. M. Doevenspeck, "Constructing the border from below: Narratives from the Congolese–Rwandan state boundary," *Political Geography* 30, no. 3 (2011): 129–142.
80. G. Dobler, "Oshikango: The dynamics of growth and regulation in a Namibian boom town," *Journal of Southern African Studies* 35 (2009): 123.
81. M. Doevenspeck, "Constructing the border from below: Narratives from the Congolese–Rwandan state boundary," *Political Geography* 30, no. 3 (2011): 129–142.
82. U. Hannerz, "Flows, boundaries and hybrids: Keywords in transnational anthropology," *Mana* 3 (1997): 12.
83. Achille Mbembe, "Provisional notes on the postcolony," *Africa* 62 (1992): 3–37.
84. T. Trefon, *Reinventing order in the Congo. How people respond to state failure in Kinshasa* (London: Zed Books, 2004).

85. V. Muzvidziwa, "Zimbabwe's cross-border women traders: Multiple identities and responses to new challenges," *Journal of Contemporary African Studies* 19 (2001): 67–79; D. K. Flynn, "'We are the border': Identity, exchange, and the state along the Bénin–Nigeria border," *American Ethnologist* 24, no. 2 (1997): 311–330.

References

Alvarez Jr., R. R. "Towards anthropology of the borderlands: The Mexican–US border and the crossing of the 21st century." In *Frontiers and borderlands: Anthropological perspective*, edited by T. Wendl and M. Röser. Frankfurt: Peter Lang, 1999: 225–238.

Anderson, J., and L. O'Dowd. "Borders, border regions and territoriality: Contradictory meanings, changing significance." *Regional Studies* 33, no. 593 (1999): 604.

Asiwayu, A. I., and P. Nugent. *African boundaries. Barriers, conduits and opportunities.* London: Printer, 1996.

Barigora, E. R. *La Croissance Spatiale et Démographique de la Ville de Goma.* Goma: Institut Supérieur Pédagogique, 2008.

Büscher, K., and K. Vlassenroot. "Humanitarian presence and urban development: New opportunities and contrasts in Goma, DRC." *Disasters* 34, no. 2 (2010): 256–273.

Buursink, J. "The binational reality of crossborder cities." *GeoJournal* 54 (2001): 7–19.

Delathuy, A. M. [Jules Marechal]. *L'histoire du Congo 1900–1910. Morel contre Léopold II.* Paris: L'Harmattan, 1996.

Division Provinciale de l'Urbanisme et Habitat du Nord-Kivu (1993). "Mémorandum préparé par le conseil préfectoral de sécurité de Gisenyi en vue de sa rencontre avec le comité de sécurité de Goma prévue le 23 décembre 1993 à Gisenyi".

Division Provinciale de l'Urbanisme et Habitat du Nord-Kivu (1994). "Proces-Verbal de la réunion de la sous-commission technique mixte chargée de la matérialisation de la ligne frontières des bornes entres le Zaire et le Rwanda tenue à Gisenyi du 24 au 25 janvier 1994".

Dobler, G. "Oshikango: The dynamics of growth and regulation in a Namibian boom town." *Journal of Southern African Studies* 35 (2009): 115–131.

Doevenspeck, M. "Constructing the border from below: Narratives from the Congolese–Rwandan state boundary." *Political Geography* 30, no. 3 (2011): 129–142.

Doevenspeck, M., and N. M. Morisho. "Navigating uncertainty: Observations from the Congo–Rwanda border." In *Borders as resources*, edited by B. Bruns and J. Miggelbrink. Wiesbaden: VS-Verlag, 2011.

Donnan, H., and T. M. Wilson. *Border approaches: Anthropological perspectives on frontiers.* Lanham: University Press of America, 1994.

Donnan, H., and T. M. Wilson. *Border identities. Nation and state at international frontiers.* Cambridge: Cambridge University Press, 1998.

Donnan, H. & T. M. Wilson. *Borders: Frontiers of identity, nation and state*. Oxford: Berg, 1999.

Doom, R., and J. Gorus. *Politics of identity and economics of conflict in the Great Lakes region*. Brussels: VUBPRESS, 2000.

Dürrschmidt, J. So near yet so far: Blocked networks, global links and multiple exclusion in the German–Polish borderlands. *Global Networks* 6, no. 3 (2006): 245–263.

Englund, H. "Ethnography after globalism: Migration and emplacement in Malawi." *American Ethnologist* 29, no. 2 (2002): 261–286.

Flynn, D. K. " 'We are the border': Identity, exchange, and the state along the Bénin–Nigeria border." *American Ethnologist* 24, no. 2 (1997): 311–330.

Gupta, A., and J. Ferguson. "Beyond 'culture': Space, identity and the politics of difference." *Cultural Anthropology* 6, no. 1 (1992): 6–23.

Hannerz, U. "Fluxos, fronteiras, híbridos: palavras-chave da antropologia Transnacional." *Mana* (Rio de Janeiro) 3, no. 1 (1997): 7–39.

Heddebaut, O. "The binational cities of Dover and Calais and their region." *GeoJournal* 54 (2001): 61–71.

Jackson, S. "Sons of which soil? The language and politics of autochtony in eastern D.R. Congo." *African Studies Review* 49, no. 2 (2006): 95–123.

Kaiser, R., and Nikiforova, E. "Borderland spaces of identification and dis/location: Multiscalar narratives and enactments of Seto identity and place in the Estonian–Russian borderlands." *Ethnic and Racial Studies* 29, no. 5 (2006): 928–958.

Kasereka, C. M. "Problème de Gestion Administrative des Quartiers Urbains Spontanés. Cas de Birere à Goma, 2000–2005." Goma: Faculté des Sciences Sociales, Politiques et Administratives, 2006.

Lefèvre, P., and Lefèvre, J.-N. *Les Militaires Belges et le Rwanda*. Bruxelles: Racine, 2006.

Mairie de Goma. *Rapport Annuel 2008 Quartier Kahembe*. Goma: République Démocratique du Congo, 2009a.

Mairie de Goma. *Rapport Annuel 2008 Quartier Mapendo*. Goma: République Démocratique du Congo, 2009b.

Mairie de Goma. *Rapport Annuel 2008 Quartier Mikeno*. Goma: République Démocratique du Congo, 2009c.

Mairie de Goma. *Rapport Annuel 2009*. Goma: République Démocratique du Congo, 2010.

Mbembe, A. "Provisional notes on the postcolony." *Africa* 62 (1992): 3–37.

Muzvidziwa, V. "Zimbabwe's cross-border women traders: Multiple identities and responses to new challenges." *Journal of Contemporary African Studies* 19, no. 1 (2001): 67–79.

Newbury, D. "From 'frontier' to 'boundary': Some historical roots of peasant strategies of survival in Zaire." In *The crisis in Zaire: Myths and realities*, edited by G. Nzongola-Ntalaja. Trenton: Africa World Press, 1986: 87–97.

Newbury, D. "Returning refugees: Four historical patterns of 'coming home' to Rwanda." *Comparative Studies in Society and History* 47 (2005): 252–285.

Newman, D., and A. Paasi. "Fences and neighbours in the postmodern world: Boundary narratives in political geography." *Progress in Human Geography* 22, no. 2 (1998): 186–207.

Nugent, P. *Sizing up asymmetry: State logics and power dynamics in the Senegambian and Ghana–Togo Borderlands.* Forthcoming.

Nugent, P. "Border towns and cities in comparative perspective: Barriers, flows and governance." In *A Companion to border studies*, edited by H. Donnan and T. M. Wilson. Oxford: Blackwell, 2012.

Pick, J. B., N. Viswanathan and J. Hettrick. "The U.S.–Mexican borderlands region: A binational spatial analysis." *Social Science Journal* 38, no. 4 (2001): 567–595.

Raeymaekers, T. "The silent encroachment of the frontier: A politics of transborder trade in the Semliki Valley (Congo–Uganda)." *Political Geography* 28, no. 1 (2009): 55–65.

République Démocratique du Congo. *Etude globale sur la situation des ménages dans la ville de Goma après l'éruption du volcan Nyiragongo le 17 janvier 2002. Rapport d'analyse.* Goma and Namur: JSIG-Goma and Ministère de la Région Wallone, 2003.

Louis, W. R. *Ruanda-Urundi 1884–1919.* Oxford: Clarendon Press, 1963.

Sematumba, O. *et al.* "Les frontières: Lieux de division où passerelles d'echange?" *Fissures* 005 (2007).

Tegera, A., and D. Johnson. "Rules for sale: Formal and informal cross-border trade in eastern DRC." *Regards Croisés* 19bis (2007a): 1–122.

Trefon, T. *Reinventing order in the Congo. How people respond to state failure in Kinshasa.* London: Zed Books; Kampala: Fountain Publishers, 2004.

Tull, D. *The reconfiguration of political order in Africa. A case study of North Kivu (DR Congo).* Hamburg: RFA Institut für Afrika-Kunde, 2005.

Turner, T. *The Congo wars: Conflict, myth and reality.* New York: Zed Books, 2007.

Vlassenroot, K., and K. Büscher. *The city as a frontier: Urban development and identity processes in Goma.* Working Paper 61. http://eprints.lse.ac.uk/28479/1/WP61.2.pdf, Crisis States Research Centre, 2009 (May 5, 2011).

Vwakyanakazi, M. "Import and export in the second economy in North Kivu." In *The real economy of Zaïre. The contribution of smuggling and other unofficial activities to national wealth*, edited by J. MacGaffey. Oxford: James Currey, 1991, 43–71.

PART III

The Border as Frontier: States, Sovereignty and Identity

CHAPTER 6

Dangerous Divisions: Peace-Building in the Borderlands of Post-Soviet Central Asia

Christine Bichsel

Introduction

This chapter[1] looks into peace-building in the Ferghana Valley, a large intramontane basin in former Soviet Central Asia. In 2002, a document of an aid agency running peace-building projects characterized the Ferghana Valley as "a culturally rich and diverse area with the potential for real growth in many spheres, but also the undeniable potential for dangerous divisions".[2] "Dangerous divisions", as referred to in this quotation, were seen by the aid agency in manifold aspects. An important one among them were the *divisions* as embodied in the political borders that transect the Ferghana Valley, separating the three states Kyrgyzstan, Uzbekistan and Tajikistan who currently share the basin. *Dangerous,* in turn, refers to a particular social imaginary of the Ferghana Valley, attributed by both academic and journalistic writing, as well as by practical attempts to mitigate a perceived potential for violence.

A body of academic and policy-oriented literature began to focus on the danger of conflict in Central Asia as of the late 1990s. While differing in details, the authors concurred that the Ferghana Valley exposes a high potential for violent conflict. They base this potential on evidence of past violent episodes and/or present tensions that may result in violence. In other words, these writings depict the Ferghana Valley as a "host of crises"[3] or a "flashpoint of conflict".[4] This literature argues that the potential for conflict is comprised of a broad array of interlinked conflictive factors such as environmental, social, political, economic, religious, demographic, military and criminal ones.[5] A consistent concern was the perception of a "mismatch" between nations and states, and a related threat assigned to territorial ambiguity and un-demarcated borders.[6] Policy recommendations for preventive action were taken up by aid agencies in the late 1990s, and since then a considerable number of peace-building projects have been implemented in the Ferghana Valley.

In the present chapter, I explore peace-building activities in the Ferghana Valley over the period of 1999–2006. My main focus is on the Swiss Agency for Development and Cooperation (SDC), a governmental aid agency to coordinate international development activities of Switzerland. In addition, I also draw on the activities of the United Nations Development Programme (UNDP) and Mercy Corps with similar peace-building frameworks. This chapter argues that peace-building projects conducted by these aid agencies reconfigured the processes that constitute territory in the Ferghana Valley through altering social action and material space at the border. As a consequence, they interfered with the ongoing processes of post-Soviet border delimitation. The chapter thus questions the presumed apolitical nature of peace-building by arguing that in its unintended outcomes it became part and parcel of state territorialization and nation-building projects in Central Asia.

My study is positioned as an "ethnography of aid".[7] It approaches international aid as an ethnographic object, and seeks to explain how it operates. Ethnography of aid explores both the theoretical assumptions underlying an approach that the aid agencies adopt, as well as the outcomes in the form of specific localized practices when approaches are applied. My research thus neither privileges nor stops at the level of textual analysis, but engages with how aid is enacted in the form of a social practice with assigned meanings and lived experiences. Empirically, I combine the analysis of project documents produced by aid agencies with data generated by interviews and participant observation. The chapter draws on my fieldwork in the Ferghana Valley between 2003 and 2007 as a PhD student (14 months) and a consultant for an aid agency (3 months).

After this introduction, I elaborate on my conceptual understanding of the border and peace-building. In the third part, I then present the context of the borders in the Ferghana Valley. In the fourth part, I introduce peace-building practices drawing on the example of the SDC. The fifth part looks into the case of Maksat and Ovchi-Kalacha on the border of Kyrgyzstan and Tajikistan. The sixth part discusses delimitation politics in the Ferghana Valley. The seventh part then reflects on peace-building in borderlands. Finally, I offer a conclusion to this chapter.

Conceptual Issues

I conceive of the borders of the Ferghana Valley as constituted by a specific and historical notion of territory. Territory, in turn, is understood as bounded space attributed with meaning. I understand it as a product of cultural work of human associations and institutions to organize themselves in relation to the social and material world.[8] Bounded space implicated with meaning is therefore an expression of social relationships and informs key aspects of individual and collective identities. At the same time, I conceive of it as a political achievement. In this sense, territory constitutes a spatial expression of social power to delimit space and to exert control over it[9] as well as to define the meaning attributed to it. In line with this second aspect of territory, I understand the concept as integrally related to the political institution of the state.[10] However, while the state is tied to territory, territory is not conditional upon the state. Rather, I understand it as a product and process unfolding at multiple and overlapping geographical scales, the state being one of them.

The term peace-building denotes post–Cold War approaches to conflict and violence. These approaches are guided by an intellectual and practical framework, which assumes that liberal political and economic structures as well as democratic forms of governance will reduce violence and foster enduring peace.[11] Such "liberal peace" in the framework of peace-building resides in respective social, political and economic regimes, structures and norms, mostly teleologically defined by the supposed state of "western" societies.[12] Equally, the underlying assumption of peace-building is that it is indeed possible for conflict-ridden societies to achieve liberal peace, given that correct steps are taken. As a consequence, agents of peace-building can foster liberal peace by "exporting" the norms and values of societies that presumably have reached a state of liberal peace.[13] A possibility for peace-building is thus the vehicle of international aid, in the framework of which aid agencies promote liberal peace through conducting relevant aid projects.

For this chapter, I assume that peace-building activities result, among many other intended and unintended outcomes, in spatial effects. More precisely, through promoting the changes required to achieve liberal peace as outlined above, peace-building reconfigures the social, political and cultural processes that constitute territory. While this is not specific to the borderlands, I suggest that it is productive to explore peace-building on the border. First, exploring the borderlands has the potential to show us with special clarity how the interplay of territory, nation and state is routinely lived and experienced in everyday life.[14] Second, the border and the center need to be understood in a dyadic and complex relationship, being mutually constitutive. Thus, an ethnographic analysis of peace-building in the borderlands provides insights into what Hastings Donnan and Dieter Haller term the "dialectical relationship between the border and the nation-state."[15]

The Borders of the Ferghana Valley

The Ferghana Valley is an almond-shaped intramontane basin surrounded by extensive mountain ranges. At the heart of the basin are plains and steppe lands that lie at an altitude of 250–500 m above sea level. Foothills that enclose this depression are slightly higher, ranging from 500 to 1,300 m. The mountain ranges then reach up to more than 5,000 m in altitude. United as part of the Soviet Union until 1991, the Ferghana Valley is at present divided among three successor states. Uzbekistan holds the eastern lowlands, which form in many respects the historical and cultural heartland of the Ferghana Valley. The surrounding foothills and most of the high mountain ranges are part of Kyrgyzstan. Finally, Tajikistan stretches into the western lowlands and, partially, the mountain ranges. They are largely identical with the former Soviet republican borders of the Kyrgyz, Uzbek and Tajik Soviet Socialist Republics (SSRs). Understanding the current borderlines in the Ferghana Valley will require a short excursion into the past for their historical emergence within the particular constitution of the Soviet statehood.

The debate on how Central Asia has been divided up into republics remains central to discussions about the nature of Soviet rule and the emergence of conflicts after independence. Popular interpretations of this process often see *divide-and-rule* strategies by Soviet leadership, and the attributed pernicious intentions to create havoc after disintegration, as an explanation for the occurrence of violence in the Ferghana Valley. In my view, however, such a perspective is not productive. Rather, I follow Francine Hirsch,[16] who conceives of the Soviet Union as an "empire of nations". She convincingly argues that the Soviet Union in contrast to western colonizers, who conceived of themselves as embodying the metropolitan center in opposition to the colonized peripheries, defined itself as a sum of its parts in the form of a union of nationalities. Moreover, dismissing the West European civilizing mission as a lie, Soviet leaders attempted to give nationhood to feudal clans and tribes to promote their—imagined—road to socialism. The nation, thus, in early Marxist-Leninist terms, should be a merely transitional stage on the temporal unfolding of the state. According to this thought, the mature Soviet Union was envisioned as a socialist union of a denationalized people. To turn so-called "backward people" into nations, which means to create new political boundaries and foster national-cultural distinctions, became thus an imperative task and a state-sponsored effort of codifying, institutionalizing and—in some cases—even inventing nations during the early years of the Soviet Union.[17] This process, usually referred to as "national-territorial delimitation", gave the Soviet Union its distinctive form.

Soviet leadership set about national-territorial delimitation in Central Asia between 1924 and 1927. At the beginning of Soviet rule, a variety of ethnic, religious, linguistic and economic divisions prevailed in the Ferghana Valley. Moreover, people may have subscribed to several identities at the same time.[18] But the Soviet Union categorized this population and assigned territory to the established major groups termed "nationalities"—these are the Uzbeks, Tajiks and Kyrgyz in the case of the Ferghana Valley—based on ethnographic, economic and administrative criteria. The process of national-territorial delimitation eventually led to the territorial definition of three national republics in the Ferghana Valley,[19] namely the Uzbek, Tajik and Kyrgyz SSRs. The process of national-territorial delimitation thus resulted in a twofold classification: the categorization of nationalities on the one hand, and the delimitation of the territories of national republics on the other hand.[20]

Rogers Brubaker[21] locates an irresolvable tension between the "national" and the "territorial" in this particular construction of the Soviet Union. He suggests that the concept of a "dual institutionalization" is helpful in order to conceptualize Soviet statehood. He states that on the one hand, the Soviet Union was constituted as a state of multiple nationalities that were defined by descent and not by residence. In this first sense, institutionalization was ethnocultural and personal. On the other hand, the Soviet Union was constituted by national republics that bore names of nationalities, usually referred to as "titular nationalities". In this second sense, institutionalization was thus territorial and political. The Soviet Union was thus a composition of first 16, and, after 1956, 15 republics. From the outset, Brubaker argues, these two forms of institutionalization were in an uneasy relationship, as there is a conceptual as well as spatial lack of congruence of territorial nationhood and personal nationality.

In practice, the national-territorial delimitation in the Ferghana Valley and in overall Central Asia turned out to be a difficult exercise.[22] From the outset, delimitation has been fraught with precedent and newly emerging conflicting claims for territory. Several commissions from the central government were sent to Central Asia in order to resolve the issues at stake. Settlements are likely to have resulted from both an accommodation of local power struggles by the central government and the implementation of all-union concerns. Yet, claims did not come to a halt with the completion of national-territorial delimitation in 1927, but were to continue until the disintegration of the Soviet Union. Repeated inter-republican border commissions assessed these claims and established revised borderlines. For the case of the border of the Kyrgyz and Tajik SSRs, there were at least three instances of border delimitation (1958, 1975, 1989). However, the actual borderlines were not always enforced, and official recognition by the relevant Soviet agencies is sometimes not documented.

During and after national-territorial delimitation, territorial claims were increasingly framed in terms of the "national", thus the very category of nationalities that the Soviet leaders had introduced in the first place. Yet, equally the form of land use was brought to the fore in such conflicts. This may on the one hand express the growing link between membership in titular nationalities and privileged access not only to land, but also to national rights and significant political, economic and cultural resources.[23] On the other hand, however, as I have argued elsewhere,[24] with the process of national-territorial delimitation, the socioeconomic distinctions in between groups in terms of lifestyle and mode of production became territorialized. As a general rule, Uzbek and Tajik groups in the Ferghana plains have a far longer history of agricultural production and sedentary lifestyles than the Kyrgyz, most of whom practiced animal husbandry and pursued a nomadic or transhumant existence in the foothills and premontane zones. The borderlines of the Ferghana Valley thus not only represented the territory of newly established Soviet republics, but to some extent also follow the territorial distinction between different socioeconomic practices like irrigated agriculture and animal husbandry.

After the collapse of the Soviet Union in 1991, the tension outlined by Brubaker became reconfigured. With regard to the "national", the former titular nationalities in the Kyrgyz, Tajik and Uzbek SSRs became the nations of the three new states. I will illustrate this in the example of a person of Kyrgyz nationality living in the Kyrgyz SSR. Whereas, formerly, her or his citizenship had been Soviet, and nationality Kyrgyz—whether or not his or her residence was the Kyrgyz SSR—the term "Kyrgyz" now assumed an ambiguous meaning of being of Kyrgyz descent and at the same time a citizen of the state Kyrgyzstan. While the term "Kyrgyzstani" exists and denotes a citizen of Kyrgyzstan, it is much less common in popular use than "Kyrgyz". In this chapter, I try to avoid confusion as much as possible by using the term Kyrgyzstani for a citizen of Kyrgyzstan. Conversely, the term Kyrgyz is used for a person of Kyrgyz ethnicity when referring to the post-Soviet period in Central Asia.

With regard to the "territorial", the former borders of the republics became the borders of the new nation-states. The successor states agreed to retain, provisionally, the previous republican borders. Thus, the *de facto* borderline until today largely follows the former republican boundaries and continues to reflect the Soviet Union's original conceptualization in terms of nationhood and nationality. Yet, independence presented the challenge of establishing a *de jure* borderline between the newly independent states in Central Asia. The three states subsequently formed bilateral (or even tripartite) commissions commonly referred to as Parity Commissions for the delimitation and demarcation of borders. However, the actual delimitation and ratification of the borderlines is still in process and fraught by numerous conflicting claims. It is, in part, these conflicting claims in combination with other claims at stake (such as contested ownership and use of water and land) that were perceived as *dangerous divisions* by analysts and aid agencies as referred to in the beginning of this chapter.

Peace-Building through Dialogue and Development

As of the late 1990s, aid agencies have promoted a wide range of activities in the Ferghana Valley. These activities included early warning systems, media and education projects, mediation networks and dialogue processes, micro-business and micro-lending programs, border management training, access to social justice, civil society initiatives and democracy-building.[25] Among the many aid agencies, I focus on the case of the Swiss Agency for Development and Cooperation (SDC) in this chapter. SDC is a governmental aid agency, which coordinates international development activities of Switzerland. Switzerland looks back on a relatively long history of engagement in Central Asia and has provided bilateral development aid since 1993. The traditional focus of SDC was on fields such as agricultural extension services, legal advice and microfinance. Toward the end of the 1990s, SDC however expanded its field of activities to peace-building in the Ferghana Valley.[26]

SDC's main aim of peace-building in the Ferghana Valley was to contribute to the prevention of conflicts in cross-border areas and multiethnic communities, as well as to improve regional cooperation in the border areas of the three countries Kyrgyzstan, Uzbekistan and Tajikistan. Two pilot projects were launched for this purpose in 1999: first, the Kyrgyz–Tajik Conflict Prevention Project, and second, the Rehabilitation of Social Infrastructure Project, operating in Kyrgyzstan and Tajikistan over the period of 1999–2002. In 2002, they were merged into the Regional Dialogue and Development (RDD) Project in the Ferghana Valley, as well as the regional focus extended to Uzbekistan.[27] During 2002–2006, SDC implemented RDD within more than ten so-called "address zones"—clusters of communities at risk of violent conflict—in Kyrgyzstan, Uzbekistan and Tajikistan.

Within the RDD framework, SDC located the danger of conflict in the Ferghana Valley in interethnic tensions over primarily natural but also other resources shared by different communities. For the aid agency, this was no abstract fear, but rather a concrete risk for specific villages and settlements. As a result, SDC mainly targeted neighboring villages separated by ethnic affiliation, multiethnic villages and adjacent villages separated by the newly established international borders, which were understood to compete for water and land. While SDC expected such disputes to play out locally, it was also concerned that, if not contained at the same level, they may spread and feed into region-wide escalation. The aid agency addressed predominantly rural communities, which it judged as socially and economically disadvantaged, therefore lacking means and skills to tackle the causes of conflict.

The approach which SDC adopted to mitigate such conflicts centered on the combination of three elements: first, building or rehabilitating infrastructure; second, establishment of and support to community-based organizations (CBOs);[28] and third, fostering joint social activities between the adversarial groups. At this point, I will not enter into a detailed discussion of this approach, which I have done elsewhere,[29] but merely offer a brief description. The first component entailed the building and rehabilitation of infrastructure for irrigation, drinking water supply, healthcare and educational and recreational facilities. This should address the structural causes of conflict, which were seen to relate to scarcity of resources and the dysfunctional state of infrastructure. The second component implied establishing and training CBOs within the communities. By means of CBOs, communities should be enabled and mobilized to constructively address the issues at stake, and turn the conflictive relationship into a more peaceful one. The third component entails the promotion of joint social activities between the communities at loggerheads. It entails the creation of social and physical spaces for conflict parties to interact, such as youth clubs, sports competitions or festivals. The cultivation of communication, trust and personal friendship is expected to improve intergroup relations.[30]

In wider perspective, RDD can be considered as being part and parcel of a larger framework, or a "new architecture of aid",[31] after the Cold War that has taken shape along the tenets of economic liberalization, privatization and democratization. Accordingly, for SDC, RDD was positioned explicitly as a part of Switzerland's support of the transition of Central Asia from authoritarian rule and central planning to pluralism and market economy in Central Asia.[32] Peace-building thus went alongside Switzerland's further development activities, which involved fostering interstate agreements, privatization and restructuring of state enterprises, reforms of macroeconomic systems and international trade and establishment of the rule of law. There-fore, I suggest that for SDC, attempts at behavioral and institutional change at the grass roots aimed not only to mitigate conflict, but should also create the conditions from "bottom up" in order to enable democratic politics and liberal market economies in Central Asia. At the same time, by reducing the risk of violence, peace-building should also remove an obstacle to the desired wider political and economic change.

In a next step, I will turn to a concrete case study, which gives insights into how SDC's activities were played out in the borderlands of the Ferghana Valley.

On the Border: Maksat village

Maksat is a small village located in southwestern Kyrgyzstan right on the bor-der with Tajikistan. The village was founded after a visit of former President Askar Akaev in 1996. Upon the President's visit, local authorities expressed their worries about ongoing spatial expansion of villagers from neighbor-ing Ovchi-Kalacha south across the border, referring to this phenomenon as "creeping migration" *(polzuchaia migratsiia)*. As they explained, more and more Tajikistani villagers build their houses and created garden plots onto Kyrgyzstani pasture, beyond what was perceived to be the official borderline. Upon this, President Akaev is said to have ordered the building of Maksat village in order to prevent further Tajikistani expansion. *Maksat*, in Kyrgyz language, roughly translates as "objective" or "goal". For this purpose, the state provided finance and instructed the Ministry of Emergency Situations to build 60-plus houses. These houses are lined up along the *de facto* border and should in this way foreclose any further claiming of land from Ovchi-Kalacha (see figure 6.1). Families from nearby villages willing to resettle were provided free of cost the newly built houses.

While at that moment the village had no access to drinking or irrigation water, Kyrgyzstani authorities promised to provide the necessary infrastruc-ture in the near future. Technically, this should be solved by means of a siphon, a tunnel and a large canal providing water from the nearby Kosy Baglan River. The water of this trans-boundary river is shared by Kyrgyzstan and Tajikistan. In order to cover the investment costs, the government signed a credit agreement with the Asian Development Bank. While the pipeline system and the tunnel were completed in 1999, the main canal remained unfinished due to financial constraints of unclear nature. The plans to pro-vide adequate provision for drinking and irrigation water to Maksat, and to develop new land in its proximity thus came to a halt, and the newly settled families remained without a water supply.

Figure 6.1 Maksat village.
Source: own picture (2003).

The issue has been taken up in 2000 by the SDC. Analyses jointly made by a Tajik and a Kyrgyz nongovernmental organization (NGO) characterized the situation as tense, with frequent skirmishes between villagers of Maksat and those of Ovchi-Kalacha mainly over access to water, land, transit and further issues.[33] The NGOs identified an "interethnic conflict" between ethnic Kyrgyz villagers of Maksat and ethnic Tajik villagers of Ovchi-Kalacha. Reasons were mainly seen in intergroup animosities, as well as in the lack of water and the absence of social infrastructure. In the following years, SDC thus conducted a number of joint social activities between Kyrgyz villagers of Maksat and Tajik villagers of Ovchi-Kalacha. These activities, as explained earlier on, should foster personal contact and improve intergroup relations. SDC also supported the building of a health point in Maksat.

In a next step, SDC set about to resolve the water issue. It suggested providing Maksat and four of its neighboring villages drinking water by means of a pipeline connection to the already-constructed siphon, and later directly to the Kosy Baglan River. For this purpose, the aid agency thus initiated a negotiation process between Tajikistani and Kyrgyzstani authorities. This process, however, did not yield the desired result in the form of a consensus. First, Tajikistani authorities voiced concerns that the provision of water to Maksat and subsequent irrigation on their land would put lower-lying Ovchi-Kalacha at risk of rising groundwater levels and flooding. Secondly, they maintained that the additional water to be abstracted for Maksat would disrupt the agreed water distribution of the Kosy Baglan River dating from 1968. According to knowledge at hand, this agreement allocates to Kyrgyzstan 21 percent of the annual water flow, and to Tajikistan 79 percent, respectively, with no stipulations about seasonal variation.[34] The Kyrgyzstani authorities rejected both concerns as unfounded. Moreover, they question the legitimacy of the former Soviet agreement, seeking to correct what they understand as a historical injustice, which prevents present-day Kyrgyzstan to develop self-sustaining and market-based irrigated agriculture. Eventually, lacking consensus, increasingly complicated negotiations and financial constraints led SDC to halt their activities in the water sector by 2003.

By 2006, only one-third of the houses were found to be permanently inhabited. Some of the originally resettled families had moved away to other regions of the country because of the lack of facilities and opportunities to work. Other families did not permanently live in Maksat, but only spent summer time there in order to herd their animals, while in wintertime returning to their villages of origin. In turn, around 12 families of ethnic Kyrgyz affiliation who out-migrated from Tajikistan had recently moved to Maksat. Most Maksat villagers either made a living as day laborers in neighboring Tajikistan, or worked as labor migrants in Russia or Kazakhstan. Subsistence agriculture and even elementary living conditions were rendered difficult by the absence of irrigation and scarcity of drinking water, respectively. Mostly, villagers either fetched water with buckets from the Tajikistani canal in Ovchi-Kalacha or bought it from a Tajikistani neighbor who had installed a pump. As an NGO report states, "Today, in the village dwell only those who have no [other] place to live, and those who live in hope of receiving a land plot to build a house no matter where."[35]

Despite the little interest of people in actually living in this area, the Kyrgyzstani authorities still tried to attract finance and promote new settlement and irrigation development projects in Maksat. In 2006, the issue of water and land in Maksat had been taken up by EuropeAid and UNDP. These aid agencies allocated finance to complete the missing main canal and provide Maksat with water from the Kosy Baglan River. GTZ Batken ("Batken Capacity Building Project for Food Security, Regional Cooperation and Conflict Mitigation") in turn supported the construction of an on-farm irrigation network for point irrigation. The latter should allow developing new agricultural land while preventing the risk of erosion and flooding of Ovchi-Kalacha. It was foreseen that Maksat villagers and young families in need of land from nearby communities would be able to use the newly developed arable land. In addition, GTZ Batken financed the building of a new school in order to provide education facilities to the children, who were expected to arrive with the resettling families, and to improve the social infrastructure of the village. Contrary to the SDC project, EuropeAid, UNDP and GTZ have restricted their activities to Kyrgyzstan and refrained from a trans-boundary approach. Moreover, they frame their project in agricultural development rather than peace-building. In sum, there is a continuing interest by Kyrgyzstani authorities to populate the area and render it suitable for irrigated agriculture. I will explore the reasons for this interest in the next part.

The Politics of Post-Soviet Border Delimitation

I suggest that the case of Maksat and Ovchi-Kalacha needs to be discussed in the context of border delimitation. In this process, a term frequently used to designate land plots in proximity of the *de facto* border to which more than one state lays claims is "disputed territory" *(spornaia territoriia)*. Formally, the Parity Commission Kyrgyzstan–Tajikistan has established a list of so-called "disputed territories", which await evaluation and final decision for their state affiliation. Yet, since independence, the term "disputed territory" has gained much wider currency and is applied in popular usage to any land plot which is contested between residents of different states. In the case of Maksat, despite the fact that it is not officially listed as a "disputed territory", I argue that in both states, Kyrgyzstan and Tajikistan, claims to this territory exist.

Two prevalent lines of argument discursively bestow legitimacy to such claims. The first one draws on the notion of historical legacy. It argues that the problem of "disputed territory" needs to be resolved on the basis of historical Soviet border agreements. Ambiguities, however, arise from spatial non-congruence of diachronic Soviet border delimitations as well as their incomplete endorsement by the responsible Soviet authorities. Thus, a fundamental point of contention is which historical map should serve as the basis for the Parity Commission's work. While Tajikistan insists on the map from delimitation in 1927, Kyrgyzstan maintains that the Parity Commission should base its decisions on the map of 1958. The two diachronic maps differ considerably, as a large part of Kyrgyzstan's present-day southwestern territory in the Ferghana Valley was initially allocated to the Tajik ASSR, at that time still part of the Uzbek SSR. According to the information available, it is likely that the territory of Maksat is located within this area.[36]

The second line of argument is referred to as delimitation according to "actual land use" *(fakticheskoe zemlepol'zovanie)*. As the expression suggests, rather than looking at the historico-legal construction of rights, this argument holds that the problem of "disputed territory" should be resolved on the basis of current land use. Following this argument, it is therefore to establish who the user is—both in terms of an individual, but even more so as a collectivity that can be categorized. Therefore, in this case, ambiguities on the one hand arise from the question whether citizenship (this is legal membership in a state acquired through residence at the time of independence) or ethnicity (this is descent in the framework of Soviet nationality) holds as salient for legitimatizing claims to "disputed territory". On the other hand, we may ask which land use constitutes in the first place, and which respective socioeconomic form (animal husbandry or irrigation) bestows legitimacy to territorial claims.

Let us thus turn back to the case of Maksat. I suggest that both the process of "creeping migration", which means the gradual movement of Ovchi-Kalacha villagers toward the village of Maksat, as well as the very establishment of Maksat itself must be understood in terms of legitimizing claims for territory with the argument of "actual land use". Settlers of Maksat originated on the one hand from surrounding villages in Batken province—on the informal condition spelled out by local authorities that they were ethnic Kyrgyz. On the other hand, inhabitants of Maksat consist of Tajikistani citizens of Kyrgyz ethnicity who migrated to Kyrgyzstan. As the acquisition of a Kyrgyzstani passport is a lengthy and costly process, but at the same time only Kyrgyzstani citizens have the right to own land plots, immigrants have often few choices but to accept the plots along the disputed borderline. While Tajikistani citizens of Tajik ethnicity are represented to undertake "creeping migration", Tajikistani citizens of Kyrgyz ethnicity are thus encouraged to settle in Kyrgyzstan—preferentially onto land in proximity of the border. Conversely, Kyrgyzstani citizens of Tajik ethnicity are prevented to settle in similar sites on the border.[37] Based on this case, I argue that it is not citizenship being expected to legitimate claims to "disputed territory" with future delimitation, but ethnic affiliation interpreted in national terms.

As for land use, I suggest that it is irrigated agriculture that primarily bestows legitimacy to claims. As I have argued elsewhere,[38] the original territorialization of socioeconomic distinctions became reconfigured during the lifespan of the Soviet Union. On the one hand, Soviet leadership accentuated these distinctions by means of regional economic specialization (cotton production in the Uzbek SSR, meat and milk production in the Kyrgyz SSR). Yet, at the same time, other Soviet policies undermined them, such as the resettlement of nomadic and seminomadic populations in the lower parts, as well as the expansion of the zone of irrigated agriculture into the foothills of the Ferghana Valley. A further shift occurred with independence. The disintegration of the big state farms that produced meat and milk and the subsequent privatization of land led many Kyrgyzstanis to turn to private agriculture to sustain their livelihoods. As a consequence, irrigated agriculture, by and large, serves at present as the predominant materially manifestation of claims to territory—also in the case of Maksat.

Both within Kyrgyzstan and Tajikistan, settlement on or cultivation of "disputed territory" or beyond the *de facto* border is tacitly tolerated, and in some instances actively encouraged. Yet, such approval stems from the district rather than national level, or possibly province government officials—with the exception of the initiation of Maksat encouraged by the former President of Kyrgyzstan. In Tajikistan, it appears that the province- and district-level officials struggle to successfully lobby for their interests and concerns with the national government.[39] Equally, in Kyrgyzstan, government officials of Batken province complain about the poor knowledge of the region and its complex borderline by politicians at national level. In combination with corruption endemic to all levels in the two countries, both villagers and district or province government officials express concerns that their interests might be overridden by decisions which merely serve the interests of politicians at national level.[40] The politics surrounding "actual land use" is therefore not only directed toward contesting the claims of geographic neighbors, but equally serves to secure particular local interests in the face of interstate power plays as well as corruption.

When it comes to aid agencies, an interlocutor stated that in the case of Maksat village and irrigation development, "the strategic interest of the authorities and the agricultural interests of the donors coincide".[41] While there is a strong interest by authorities to address the problem of scarcity of arable land in neighboring municipalities and provide young families new land plots, local authorities also have a distinct stake to claim this land in order to further their strategic goals in the delimitation process. In absence of federal support and finance, the development of the land in Maksat significantly increases the chances of the district and the province for a result of delimitation favorable to Kyrgyzstan. To me, it seems that this is symbolically expressed by the spatial configuration of the newly attributed plots as part of the GTZ Batken irrigation development activities. As an official formulated it, "We will build the second row [of houses] with this project".[42]

By virtue of their very presence, Maksat villagers provide a service to the state that—in theory—other governmental institutions should assume. At the same time, the government has so far failed to provide them with the essential social and physical infrastructure as originally promised and used as an incentive for resettlement. Ironically, it is the poor and vulnerable who carry the cost of this unofficial strategy to acquire and defend territory for the state. However, this constellation is carefully hidden by political actors, who preferred conflicts between Maksat and Ovchi-Kalacha to be represented as "ethnic". This raises a number of questions about the concept of "interethnic conflict" as conceptualized in the peace-building approach of SDC into which I will look next.

Peace-Building in the Borderlands

The Regional Dialogue and Development (RDD) Project of the SDC was based on the assumption that the Ferghana Valley is at risk of interethnic conflict. So their activities are framed that such conflict can be transformed peacefully with mutually beneficial solutions, represented in a "consensus" on issues at stake. The support of civil society organizations, negotiations to accommodate and balance the needs and interests and improvement of behavioral patterns and attitudes would reduce the tensions and enable such a consensus. Yet, the interpretation of the tensions as "interethnic conflict" by SDC is put into question after the exploration of the case of Maksat and Ovchi-Kalacha. It becomes manifest that the reasons for animosities may less lie in relational or behavioral aspects of the two groups. Rather, it is their respective political leaders that—while not always intentionally—provide the sources of and are to a certain extent interested in conflictive relations, as this guarantees the defense of the border.

In the absence of other means, Kyrgyzstani (and Tajikistani) authorities exploit citizens (and, to some extent, noncitizens of Kyrgyz ethnic affiliation) to defend the state border and make claims to disputed land. The politics of "actual land use", it is suggested, serves to produce a specific attachment to land by claiming and capturing plots. These claims, over time, potentially turn into recognized residence and land rights. Such a strategy encourages people to settle or cultivate land, which they believe to rightfully claim. Yet these claims are met by similar counterclaims. The resulting tensions and sometimes outbreaks of violence may not only generate strong feelings of animosity, but also produce a new form of attachment to places. By fighting for it, as it was once pointed out to me by a Kyrgyzstani government official, people learn to "appreciate the land". In this particular understanding, conflicts and, possibly even more so, violence produce property relations along ethnonational lines, which can subsequently be consolidated into state territory.

As a consequence, it is not surprising that such conflicts are impervious to the mitigation strategies as deployed by the SDC. On the contrary, I suggest that the aid agencies' approach may have led to a further reification of categories in which the tensions between Maksat and Ovchi-Kalacha are framed. First, reification occurred through the representation of these categories to a wider public. With the use of "Kyrgyz" and "Tajik", authors of project documents and reports of conflict analyses often unquestioningly repeated the expressions of these categories by informants and interpreted them in terms of "ethnicity". Mostly, reports failed to acknowledge the differentiation between ethnicity and citizenship. Many of them base their argument on the assumption that solidarity among people will automatically arise from the shared affiliation with an ethnic group. Second, reification to some extent also happened through the very implementation of the approach, which stressed ethnicity as the category within which joint social projects and thus encounters of communities were framed.

SDC's activities were originally designed to compensate for the state's "absence" in terms of the government's apparent failure of service delivery in the fields of infrastructure building and conflict mitigation.[43] At the same time, implementation of peace-building occurred by means of collaboration mainly with NGOs and CBOs, thus presumably circumventing the ideologically suspect, operationally ineffectual and often corrupt state agencies. Yet, as the case of Maksat shows, the seemingly absent state powerfully marks its presence through pursuing two of its core projects: nationbuilding and territorialization at its borders under construction. To offer support to the particular way these state projects are currently framed in Central Asia must thus be understood as an unintended outcome, which certainly runs counter to the objective of peace-building aiming to create the conditions from "bottom up" for neoliberal reforms in Central Asia.

Conclusion

In sum, I suggest that the SDC is not oblivious to the border, but rather that it misrecognizes its nature and constitution. Rather than being a line drawn on the ground endowed with features that disrupt relationships which can be mended,[44] it is an expression of the constitution of territory and the formation of nations over time as described in this chapter. The border is therefore not a place where conflict is located, but a space where social processes become manifest and may be articulated in the form of conflicts. The border is thus, as Georg Simmel stated, not a spatial fact with sociological effects, but a sociological fact spatially expressed.[45]

The analysis of peace-building in the borderlands provides insights on the complex and dynamic interactions of state, nation and territory. As I have shown, the conflictive land claims in this case study emerge from a specific constellation of ideological work relating to nationalism, exploitation of both cultural attachment to land as well as subsistence needs and relegation of violence involved in delineating the nation to everyday transactions of the population. Attempts to understand peace-building in Maksat as a consequence of either Central Asian political rationality with its background in Soviet history, or the imposition of neoliberal development aid with a civilizing mission fall too short of grasping the issues at stake.

Notes

1. Funding for research on which this chapter is based was provided by the Swiss National Centre of Competence in Research (NCCR) North–South: Research Partnerships for Mitigating Syndromes of Global Change. The NCCR North–South program is co-funded by the Swiss National Science Foundation and Swiss Agency for Development and Cooperation. This chapter has been written during a fellowship granted by the Swiss National Science Foundation. It was first presented at international workshop "Bringing the margins back in: War making and state making in the borderlands", Ghent, February 12–14, 2010, and has much benefited from participants' comments and suggestions. Parts of this chapter have been published earlier in a book publication with Routledge, titled *Conflict transformation in Central Asia: Irrigation disputes in the Ferghana Valley.*
2. Mercy Corps, *Ferghana valley field study. Reducing the potential for conflict through community mobilization* (Portland, OR: Mercy Corps, 2003).
3. R. Slim, "The Ferghana Valley: In the midst of a host of crises," in *Searching for peace in Europe and Eurasia: An overview of conflict prevention and peacebuilding activities,* ed. P. van Tongeren, H. van de Veen and J. Verhoeven (London: Lynne Rienner, 2002).
4. A. Tabyshalieva, *The challenge of regional cooperation in Central Asia. Preventing ethnic conflict in the Ferghana Valley* (Washington, DC: United States Institute of Peace, 1999), vii.
5. N. Lubin, K. Martin and B. R. Rubin, *Calming the Ferghana Valley. Development and dialogue in the heart of Central Asia,* ed. The Centre for Preventive Action, Report on the Ferghana Valley Project (New York: The Century Foundation Press, 1999).
6. See also M. Reeves, "Locating danger: *Konfliktologiia* and the search for fixity in the Ferghana Valley borderlands," *Central Asian Survey* 24, no. 1 (2005): 67.
7. E. Crewe and E. Harrison, *Whose development? An ethnography of aid* (London: Zed Books, 1998); D. Mosse, *Cultivating development: An ethnography of aid policy and practice* (London: Pluto Press, 2005); J. Gould, "Introducing aidnography," in *Ethnographies of aid. Exploring development texts and encounters,* ed. J. Gould and H. S. Marcussen (Roskilde: University of Roskilde, International Development Studies, 2004).
8. D. Delanty, *Territory. A short introduction* (Oxford: Blackwell, 2005), 10.
9. R. Sack, *Human territoriality. Its theory and history* (Cambridge: Cambridge University Press, 1986).
10. S. Elden, "Missing the point: Globalization, deterritorialization and the space of the world," *Transactions of the Institute of British Geographers* 30, no. 1 (2005).

11. O. P. Richmond, *The transformation of peace, rethinking peace and conflict studies* (Basingstoke: Palgrave Macmillan, 2005); R. Mac Ginty, *No war, no peace: The rejuvenation of stalled peace processes and peace accords* (Basingstoke: Palgrave Macmillan, 2006).

12. R. Paris, "Peacebuilding and the limits of liberal internationalism," *International Security* 22, no. 2 (1997).

13. O. P. Richmond, *The transformation of peace, rethinking peace and conflict studies* (Basingstoke: Palgrave Macmillan, 2005); R. Mac Ginty, *No war, no peace: The rejuvenation of stalled peace processes and peace accords* (Basingstoke: Palgrave Macmillan, 2006), 110.

14. H. Donnan and D. Haller, "Liminal no more. The relevance of borderland studies," *Ethologia Europaea* 30, no. 2 (2000): 15.

15. H. Donnan and D. Haller, "Liminal no more. The relevance of borderland studies," *Ethologia Europaea* 30, no. 2 (2000):18.

16. F. Hirsch, *Empire of nations. Ethnographic knowledge and the making of the Soviet Union* (Ithaca, NY: Cornell University Press, 2005).

17. F. Hirsch, *Empire of nations. Ethnographic knowledge and the making of the Soviet Union* (Ithaca, NY: Cornell University Press, 2005), 203–204.

18. See, for example, P. G. Geiss, *Nationenwerdung in Mittelasien*, vol. 269, Europäische Hochschulschriften, Reihe 31, Politikwissenschaft (Frankfurt: Peter Lang, 1995).

19. In 1924, the national-territorial delimitation first established the Uzbek SSR. The Tajik SSR was first constituted as an autonomous national republic (ASSR) within the Uzbek SSR and gained republic status in 1929. The Kyrgyz SSR was initially incorporated into the Russian Soviet Federative Socialist Republic (RSFSR) as the Kara-Kyrgyz autonomous region AO (until 1925), the Kyrgyz AO (until 1926) and then the Kyrgyz ASSR until it became a full republic in 1936.

20. A. Haugen, *The establishment of national republics in Soviet Central Asia* (Basingstoke: Palgrave Macmillan, 2003); F. Hirsch, *Empire of nations. Ethnographic knowledge and the making of the Soviet Union* (Ithaca, NY: Cornell University Press, 2005); A. Koichiev, "Ethno-territorial claims in the Ferghana Valley during the process of national delimitation, 1924–7," in *Central Asia. Aspects of transition*, ed. T. Everett-Heath, Central Asia Research Forum Series (London: RoutledgeCurzon, 2003).

21. R. Brubaker, "Nationhood and the national question in the Soviet Union and Post-Soviet Eurasia: An institutionalist account," *Theory and Society* 23, no. 1 (1994): 49–60.

22. Compare A. Haugen, *The establishment of national republics in Soviet Central Asia* (Basingstoke: Palgrave Macmillan, 2003).

23. F. Hirsch, *Empire of nations. Ethnographic knowledge and the making of the Soviet Union* (Ithaca, NY: Cornell University Press, 2005), 318.

24. C. Bichsel, *Conflict transformation in Central Asia. Irrigation disputes in the Ferghana Valley* (London: Routledge, 2009).

25. L. De Martino, *Peace initiatives in Central Asia: An inventory* (Geneva: Cimera, 2001).
26. W. Fust and D. Syz, "The Swiss Regional Mid-Term Programme Central Asia 2002–2006," Swiss Agency for Development and Cooperation and State Secretariat for Economic Affairs. <http://www.deza.ch/ressources/product_40_en_1137.pdf.>.
27. SDC, "Uzbekistan, Kyrgyzstan, Tajikistan: Regional dialogue and development project in the Ferghana Valley (Rdd)." (Bern: Swiss Agency for Development and Cooperation, Department for Cooperation with Eastern Europe and the CIS (unpublished document), 2002).
28. The term community-based organization (CBO) is understood as a membership-based association consisting of village or municipality representatives. Members are mostly volunteers and nonpaid. CBOs are mainly formed with the goal of self-help. Their scope of operation is usually limited geographically to the administrative entities they represent.
29. C. Bichsel, *Conflict transformation in Central Asia. Irrigation disputes in the Ferghana Valley* (London: Routledge, 2009).
30. SDC, "Uzbekistan, Kyrgyzstan, Tajikistan: Regional dialogue and development project in the Ferghana Valley (Rdd)." (Bern: Swiss Agency for Development and Cooperation, Department for Cooperation with Eastern Europe and the CIS (unpublished document), 2002).
31. D. Mosse, "Global governance and the ethnography of international aid," in *The aid effect. Giving and governing in international development*, ed. D. Mosse and D. Lewis (London: Pluto Press, 2005).
32. W. Fust and D. Syz, "The Swiss Regional Mid-Term Programme Central Asia 2002–2006," Swiss Agency for Development and Cooperation and State Secretariat for Economic Affairs. <http://www.deza.ch/ressources/product_40_en_1137.pdf>.
33. Fair Process, "Otchet Po Analizu Situatsii V Sele Maksat." (Batken: NGO Fair Process (unpublished report), 2006).
34. In 1992, the new Central Asian states confirmed with the Almaty Agreement on Water Resources that they would continue to observe the existing quotas dating from the Soviet Union for the time being, but did not foreclose possible changes later.
35. Fair Process, "Otchet Po Analizu Situatsii V Sele Maksat." (Batken: NGO Fair Process (unpublished report), 2006).
36. Author's interview with former member of PC Tajikistan–Kyrgyzstan, Batken, April 2007.
37. Fair Process, "Otchet Po Analizu Situatsii V Sele Maksat." (Batken: NGO Fair Process (unpublished report), 2006).
38. C. Bichsel, *Conflict transformation in Central Asia. Irrigation disputes in the Ferghana Valley* (London: Routledge, 2009).
39. J. Odum and E. Johnson, "The state of physical infrastructure in Central Asia: Developments in transport, water, energy, and telecommunications," *NBR Analysis* 15, no. 5 (2004): 99.

40. See also UNDP, "Coexistence for Northern Tajikistan and Southern Kyrghyzstan," United Nations Development Programme, Cross-Border Cooperation Project, 2004. <http://www.pdp.undp.kg/AnnualEWR2004eng.pdf>.
41. Author's interview with former member of PC Tajikistan–Kyrgyzstan, Batken, April 2007.
42. Personal communication with local government official, Maksat, April 2007.
43. SDC, "Uzbekistan, Kyrgyzstan, Tajikistan: Regional Dialogue and Development Project in the Ferghana Valley (Rdd)." (Bern: Swiss Agency for Development and Cooperation, Department for Cooperation with Eastern Europe and the CIS (unpublished document), 2002).
44. See also C. Bichsel, "In Search of Harmony: Repairing infrastructure and social relations in the Ferghana Valley," *Central Asian Survey* 24, no. 1 (2005).
45. H. Donnan and D. Haller, "Liminal no more. The relevance of borderland studies," *Ethologia Europaea* 30, no. 2 (2000).

References

Bichsel, C. "In search of harmony: Repairing infrastructure and social relations in the Ferghana Valley." *Central Asian Survey* 24, no. 1 (2005): 53–66.
Bichsel, C. *Conflict transformation in Central Asia. Irrigation disputes in the Ferghana Valley*. London: Routledge, 2009.
Brubaker, R. "Nationhood and the national question in the Soviet Union and Post-Soviet Eurasia: An institutionalist account." *Theory and Society* 23, no. 1 (1994): 47–78.
Crewe, E. and E. Harrison. *Whose development? An ethnography of aid*. London: Zed Books, 1998.
De Martino, L. *Peace initiatives in Central Asia: An inventory*. Geneva: Cimera, 2001.
Delanty, D. *Territory. A short introduction*. Oxford: Blackwell, 2005.
Donnan, H. and D. Haller. "Liminal no more. The relevance of borderland studies." *Ethologia Europaea* 30, no. 2 (2000): 7–22.
Elden, S. "Missing the point: Globalization, deterritorialization and the space of the world." *Transactions of the Institute of British Geographers* 30, no. 1 (2005): 8–19.
Fair Process. *Otchet Po Analizu Situatsii V Sele Maksat*. Batken: NGO Fair Process (unpublished report), 2006: 11.
Fust, W. and D. Syz. "The Swiss Regional Mid-Term Programme Central Asia 2002–2006." Swiss Agency for Development and Cooperation and State Secretariat for Economic Affairs 2002. <http://www.deza.ch/ressources/product_40_en_1137.pdf> 1 November 2005.
Geiss, P. G. "Nationenwerdung in Mittelasien." Europäische Hochschulschriften. Reihe 31, Politikwissenschaft. Bd. 269. Frankfurt: Peter Lang, 1995.
Gould, J. "Introducing aidnography." In *Ethnographies of aid. Exploring development texts and encounters*, edited by J. Gould and H. S. Marcussen. Roskilde: University of Roskilde, International Development Studies, 2004: 1–13.
Haugen, A. *The establishment of national republics in Soviet Central Asia*. Basingstoke: Palgrave Macmillan, 2003.

Hirsch, F. *Empire of nations. Ethnographic knowledge and the making of the Soviet Union*. Ithaca, NY: Cornell University Press, 2005.

Koichiev, A. "Ethno-territorial claims in the Ferghana Valley during the process of national delimitation, 1924–7." In *Central Asia. Aspects of transition*, edited by T. Everett-Heath. London: RoutledgeCurzon, 2003: 45–56.

Lubin, N., K. Martin and B. R. Rubin. *Calming the Ferghana Valley. Development and dialogue in the heart of Central Asia*. Edited by The Centre for Preventive Action, Report on the Ferghana Valley Project. New York: The Century Foundation Press, 1999.

Mac Ginty, R. *No war, no peace: The rejuvenation of stalled peace processes and peace accords*. Basingstoke: Palgrave Macmillan, 2006.

Mercy Corps. *Ferghana Valley field study. Reducing the potential for conflict through community mobilization*. Portland, OR: Mercy Corps, 2003: 39.

Mosse, D. *Cultivating development: An ethnography of aid policy and practice*. London: Pluto Press, 2005.

Mosse, D. "Global governance and the ethnography of international aid." In *The aid effect. Giving and governing in international development*, edited by D. Mosse and D. Lewis. London: Pluto Press, 2005: 1–36.

Odum, J. and E. Johnson. "The state of physical infrastructure in Central Asia: Developments in transport, water, energy, and telecommunications." *NBR Analysis* 15, no. 5 (2004): 59–114.

Paris, R. "Peacebuilding and the limits of liberal internationalism." *International Security* 22, no. 2 (1997): 54–89.

Reeves, M. "Locating danger: *Konfliktologiia* and the search for fixity in the Ferghana Valley borderlands." *Central Asian Survey* 24, no. 1 (2005): 67–81.

Richmond, O. P. *The transformation of peace: Rethinking peace and conflict studies*. Basingstoke: Palgrave Macmillan, 2005.

Sack, R. *Human territoriality. Its theory and history*. Cambridge: Cambridge University Press, 1986.

SDC. "Uzbekistan, Kyrgyzstan, Tajikistan: Regional dialogue and development project in the Ferghana Valley (Rdd)." Bern: Swiss Agency for Development and Cooperation, Department for Cooperation with Eastern Europe and the CIS (unpublished document), 2002: no pagination.

Slim, R. "The Ferghana Valley: In the midst of a host of crises." In *Searching for peace in Europe and Eurasia: An overview of conflict prevention and peacebuilding activities*, edited by Paul van Tongeren, Hans van de Veen and Juliette Verhoeven. London: Lynne Rienner Publishers, 2002: 489–515.

Tabyshalieva, A. *The challenge of regional cooperation in Central Asia. Preventing ethnic conflict in the Ferghana Valley*. Washington, DC: United States Institute of Peace, 1999: 28.

UNDP. "Coexistence for northern Tajikistan and southern Kyrghyzstan." United Nations Development Programme, Cross-Border Cooperation Project, 2004. <http://www.pdp.undp.kg/AnnualEWR2004eng.pdf> 1 November 2005.

CHAPTER 7

State-Making and the Suspension of Law in India's Northeast: The Place of Exception in the Assam–Nagaland Border Dispute

Bert Suykens

Post 9/11, exceptionalism has won popularity to describe the variety of processes resulting from a new security discourse, the war on terror and the treatment of terrorism suspects.[1] Indeed, the central case to argue and counterargue the usefulness of the concept of the state of exception is the "modern camp" in Guantanamo Bay.[2] Other key cases include the analysis of (illegal) migrants[3] and, interrelated, of the securization of border regimes,[4] where the discussion on the inside and the outside of the state and the sovereign power seems to be most profound. Little attention has however been awarded to exceptionalism away from this security and terrorism discourse. Moreover, cases are often only used to make a theoretical argument about the state of exception, and the attention to a particular case seems to be little more than a corollary of a theoretical positioning.

In this article I want to focus on a specific *place* of exception, and analyze *how* the exception takes place, *where* it takes place. I use the state of exception—"the suspension of rules and conventions creating a conceptual and ethical zero-point from where the law, the norms and the political order can be constituted"[5]—as a starting point. Rather than focusing on the theory of the exception,[6] I want to understand how it is in fact practiced in specific localities.[7]

I more specifically want to investigate how political order is being constituted in the place of exception—"where the state of exception can be located and the particular bodies, and specific actions, which trigger the decision on the exception can be understood"[8]—and what the relation is between the removal of "normal law" and state-making, understood as an ongoing process, rather than a "mythic initial moment".[9] I indeed conclude that, although law is often seen as central to the state, state-making and the suspension of law are not mutually exclusive.[10]

I will draw on the specific case of the border dispute between Nagaland and Assam, two states located in northeast India. This case forces us to depart from most work on exceptionalism in that it forces us to engage with a much more diffuse and layered notion of sovereignty, rather than a single sovereign.[11] The Disputed Area Belt (DAB) between Assam and Nagaland offers a prime locus to better understand the struggle to constitute a political order in a situation of "unsettled sovereignty",[12] where the link between sovereignty and territory is far from straightforward. In this case, the exception has become a tool to control this link. In short, in the 1970s, the two state governments concluded interim agreements to control the border dispute—at the instigation of the central government. These agreements were meant to temporarily install a status quo until a solution, with the support of a centrally appointed arbitrator, could be reached. These interim agreements suspended "normal" law in the area under dispute. They should not only have stopped further settlement into the DAB, but indeed made any change that could alter the balance between the two states subject to interstate negotiation and agreement. This should have frozen the data, in order to find a solution on the border conflict. Yet, in the absence of a definitive agreement over the delimitation of the border, the interim agreements have become permanent and so has the exceptional regime that they installed. In effect, this border conflict has resulted in the suspension of "normal" law and produced a status quo,[13] a "suspended temporality".[14] Although, at first sight, this regime can only be detrimental, we will show that it also offers opportunities.

Although by default located at extremities, border regions—both internal and external—can be at the heart of the "meaning of the nation".[15] Political borders, international or internal, offer prime locales to look at the "tight linkages between the territory, the people and the state".[16] In this case, people that are excluded and marginal can at the same time become of central importance to the state and state agents as they symbolize the inclusion of certain disputed territory within a particular nation. This inversion of the relation between the periphery and state can help people living under the exception at the margins to claim public goods, and conversely compels the competing authorities to grant exemptions and try to defuse the exceptional regime—at least for "their" population. The different potentialities in constructing a new political order in the border—a process that has continued notwithstanding the perceived standstill—make that "people [. . .] can enter into a negotiation of identity and political space that produces different political outcomes".[17] In essence, the place of exception reveals itself as creative[18] in the efforts of both populations and states to control rights, people and territory.

Finally, this case clearly highlights the continuities and the historicity of exceptional regimes. As I will show more clearly later, the original legal status of the territory, which became disputed, as forest land is crucial. Because of this status, no human population was and is allowed to reside in the area. Yet, massive encroachments on the Reserved Forest land—which effectively transformed the DAB from a forest to an agricultural zone—help to support the claims made by both states in the border conflict. Populations became a tool to claim territory. Moreover, the imagination of a historic distinction between the plains people of Assam and the hill tribes of Nagaland[19] is central to understand the difficulties in negotiating a political solution for the border dispute and to the claims and counterclaims made in the DAB.

Fieldwork in November–December 2008 in the DAB of Golaghat district and in Nagaland, as well as government papers and civil society reports form the main basis for this article. The rest of the article will be organized as follows: (1) I will discuss the installation of the status quo under the interim agreements, under which "normal" law was suspended; show that this suspension is rooted in a longer history[20] of (2) exclusion between hills–plains populations, and (3) illegal, but government-sponsored, encroachment into forest area; (4) show the contemporary interlinking of maintenance–contestation and public–private in the everyday negotiation in a place of exception; (5) reveal the opportunities for non-state contestation and highlight the possibility of this unregulated population to look for support beyond the state by looking at the role of the Naga underground in the DAB.

The Interim Agreements and the Suspension of "Normal Law"

In August 1971, the Indian Ministry of Home Affairs appointed K. V. K. Sundaram as adviser to the border dispute, as the two state governments could not agree to delimitation. Awaiting his report, four *interim* agreements, of which the fourth refers to Doyang Reserved Forest,[21] were signed in 1972. These agreements were only meant to be temporal measures to maintain "peace and tranquility". As the Nagaland government rejected the Sundaram report of 1976,[22] these exceptional and temporal agreements have been active till now. Moreover, an interstate meeting in 1979, called after a violent confrontation in Chungajan, cemented the place of exception in the Assam–Nagaland border. The interim agreements were meant to suspend and contain the DAB in time and space, until a solution could be reached. According to the agreements, everything that might affect the status quo has to be decided upon by interstate negotiation. The status quo became the prime locus to negotiate the "unsettled sovereignty"[23] over this former buffer area.

Interstate violence has regularly marred the system of continuous negotiation. The central case in this respect—albeit not the only one—is the Merapani incident of June 4–6, 1985, where Nagaland's and Assam's armed police clashed. Twenty-eight police officers and 13 civilians died in the 3-day violence.[24] While both governments put the blame for the armed confrontation with each other (Government of Assam, 1985; Government of Nagaland, 1985),[25] it must be clear that these incidents continuously reenact the process that led to the installation of the regime of status quo, going around negotiating and toward confrontation. While political negotiation normally contains violence, violence and violent conflict have not been removed from the DAB. In the end, as a legal solution for the area has not been reached, the political opponents are sometimes forced to show muscle power to maintain their political influence in the DAB.

As a consequence of the Merapani incident, in 1985, it was agreed to put the maintenance of law and order in the whole DAB in the hands of the Central Reserve Police Force (CRPF) (and in lesser numbers, the Assam Rifles). They, as a "neutral force", under the direction of both Assam and Nagaland, now became the guards of the place of exception, who should see to the maintenance of the status quo. In an interview, a member of the force most lucidly illustrated their contradictory role:

> We man Border Outposts, mostly located on the big roads and more or less between the Assamese and the Naga. You know, Border Outposts are normally located at the border of our country, to defend our country from foreign aggression. Is this the border of India?

While both states want to make sure their opponent does not infringe on the interim terms of the status quo, they also try to alter the relations of power in the DAB. The Nagaland government has for instance organized overlapping subdivisions in the DAB. This is where the "unsettled sovereignty"[26] gets its complete form. In 1991, two subdivisions, Niuland and Kohobotu, were established in Diphu Reserved Forest (Sector A), and in 2006, two more subdivisions, Uriamghat and Hukai, were established in Rengma Reserved Forest (Sector C).[27] Certainly Niuland and Kohobotu, which are administered as a part of Dimapur District, are well established, with an Additional Deputy Commissioner residing in Niuland. I will later elaborate further on the complicated and ambiguous nature of the states' positions as the states purport to maintain the status quo vis-à-vis each other and they contest it at the same time, using populations and goods to alter the status quo.

The failure of the central government to arbitrate in the matter and propose a settlement is critically visible in the disappointing results of the different commissions installed by the Home Ministry and the Supreme Court—Sundaram (1976), Shastri (1985), Pillai (1997) and currently Variava (since 2006)—to find a solution, or at least take the negotiations to a new level. The Sundaram report was rejected by Nagaland—as it also rejected most of Nagaland's claims to territory—and the Pillai report even by both states. Disillusion with the real commitment of Delhi to solve the border problem is also very common in the DAB itself: "They sit in Delhi and Gauhati and write their report. Maybe they will come here for one day, maybe two. How can they understand our problems? We have lived here for the last 30 years". Many Naga civil society organizations did not even bother to send a memorandum to former Justice S. N. Variava—unlike their Assamese counterparts—to make their claims: "Assam will come with all the official documents. All I know is what my forefathers told me. Our Ancestral domain was up to Furkating [the railway junction near Golaghat town]. It is our land".[28]

Hills–Plains and Colonial Territoriality

The border dispute has to be understood in the context of the imagination of a distinction between hill (Naga) and plains (Assamese) populations.[29] The DAB, especially its section on Golaghat, forms a zone of contact or friction between these two "societies". As such, it is also a zone where these self-evident distinctions are and were questioned. As James Scott remarks for a larger area from highland Vietnam to the northeast of India: "The colonial ethnographers' map said they were A, but they said they were B and had always been".[30]

For the British colonizers, the current DAB formed a threshold between their sovereignty and its borders. The Inner Line Regulation formally delineated this threshold. The line was drawn along the foothills, and

> [b]eyond the line the tribes [were] left to manage their own affairs with only such interference on the part of the frontier officers in their *political* capacity as may be considered advisable with the view to establishing a *personal* influence for good among the chiefs and the tribes.[31]

Making the British administration not extend to the areas beyond the Inner Line and relying on the "political" and "personal" influence of its officers located at the border excepted the hills from becoming a part of the British empire *in toto*. Moreover, Edward Gait, a colonial administrator and historian of Assam, wrote in 1926 that

> it was not always convenient to define the actual boundary of the British pos-
> sessions, this line does not necessarily indicate the territorial frontier but only
> the *limits of the administered area*; It is known as the "Inner Line" and . . . it
> does *not* in any way *decide the sovereignty* of the territory beyond.[32]
>
> (emphasis added)

While the Inner Line did not limit the sovereignty of the British Empire over any territory, the people living in the territory in question did not fall under the British administration. Consequently, the Inner Line Regulation exempted the "unadministered Naga Hills" from its laws.

As Sanjib Baruah has convincingly argued, the creation of the Inner Line in 1873 profoundly hardened the "boundaries between the hill 'tribes' and the plains peoples of Assam".[33] He clearly shows that in the case of the Assamese and the Naga, "substantial political, economic, and cultural relations"[34] did exist, although after colonization the difference between the "modern" and the "primitive" was exacerbated. The hills were reserved for the unadminis-trable "savage tribes"[35] and the plains for civilized rule. While the plains were subdued by law, "[t]he story of the early British relations with these tribes is one of perpetual conflict".[36] This strict depiction of the Naga as living in the hills is still very apparent in the postcolonial official writing on the border area. In an official report on the Assam–Nagaland border dispute, Sundaram clearly states that

> the plains area was at no time occupied or inhabited by any Naga tribe. It is
> well known that the Nagas built their villages on the top of the hill ranges and
> did their jhum [shifting] cultivation on the hills [*sic*] slopes.[37]

A Naga occupying or inhabiting a plain seems to go against all common knowledge.

The delineation of administered and unadministered territories and districts changed over time as the pressure to put more land under cultivation—partly for rubber and tea plantations—pushed the internal boundary deeper into the foothills.[38] While Alexander Mackenzie, following Dalton's *Ethnology of Bengal*, in 1884 discussed the "Nagas to the east and those to the west of the Dhunsiri [Dhansari]" and "Nagas to the west of the Doyeng [Doyang]",[39] these areas west of both rivers are currently located in Assam. Indeed, it is exactly the areas west of the Doyang River, between the Doyang and the Dhansari, that form the main bone of contention between Nagaland and Assam.

A comprehensive discussion of the different transfers of land inside and outside the Naga areas falls largely outside the scope of this chapter. The exact delimitations are far from an exact science, as the descriptions of the boundary are far from clear and comprehensive, while on-the-ground markers, like old boundary pillars, are not always easily retraced or available. However, the comparison of three indicative maps (figures 7.1–7.3), of the situation in 1874, that in 1898 and the contemporary map of Assam–Nagaland, reveals some trends.[40]

The repeated transfer of land outside the Unadministered Naga Hills and into the Naga Hills District[41] and certainly Sivasagar District and the consequent reterritorialization of the Naga and Assamese areas, and between administration and un-administration lie very much at the heart of the dispute. The central crux is the notification of 1925, which consolidated the boundary changes since 1866—the constitution of the Naga Hills District—and gave permanence to the exclusion (from 1898), central to the current debate, from the Naga Hills District of the area between the Dhansari and Doyang rivers, which is currently part of the Golaghat District. While the Naga refer to the 1925 transfers as a colonial sham, for the Assamese, the 1925 notification of the Naga "cannot claim any areas outside its boundary as morally, legally or constitutionally to it".[42]

The creation of the state of Nagaland, in 1963, did little to change the claims.[43] Insurgent groups, fighting for an independent Nagaland, have

Figure 7.1 Assam–Nagaland border, ca. 1878.

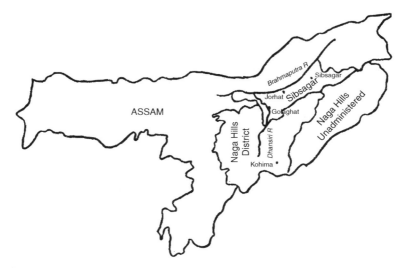

Figure 7.2   Assam–Nagaland border, ca. 1898.

Figure 7.3   Assam–Nagaland border, ca. 2010.

been active in the Naga areas since Indian independence. Symbolically, some Naga leaders even declared Naga independence from the British—and consequently also from India—one day before Indian independence. In the 16-point agreement leading to the creation of this state, the moderate Naga leaders who supported the creation of the state reiterated the demand for "the consolidation of forest areas" and "the inclusion of the Reserve Forest and of contiguous areas inhabited by the Nagas". This demand is important when considering the current situation of the DAB. Four Reserved Forests (Doyang, Rengma, Nambor South and Diphu), corresponding to four sectors currently under the DAB (respectively D, C, B and A), are located alongside the current Nagaland border in Golaghat. This forest belt was used as a buffer and a no-man's-land to demarcate the Inner Line, and to protect the plains from Naga raids by marking a clear division. Forest law in India, both during British times and after independence, is very strict. Reserved Forests are government property and—although things might change when the Tribal (Recognition of Forest Rights) Act 2006 is implemented—any use of the forest, not under Forest Department supervision, is very restricted, although frequently challenged.[44] Yet the disputed nature of the forest tracks allowed breaking this restrictive regime.

Illegal Encroachment and State-Making in the DAB

What can I do? You have seen it, there is no forest left. I cannot protect what is not there.

(Forest official, Golaghat)

After independence, encroachment took place on a massive scale in these forest areas, from the Assamese side in Doyang and from the Naga side in Diphu and from both sides in Rengma and Nambor South. This encroachment is related to two main postcolonial developments in the region: the pressure on land in Assam and the Naga insurgency. The lack of government control on these encroachments was not the result of state incapacity. Clearly, allowing for encroachment was instrumental to state politics in the border areas, as people could better support state-making in the disputed area than could trees.

Encroachment from the Assam side gathered steam in the 1960s after the Assam government settled some retired army personnel between Chungajan and Bokajan and issued private land titles (*patta*) to them in 1962.[45] Landless peasants—or peasants from floodplains—from Lakhimpur, Bangladeshi migrants and refugees and ex–tea garden laborers or their children all encroached on the forest in search for fertile lands. Certainly around

Merapani in Doyang Reserved Forest (sector D), from 1911 designated as an official forest village, encroachment skyrocketed, and, currently, the whole of Doyang Reserved Forest has disappeared. Many schools, both Assamese government as well as private schools, have been opened since 1971. The principal of the first school to open in the Merapani area reminisced clearly that the demand had come from the state government to open an Assamese-language school for the growing population. In this case, the timing—1971—is important, 1 year before the interim agreements would be signed (see further).

Encroachment from the Naga side also started in the 1960s. In the 1950s, Diphu, Nambor and Rengma Reserved Forests were often used as bases and as a safe passage to what is now Karbi Anglong. After the 16-point agreement and the creation of the state of Nagaland in 1963, many Naga, mostly Sema, moved into the former base areas and started cultivation. The result has been the same as in Doyang Reserved Forest: the forest has now disappeared. Mirroring the activities of the Assam state government, Nagaland has also started building Naga schools and making illegal occupations of forest land licit.

Notwithstanding that the whole area has been brought under agriculture from both the Assam and Nagaland sides, the land remains officially forest land. No *patta* has been given, nor does any legal protection pertain to the lands in the area.[46] However, while the practice of encroachment itself is illegal, it was at the same time tacitly allowed and even encouraged by the state governments in a growing struggle to maintain territorial rights over this disputed land. Official government support for the encroachers and unofficial government encouragement to new settlers has been common. For both state governments, the numbers game, allowing as many of "its own kind" as possible to live illegally in the wasteland, supported their claims to a particular territory. These encroachments were not the result of state demise, as the state also used their capacity to destroy houses and evict people "from the other side" in the disputed area[47] to cement their claims.

From being at the fringes of the colonial and postcolonial Assam, the encroachers became central for both states to assert their territorial stakes. Both governments wanted to prove that this area had been part of the Ahomiya (Assamese) or Naga (Rengma, Lotha and Sema) ancestral domain. Although the encroachers were living in illegality, they became the cornerstone of their community. Much of these discussions are of course reminiscent of Akhil Gupta and James Ferguson's well-known discussion of the politicized "imagination of places"[48] and Liisa Malkki's assessment of the "territorialization of national identity".[49] In this case, allowing people to move into illegality—or in other words making encroachment licit—formed a central part of the territorial state-making of both Assam and Nagaland.

The interim agreements tried to freeze illegal encroachment into the DAB, but also removed the option of regularization. The forest land, as an opportunity for landless peasants, transformed; while earlier encroachment was tacitly allowed, now each state tried to put a halt to each other's infringements. Consequently, the open encroachments stopped and the suspension of "normal" law installed a new regime in the area. Yet, while this exceptional measure at first sight might have indeed stopped further encroachments, after the interim agreement, this process would continue. While people who had earlier migrated into the "wasteland" in search for scarce land became encroachers, but were encouraged by the state governments (e.g., by services like schools), after 1979 they were no longer illegal. The status of people living in the border zone has become undecided and outside normal law. The strategies employed in the border area changed. People were still able to move and settle inside the DAB, although their tactics and those of both state governments changed.

Private–Public Goods and the Interstate Maintenance–Contestation of the Exception

The maintenance of the status quo necessitates a permanent negotiation, as any change in the DAB is officially the subject of an agreement by both states. Yet simultaneously both states try to secure privileges for "their" population. Not only are public goods used by both states to maintain and support their claims on a particular area, but private goods are also rendered public. In fact, every life in the DAB has a clear public function. As such, the dichotomy between private/public does not hold in this place of exception.

First, the role of public goods in forming state claims is the most obvious. In an effort to inhibit the competing government to use infrastructure as a weapon to secure their hold—in line with the rationale of the status quo—the road network has suffered the most as no new roads can be laid out. Electricity supply is largely absent. On the other hand, by recognizing schools—or for that matter churches and temples—that have been set up "by local people with their own efforts without Government help" (from the records of a 1981 meeting between Assam and Nagaland in Kohima), both states have been able to extend their networks of power, inducing private persons to start such public services (e.g., the first, 1971, school) with the promise to recognize them as soon as they are established, certainly diffusing the public–private divide. A more complex symbolic public good is the Nagaland State Transport bus services, which form a kind of moving infrastructure to highlight Nagaland's presence. Using the DAB roads is quicker than reaching Wokha and Mokokchung from Dimapur through hilly Nagaland. The service, with very regular stops along the way, is almost exclusively used by the Naga living in the DAB and is clearly perceived by Naga interviewees as a direct link to Nagaland and in fact the proof that they form intrinsic part of Nagaland.

Second, private housing forms one of the main stumbling blocks for people living in the DAB. Not only do new families immigrate to the area, but established families also expand and need more room for their family. Notwithstanding, quite a few hardware shops sell building materials in Merapani, in the heart of Sector D. As putting new houses up is not allowed according to the interstate agreements, most of these illegal buildings are locally described as "renovations". The CRPF is not known to have demolished too many buildings, certainly not from the Assamese majority population in Doyang or the Naga majority population in Diphu Reserved Forest. Anil Barua, an Assamese schoolteacher, for instance, built his entirely new "renovation" only a few years ago. Initially the CRPF had threatened to remove the structure, but he was able to prove it was only a renovation, albeit of a small garden shed of his neighbor's house. Some CRPF members also quite readily and quite unofficially admitted that, although the interim agreements stipulate that they have to demolish all new structures, under political pressure they allow for the licit "renovations" and only destroy excessive "illegal" structures. For people like Anil the current status quo offers some protection, as his house, located inside a Reserved Forest, is of course illegal. He did not consider this to be a major problem, as to him—a proud Ahomiya—living there supported the claims of Assam, a state he was certain would win the struggle over the DAB and would regularize his situation.

For both states, private infrastructure clearly serves a public function, as indication of one of the state's domination over a specific population in a specific territory. Property rights are removed from the legal and personal to the public realm and the externalities of the private goods render the division between private and public goods meaningless. Indeed, the popular maxim "possession in nine-tenths of law" does not hold true in the disputed border zone. The maintenance of possession has clearly been removed from the legal terrain. It has moved toward a threshold where agents, like the CRPF commanders or their relations in the administration, by virtue of their role in maintaining the status quo—as the prime local agents of the exception— grant the temporary suspension of the status quo. However, as the final decision, which territory belongs to whom, and which rights will be granted by which state, remains the subject of political negotiation, people are granted only what we could call "interim rights", which only hold as long as the current politically negotiated situation persists.

Land ownership is also a matter where private rights and public ownership become confused. *Patta* have not been issued in the DAB, initially because of its nature as Reserved Forest land. These land rights form an important grudge of people in the DAB against the government.[50] Given the interim agreements, granting *patta* remains however very precarious.[51] As administrative sanction has not been secured, direct intergroup negotiation at the local level is used to solve disputes. Yet the outcome of these negotiations often gets a complicated semiofficial status. To maintain "cordial relations", a peace committee, with members from both Nagaland and Assam, is active in a particular part of Doyang Reserved Forest. They negotiate between the two communities, mostly to settle land disputes. Their activities were often derogatorily described in interviews as "purely political". This description illustrates perfectly the everyday reality of life in the border zone. As ownership rights cannot be referred back to the state, the delimitation of these rights, and consequently disputes about them, has to be settled by direct negotiation between farmers and their leaders (often *goanburas* or village heads). The negotiations within the peace committee take place in the "neutral" CRPF camp. This venue indeed gives a legal gloss to the outcome of the negotiations. While the CRPF admitted that the outcome of these negotiations—the minutes of the meetings, of which a copy is also kept by the CRPF—has no validity in any court, the decisions acquire a complex juridical-political status in the border zone and seem to open up a space between the legal and the illegal. As the alternative for these informal accords is a complex interstate discussion, local settlement has clear advantages (both for the parties and for the CRPF), although the enforcement of these decisions only holds as long as a political settlement between the Assam and Naga states holds.

An Assam police officer was quite blunt in giving his assessment of the complicated nature of state–society relations in the DAB: "[t]he interim agreements force people to bribe the administration and the CRPF. As a status quo is impossible to maintain, we have to bribe them. It is an official system of bribes". He clearly professed that the maintenance of the status quo had installed a system of under-the-table negotiations. Quite a lot of research in and on India has focused on bureaucratic corruption and the use of public office for private gains.[52] In the DAB, this bureaucratic corruption has a very ambiguous meaning. While most commonly bribes are used to make the illegal legal, bending the law in such a way is a fiction in the DAB. What is done in effect is momentarily suspending, case by case, the status quo and to give semblance to a legal reality, where in fact there is none. These bribes can only hold as long as the border remains under dispute, creating a regime of "suspended temporality".[53] As every fact recorded in the administrative files of the border administration is open for renegotiation—when and if a solution on the DAB would be reached—the "renovations", whether or not officialized through bribes, remain in the end prone to destruction. At the same time, administrators in the DAB who accept private gains—bribes—to help securing private benefits for their clients are not simply undermining the state. The administrations help securing infringements on the status quo—mostly by using their relations with the CRPF—which actually supports the process of state-making for their "side". One could argue that by choosing whom to bribe, people living under the exception are not only trying to secure private benefits, but they are also supporting the state-making project of one of the contenders for sovereignty over the area: they are providing legitimacy to Assam or Nagaland.

The Naga Underground: Protecting Nagalim

Voicing a local concern, national newspaper *The Hindu* (December 26, 2006) placed the responsibility for Naga encroachments in the DAB with Assamese politicians and administrators. Although the responsibility for progress on the official level lies indeed with Assam and Nagaland, their influence and governance over the DAB is far from complete. The different factions of the National Socialist Council of Nagalim/Nagaland (NSCN)[54] are very active in the DAB, clearly defying the authority of the Assamese government in the Naga-controlled areas of the DAB. Assamese state officials do not enter the southern part of the DAB without a large CRPF support, out of fear of getting ambushed by the NSCN operatives. Although the NSCN factions have entered into a peace agreement with the Indian state and are officially not allowed to enter the DAB armed, the insurgents feel it is their duty to protect all Naga living in the ancestral domain or Nagalim, which is proposed to extend across the borders of Nagaland state into parts of neighboring Indian states Assam, Manipur and Arunachal Pradesh and into Burma. As such, securing the DAB is considered a first step in securing the whole of Nagalim, the unification of all Naga-inhabited areas. Moreover, many Naga leaders consider the NSCN members as "national workers", and their administrative structures—the Government of the People's Republic of Nagalim—as a legitimate and powerful authority. As a result, these insurgents levy taxes on both the Naga and non-Naga living in the DAB. In one telling instance, the aforementioned peace committee negotiated directly with the NSCN to stop taxing the non-Naga in their area, as these harassed the Naga repeatedly over this taxation. In return for these taxes, the insurgents support the claims to include the DAB in a Greater Nagaland and protect the Naga from harassment by Assamese state officials. While Anil Barua had to prove his "renovation", one of his Naga counterparts, Neheto Sema, resident of Niuland subdivision, did not have any fears about his house being demolished. By giving tax to the NSCN (Unification) (NSCN(U)), he secured their support against harassment by the CRPF or the Assamese state. Neheto did not consider this to be protection money, but considered the NSCN(U) to be best able to include the DAB in Nagaland. In the Naga-dominated sectors, the CRPF—with the covert cooperation of the Assam Police—has tried and failed to curb this insurgent taxation. A high CRPF commandant admitted the difficulty—near impossibility—to control the Naga areas away from large roads.

Although a complete discussion of the Naga conflict falls outside the scope of this chapter, the NSCN clearly wants to extend its control over the DAB. It tries to install a new regime in the border area, unrestricted by interim agreements and openly defying the status quo. As they are not bound by these agreements, they have a comparative advantage to the Naga state in protecting the Naga encroachments. Although interviewees on the Assamese side did not so clearly distinguish between the Nagaland state and the Naga underground, and while the Naga state and insurgent operators often pursue the same goals, the NSCN is as much an alternative to both states' politics in the DAB. By disallowing Assamese officials to visit the area, the NSCN at the same time increases the authority of the Nagaland state as the official enforcer of the state, but in the practice of authority (instead of law, or the official position of the state of Nagaland) uses the DAB as an opportunity to impose their political frame. This dual process makes the aforementioned "juridical-political status" of those living in the DAB even more "undecidable"[55] (Vaughan-Williams 2008: 333).

Conclusion

What was at first intriguing to me was the veritable banal reason for the imposition of the exceptional measures in this case. Not a civil war, nor an insurgency (of which the area abounds) or violent acts of terrorism lie at the heart of the prolonged state of exceptionalism. Although I have argued that the history of the exception dates back to British policies regarding the Inner Line and Forest Reserves, the role of the encroachers is central to understand this place of exception. They, looking for land, voluntarily entered into the "wasteland". With the creation of Nagaland in 1963 and the start of the border dispute, they than became the inhabitants of a place of exception, precisely because their presence urged a decision on their status. The continuous reaffirmation of a "unity between place and people"[56] made a formal delimitation of the Assamese and Naga "ancestral domains" heavily contested. The decision to maintain a populated place as an imagined wasteland space (Reserved Forest), as an area where only nature dwells, negated the necessity to bring law to the encroached area and turned it into a place of exception, with the exception as a status quo. While British territoriality had mostly tried to divide territories, the status quo lifted the territory under dispute out of the normal legal order.

Consequently, as I hope to have argued, something as apparently mundane as an interstate boundary dispute can make a place of exception, a place where not law, but negotiation has to decide on everyday life, or, more precisely, where one moves from law (e.g., forest law) to politics and where politics is phrased in the semblance of law, where the continuous decisions on exceptions are made a corollary of the illegal encroachment of the DAB by people.

Yet, at the same time, by allowing for encroachment, supporting the provision of public/private goods and recognizing illicit constructions and services, both states and rebel groups continue state-making in the disputed border zone. The unsettled sovereignty opens up a space to creatively use populations and public/private goods to sustain and further their state projects. Consequently, and what I finally have tried to show, the state of exception, where it takes place, is not an absolute object, but is subject to contestation, even by those who have installed it in the first place. We can thus also understand actual regimes of exceptionalism by taking into account the everyday transgression of the status quo by states as a tool for state-making. Exceptionalism takes place in a quagmire of decisions, maintenance activities and contestations. It is a dynamic and layered project, with forces both inside and outside taking part in its actual functioning. By using the exception as a lens, I hope not only to have shown the working of a localized place of exception, but also to have made the DAB as a place of exception more intelligible.

Notes

1. J. Huysmans, "International politics of exception: Competing visions of international political order between law and politics," *Alternatives: Global, Local, Political* 31 (2006): 135–165.
2. D. Gregory, "The black flag: Guantanamo Bay and the space of exception," *Geografiska Annaler: Series B, Human Geography* 88 (2006): 405–427; C. Minca, "The return of the camp," *Progress in Human Geography* 29 (2005): 405–412; for a critique, see F. Johns, "Guantánamo Bay and the annihilation of the exception," *European Journal of International Law* 16 (2005): 613–635; S. Reid-Henry, "Exceptional sovereignty? Guantanamo Bay and the re-colonial present," *Antipode* 39 (2007): 627–648.
3. J. Edkins and V. Pin-Fat, "Through the wire: Relations of power and relations of violence," *Millennium: Journal of International Studies* 34 (2005): 1–24; M. B. Salter, "When the exception becomes the rule: Borders, sovereignty, and citizenship," *Citizenship Studies* 12 (2008): 365–380.

4. L. Amoore, "Biometric borders: Governing mobilities in the war on terror," *Political Geography* 25 (2006): 336–351; T. Basaran, "Borders, territory, law," *International Political Sociology* 2 (2008): 322–338.
5. T. B. Hansen and F. Stepputat, "Sovereignty revisited," *Annual Review of Anthropology* 35 (2006): 301.
6. See, among others, C. Schmitt, *Political theology: Four chapters on the concept of sovereignty* (Chicago, IL: The University of Chicago Press, 2005 [1934]); G. Agamben, *State of exception* (Chicago, IL: Chicago University Press, 2005); S. Prozorov, "X/Xs: Towards a general theory of the exception," *Alternatives: Global, Local, Political* 30 (2005): 81–112; J. Huysmans, "The jargon of the exception: On Schmitt, Agamben and the absence of political society," *International Political Sociology* 2 (2008): 165–183.
7. See also R. Jones, "Agents of exception: Border security and the marginalization of Muslims in India," *Environment and Planning D: Society and Space* 27 (2009): 879–897; V. Das and D. Poole, eds. "State and its margins: Comparative ethnographies," in *Anthropology in the margins of the state*, (Santa Fe, NM: School of American Research Press and James Currey, 2004), 3–34.
8. R. Jones, "Agents of exception: Border security and the marginalization of Muslims in India," *Environment and Planning D: Society and Space* 27 (2009): 883.
9. G. Steinmetz, ed. "Introduction: Culture and the state," in *State/culture: State-formation after the cultural turn*, (Ithaca, NY: Cornell University Press, 1999), 9.
10. See also, M. Neocleous, "The problem with normality: Taking exception to 'permanent emergency'," *Alternatives: Global, Local, Political* 31 (2006): 191–213.
11. C. Schmitt, *Political Theology: Four chapters on the concept of sovereignty* (Chicago, IL: The University of Chicago Press, 2005 [1934]); G. Agamben, *State of exception* (Chicago, IL: Chicago University Press, 2005).
12. T. B. Hansen and F. Stepputat, "Introduction," in *Sovereign bodies: Citizens, migrants and states in the postcolonial world*, ed. T. B. Hansen and F. Stepputat (Princeton, NJ: Princeton University Press, 2005), 27.
13. This term came up in most of the interviews conducted in the DAB.
14. N. Vandekerckhove, "No land, no peace: Dynamics of violent conflict and land use in Assam, India," Unpublished PhD dissertation, Ghent University, 2010.
15. N. Megoran, "The critical geopolitics of the Uzbekistan–Kyrgyzstan Ferghana Valley boundary dispute, 1999–2000," *Political Geography* 23 (2004): 731–764.
16. R. Jones, "Agents of exception: Border security and the marginalization of Muslims in India," *Environment and Planning D: Society and Space* 27 (2009): 882.
17. T. Raeymaekers, "The silent encroachment of the frontier: A politics of transborder trade in the Semliki Valley (Congo–Uganda)," *Political Geography* 28 (2009): 63.
18. V. Das and D. Poole, eds. "State and its margins: Comparative ethnographies," in *Anthropology in the margins of the state*, (Santa Fe, NM: School of American Research Press and James Currey, 2004), 19.

19. S. Baruah, *India against itself: Assam and the politics of nationality* (New Delhi: Oxford University Press, 2002), 29; see also J. Scott, *The art of not being governed: An anarchist history of upland Southeast Asia* (New Haven, CT: Yale University Press, 2009).

20. See the critique of M. Neocleous, "The problem with normality: Taking exception to 'permanent emergency'," *Alternatives: Global, Local, Political* 31 (2006): 191–213.

21. The other three Reserved Forests in the Doyang–Dhansari valley did at this time not fall under the agreements.

22. K. V. K. Sundaram, *Report of the Advisor K.V.K. Sundaram on the Assam–Nagaland boundary* (New Delhi: GoI, Ministry of Home Affairs, 1976).

23. T. B. Hansen and F. Stepputat, eds. "Introduction," in *Sovereign bodies: Citizens, migrants and states in the postcolonial world*, (Princeton, NJ: Princeton University Press, 2005), 27.

24. For an official overview, see R. K. Shastri, *Report of the commission of inquiry on the incidents relating to the Assam–Nagaland border conflict (April–June 1985)* (New Delhi: GoI, Ministry of Home Affairs, 1987).

25. Government of Assam, *Facts about the Assam–Nagaland border* (Guwahati: GoA, 1985); Government of Nagaland, *Untold story about Merapani* (Kohima: GoN, 1985).

26. T. B. Hansen and F. Stepputat, eds. "Introduction," in *Sovereign bodies: Citizens, migrants and states in the postcolonial world*, (Princeton, NJ: Princeton University Press, 2005), 27.

27. H. Gohain, "Violent borders: Killings in Nagaland–Assam," *Economic and Political Weekly* 42 (2007): 3281–3282.

28. According to another claim, which was repeatedly made—but which is emblematic, but difficult to investigate—the Government of Nagaland had sent all the documents, including a map, that proved their claims to the Government of Assam, which however lost/destroyed all the documents. See also N. Kinghen, *Facts about the Nagaland–Assam boundary affairs* (Wokha: Lotha Hoho, 1985).

29. S. Baruah, *India against itself: Assam and the politics of nationality* (New Delhi: Oxford University Press, 2002), 21–43.

30. J. Scott, *The art of not being governed: An anarchist history of upland Southeast Asia* (New Haven, CT: Yale University Press, 2009), 242.

31. Alexander Mackenzie, *The north-east frontier of India* (New Delhi: Mittal Publications, 2007 [1884]), 89–90.

32. Edward Gait, *A history of Assam* (Guwahati: Bina Library, 2008 [1926]), 387.

33. S. Baruah, *India against itself: Assam and the politics of nationality* (New Delhi: Oxford University Press, 2002), 29.

34. S. Baruah, *India against itself: Assam and the politics of nationality* (New Delhi: Oxford University Press, 2002), 31; see also B. Kar, "When was the postcolonial? A history of policing impossible lines," in *Beyond counter-insurgency: Breaking the impasse in northeast India*, ed. S. Baruah (New Delhi: Oxford University Press, 2009), 49–77.

35. B. C. Allen *et al.*, *Gazetteer of Bengal and north-east India* (New Delhi: Mittal Publications, 2008 [1905]), 469.
36. B.C. Allen et al., *Gazetteer of Bengal and north-east India* (New Delhi: Mittal Publications, 2008 [1905]), 469.
37. K. V. K. Sundaram, *Report of the Advisor K.V.K. Sundaram on the Assam–Nagaland boundary* (New Delhi: GoI, Ministry of Home Affairs, 1976), 25.
38. See, for a discussion of the foothills, D. Kikon, "Borders, bagaans and bazaars: Locating the foothills along the Naga Hills in northeast India: An essay," *Biblio: A review of books* 8 (2008): 21–23.
39. A. Mackenzie, *The north-east frontier of India* (New Delhi: Mittal Publications, 2007 [1884]), 77.
40. These maps are meant as illustration and are not to scale and only indicative. For easy reference, the outline of Assam is the current state boundary.
41. We must be careful to equate the name Naga Hills District only with Naga tribes. Currently, what was the Naga Hills District has been divided, with a part in Nagaland state, but also a part in Karbi Anglong district, with large Karbi and Dimasa populations, although with a Naga presence.
42. B. Bhattacharyya, *The troubled border: Some facts about boundary disputes between Assam–Nagaland, Assam–Arunachal Pradesh, Assam–Meghalaya and Assam–Mizoram* (Guwahati: Lawyer's Book Stall, 1995), 16.
43. From undivided Assam, the new states of Arunachal Pradesh, Nagaland, Mizoram and Meghalaya were separated during the 1960s and 1970s. Nagaland still falls outside the normal territory of India as Indian nationals still officially need an Inner Line Permit to enter Nagaland, and foreign nationals need the very restrictive Protected Areas Permit. It is telling that the Nagaland Security Regulation, 1962 (no. 5 of 1962), giving wide prerogatives to the police and armed forces, was voted even before the State of Nagaland Act, 1962 (no. 22 of 1962) (Human Rights Watch, *Getting away with murder: 50 years of the Armed Forces (Special Powers) Act* (New York: HRW, 2008)). See also "Fifty-year disturbance: The Armed Forces Special Powers Act and exceptionalism in a South Asian periphery," special issue of *Contemporary South Asia* 17, 2009.
44. B. Suykens, "The tribal–forest nexus in law and society in India: Conflicting narratives," *Critical Asian Studies* 41 (2009): 381–402; see also S. Jewitt, "Europe's 'others'? Forestry policy and practices in colonial and postcolonial India," *Environment and Planning D: Society and Space* 13 (1995): 67–90.
45. C. Kindo and D. Minj, "Impact of Assam–Nagaland territorial dispute in the district of Golaghat, Assam," in *Conflict mapping and peace processes in northeast India*, ed. Lazar Jeyaseelan (Guwahati: North Eastern Social Research Centre, 2008), 25.
46. For a discussion of the land problem in one part of the DAB, Nambor Reserved Forest, see A. Saikia, "Forest land and peasant struggles in Assam, 2002–2007," *Journal of Peasant Studies* 35 (2008): 39–59.

47. See also B. Bhattacharyya, *The troubled border: Some facts about boundary disputes between Assam–Nagaland, Assam–Arunachal Pradesh, Assam–Meghalaya and Assam–Mizoram* (Guwahati: Lawyer's Book Stall, 1995), 23.
48. A. Gupta and J. Ferguson, "Beyond 'culture': Space, identity, and the politics of difference," *Cultural Anthropology* 7 (1992): 11–12.
49. L. Malkki, "National geographic: The rooting of peoples and the territorialization of national identity among scholars and refugees," *Cultural Anthropology* 7 (1992): 24–44.
50. A. Saikia, "Forest land and peasant struggles in Assam, 2002–2007," *Journal of Peasant Studies* 35 (2008): 39–59.
51. At regular intervals, different government ministers have proposed to give *patta* to the people living in the DAB, which seems almost impossible to negotiate between the two states (interview with former Assamese Minister of Agriculture, Golaghat district, December 2008).
52. A. Gupta, "Blurred boundaries: The discourse of corruption, the culture of politics, and the imagined state," *American Ethnologist* 22 (1995): 375–402; S. K. Das, *Public office, private interest: Bureaucracy and corruption in India* (New Delhi: Oxford University Press, 2001); V. Das, "The signature of the state: The paradox of illegibility," in *Anthropology in the margins of the state*, ed. V. Das and D. Poole (Santa Fe, NM: School of American Research Press and James Currey, 2004), 225–252.
53. N. Vandekerckhove, "Only ghosts are ruling the forest: Land tenure and the distant state in the Kachugaon Reserved Forest, Assam," *Current Anthropology*, forthcoming, under review.
54. For more info, see Marcus Franke, *War and nationalism in South Asia: The Indian state and the Nagas* (London and New York: Routledge, 2009).
55. N. Vaughan-Williams, "Borders, territory, law," *International Political Sociology* 2 (2008): 333.
56. A. Gupta and J. Ferguson, "Beyond 'culture': Space, identity, and the politics of difference," *Cultural Anthropology* 7 (1992): 17.

References

Agamben, G. *State of exception.* Chicago, IL: Chicago University Press, 2005.
Allen, B. C., *et al. Gazetteer of Bengal and north-east India.* New Delhi: Mittal Publications, 2008 [1905].
Amoore, L. "Biometric borders: Governing mobilities in the war on terror." *Political Geography* 25, no. 3 (2006): 336–351.
Baruah, S. *India against itself: Assam and the politics of nationality.* New Delhi: Oxford University Press, 2002.
Bhattacharyya, B. *The troubled border: Some facts about boundary disputes between Assam–Nagaland, Assam–Arunachal Pradesh, Assam–Meghalaya and Assam–Mizoram.* Guwahati: Lawyer's Book Stall, 1995.
Das, S. K. *Public office, private interest: Bureaucracy and corruption in India.* New Delhi: Oxford University Press, 2001.

Das, V. "The signature of the state: The paradox of illegibility." In *Anthropology in the margins of the state*, edited by V. Das and D. Poole. Santa Fe, NM: School of American Research Press and James Currey, 2004: 225–252.

Das, V. and D. Poole, eds. "State and its margins: Comparative ethnographies." In *Anthropology in the margins of the state*, Santa Fe, NM: School of American Research Press and James Currey, 2004: 3–34.

Edkins, J. and V. Pin-Fat. "Through the wire: Relations of power and relations of violence." *Millennium: Journal of International Studies* 34, no. 1 (2005): 1–24.

Franke, M. *War and nationalism in South Asia: The Indian state and the Nagas.* London and New York: Routledge, 2009.

Gait, E. *A history of Assam.* Guwahati: Bina Library, 2008 [1926].

Gohain, H. "Violent borders: Killings in Nagaland–Assam." *Economic and Political Weekly* 42, no. 32 (2007): 3280–3283.

Government of Assam. *Facts about the Assam–Nagaland border.* Guwahati: GoA, 1985.

Government of Nagaland. *Untold story about Merapani.* Kohima: GoN, 1985.

Gregory, D. "The black flag: Guantanamo Bay and the space of exception." *Geografiska Annaler: Series B, Human Geography* 88, no. 4 (2006): 405–427.

Gupta, A. "Blurred boundaries: The discourse of corruption, the culture of politics, and the imagined state." *American Ethnologist* 22, no. 2 (1995): 375–402.

Gupta, A. and J. Ferguson. "Beyond 'culture': Space, identity, and the politics of difference." *Cultural Anthropology* 7, no. 1 (1992): 6–23.

Hansen, T. B. and F. Stepputat, eds. "Introduction." In *Sovereign bodies: Citizens, migrants and states in the postcolonial world*, Princeton, NJ: Princeton University Press, 2005: 1–38.

Hansen, T. B. and F. Stepputat. "Sovereignty revisited." *Annual Review of Anthropology* 35 (2006): 295–315.

Human Rights Watch. *Getting away with murder: 50 years of the Armed Forces (Special Powers) Act.* New York: HRW, 2008.

Huysmans, J. "International politics of exception: Competing visions of international political order between law and politics." *Alternatives: Global, Local, Political* 3, no. 2 (2006): 135–165.

Huysmans, J. "The jargon of the exception: On Schmitt, Agamben and the absence of political society." *International Political Sociology* 2, no. 2 (2008): 165–183.

Jewitt, S. "Europe's 'others'? Forestry policy and practices in colonial and postcolonial India." *Environment and Planning D: Society and Space* 13, no. 1 (1995): 67–90.

Johns, F. "Guantánamo Bay and the annihilation of the exception." *European Journal of International Law* 16, no. 4 (2005): 613–635.

Jones, R. "Agents of exception: Border security and the marginalization of Muslims in India." *Environment and Planning D: Society and Space* 27, no. 5 (2009): 879–897.

Kar, B. "When was the postcolonial? A history of policing impossible lines." In *Beyond counter-insurgency: Breaking the impasse in northeast India*, edited by S. Baruah. New Delhi: Oxford University Press, 2009: 49–77.

Kikon, D. "Borders, bagaans and bazaars: Locating the foothills along the Naga Hills in northeast India: An essay." *Biblio: A review of books* 8 (2008): 21–23.

Kindo, C. and D. Minj. "Impact of Assam–Nagaland territorial dispute in the district of Golaghat, Assam." In *Conflict mapping and peace processes in northeast India*, edited by L. Jeyaseelan. Guwahati: North Eastern Social Research Centre, 2008: 8–53.

Kinghen, N. *Facts about the Nagaland–Assam boundary affairs.* Wokha: Lotha Hoho, 1985.

Mackenzie, A. *The north-east frontier of India.* New Delhi: Mittal Publications, 2007 [1884].

Malkki, L. "National geographic: The rooting of peoples and the territorialization of national identity among scholars and refugees." *Cultural Anthropology* 7, no. 1 (1992): 24–44.

Megoran, N. "The critical geopolitics of the Uzbekistan–Kyrgyzstan Ferghana Valley boundary dispute, 1999–2000." *Political Geography* 23, no. 6 (2004): 731–764.

Minca, C. "The return of the camp." *Progress in Human Geography* 29, no. 4 (2005): 405–412.

Neocleous, M. "The problem with normality: Taking exception to 'permanent emergency'." *Alternatives: Global, Local, Political* 31, no. 2 (2006): 191–213.

Prozorov, S. "X/Xs: Towards a general theory of the exception." *Alternatives: Global, Local, Political* 30, no. 1 (2005): 81–112.

Raeymaekers, T. "The silent encroachment of the frontier: A politics of transborder trade in the Semliki Valley (Congo–Uganda)." *Political Geography* 28, no. 1 (2009): 55–65.

Reid-Henry, S. "Exceptional sovereignty? Guantanamo Bay and the re-colonial present." *Antipode* 39, no. 4 (2007): 627–648.

Saikia, A. "Forest land and peasant struggles in Assam, 2002–2007." *Journal of Peasant Studies* 35, no. 1 (2008): 39–59.

Salter, M. B. "When the exception becomes the rule: Borders, sovereignty, and citizenship." *Citizenship Studies* 12, no. 4 (2008): 365–380.

Schmitt, C. *Political Theology: Four chapters on the concept of sovereignty.* Chicago, IL: The University of Chicago Press, 2005 [1934].

Scott, J. *The art of not being governed: An anarchist history of upland Southeast Asia.* New Haven, CT: Yale University Press, 2009.

Shastri, R. K. *Report of the commission of inquiry on the incidents relating to the Assam–Nagaland border conflict (April–June 1985).* New Delhi: GoI, Ministry of Home Affairs, 1987.

Steinmetz, G. "Introduction: Culture and the state." In *State/culture: State-formation after the cultural turn*, edited by G. Steinmetz. Ithaca, NY: Cornell University Press, 1999: 1–50.

Sundaram, K. V. K. *Report of the Advisor K.V.K. Sundaram on the Assam–Nagaland boundary.* New Delhi: GoI, Ministry of Home Affairs, 1976.

Suykens, B. "The tribal–forest nexus in law and society in India: Conflicting narratives." *Critical Asian Studies* 41, no. 3 (2009): 381–402.

Vandekerckhove, N. "No land, no peace: Dynamics of violent conflict and land use in Assam, India." Unpublished PhD dissertation, Ghent University, 2010.

Vaughan-Williams, N. "Borders, territory, law." *International Political Sociology* 2, no. 4 (2008): 322–338.

Vaughan-Williams, N. "Security, law, borders: Spaces of exclusion." *International Political Sociology* 2, no. 4 (2008): 322–338.

PART IV

"Bringing the State Back In": Borders, War Economies and Peace Economies

CHAPTER 8

Get It While You Can: Governance between Wars in the Uganda–South Sudan Borderland[1]

Wolfgang Zeller

Introduction

"Why do you keep that back door of your office open?" The Ugandan immigration officer at the Oraba/Kaya border post grins knowingly. "You can see this bad and steep road we have here. Those big trucks for Sudan and Congo, some of them cannot stop. We hear a commotion; a truck horn is blowing, people shouting. Then we must run. They have crushed our office before".

The hazardous slope outside the border post is part of a major transport route winding its way from the Kenyan port of Mombasa 1,700 km away to Juba, the political and economic center of South Sudan. At Oraba, a rusty cable strung across muddy potholes symbolizes the Ugandan–Sudanese border. It holds up the blond driver of a battered Land Cruiser and his Ugandan girlfriend, but not for long. The Swedish man is well known here. He imports gourmet food and alcohol from overseas for a well-endowed clientele of Sudan People's Liberation Army (SPLA) officer-bureaucrats and western development aid workers in Juba. My next interview with the head of the local Uganda Revenue Authority office across the road is slow-going and official, but between a beer and a Champion's League satellite broadcast at the new motel bar, he gets more talkative about his past and future. Apparently a well-educated man, he claims his father is a former Ugandan government minister and is convinced there will soon be war again in South Sudan. "That will be good for me. Then I will start a business here, on the safe side of the border. I have all the connections and can easily make ten times my current salary".

Several protracted and interrelated conflicts and the streams of refugees they set off have been washing over the Ugandan–Sudanese borderland like waves since the outbreak of the first North–South civil war on the eve of Sudan's independence on January 1, 1956. In Uganda, independence from Great Britain on October 9, 1962, soon turned out to be the beginning of changing but consistently violent postcolonial regimes. Each incumbent took power militarily and committed major atrocities against real and suspected opponents. As a direct result of this continuous volatility, official norms of governance have been in suspension for decades and the exception has become the rule. Over time, the cracks, gaps and gaping holes of eroding administrative brickwork—to the extent that it ever had a real-life presence here in the colonial and postcolonial period—have been filled with what I call *borderland governance.*

Niles Hansen defines borderlands as "sub-national areas whose economic and social life is directly and significantly affected by proximity to an international boundary".[2] Since international boundaries are limits to jurisdiction, all borderland settings are by definition characterized by the presence of more than one regime of official regulation. The stakes are high for the central state authority to demonstrate it is indeed fully in control right up to, but also not across, that red dotted line. Here lies the root for what, according to Paul Nugent and Anthony I. Asiwaju, imparts a paradoxical quality to all boundaries: landscapes, history and daily life generally "spill over" state boundaries, in particular in postcolonial Africa.[3]

Various scholars in recent years have become interested in what Nikolas Rose and Michael Watts call "(un-)governable spaces",[4] where the exercise of public authority becomes associated with—or challenged by—multiple, partly overlapping, territories, regulatory regimes and group identifications.[5] Veena Das and Deborah Poole develop the concept of margins of the state, which is not exclusively territorial, but also embraces the relevance of territorial boundaries as margins. Rather than seeing these as wild, uncontrolled or unstable frontier zones that are waiting to be pacified, the margins often manifest as socially productive zones in their own right. Margins can thus be sites where lawmaking and other activities of the central state's representatives are not just evaded, but actively transformed and "colonized" by other more or less organized practices, thus generating important political and economic outcomes that may have a decisive impact on state formation in a broader sense.[6]

Besides institutional and regulatory pluralism, another key feature of *borderland governance* is the often dynamic, sometimes volatile nature of conditions in borderlands. Major changes in the political and economic environment, new infrastructure or a combination of these can transform a sleepy backwater border post into a bustling node of transnational business in a matter of years or even months. Whether such booms are sustainable is another matter, though. Dobler describes how, following the end of the Angolan civil war, the Namibian border town Oshikango went through several phases of rapid development—from the early days reminiscent of a Wild West boomtown to the arrival of more established and cautious large enterprises. State actors soon followed in the tracks of the entrepreneurial pioneers, and the measures they sought to introduce in order to cash in on and regulate the boom eventually choked off some of the conditions that had driven it in the first place.[7] The town of Bibia, which I examine in this chapter, has clear similarities with Oshikango in its "wild days": since open conflict subsided in southern Sudan in 2005 and in northern Uganda in 2006, this border town and the greater region have experienced a rapid expansion of investment, construction and cross-border trade. From the official point of view of the Ugandan government, the area in 2006 constituted a no-man's-land void of legitimate institutionalized forms of administration. With massive support from aid donors, the Ugandan government has in recent years continued in its long-term effort to assert control over northern Uganda, albeit with a shift in emphasis from coercive/military action to "reconstruction and development". It is important to understand that this process does not take place in a regulatory and political vacuum. From what I have observed, there was no institutional tabula rasa in the borderland in 2005/2006, and from the vantage point of various more or less well-established actors in the area the central government continues to encroach upon their territory and room for maneuver. Considering the recent history of continuous warfare and atrocities in the South Sudan borderland, this is anything but a politically neutral and technocratic process of "development".

A crucial element of the setting examined in this chapter is the continuing political volatility of the Ugandan–South Sudanese borderland, which has two dimensions. First, there is a long history of opposition among the Acholi people of northern Uganda against the National Resistance Movement (NRM), the ruling party led by President Yoweri Museveni. Second, there is widespread anticipation of more conflict to break out in the region in the near future. Whether this will really happen or not is not of primary relevance to the analysis here. What counts is the *expectation*—by both residents and frontline representatives of state authority—that the long years of living with the exception as the rule are not yet over.

At this point, it is necessary to engage explicitly with the argument made by Giorgio Agamben, who draws on Carl Schmitt's definition of the sovereign as "the one who decides on the state of exception" to conceptualize the deliberate perpetuation of an *Ausnahmezustand* (state of exception) as a way of the central state maintaining its power and projecting it into the margins.[8] I feel that this adequately describes one important aspect of events in northern Uganda and the greater region in recent years. Members of the Ugandan political and military leadership have for years argued that exceptional situations call for exceptional measures, meanwhile pursuing their own political and economic interests with very little restraint. As one result, the population of an entire region has been more or less forcefully removed from their land—which happens to be highly fertile—into 240 so-called "internally displaced people (IDP) camps". The claims to "protect" the civilian population and pursue "terrorists" have given the Ugandan government diplomatic and military leverage over powerful allies. Under the banner of "peacemaking", the Ugandan armed forces have ventured across the borders of Sudan, the Democratic Republic of Congo (DRC) and the Central African Republic (CAR) into areas that are rich in natural and mineral resources. Through their own, however well-intended, attempts to soften the impact of these actions on the wider population, a great number of international donor agencies have themselves become part of the perpetuation of a humanitarian quagmire. The Ugandan leadership's current assertions of political and administrative power in the former war zone often have a distinct military-like quality. Descending suddenly and with great force onto the borderland, they create temporarily and spatially limited, controlled situations within which the government can safely operate, and then retreat behind safe lines when the operation is deemed to be complete. And yet, the argument—that those at the center of state power make use of and perpetuate a state of exception to serve their own purpose—provides only a partial explanation for how power is constituted in the Ugandan–Sudanese borderland. Other forms of power at play here do not appear in the form of a single, coherently organized project. As a result, the conditions awaiting agents of the central state in this area compromise them into adapting to the borderland way of doing things. They find it necessary to cooperate with other powers that be—and their regulatory regimes—to achieve official objectives or because the opportunities to increase the state salary are too tempting to ignore. This is directly linked to the location on the edge of the state territory. Being on the edge of war is very important as well. Both the government's sudden, forceful and military-style attempts to reclaim the borderland and the wheeling and dealing in border boomtowns reeking of dust, diesel and beer appear to bear testimony to the same basic premise for action: "Get it while you can". A deep-seated and ambiguous anticipation prevails that the current conditions of relative peace will not prevail. It is ambiguous because of the interplay of danger and opportunity it entails, which is so typical for border boomtowns: one might get rich quickly but lose out if one is still around when circumstances take a turn for the worse. It is this ambiguity, which I consider to be a fundamental element of governance in borderlands with protracted violent conflict.

In the following sections, I will explore *borderland governance* further by taking the reader on a road trip from the Ugandan capital, Kampala, to the Sudanese border. Along the route, I will highlight examples of past and ongoing initiatives by the Ugandan government to assert its control over the former war zone, and show how these align or collide with other actors and institutions they encounter on the ground in the borderland. The first stop along the way is the town of Gulu in northern Uganda, now a fast-growing urban center with private enterprises, Ugandan government institutions and a lively circuit of development agencies engaged in the business of post-conflict development aid. Proceeding north toward the Sudanese border along a newly reconstructed major traffic artery, we then pass through the town of Atiak. Turned into an IDP camp under the Ugandan military's "protected village" scheme, Atiak was the site of a major massacre committed by members of the Lord's Resistance Army (LRA) in 1995. The journey ends further down the same road at the border post of Bibia. Like Oraba, this fast-booming town lies along a major transport route connecting the urban centers of Uganda and Southern Sudan with the greater region's main hub for global trade: Kenya's port of Mombasa. I will introduce a select cast of movers and shakers staying in or passing through Bibia, and highlight how and on what they thrive and survive in their bustling environment. I will then discuss and draw my final conclusions regarding the nature of *borderland governance*.

From Kampala to Gulu: "You Are All Here"—The Borderland from War Zone to Opportunity

Some four hours into the asphalt road journey from Kampala to Gulu, the bridge across the Victoria Nile at Karuma is a gateway into what until recently was a theater of war (figure 8.1). Uganda's violent history entered a new chapter after President Yoweri Museveni and his NRM party took power in 1986. A year later, the atrocities they committed against the Acholi people of northern Uganda led to the formation of the Lord's Resistance Movement and Army (LRM/A), which has fought a guerrilla insurgency ever since. From 1996, with economic development in the southern part of the country gaining momentum, the entire area between the Nile and the border with Sudan became a combat zone. Across the border, the second civil war between Sudan's Muslim-dominated north and predominantly Christian south was raging at the same time. As part of the Ugandan government's

Figure 8.1 Development town: Aid agency and commercial bank signs at a traffic junction in central Gulu. Photograph by the author.

counterinsurgency strategy, virtually the entire population of Acholiland was forced to abandon their livelihoods and moved into so-called "protected villages" for IDPs. The humanitarian label obscures that many of these new settlements were rather forced internment camps.[9] Here the Ugandan government kept what they considered a politically volatile population under close supervision, more or less adequately fed and sheltered with donor money.

In 2002, the Uganda People's Defence Force (UPDF) launched Operation Iron Fist. This massive attempt to hammer through a military victory over the LRA involved prolonged cross-border operations on the territory of Sudan, where the LRA had meanwhile established its guerrilla stronghold. The offensive backfired. The LRA retaliated against both civilian and military targets, resulting in more widespread suffering for the regional population than ever before, on both sides of the border. Stuck between two wars, the Acholi-inhabited areas became a no-man's-land with isolated and temporary pockets of government control. Gulu made international news headlines in 2005 as tens of thousands of so-called "night commuters" sought shelter from the raids and abductions that terrorized the surrounding rural villages. The border with Sudan was officially closed at the time and the only immigration and customs unit issuing documents for travel and transport between Sudan and Uganda was in Kampala.

A study funded by the Swedish International Development Cooperation Agency (SIDA) reported in 2008 that "a renewed sense of possibility has emerged regarding the rebuilding of the Northern Ugandan Economy".[10] As key reasons, it cited the 2005 Comprehensive Peace Agreement (CPA), which paved the way toward South Sudan's independence in 2011 and the (ultimately unsuccessful) attempt to reach a negotiated settlement between the LRA and Ugandan government in the 2006–2008 Juba peace process. Those on board the white SUVs of aid agencies and diplomatic missions traveling south from Gulu to Kampala on fresh World Bank–funded tarmac[11] were reporting back to headquarters that things were getting better up north. The consensus in early 2009 was that security is sufficient to go ahead with development in northern Uganda. Gradually, the extensive no-man's-land of the war zones of northern Uganda and southern Sudan was being brought under government control. Donor agencies were financing and coordinating the construction of roads, water and sanitation, electricity and administrative infrastructure projects. Numerous programs were facilitating the return of people to their farmlands and villages of origin. Large areas in the regional development hubs of Gulu, Kitgum and Juba turned into sprawling construction sites for new banks, hotels, shops and petrol stations. Donor agencies established offices in leafy neighborhoods, and luxury consumables were available to those who could afford them.

Uganda's political elite meanwhile was skillfully milking development aid funds for their own purposes. The Northern Uganda Recovery Programs (NURP I and II), which began in 1996, and the Northern Uganda Social Action Fund (NUSAF), an initiative of the Ugandan government primarily funded by the World Bank, have in the past gained notoriety for systematic wastefulness and corruption.[12] At its official launch in 2007, the 3-year Peace, Recovery and Development Plan (PRDP) overseen by the Office of the Prime Minister of Uganda had a budget of 400 million euros, 70 percent of which was to be donor funded. By mid-2009, the PRDP was still largely bogged down in controversy and a failure to come up with clear and transparent guidelines for the selection of individual projects. The Ugandan government had revised its contribution for the 2008/2009 budget to a sum below the cost of a new executive jet for President Museveni.[13] Integrated sections of the PRDP, like the 30-million-euro Northern Uganda Rehabilitation Programme (NUREP) funded by the European Commission, were nevertheless able to function on their own and moving ahead with implementation.[14]

Without the support of external donor funding, the Ugandan Ministry of Information and National Guidance has in recent years organized boot camps for so-called "political education" of civil servants and youth in nearly all districts of Acholiland. Participants were lectured on "patriotism and history" taught from the viewpoint of the ruling NRM party. Physical exercise and the encouragement of obedience through corporal punishment were also on the curriculum. Trainings like these had been carried out in Uganda for decades, but were few and sporadic in northern Uganda during the war. In 2007, President Museveni stated that he wished to make it compulsory "for all able-bodied Ugandans" to complete such programs (*Daily Monitor* July 25, 2007). Government agencies and private security companies also used the training events to recruit unemployed youth into their services, and later in NRM's mobilization campaigns for Uganda's 2011 national parliamentary and presidential elections.

In October 2009, another state initiative with a distinctly top-down and militaristic character took place near the Ugandan–Sudanese border and outside the town of Kitgum. Some 1,200 troops, about half of them US military, and the rest from Uganda, Burundi, Kenya, Rwanda and Tanzania, took part in an exercise supposed to "improve interoperability and build partner capacity to respond to complex humanitarian emergencies".[15] It took the form of a simulated coordinated response to a natural disaster, a pandemic flu outbreak in Uganda and other humanitarian crises. Concerns raised by the exercise planners at the US military's Africa Command headquarters in Stuttgart, Germany, regarding possible "crowd control" problems were justified, as to the war-experienced residents of Kitgum the display of military might descending from the skies in helicopters was frightfully familiar. A trial immunization campaign, which took place as part of the exercise, had only limited resources, however. As a result, several thousand residents who had been queuing up in vain, hoping to receive some form of treatment (for or against what exactly had not been communicated to them), were left disappointed when the exercise teams packed up and took to the skies again.

The last two examples[16] illustrate both how a militaristic operational logic "leaks" over into less overtly coercive measures designed to bring state control back into the borderland—and how politically volatile these initiatives are. The following example gives further evidence of this continuation of warfare as governance, as well as the networked nature of the actors involved. Following the collapse of the Juba peace process, on December 14, 2008, a coalition of Ugandan, South Sudanese and Congolese armed forces launched Operation Lightning Thunder (OLT) in the LRA's suspected new hideout, Garamba National Park in the borderland of DRC and South Sudan. It received diplomatic, logistical and material support from the US government and military. Like Operation Iron Fist, it failed to hunt down LRA leader Joseph Kony and most of his men, instead sparking a new LRA killing spree and refugee crisis in that area, which soon spilled over into the territory of the Central African Republic.[17] The prospect of either rebel or government forces (or both) gaining access to suspected deposits of diamonds and other high-value minerals in this vast and largely unexplored area evoked memories of the lucrative extraction schemes that Ugandan and Congolese government troops, rebel groups, transnational traffickers and even members of the UN forces in eastern Congo have been previously known to be involved in.[18] Senior officers in the Ugandan army have in the past also diverted state pension funds for veterans and salaries for thousands of soldiers who only existed on paper into their own pocket. In another scam, officers resold fuel, provisions and ammunition that had supposedly been used in the battlefield. UPDF's costly cross-border adventures are carried out in nearly perfect insulation from public scrutiny. Enquiries are rejected with reference to "security concerns", while journalists, activists and opposition politicians who insist on asking too many questions are subjected to more hands-on measures.

The Ugandan government has been typically tight-lipped regarding the details of OLT, which undeniably failed to meet its official key objective: to arrest LRA leader Joseph Kony. The UPDF claims that they raided the supposed command camp of the LRA in Garamba Park, found it deserted, but managed to retrieve the LRA leader's laptop. In a press conference held on March 16, 2009, UPDF speaker Lieutenant Colonel Felix Kulayigye announced that the computer contained "a list of LRA financiers and sympathizers" and that "the list is big". He declined to mention names, but said "politicians, civil servants, bankers, the media and NGOs" were among them. "Time will come when we will mention them. Personally, I know some", he added.[19]

The Ugandan government's attempt to reassert control over its side of the borderland is embedded in a transnational web of donors and allies, and, whether coercive or benevolent in nature, there is always an element of ambiguity what the actual intentions are of those involved. Are the schemes of Ugandan government and army members trying to secure political and material advantages merely isolated incidents or are they part of more general patterns of governance and realpolitik in this post(?)-conflict setting? Can a line be drawn between donor agencies selflessly working to help ordinary people overcome the trauma of war and a government that has brutalized its own people? Are the politics of peace fundamentally different from those during open warfare? Instead of answering these questions, I will end this section with an attempt to understand what a senior member of the Ugandan military makes of the recent flurry of development activities in northern Uganda and the greater region. On April 23, 2009, a high-profile workshop sponsored by the Danish government was held in Gulu to discuss the "lessons learned" from the (by that time already failed) Juba peace process. Lieutenant Colonel

Kulayigye attended the meeting. He reiterated the government point of view that a military solution was the only possible way forward and that OLT had been a great success. During a coffee break, Kulayigye made a less rehearsed comment about the issue of American military support for OLT, which he had earlier declined to acknowledge. When I pointed out the Americans were militarily and politically engaged in the region and had "strategic interests" there, he responded: "Yes, but you are *all* here". This statement lends itself to various interpretations. I offer the following: The Ugandan government is not the only major player in the reconstruction of the country's northern part and is keenly aware of this, and of the country's geostrategic importance. Northern Uganda's depopulated rural areas have great potential for agribusiness investment. Substantial reserves of oil and uranium have been discovered in Uganda and Southern Sudan in recent years. Eastern DRC has very significant deposits of strategic minerals, and the greater region is widely regarded as a frontier zone of Islam and Christianity. Kulayigye was only stating the obvious: fair-skinned people like myself from each and every industrialized country were indeed "all here", and for good reasons—this land is very rich in resources and opportunities. And Gulu has become an important hub to access them.

From Gulu to Atiak: Fearing Past and Future Wars

The distance by road from Gulu to Bibia on the border with South Sudan is about 100 km and the town of Atiak lies 65 km north of Gulu along the same road, Highway A104 (figure 8.2). With funding from the World Bank, this nightmare of mud and potholes was transformed into a smooth asphalt band during 2011. Tarring of the remaining 120 km from the border to South Sudan's new capital Juba also commenced in February 2011, with funding from the United States Agency for International Development (USAID) and the South Sudanese government. Heavy lorry traffic on the road has increased noticeably since 2007, a clear sign of South Sudan's growing hunger for imported consumer goods and its attempts to shake off the Khartoum government's grip on the vital supply lines of Juba. For a brief period in 2007, Atiak had been the most forward immigration and customs checkpoint maintained by the Ugandan government in this part of the borderland. By 2009, however, Atiak saw little more of the increasing traffic than passing clouds of dust. The memories of another chapter of Atiak's more recent history are not likely to move on as quickly, though.

On April 20, 1995, some 300 LRA fighters rounded up the civilian inhabitants of Atiak and declared they were traitors for allowing UPDF to move them into this "protected village". Around 200 men and boys were killed

Figure 8.2 Memorial site in Atiak on the 14th anniversary of the massacre. Photograph by the author.

by firing squads while women and girls were forced to watch.[20] The small local UPDF deployment, which was supposed to protect the inhabitants, was located at the center of the village—behind a human shield of civilians—and escaped the massacre. The incident marked the beginning of a new phase of the war in Acholiland. A year later, the Ugandan government declared all territory outside the marked boundaries of "protected villages" as "rebel areas". No one could move without fear of being instantaneously killed or arrested under suspicion of insurgency activity. Atiak was also subjected to this policy, and according to local sources this was a period of extensive violence and forced recruitment carried out by government forces.[21] Both warring parties, in other words, brutalized the people of Atiak. Throughout Acholiland, residents have often expressed the feeling that they were caught between two fires during the war.[22] The atrocities inflicted on the population by the LRA tended to be more extreme and spectacular than the often subtle and structural violence by the UPDF, but both have left deep wounds. From conversations with the inhabitants of Atiak and other settlements in northern Uganda, four distinct but closely connected concerns emerge, all of which question the dominant official narrative of a new era of peace.

The first issue causing concern for a peaceful future on both sides of the borderland is the situation in Sudan. South Sudan became a sovereign independent state on July 9, 2011. However, the implementation of key components of the 2005 CPA including the demarcation of sections of the new border remains highly contested beyond the date of independence. Armed factions in a South Sudan awash with weapons are proliferating and it remains to be seen if the SPLA government can manage the transition from guerrilla fighters to democratic government while at the same time asserting the monopoly of legitimate violence.

The second concern is rooted in the unclear whereabouts of the LRA's enigmatic leader Joseph Kony. The Ugandan government and development agencies argue it is extremely unlikely that Kony and the LRA will be able to terrorize northern Uganda again. His powerful presence is still felt throughout the region, nevertheless. One former senior member of the LRA had this view on the matter: "Oh, don't think they are not here [in northern Uganda]. There is no limit to those guys. Believe me, I know that the LRA is everywhere!" The same informant was skeptical that the war has ended for good: "Even if you kill Joseph Kony the war can drag on and on. Someone else will just take over. And don't be fooled, the UPDF will make sure people get reasons to continue fighting".[23] In northern Uganda it is a well-established fact that the boundaries of who is in the LRA and who is not are blurred. Like any guerrilla army, its members and associates often lead double lives—one "in the bush", the other "in town"—with constant movement back and forth between these two states of existence.[24] A senior employee of Gulu University explained the delicate situation he finds himself in on any given day:

> The LRA are here in Gulu, even in my office they just visit or call me. Now, as you have seen we have many Americans coming, like those Christian students, all these donors, and even UPDF visit my office also. So you can imagine I feel a little bit hot sometimes.[25]

A third concern is that of recurring political violence. Opposition against Museveni and his government continues to be strong among the Acholi, and government harassment of opposition politicians and their supporters is a routine exercise throughout Uganda. Election times in particular are periods of heightened suspicion, acute fear and political witch hunts. Journalists, politicians and activists are routinely arrested and prosecuted on dodgy charges, are beaten up by unknown thugs or disappear altogether. "Things will turn really bad with elections", one member of staff at a Gulu-based research institution put it in 2009. This turned out to be an accurate prediction of events before and especially after the 2011 election. Asked if he hoped for a regime change, he responded:

> I have to vote for Museveni and told my family to do the same. Museveni has to win, that is our only chance of avoiding total chaos. He will never accept

defeat, not by voting, not by arms. If someone else is elected, be sure to leave this country immediately. He cannot accept defeat and he has the love of very many soldiers.[26]

The fourth issue is land tenure—a political and social minefield in Acholiland. As IDP (internally displaced persons) camps across northern Uganda like the one in Atiak are gradually dissolved, many inhabitants no longer have anywhere to return to. Former neighbors cannot determine the location of tenure boundaries anymore, since family members who could recognize landmarks have died. The physical landscape has in many places changed dramatically as the UPDF used scorched-earth tactics during the war as part (or arguably under the pretence) of counterinsurgency measures. The persons and institutions representing customary Acholi land tenure have thus become a casualty of protracted warfare themselves. In some cases, entire clans now lay claim to the same areas of land and face the prospect of drawn-out court battles. While such problems are a common by-product of long-term conflict, other evidence suggests that access to the Acholi's highly fertile land has been playing a key role in the beginning and escalation of this conflict all along. Members of Uganda's ruling elite all the way up to the president's family have since the early 1990s made various statements, both public and classified, in which they acknowledge the commercial potential of the Acholi areas, while denouncing the alleged inability of the inhabitants to put the land to productive use. They now stand accused of profiteering from large-scale agricultural schemes set up in areas rendered vacant when the UPDF forced people to move off their ancestral lands into the camps.[27] In 2003, the president's brother and former senior army officer Salim Saleh himself proposed his vision for a public–private scheme titled "Security and Production Programme", under which all Acholi customary land that was "not tilled, being grazed on, or privately registered" would be turned into militarized working farms, with local youth recruited and trained by the government to protect the fields. The scheme was met with fierce opposition from many Acholi, but large areas have since been incorporated into fenced plots owned by "big men" and guarded by UPDF troops or private security companies with ties to the leadership.[28] Widespread encroachment of illegal charcoal production further adds to the deterioration of the Acholi cultural landscape. The fuel enters long-distance trade networks controlled by politically well-connected entrepreneurs, which supply urban markets like Kampala and Juba. The land question is therefore charged with fear that the seeds of future conflict have been already sowed. A Gulu-based lawyer working on land tenure cases explains: "Maybe one war is over, but land is the next one. And that is a serious one because no force or superpower in the world can do anything about it".[29] In Atiak, many residents hesitate to return to their ancestral land and sow what they do not expect to reap. Trade along the new transnational transport route now running through Atiak affords other possibilities to make a living, but after the Atiak border checkpoint moved 35 km further on up the road in 2007, the new place of opportunity became the town of Bibia.

From Atiak to Bibia: A Ugandan Border Boomtown

Bibia can be best described as three towns in one: IDP camp, garrison town and frontier Las Vegas. Each of these has its own logic but all are a direct result of its setting on the border. Bibia is the last settlement along Highway A105 until, after another 8 km of road through the no-man's-land, it reaches a road and pedestrian bridge crossing a sidearm of the Nile and the actual boundary. On the other side of the bridge lies the South Sudanese border checkpoint and town of Nimule (figure 8.3).

The IDP camp of Bibia consists of a densely built area of deteriorating grass-thatched huts that used to shelter up to 6,500 inhabitants at the height of the war, a small health station, a school and a church. Bibia was previously in the worst affected and least accessible part of northern Uganda's war zone. Some of the earlier inhabitants have moved back from IDP camps into the

Figure 8.3 In transit: Taking a rest in Bibia before crossing the border into South Sudan. Photograph by the author.

area between Bibia and Nimule, though in interviews they are reluctant to speak about the past as much as they are about what may come. As one villager put it, somewhat cryptically, when asked about his expectations: "The future—we can't go there".[30] In mid-2009, only some 400 people were still permanently living in the Bibia IDP camp as donor agency and government efforts were under way to (re)settle the rest. However, many of the last inhabitants were mentally ill, were substance addicted or had no next of kin left alive. Living casualties of war, they were not to be moved easily, despite mounting pressure. In September 2011, Resident District Commissioner and NRM party member Milton Odongo announced plans to evict the by then remaining 150 inhabitants. He argued the dilapidated buildings of the former camp were a "security threat", while a property developer, who now owned the land occupied by the remnants of the IDP camp, claimed it was "obstructing development".[31]

Close to the IDP camp—though clearly separated from it—lays a small military camp. It consists of a circle of army tents for about 100–150 UPDF soldiers surrounding a few more permanent structures at its center. Between the IDP and military camp areas, and just beside the main highway, lies the border checkpoint of Bibia. This has clearly been the single most important factor in the relative boom Bibia has experienced in recent years. Any vehicle arriving from or going to Sudan has to stop here. The 8 km between Bibia and the border is therefore technically a no-man's-land. It was not always so. The old Ugandan customs and immigration station close to the Nimule Bridge is now a cluster of ruins riddled with bullet holes and pro-LRA graffiti. A new Ugandan border checkpoint and police station have been under construction near the old site since 2008, but they were still not completed 3 years later. While concerns over South Sudan's future stability persist, the Ugandan authorities apparently are in no hurry to establish a permanent presence on the borderline. Privately funded construction projects meanwhile establish more facts on the ground in Bibia.

By 2009, it had all the characteristics of a frontier boomtown in the American Wild West, transplanted into twenty-first-century Africa. The 200 m of Highway A104 leading up to the checkpoint was lined on both sides with hastily built structures at various stages of completion. Corrugated iron roofs rattling in the dusty wind were sheltering small kiosks, basic overnight hotels, eateries and bars with pool tables, plenty of alcohol and young women looking for "boyfriends" among the truckers and soldiers. A town dentist advertised hands-on pain relief. The magic of reanimating mangled truck axles with a hammer and a blowtorch was performed in roadside workshops by greased-smeared explorers of the frontiers of mechanical ingenuity. Bibia's main street was open for business 24/7, its soundtrack consisting of pumping

rhythm, power generators, truck engines and occasional outbursts of intox-
icated patrons. Airtime vouchers and cell phone battery chargers were for
sale, and high above it all stood a brand-new transmission tower sending
Uganda Telecom's 3G network signal deeply into Southern Sudan. On any
given morning, a long line of trucks was waiting for the immigration and
customs offices to open at 7 am. The border is not only good for business; it
is the business of Bibia.

On the afternoon of April 27, 2009, a Toyota Land Cruiser pulled up at
the border checkpoint. A senior member of a Pakistani family dynasty special-
ized in importing used vehicles from Asia into Eastern and Southern Africa
entered the Uganda Revenue Authority (URA) station with his assistant and
emerged thirty minutes later, checking lists and taking notes. The purpose of
his visit: to track down several vehicles, which had recently disappeared from
the company parking lot in Kampala. The businessman quite openly admitted he had just paid a minor bribe to a URA official in order to speed up the
process of cross-checking official records. He explained the Sudanese border
to him represented the horizon of utter chaos and that he had no interest to
cross it. He was only interested in the paper trail of his stolen merchandise so
he could keep his books in order, as required by Ugandan law. The URA officers were merely selling him a service he should not have to, but was willing
to pay for.

Stolen cars are not the only commodities crossing the Ugandan–Sudanese
border through Bibia without full or correct documentation. Fred Oroma
(name changed) is a man who knows, and is eager to talk about this topic.
Sipping his second or third afternoon beer while observing the passing trucks
with expert glances, he occasionally shouted instructions to an assistant to
look under a tarpaulin. Oroma is working for the Bank of Uganda. To gather
more accurate economic data, the bank in cooperation with the Ugandan
Bureau of Statistics has since 2005 prepared an annual Informal Cross Border Trade Survey Report. Fred Oroma and his colleagues operate at all of
Uganda's major road border-crossing points, collecting their own independent export and import data and reporting them back to headquarters in
Kampala. Oroma claimed he knew exactly who smuggles what across the
Bibia border, but that it was not his job to prevent it from happening.
A cynical and intelligent man, he claimed to see the larger picture of what
he described as a "great conspiracy". He backed his views with details on
big-shot politicians supposedly in cahoots with transport companies moving commodities across the border and past fiscal regulations at astronomical
profit. Alcohol eventually triumphed over Fred Oromo's attempts to construct a coherent narrative, but his surveyor colleagues at the Oraba and
Mayo border posts hundreds of kilometers away later recognized his name,
and confirmed and added further details to his claims.

Figure 8.4 Open for business: Bibia currency traders' office. Photograph by Cecilie Lanken Verma.

One group of young men making a handsome profit at the Bibia border is the Association of Currency Traders. To stay in business, membership in this association is imperative and freelancing is not an option. Most of the traders maintain a second home in Kampala. Between them, the dealers are fluent in all regional dialects spoken in Uganda. "When Ugandans come back from Sudan they like to see that 'oh, there is somebody from my home, I can trust to change my money here'". Victor (name changed), a smart-looking young man, was tending to one of 16 tables lined up outside the border checkpoint and stacked with neat piles of cash. At intervals, some of the tables seemed completely unattended. "We can walk away any time", Victor said.

> If someone should take something they will not get out of here alive. The police are right here, the UPDF right there and the people you see around town, many of them are wearing normal dress but they are from the barracks. You do not want to temper and people all know it.

That does not mean that nobody tries his luck. In April 2011, one of Bibia's currency traders was shot dead, reportedly by unknown thugs, who robbed him of 75 million Ugandan shillings.[32] A week later, however, a man who tried to grab an unspecified amount of cash from one of the exchange tables was lynched by an angry mob.[33]

Security is a key aspect of Bibia's day-to-day existence and closely entwined with its commercial side. Although this is not immediately obvious, Bibia is a garrison town swarming with Ugandan and South Sudanese military personnel. The same is true for Nimule on the other side of the border, where UPDF maintain one of their garrisons on South Sudanese soil. Upon closer inspection the range of actors populating the field of "security" goes well beyond the more-or-less uniformed men in government service, though. Numerous characters claim they are "private security guards" and "informants". They seem to spend most of their time lurking around the various bars or near the immigration and customs offices. The following anecdote,[34] however, is evidence of a more hands-on approach by yet another security force to be reckoned with in Bibia.

As the town itself and traffic through it are growing, clean drinking water is an increasingly rare commodity in Bibia. Of the four local boreholes, access to three is reserved for the school and clinic. Only the fourth borehole, located just off Bibia's main street, is not fenced off, and an all-female well association has formed itself to control access to it. Members of the association can pump for free, but the women charge between 500 and 1,000 Ugandan shillings per 25-liter jerry can from anyone they consider an "outsider". They will enforce their privilege, if necessary. In March 2009, a Ugandan army soldier passing through demanded a jerry can of water to replenish the radiator of his vehicle. The well association's members demanded he should pay and wait in line. The soldier became angry and tried to force his way to the pump. A fight broke out during which the women attacked the soldier; then some of their husbands gave the man a more severe beating, before finally releasing him to the local army barracks.

By taking the law into their own hands, some dwellers of Bibia seem to challenge the state monopoly on legitimate violence. However, state security forces actually encourage vigilantism. To protect the borderland from "outlaws" and "criminals", Ugandan police and army have organized "sensitization" campaigns and instructed borderlanders to report "subversive activities" to the authorities. The chief of police in Bibia sees the people as "the eyes and ears of the government" who "must report when they see, hear, and suspect things that are harmful for the peace".

Hand in hand with the prominent role of security in everyday life in Bibia goes that of information. The fast-shifting conditions in a borderland where dynamic economic growth and insecurity coexist raise the stakes to obtain and verify information, while making it difficult for those who are not part of the relevant knowledge networks to do so. Border checkpoints and their surroundings always entail an element of surprise and confusion—especially for newcomers. This is the case for even the most "officially" regulated borders. In Bibia, there are various well-established procedures for customs and immigration, but also currency exchange and the purchase of, for example, water, lodging and sex. The rules that apply are rarely made explicit, however. Information and making a credible claim to having it therefore becomes a crucial asset. An extraordinary amount of the daily activities in Bibia accordingly revolves around the collection and redistribution of information. This is by no means a localized affair. Knowledge about changes in infrastructure and regulatory regimes hundreds of kilometers away is constantly exchanged and those who aspire to display a more sophisticated understanding of the larger issues will talk fluently about supply and demand changes in faraway places, "the global economic downturn" and how it affects the daily flows of commodities and people through Bibia. Because the border itself is always a location of heightened economic activity, various entrepreneurs of knowledge are thriving here. Just the value of the information they claim to have and whom they are working for is, again, ambiguous.

The importance given to the fleeting nature of information in Bibia adds further to the impression that the town is not only a transit point, but also itself a transitory phenomenon. The real power to effect change onto Bibia lies in the goods and people that are passing through. The truck drivers, well known to restaurant owners and checkpoint personnel, clearing their goods with apparently no official procedure at all and effortlessly dropping off and picking up a young female passenger—they are as much in transit as everyone else. This raises the question if there is anything about Bibia that is not merely transitory.

Conclusion

In this chapter, I have set out to gain a better understanding of the parameters that condition what I call *borderland governance,* by accounting for what kind of people, institutions and practices emerge as successful in a border area with protracted uncertainty. Borderlands are always zones of regulatory ambiguity, and during open conflict the opportunity to make up and enforce different (formal and nonformal) regimes of regulation is particularly prevalent. The border itself provides access to alternative regulatory regimes. Those who are skillful can play these out against each other to their own advantage, as both the LRA and UPDF have demonstrated. In the case of northern Uganda, this zone is narrowing geographically now that open conflict has subsided and a new wave of investment in the infrastructure and institutions of formal state regulation and commerce is under way. Officially,

Figure 8.5   In the no-man's-land: Between Bibia and Nimule. Photograph by Cecilie Lanken Verma.

a project of the state's regulatory power emanating from the center into the periphery is currently under way, supposedly overcoming and replacing what existed before.

I am left with many unanswered questions regarding the medium- and *longue-durée* trajectories of the people, practices and places I have observed along the journey to Bibia. Did I encounter pioneers and soldiers of fortune that are temporarily successful in uncertain conditions? Did I meet with seasoned players, whose inside knowledge and ability to bend and define the rules afford them with a staying power beyond the short term? If the current absence of large-scale organized violence does prevail, despite the expectations of many, I may well have witnessed emerging forms of social structure and regulation with a distinct local flavor. Perhaps in the long run, not everyone turns out to be in Bibia merely to "get it while they can" after all. A well or currency traders' association may eventually become a more established and formalized civil society actor or element in a future town council. Yet, the transitory nature of life with protracted conflict has for a long time fed an urgency to make fast profit before it is too late, not just in Bibia. In my conception, *borderland governance* is not a condition exclusively endemic to Uganda's territorial margins that will be "cured" as part of a project where rationalized and formalized regulatory power is successfully projected from the center to the periphery. As I have shown, institutional pluralism, volatility and ambiguity are not just characteristic of the way everyday life in Uganda's northern borderland with South Sudan is governed. The agents of the Ugandan state are clearly themselves using methods straddling and transgressing the boundaries of legality and territory to pursue their political and private business interests—in times of open warfare as well as in times of relative peace. The attributes of *borderland governance* and the urgency to "get it while you can" are therefore as much at the heart of practices at the center as they are in the margins of the Ugandan state. The margins in this sense are not colonizing the center. The two are mirroring each other, and as the Ugandan state projects its power into the periphery, what it encounters there is merely a reflection of what is already at its very heart. It comes, in other words, face to face with its own violent reflection.

Notes

1. Cecilie Lanken Verma has contributed invaluable feedback on an early draft of this chapter and allowed me to use some ethnographic material, as well as two photographs from her own work in northern Uganda. Critical feedback from Kristof Titeca and the editors of this volume is also gratefully acknowledged. The fieldwork for this chapter was made possible by a research grant from the Finnish Ministry of Foreign Affairs.

2. N. Hansen, *The border economy: Regional development in the Southwest* (Austin, TX: University of Texas Press, 1981): 19.

3. P. Nugent and A. Asiwaju. *African boundaries. Barriers and conduits* (London: Pinter, 1996), 1.

4. Rose 1999; Watts 2003, 2004; see also Swyngedouw 1997.

5. Lund 2006; Engel and Mehler 2005; Roitman 2005.

6. V. Das and D. Poole, *Anthropology in the margins of the state* (Santa Fe, NM: School of American Research Press, 2004), 8; see also J. Scott, *The art of not being governed: An anarchist history of upland Southeast Asia* (New Haven, CT: Yale University Press, 2009); H. Donnan and T. M. Wilson, *Borders: Frontiers of identity, nation and state* (Oxford and New York: Berg, 1999).

7. G. Dobler, "Oshikango: The dynamics of growth and regulation in a Namibian boom town," *Journal of Southern African Studies* 35, no. 1 (2009): 115–131; see also W. Zeller, "Danger and opportunity in Katima Mulilo: A Namibian border boomtown at transnational crossroads," *Journal of Southern African Studies* 35, no. 1 (2009): 133–154.

8. G. Agamben, *State of exception* (Chicago. IL: University of Chicago Press, 2005): 1.

9. Finnström 2008; Whitmore 2010; Dolan 2009.

10. International Alert, "Building a peace economy in northern Uganda," *Investing in Peace* 1 (2008): 6.

11. According to the Director of Planning of the Uganda National Roads Authority, all roads leading up to Uganda's major border posts with (South) Sudan and the Democratic Republic of Congo are currently being upgraded, rehabilitated or reconstructed with World Bank funding.

12. P. Lukwiya, "Aid still too far," *MS Uganda Newsletter,* November 2007, <http://www.ms.dk/sw88090.asp> (November 3, 2009); R. Atkinson, "Fool's day at office of the Prime Minister," *The Independent,* April 12, 2009; International Alert, "Building a peace economy in northern Uganda," *Investing in Peace* 1 (2008): 28.

13. Daily Monitor, "Sh82b presidential jet report vanishes", October 18, 2008 ("Sh82b" means "82 billion Ugandan shillings"); International Alert, "Building a peace economy in northern Uganda," *Investing in Peace* 1 (2008): 26ff.; J. Beyond, "Is the PRDP politics as usual? Update on the implementation of Uganda's Peace, Recovery and Development Plan." *Briefing Note* 2 (2008): 4.

14. Interview Gerstel 2009 in P. I. Dolo, "Adolf Gerstel, Deutscher Entwicklungs Dienst (DED)," Moyo district local government, Gulu, May 12, 2009.

15. K. Williams, "Natural fire 10: Joint multinational exercise ends with strong emphasis on partnership, cooperation," <http://www.africom.mil/getArticle.asp?art=3652.> (November 5, 2009).

16. Important details for both of these were contributed by Cecilie Lanken Verma.

17. Humanitarian and development partnership team, "Central African Republic," *News bulletin* 17 (2009).

18. T. Raeymaekers, *Network war. An introduction to Congo's privatised war economy* (Antwerp: International Peace Information Service, 2002).

19. New Vision, "Army finds list of rebel financiers," New Vision, Uganda, March 17, 2009.

20. Justice and Reconciliation Project, "Remembering the Atiak massacre," *Field note* 4 (Vancouver: Liu Institute for Global Issues, and Gulu-Uganda: The Gulu District NGO Forum, April 2007): 2.

21. Justice and Reconciliation Project. "Remembering the Atiak massacre." *Field note* 4 (Vancouver: Liu Institute for Global Issues, and Gulu-Uganda: The Gulu District NGO Forum, April 2007): 8.

22. S. Finnström, *Living with bad surroundings. War, history and everyday moments in northern Uganda* (Durham, NC: Duke University Press, 2008); M. Schomerus, *Perilous border: Sudanese communities affected by conflict on the Sudan–Uganda border* (London: Conciliation Resources, 2008): 8.

23. Anonymous informant, 2010.

24. C. Lanken, "Somebody from the bush. Rethinking abduction, homecoming and storymaking in war-torn northern Uganda," Unpublished MA thesis (University of Aarhus, 2007).

25. Anonymous informant, April 2010.

26. Anonymous informant, May 2010.

27. M. A. Rugadya, E. Nsamba-Gayiiya and H. Kamusiime, *Analysis of post-conflict land policy and land administration: A survey of IDP return and resettlement issues*

and lessons (Kampala: World Bank, 2008); R. Atkinson, "Fool's day at office of the Prime Minister," *The Independent*, April 12, 2009, 5; T. Whitmore, "Genocide or just another 'casualty of war'? The implications of the memo attributed to President Yoweri K. Museveni of Uganda," *Practical Matters* 3 (2010): 1–49.

28. T. Whitmore, "Genocide or just another 'casualty of war'? The implications of the memo attributed to President Yoweri K. Museveni of Uganda," *Practical Matters* 3 (2010): 1–49.
29. Anonymous informant, October 2009.
30. Anonymous informant interviewed by Cecilie Lanken Verma, May 2009.
31. J. Wacha 2011, "100 families living in former Bibia IDP camp face eviction," Uganda radio network, September 1, 2011. <http://ugandaradionetwork.com/a/story.php?s=36515#ixzz1ZQvn7QRV> (September 20, 2011).
32. In 2009, 1,000 Ugandan shillings (USh) equaled about 30 cents (euro).
33. D. Olaka, "Angry mob lynch one in Bibia," Uganda radio network, May 2, 2011. <http://ugandaradionetwork.com/a/story.php?s=33307#ixzz1a6Wf3XCS> (September 20, 2011).
34. This was relayed to me by Cecilie Lanken Verma.

References

Agamben, G. *State of exception*. Chicago, IL: University of Chicago Press, 2005.
Atkinson, R. "Land issues in Acholi in the transition from war to peace." *The Examiner* 4 (2008).
Atkinson, R. "Fool's day at office of the Prime Minister." *The Independent*, April 2009, 12.
Beyond, J. "Is the PRDP politics as usual? Update on the implementation of Uganda's Peace, Recovery and Development Plan." *Briefing Note* 2 (2008).
Das, V. and D. Poole. *Anthropology in the margins of the state*. Santa Fe, NM: School of American Research Press, 2004.
Dobler, G. "Oshikango: The dynamics of growth and regulation in a Namibian boom town." *Journal of Southern African Studies* 35, no. 1 (2009): 115–131.
Dolan, C. *Social torture. The case of northern Uganda, 1986–2006*. New York: Berghahn, 2009.
Dolo, P. I. "Adolf Gerstel, Deutscher Entwicklungs Dienst (DED)," Moyo District Local Government, Gulu, May 12, 2009.
Donnan, H. and T. M. Wilson. *Borders: Frontiers of identity, nation and state*. Oxford and New York: Berg, 1999.
Engel, U. and A. Mehler. "Under construction: Governance in Africa's new violent social spaces." In *The African exception*, edited by U. Engel and G. R. Olsen. Aldershot: Ashgate, 2005: 87–102.
Finnström, S. *Living with bad surroundings. War, history and everyday moments in northern Uganda*. Durham, NC: Duke University Press, 2008.
Hansen, N. *The border economy: Regional development in the Southwest*. Austin, TX: University of Texas Press, 1981.

Humanitarian and Development Partnership Team. "Central African Republic." *News bulletin* 17 (2009).

ICBT report. *Informal cross border trade survey report 2007*. The Uganda Bureau of Statistics and Bank of Uganda, 2007. <http://www.bou.or.ug/bouwebsite/export/sites/default/bou/bou-downloads/publications/TradeStatistics/ICBTReports/ICBT_REPORT_2007.pdf> (August 10, 2011).

International Alert. "Building a peace economy in northern Uganda." *Investing in peace* 1 (2008).

International Crisis Group. "Sudan: Preventing implosion." *Africa Briefing* 68: December 17, 2009.

Justice and Reconciliation Project. "Remembering the Atiak massacre." *Field note* 4. Vancouver: Liu Institute for Global Issues, and Gulu-Uganda: The Gulu District NGO Forum, April 2007.

Lanken, C. "Somebody from the bush. Rethinking abduction, homecoming and storymaking in war-torn northern Uganda." Unpublished MA thesis, University of Aarhus, 2007.

Leopold, M. *Inside west Nile*. Oxford: James Currey, 2005.

Lukwiya, P. "Aid still too far." *MS Uganda newsletter*, November 2007. <http://www.ms.dk/sw88090.asp> (November 3, 2009).

Lund, C. "Twilight institutions: An introduction." *Development and Change* 37, no. 4 (2006): 673–84.

Daily Monitor, "Sh82b presidential jet report vanishes." October 18, 2008.

Daily Monitor. "Gulu's impressive outlook four years after Kony is gone." July 25, 2007. <http://www.monitor.co.ug/SpecialReports/-/688342/883452/-/item/0/-/vcbs7nz/-/index.html> (August 20, 2011).

New Vision. "Army finds list of rebel financiers." *New Vision*, Uganda, March 17, 2009.

Nugent, P. *Smugglers, secessionists and loyal citizens on the Ghana–Togo Frontier: The lie of the borderlands since 1914*. Oxford: James Currey, 2002.

Nugent, P. *Africa since independence. A comparative history*. Basingstoke: Palgrave Macmillan, 2004.

Nugent, P. and A. Asiwaju. *African boundaries. Barriers and conduits*. London: Pinter, 1996.

Olaka, D. "Angry mob lynch one in Bibia." Uganda radio network, May 2, 2011. <http://ugandaradionetwork.com/a/story.php?s=33307#ixzz1a6Wf3XCS> (September 20, 2011).

Raeymaekers, T. *Network war. An introduction to Congo's privatised war economy*. Antwerp: International Peace Information Service, 2002.

Raeymaekers, T. "The silent encroachment of the frontier: A politics of transborder trade in the Semliki Valley (Congo–Uganda)." *Political Geography* 28, no. 1 (2009): 55–65.

Roitman, J. "Productivity in the margins: The reconstitution of state power in the Chad Basin." In *Anthropology in the margins of the state*, edited by V. Das and D. Poole. Santa Fe, NM: School of American Research Press, 2004: 191–224.

Rose, N. *The powers of freedom. Reframing political thought.* Cambridge: Cambridge University Press, 1999.

Rugadya, M. A., E. Nsamba-Gayiiya and H. Kamusiime. *Analysis of post-conflict land policy and land administration: A survey of IDP return and resettlement issues and lessons.* Kampala: World Bank, 2008.

Schomerus, M. *Perilous border: Sudanese communities affected by conflict on the Sudan–Uganda border.* London: Conciliation Resources, 2008.

Scott, J. *The art of not being governed: An anarchist history of upland Southeast Asia.* New Haven, CT: Yale University Press, 2009.

Swyngedouw, E. "Neither global nor local—'Glocalization' and the politics of scale." In *Spaces of globalization. Reasserting the power of the local,* edited by K. Cox. New York: The Guilford Press, 1997: 136–166.

United Nations High Commissioner for Refugees. "UNHCR country operations profile—Uganda." 2011. <http://www.unhcr.org/pages/49e483c06.html> (August 6, 2011).

United States Africa Command. "Natural fire 10: Joint multinational exercise ends with strong emphasis on partnership." Cooperation, 2009. <http://www.africom.mil/getArticle.asp?art=3652&lang=0> (August 6, 2011).

Wacha, J. "100 families living in former Bibia IDP camp face eviction." Uganda radio network, September 1, 2011. <http://ugandaradionetwork.com/a/story.php?s=36515#ixzz1ZQvn7QRV.> (September 20, 2011).

Watts, M. "Development and governmentality." *Singapore Journal of Tropical Geography* 24, no. 1 (2003): 6–34.

Watts, M. "Antinomies or community: Some thoughts on geography, resources and empire." *Transactions of the Institute of British Geographers* 29 (2004): 195–216.

Whitmore, T. "Genocide or just another 'casualty of war'? The implications of the memo attributed to President Yoweri K. Museveni of Uganda." *Practical Matters* 3 (2010): 1–49.

Williams, K. "Natural fire 10: Joint multinational exercise ends with strong emphasis on partnership, cooperation." <http://www.africom.mil/getArticle.asp?art=3652> (November 5, 2009).

Zeller, W. "Danger and opportunity in Katima Mulilo: A Namibian border boomtown at transnational crossroads." *Journal of Southern African Studies* 35, no. 1 (2009): 133–154.

CHAPTER 9

When Civil Wars Hibernate in Borderlands: The Challenges of the Casamance's "Forgotten Civil War" to Cross-Border Peace and Security

Aboubakr Tandia

Introduction

After 29 years, the Casamance conflict is still raging in Senegal, becoming probably one of the longest civil wars in Africa and even beyond. It has not only become a stalemate for belligerents, peacemakers and other main actors, but it also challenges the way scholars and other specialists talk and think about the duration and even the notion of "civil" war. Not forgetting that defining a *civil war* is in itself challenging,[1] I argue that the Casamance conflict can be described as "civil" when analyzed with reference to its *civilian* nature. In other words, the focus of this analysis is on the effects of this war on the populations or citizens, and their role and relationship with the conflict. Of particular concern are the responses formulated by civil populations in the borderlands.

I will analyze the Casamance conflict by considering borderlands as the primary scene for the territorialization of this regional civil order. However, I should first of all substantiate the underlying assumption that the Casamance conflict cannot, or not any more, be viewed as a *civil war* in a narrow sense. On the one hand, the national policy framework, which depicts this conflict as a somehow intolerable secession, has proven incorrect. On the other hand, regional interactions between belligerents and neighboring Gambia and Guinea-Bissau aimed at containing this regional conflict have proven fatal to successive governments and the insurgency. Do these two situations authorize calling the Casamance hot spot a *civil war*?

I assume yes, because they reflect a state-oriented conception of intrastate conflicts and peace, as well as a classical macro-geopolitical paradigm about the Casamance conflict *per se*.[2] This paradigm assumes that intrastate conflicts only threaten and concern state order, whereby these categories reduce civility and territoriality to statehood. I also presume that it is time to look at the Casamance conflict in its dynamic character, both in terms of spatial, territorial and human terms. Such dynamics include the failure of various attempts to resolve the conflict, the unprecedented level of violence and increasing propaganda around the conflict on behalf of belligerents. In the same vein, it is hardly possible to overlook how the conflict has now crystallized the attention of both the local media and civil society organizations, among which 90 nongovernmental organizations (NGOs) are seeking peace.

Consequently, I focus in this chapter on the borderland dynamics of the conflict, which were until now under-considered and are reflected through its territorial character and their effects on ordinary people. Accordingly, this chapter basically argues that if the conflict is sustained by the increased spread of violence, especially from the insurgency that follows survival and predatory logics encroached in the regional war economy, it is made a civil war through more complex processes of state–society negotiations of (dis)order resulting from or related to such violence in the borderlands. The hibernation of this war precisely consists of the cyclical reconfiguration of its structural causes and manifestations. Inevitably and constantly involving local actors, spaces and socioeconomic and political dynamics, this process consequently challenges grassroots initiatives of peace and security building in the absence or failure of official state and interstate strategies to end it. It does not mean that they cannot be taken as defining patterns of statehood. Actually the point can be made that, although cross-border politics of self-reliance reflect uneven state-making, they are also supportive and in need of statehood both symbolically and structurally, given that they resemble and comprise elements of counterinsurgency. That is why and how they appear as *civil* strategies and responses to both structural and direct violence, suggesting therefore its civil character.

I will first pinpoint the persistence of causal patterns of the civil war through its territorial character and its interconnections with the post–civil war situation in Guinea-Bissau. These preliminary observations serve to evaluate the extent to which borderlands have become the back yard of regional warfare. I then consider how this regional complexity intermingling with local borderland politics maintains the civil war in the margins through a regional war economy. Finally, I endeavor to demonstrate how this situation challenges cross-border peace and security building somehow aimed at containing this prolonged "civil" war. I conclude with an exploration of future positions for belligerents to consider if they have failed to transform the conflict toward either peace or war.

The Territorial Characters of the Casamance Conflict

The Casamance region was the last to fall into colonial dominion and as such received much less attention in the process of state-building than did northern Senegal. Despite its commitment to Pan-African ideals, the postindependence regime of Senghor replicated this colonial attitude and assigned the same *special status* to the region. It was the rather menial role of providing resources to the country, and of being a haven for civil servants and other privileged and influential social groups and networks formed by the urban industrial elites and rural marabouts of the peanut economy. This has been referred to as the multidimensional *marginalization* of the Casamance people and region. It actually reflects the devalued territoriality allocated to the region in the sense that territory and territorialization are inherently endowed categories of a state formation process.[3]

It is not surprising that the Casamance region and its inhabitants reacted negatively to the reduced political role it had been given by national postcolonial politics. The region and its people have a long tradition of political participation. Struggle was already evolving in 1947, for example, in the earlier vocation of the Mouvement des Forces Démocratiques de la Casamance (MFDC) as a regional party. The political exclusion of the region has been accentuated in national multiparty politics, where regional leaders only played the role of local clients and puppets for central decision-makers mainly of northern descent.

Political marginalization was closely related to several forms of economic and sociocultural exclusion, which were however more effective in the imaginations of the Casamançais than in the reality on the ground. The region has for a long time fulfilled the function of a natural resource base that sustains the Senegalese economy and state clientelism.[4] In the extraverted economy, it was especially providing rice as a basic commodity to satisfy the food demands of northern urban centers, while facing at the same time the competition of low-cost importations by trade networks animated by religious centers in the north (mainly the Mouride bastion of Touba) and in the region (Fula religious leaders of Madina Gonasse).

This is closely linked to a *social marginalization* of a population that was seen as rural and constituting the unwavering labor force for northern regions. The *cultural exclusion* of the region was based on its religious particularity.

Most of the 5 percent Pagans and Christians of the country are concentrated there, in the sense that this and the attachment of the population to its traditions were seen as a sign of backwardness.[5]

All these patterns of exclusion of the Casamance region stem from a *territorial marginalization,* which dates back to the colonial perception of the region as a hostile, savage and obscurantist territory. Since the very creation of the state, national leaders have been framing the popular perceptions of the region as *"la région naturelle de Casamance"*, meaning the wetland, the lungs of the national economy, the bush lived by the *Gnak* (forest people) and the retarded mentality.[6] Such a territorial ascription was manifested through the endless and stubborn efforts of the Senegalese government in describing in the school curricula[7] as well as in official records the particularity of the region as the granary of the country.[8] This was coextensive with a social and cultural territorialization that defined the Casamance identity as a multiethnic one in order to negate the regional identity whose homogeneity was constructively convoked by the rebel movement in its political discourse. Another particularity of the region is its affinities with Guinea-Bissau in both geographical and historical terms. Furthermore, the Casamance region neighbors the Gambian enclave that was constituted in the course of colonization.[9] Different Casamance ethnic groups expressed solidarity with Gambia because of frustrations and deprivations suffered in the national fate within the Senegalese state.[10] The endeavors of these groups to safeguard and exalt their traditions increased the difficulties of the nationalist territorial strategy, which was to thwart the rebellion's instrumentalization of these spatial and social representations through political mobilization. Both insurgency and government used the language of territory to describe the social and physical maps as well as the frustrations and lamentations of the Casamance region in the conflict.[11] But, as we will see later, both actors in the long run failed to manipulate the territorial representations of the region, which has become one of the main obstacles to the settlement of the conflict.

The situation in Guinea-Bissau also reflects the territorial character of the Casamance conflict. From a historical perspective, borders are also expressions and products of histories constructed by strong social and cultural ties among ethnic groups that live along them. The geopolitical configuration of the conflict reflects an intermingling of internal and external territories and social spaces.[12] If the territorial representations constructed and manipulated by the rebel movement and the Senegalese government constitute important stakes, it is because they refer to the trans-boundary range of the Casamance identity. Appropriating this trans-boundary regional identity is all the more crucial to belligerents than it is firmly rooted in the lively immemorial ties dating back to the ancient kingdoms of Gabu and Fouladou. This becomes obvious in the constant fear of the Senegalese government that the so-called *3B* axis

(*Banjul*, *Bignona* and *Bissau*) emerges on the ruins of these precolonial entities.[13] Thus, it explains why the Casamance conflict has always strained the relationships between Senegal and neighboring Guinea-Bissau and Gambia with which border disputes and localized conflicts erupted first in 1997 and a second time in 2003 and 2005. So given that the external territorialities of the conflict determine the actors' strategies, the situation in Guinea-Bissau and Gambia may obviously have some implications on the Casamance conflict and vice versa. Therefore, the borderlands between Senegal, Gambia and Guinea-Bissau can be alienated despite the many sociocultural and economic patterns of their *interdependence* and *coexistence*. Oftentimes, interactions among peoples are undermined by the unstable situation in Guinea-Bissau opportunistically exploited by the insurgents and different governments.

Spillover Effects of State Failure in Guinea-Bissau and One-Man-Rule in Gambia

Despite the current lull in the national political struggle, the situation in Guinea-Bissau will continue to influence the Casamance war, especially as the former's stabilization is rather uncertain and fragile.[14] Solidaristic impulses from the Bissau-Guinean military and politicians will probably resurface, primarily because identitary ties are now breeding material interests shared with military and political leaders of the MFDC. Despite constant efforts of the Senegalese government to patronize the country's moderate politicians and transition, business opportunities yielded by the country's narcotrafficking and militarized politics are still enormous for shareholders in power, in the bush and beyond the Atlantic.[15] When it comes to borderland conflictuality, there are few scenarios where state failure affects borderland attitudes toward the politics of cross-border management.

Undoubtedly, the recent civil war in Guinea-Bissau (1998–2000) can be explained by the historicity and territoriality of violence, which constantly captures the state in a vicious circle of government collapse, strong militarization of politics, ethnicization and criminalization of the military as well as the constant circulation of weaponry inherited from the liberation war.[16] The porosity of the border and the dense human and commercial traffic, which are still greatly criminalized, favors drug farming and trafficking. This criminal tendency has been uncontrollable whenever the connections of the rebellion within the Bissau-Guinean military waned or disappeared, as it had been the case until recently since the assassination of Bissau-Guinean Brigadier Ansoumane Mané, who was deemed to be a supporter of the Casamance rebellion and a promoter of the reinvention of the Gabu kingdom in the form of a state comprising the south of Senegal and Guinea-Bissau.[17]

President Jammeh of Gambia has always denied implication of his government in the Casamance war and still does so. Neither has he reckoned the presence of MFDC combatants in the border areas, where the leader of the armed wing Attika ("warrior" in Jola), Salif Sadio, has his strongholds of Darsilami and Kajaalong bordering the Gambian village called Jifanta. Yet he is assisting Salif Sadio and his men, who move within the Gambia without being disturbed.[18] The case of the shipment of weapons (see table 9.1) seized on October 21, 2010, by the Nigerian navy provides additional evidence that Gambia has been providing weaponry to the MFDC, whether directly through the routes connecting cross-border weekly markets with the monitoring of the presidential guard, or indirectly through the regional routes of light weapons and combatants from the Mano River Basin to Libya, Ivory Coast and Burkina Faso. It is noteworthy that Gambia has also been managing the international connections of the MFDC with, for example, Libya and Burkina Faso since the MFDC's involvement in the guerrilla war from the late 1990s. In effect, even though in a less intense mode in comparison to the 1970s and 1980s, Libya included the MFDC in its customer list of insurgencies that could be used to handle resistances to its continental power politics in West Africa. As it was the case in the wars in Liberia and Sierra Leone until the mid-1990s, Burkina Faso was used as a regional hub to cover and manage these connections. Today, Iran and Ivory Coast are frequent trade partners as shown by the shipment of weapons seized in Nigeria. Border villages where civilians are used as labor force[19] are discreetly ambushed hubs for the cultivation and trafficking of cannabis in places such as Kanilai, Bouyam and the Mangana Forest, just as in Bissau-Guinean border villages of Gabu and Cacheu regions.[20] Gambian officers among the guards of President Jammeh provide the MFDC with the information to trace out the movements and earmark the confinements of the Senegalese military and civilian targets (traders, displaced, refugees, travelers). Indeed, for more than a decade now, the deals between Jammeh and rebel leader Salif Sadio and his men have extended far beyond the securing of land and corridors for cannabis cultivation and trafficking; they have included the displacement of entire villages as well as the smuggling of arms, timber, peanuts, cashew nuts and cereals. The regional and transnational reach of this business has often bred Senegalese suspicions toward officers and field soldiers from a few segments of defense and security forces in Guinea-Bissau.[21]

The impact of this regional situation is still unpredictable given the uncertain direction of internal politics in Gambia and the diplomatic mess provoked by the Iranian warfare shipment, as well as both dormant wars in the Casamance and Guinea-Bissau, especially since the rebellion is torn apart into scattered factions indistinguishable from non-identified armed groups.

Table 9.1 Chronology of the conflict, 2010

Date	Senegal	Neighbors
January 4	Rebel attack in villages of Sanou 1, 2 and 3: 579 people are expulsed. They have been relocated in Bégène, a border village in northeast Guinea-Bissau.	Gambia: The next day, January 5, visit of President Wade.
February 4	In village of Bassada (Sédhiou region), attack of armed groups presumed to belong to the MFDC: car hijacking of six vehicles and a passenger killed.	
February 6	Rebel incursion in village of Mahmouda Chérif (Communauté rurale of Katabal).	
March 1	President Wade says on a radio broadcasting show, *La Tribune* on Ocean FM (Dakar), that his predecessor has been wrong in declaring former MFDC political leader Diamacoune Senghor dead in 2007. He also declares that his government will never help the MFDC reunite and minimizes increase of violence on roads and villages in Casamance.	
March 17	Bourama Samba and Lamarana Boubacar Coly alias Thierry Henry are arrested by army patrol Bélaye (Bignona) in the framework of army operations. The rebel leaders were returning from a headquarters meeting in Sao Domingo (Guinea-Bissau). There were reports of some attempts of government high officials to free them.	
	Army bombing against rebel confinements in Kassana and Mamatorro, 10 km south of Ziguinchor.	
March 19	Two rebels arrested since March are freed by the police following pressure of MFDC internal wing	
March 22	Rebel attack in border village of Saré Yoba 30 km south to Kolda. No losses were reported, while a week before there were losses of three soldiers and ten wounded in the army detachment.	
	Postponement of the trial of the two Hungarian mercenaries Geza Gal and Nazy Zoltan arrested since 2007.	
March 27	Leader of MFDC external wing Mamadou Nkrumah Sane interrogated by France's Direction Centrale du Renseignement Intérieur about the appropriateness of his exile in France where he has been since 1968.	
March 31	Rebel ambush against army patrol: one soldier killed and five wounded.	
	Leader of MFDC Front Nord César Atoute Badiate threatens government over arrest of his men Teuw Sambou, Pape Tamsir Badji and Ansoumana Diédhiou on March 17.	

Table 9.1 (Continued)

Date	Senegal	Neighbors
April 1		Guinea-Bissau: General Antonio Indjai overthrows army chief officer José Zamora Induta, while Prime Minister Carlos Gomez was kidnapped and released. President Bacai Sanhá was recovering from disease. General Indjai succeeded in exfiltrating navy chief Buba Na Tchuto in Gambia.
April 13	Rebel attack in the village of Oukout (Oussouye): four shops pillaged. Rebel victims are loaded with loot toward insurgency confinement toward Guinea-Bissau border.	
April 14	Rebel attack of the *gendarmerie* post in Bounkiling	
April 15	Rebel attack in Saré Niakao while army was securing sector in preparation of the weekly market of the neighboring village of Saré Yoba, eastern Kolda. Populations from fifteen villages moved away and six soldiers were killed in gunfire against army troops.	
April 19	During press conference, army accuses the national media of igniting the conflict and exposing army troops by releasing information on military movements.	
April 25	On the way to Ziguinchor for attending local festival ZigFest, the convoy of the Ministry of Armed Forces was attacked by rebel group. No wounded or dead reported. MFDC Front Nordleader César Atoute Badiate claims attack and says it is a symbol that independence is still the unwavering objective of insurgency.	
April 29	Five elements of the MFDC freed from Gambian prisons on the previous Monday disappear in Bignona.	
May 7	Rebel attack against army positions in Effok and Emay (Oussouye) while chief army officer was inspecting troops and declared that he felt no insecurity in the region.	
May 12	Rebel attack of carters and smugglers and armed robbery of shops in Bourofaye Jola, southern Ziguinchor, near the border. Rebel groups accused their victims of trespassing their strongholds. Economic operators were	

also stripped of their property and victims loaded with loot. Physical cruelty against them was reported as well as mutilations against young men who went for cashew nuts a week before.

Date		
May 24		Guinea-Bissau: Rumors of Prime Minister Carlos Gomez losing grip on power circulate as army chiefs are securing more influence on military and politics.
June 4	Rebel attack on army positions in Maniora, north Ziguinchor region: Military sources reported a car hijacking in the morning, which got four vehicles (a bus, two taxis, and a lorry tank) to the insurgents.	
June 5		Gambia: 12 people arrested and seizure of 2 tons of cocaine worth US$1 billion, more than the country's GDP set at US$851 million in 2009.
		Inspector General of Police Ensa Badjie, detained since March during waves of arrests, is on trial with other 51 detainees. Reports highlight power struggle within police forces between pro-drug and anti-drug factions, with political implications.
July 4	Rebel attack against the *gendarmerie* post of Bounkiling. A few civilians were wounded.	
July 18		Gambia: Navy chief Sarje Fofana and army chief Langtombong Tamba are accused of implications in failed coup in 2006 and 2009. Government critics say it is using allegations of coup plots to intimidate potential rivals and settle scores.
August 5		The Senegal–Gambia Joint Commission mediates disputes between communities of Touba-Tranquille and neighboring villages in the Gambia. Cross-border cooperation and peace initiative are agreed upon between community leaders.
October 13	Book of French Scholar Jean-Claude Marut *Le conflit de Casamance: Ce que disent les armes* (Paris: Karthala, 2010) is banned from the airport. Author is authorized	

228

Table 9.1   (Continued)

Date	Senegal	Neighbors
	press conference on the next day after interrogations in the state house of Ziguinchor. Marut criticized both government and insurgency for their lack of will to end conflict.	
October 21		Gambia–Senegal: Arms shipment of 13 containers of heavy weaponry (grenades, rockets and smoke shells) is seized by Nigerian navy. Leaving the Iranian port of Bandar Abbas, it was heading to Banjul.
October 22		Guinea-Bissau: President Malam Bacai Sanhá is admitted to hospital in Dakar.
October 30	Army's thorough search in Diarang and Badiouré (Bignona).	
October 31	Rebel ambush against army position in Bignona: three soldiers were killed.	
November 10		Gambia: President Jammeh declares that he has for the second time escaped a coup plot. Twelve are arrested including Director of Gambian National Intelligence Agency Lewis Gomez.
November 12	National Assembly increases budget of Ministry of Armed Forces by CFA11 billion. Insecurity in Casamance and trans-boundary criminality were the main reasons for the budget rise.	Nigeria: Government reveals to UN Security Council seizure of arms shipment.
November 15		Gambia: President Jammeh denies ownership and implication in the October 21 seizure of arms shipment by Nigerian navy
November 22		Gambia recalls envoy in Iran and sends back Iranian ambassador. President Jammeh declares move is directly linked to arms shipment affair.
November 23	*Gendarmerie* of Pata, 66 km north of Kolda, arrest a local drug tycoon while he was carrying from Gambia border ten bags of cannabis.	

November 25	MFDC Secretary General Jean Marie Biagui announces in a press release the organization of insurgency's great meeting for January 14–15, 2010.
November 26	A gang of 18 path-cutters is dismantled in Kolda with a load of three Kalashnikovs, three guns and 200 kg of cannabis. Among them, two mercenaries participated in the 1998 mutiny in Guinea-Bissau.
December 1	Gambia: His Excellency Essa Bokaar Sey, former Gambian diplomat, reveals to the online journal *Bitimrew.net* that President Jammeh is the main sponsor and mentor of Salif Sadio leader of the MFDC Front Sud and former commander of the military wing Attika. He declares that Jammeh and Sadio work on a drug and arms business, which has cost many lives among the military and officials of Gambia. He also gives details of the relationships between Sadio, Jammeh and Laurent Gbagbo, whom Salif met in 2008 in Gambia. This information is also given by another online journal, *Freedom Newspaper*. Sadio would even hold a diplomatic passport of the Gambia since 2003 and visited Ivory Coast and Libya in 2008.
December 2	MFDC Paris external wing members, Mamadou Goudiaby, Madia Sonko and Lansana Goudiaby, contradict Jean Marie Biagui over insurgency's general meeting. They insist that nothing has been decided about this meeting and call on all members to wait for the official planning of the Pilot Committee. Leader of Front Nord César Atoute Badiate also disavows Secretary General Biagui in a press release.
December 5	President Wade declares sorrow and surprise over arms shipment affair. He talked about guarantees secured by his government, whereas the UN Security Council's investigation results were being awaited.
	Gambia: President Jammeh announces death sentence of army chief Langtombong Tamba while head of intelligence services has already been assassinated.

Table 9.1   (Continued)

Date	Senegal	Neighbors
December 7	Kamougué Diatta accuses government and some NGOs of manipulating César Atoute Badiate and other rebels, driving them to refuse MFDC general meeting.	
December 14	Senegal recalls envoy in Iran officially for consultation, maybe to save exceptional economic relationships between the two countries. Iranian automobile constructor Iran Khodro opened an assemblage unit in Thies in 2007.	
December 16		Gambia: President Jammeh says arms shipment was for Nigeria and that Senegal and President Wade were campaigning against him at the international level. Iran declares arms shipment was for a private security council based in a West African country. President Jammeh claimed that Senegal instead was hosting his enemies.

Extending the Casamance war eastward and northward,[22] the whole criminalized and insecure environment has two fundamental and concomitant effects. On the one hand, the rebellion takes advantage of the insecure and porous borders to run a predatory and violent war economy, which on the other hand jeopardizes the demographics and economy of borderland communities. The way both conflicts in Casamance and Guinea-Bissau evolved through time as well as their interconnectedness explain a lot of how and why the Casamance conflict continues to hibernate in the borderlands.[23]

Criminalization, War Economy and Borderland Insecurity Dilemmas

From a historical perspective, criminalization refers more broadly to the militarization of politics and state-making as a whole. However, from an empirical standpoint, it can be restrained to the construction of war economies, given that wars are sustained through politics and accumulation at once.[24] It in effect describes situations where accumulation processes are— in contexts of state weakness, absence or privatization—driven by modes of governance based on violent (though legal) or armed forms of extraction, involving sometimes holding people to ransom, mainly civilians in times of war.[25] Due to the incommensurable opportunities of border areas, a systematic control of resources is fundamental. In the context of the unstable situation and the protracted wars, accumulation and violence are mutually sustained. I would then conceive criminalization as something inherent to the war economy, meaning the system of producing, mobilizing and allocating resources to sustain violence and vice versa.[26] Thus, I will specifically focus on the territorial aspect of criminalization, as it is also consistent with the not less important military pattern.

Definitely, this war economy is not only dedicated to the personal accumulation and greed of leaders and combatants. It also enables to gather war expenditures, which is more ambitious and tallies with the argument of a remobilization of insurgency. Additionally, the insurgency's main business has become the trafficking of marijuana from its rear bases on the Gambian borders and cocaine throughout the southern borders with Guinea-Bissau, from the coastal environments of Ziguinchor and, as of recently, toward Kolda region in the eastern parts of Casamance.[27] The MFDC has also been involved in the smuggling of arms for many decades now. Otherwise it would not have been able to successfully maintain its gun power demonstrated in regular attacks. The stock of weaponry leftovers from the liberation war and Mano Basin hot spots is recycled in an unending transition in Guinea-Bissau.[28] Undoubtedly, however, the most interesting aspect of this war economy is its spreading throughout the Casamance and beyond its borders, with destructive repercussions on the borderland economy.

The overall scenario of scarcity, chaos and conflictuality indeed unfolds some factors that interact as insecurity dilemmas for borderlanders: transboundary criminality (cattle rustling, path cutting, armed robbery), mine bombing, forced migration, land tenure, poverty and conflicts. As we intend to highlight, in response to such challenges communities have drifted to conflictuality, which in turn nurtures the civil war in the borderlands. Resulting frustrations resemble strongly the rebellion's complaints against the Senegalese government. Moreover, borderlands appear as nests of insecurity because of unsuspected spreads of armed groups.[29]

Cattle rustling is a serious insecurity challenge as it is closely related to conflicts that arise between farmers and herdsmen over pastureland. Managing rural spaces of farming and herding is a thorny issue, all the more so when the displaced from battlefields and landmine-polluted areas ultimately overpopulate their novel settlements or demand new farming tools they have lost while moving around. The *border effect* between territories of Senegal and Guinea-Bissau is manifested through criminality-induced conflicts. It is more common to see Bissau-Guineans rustle their Senegalese counterparts, which fosters tensions and community violence. A decrease in the size of the livestock causes conflicts, because the cattle are also used for farming. An increase in the livestock destroys rice fields, as there are not enough herdsmen to watch over them. This situation fuels conflicts that often degenerate, as no particular solutions are available in the short term. As victims are poorly compensated, the rancor among families and villages does not subdue. Instead, populations are prone to systematic arms carrying, a local consequence of the territoriality and history of violence deriving from the liberation war in Guinea-Bissau and the Casamance conflict. Moreover, this situation rules out the possibility to resort to traditional mechanisms of conflict resolution when it does not render them inefficient in the framework of cross-border peace and security-building strategies.

Another challenge for borderlanders is the spread and sustenance of human insecurity. Impoverishment has been worsened by the lack of social infrastructures and the remoteness from main roads and markets. Without cattle and farming equipment, populations have witnessed aggravated living conditions, namely poor sanitation and malnutrition. Many health centers are inaccessible because they are located near insurgent rear bases or landlocked around mine-bombed perimeters. This explains why some people take the risky challenge of striking deals with rebel factions in order to survive, or else offer their service to armed groups in cattle rustling, path cutting and several banditry activities. In their turn, these survival strategies clearly sustain the civil war by breeding its root causes, including enclavement and economic gaps.

As the war in Casamance and instability in Guinea-Bissau has generated migration flows of displaced communities, there is a tendency toward demographic imbalances. While there is an increase in population density in areas that receive displaced and refugee flows and populations expulsed by insurgents, other regions have become depopulated, notably those under control of factions or close to rebel camps. Naturally, these displaced, who are not always counted as refugees or displaced in relief policies, are likely to become recruits for the insurgency or criminal gangs. In places overwhelmed by poverty and cattle rustling, they are sometimes hardly welcome. For example, migrants who become herdsmen in their host families are often indulging in cattle rustling, thus exposing themselves to suspicion, if not violence. In addition to the displaced, sedentary or itinerant migrants, mostly cross-border traders and peasants coming from the northern and central parts of Senegal, also pretend to farmwork and herding. Here again root causes of the civil war are looming, given that these spontaneous settlers from the north are reputed to have exhausted their own land because of their intensive agricultural and forestry practices. Yet, and this is also an object of contention and a cause of tension, they profit from connections with local power repositories, notably religious leaders and traditional chieftaincies in the northern villages of Kolda and further to the Mouride town of Touba or the Fula religious center of Madina Gonasse. Closely related, access to land in a context of poverty and poor employment opportunities raises challenges for natural resource management. In some domains such as forestry and land tenure, cutting permits and farming land are unequally granted by local councillors. The latter often consider the tempting offers from new settlers and local big traders based in urban centers regardless of the consequences of such attitudes on rural borderland livelihoods.[30] This situation cannot be understood without being related to the very social dimension of locally induced conflicts. Actually, such new conflicts evoke class divides that are carved out upstream by mobility and downstream by waste and scarcity of land induced by mine bombing, criminality and local patrimonial governance.

Though reflecting the root causes of the Casamance civil war, these dynamics are actually more indicative of the war-making potential of extraverted state–society relationships in both the Casamance and neighboring Guinea-Bissau:

> Those who help cattle rustlers are many. Government itself is a participant by way of its inaction. Government is the first to blame and the police as well. Cattle rustlers operate in total impunity and are freed as you take them to the police.[31]

Among the Senegalese Fula of Fouladou in High Casamance, a commonplace phrase to hear is the following: "They [the northerners] are taking away our resources". A farmer complaining about migrants and local politics lamented as follows: "We happen to ask ourselves whether we should not have done like our Jola brothers in Low Casamance", referring obviously to the current irredentism.[32] How therefore, and by which means, are these communities able to carry out collective self-reliance actions toward addressing peace and security dilemmas? Are there any resources for that?

Ties That Bind and Linkages That Pacify: Cross-Border Peacemaking and Security Building

An important issue in trans-boundary politics in civil war contexts is how sociocultural ties are reproduced at the micro level, though implicating subnational institutions and trans-local communities that straddle borders to engage in transnational linkage politics.[33] A related issue is also how such trans-local forms of political mobilization make use of the sociocultural basis that supports transnational linkages.[34] In the management of local conflicts, new strategies of pacification are easier to find and implement, especially as they are justified on the basis of the transnational communitarian identity and interests that transcend the border as a barrier. The cross-border peace-building activity proceeds from the bridging effects of borders as conduits and opportunities as much as the fiction of a unified borderland community is effectively developed through transborder discourses and imaginaries that construct the normative and moral basis for creating linkages.[35] By "linkages that pacify", I mean those new governmentalities based on what Steven Vertovec calls "common consciousness of bundle experiences"[36] encroached in cross-border governance activities. These operate through para-diplomatic political forms of peaceful coexistence and borderland securing as partly stimulated by decentralization.[37]

Indicative of the transnationalization of the war, the trans-local management of the whole tropism of wariness is undertaken by modern local government and administrative institutions as well as by traditional authorities. Indicative of the "pooling of authorities", this blend of leadership in borderland communities cooperates across borders to restore peace and correct the straining effects of the Casamance conflict. These settings are marked by institutional pluralism, in which traditional and modern legitimacies are both repositories of community trust and authority to take the lead of loyalty building in the negotiation and implementation of collective actions of pacification. Cross-border cooperation for peace is legitimized by borderland communities through a kind of transborder *homeland nationalism* that dictates collective efforts beyond borders and regardless of the sociopolitical status of actors within local power structures. According to most approaches of *transnationalism from below*, identity and territory are often turned into resources for circumventing the state. But here, linkages show the contrary. They are grounded not only on imaginaries of immemorial ties and ethnic solidarity, but also on national identification, as exemplified in the appeal by peacemakers to and lamentations over the local territorial administration of the state.[38]

In relation to the conflict as such, the little identification of people with the insurgent cause can to a great extent be explained by the vitality of these ties and the linkages that mobilize them as resources, especially as their national belonging is reasserted and reinforced.[39] The resulting cosmopolitan discourse of communitarian transnationalism creates a consciousness of militancy against various forms of insecurity and of conflict prevention among borderland communities. However, local power structures are not confined to borderlands, as their linkages connect them to interstate committees, which often stand as intergovernmental mechanisms of conflict management between Senegal and its neighbors.[40]

Pluralism is also a pattern the borderland political scene shares with national governmental scenes as local powers include grassroots organizations and individual figures like traditional and religious leaders (imams and brotherhood leaders). This shows again how borderlands can develop as trans-local scales of multilevel and multi-actor spaces where conflict management is a pattern of transnational politics involving balances as well as asymmetries in relationships that can be yet collaborative. The politics of cross-border pacification are thus an empirical evidence of how the Casamance war, and civil war hibernation, becomes an ambivalent process of political order making and of negotiation of state-making.[41]

The conflicts between Bissau-Guinean and Senegalese communities in the borderland areas, from Salikegne up to Tanaff in southern Kolda, have been taken as a good justification by the Mouvement des Jeunes pour la Paix et l'Intégration (MJPI) to take part in this (re)ordering process as a grassroots cross-border organization dedicated to politics of peace and integration in the border region. Sensitizing about the causes, the perpetrators and the consequences of the war has been a shared concern and object of commitment with a high diversity of actors such as local councillors, local administrations, security and defense forces, traders and populations.

The retrieval of the Senegalese army from many southern villages is therefore difficult to understand for local communities, as it leaves to bandits much more room for maneuver.[42] With many cells functioning in Guinea-Bissau, the vigilante committees set up by the "other" youth, calling themselves the *youth at war*, fight against the war and its consequences. They are sponsored by local councils and secure logistical support from the security forces in Senegal and Guinea-Bissau. But, despite the patronage of certain local authorities, and criminal gangs sometimes, the youth are not always successful in handling trans-boundary criminality.[43] Backed by some local NGOs, these youth sensitize about peace culture and mine clearance in central and western parts of Casamance such as Kagitt, Dialam and Effock.[44] It is quite interesting to realize that in some areas people do not feel they are directly suffering from the conflict: they do consider there is no war anymore. Recollecting the liberation war of Guinea-Bissau and the guerrilla wars of the MFDC in the 1990s, such communities rather talk about post-conflict reconstruction.[45]

Cross-border cooperation among sanitation, educational, agricultural and animal breeding services between Guinea-Bissau and Senegal is also intended to break the walls of confinement and revive social basic infrastructure, reminding people of their belonging to *here* and *there*.[46] Furthermore, this has helped to prevent and resolve many socioeconomic conflicts, especially as they are most of the time patronized by local authorities.[47] The linkages of social policy also benefit from cultural heritages preserving the ties on which are grounded these governmentalities of conflict transformation. Many festivals covering domains such as sports (football and wrestling) and culture (dance, music, craftsmanship) have been established on a seasonal basis to bring borderland communities together, integrate and make them forget frustrations brought about by lack of dispensaries and schools and the collapse of livelihood economies.[48] Through joint ventures between the MJPI and other NGOs like the Enda-Dialogue Politique, community radio broadcasting helps mediate the borderland politics of peace.[49] Their utility has been obvious, for example, by means of provoking and facilitating exchanges through contacts they established between the nurseries[50] of Guinea-Bissau and Senegal: as a result, borderland communities now share many services, including vaccination and first aid.

As tensions often rise over farming activities along wetlands straddling borders, the Communauté rurale of Medina El Hadj and the Commune of Salikegne for instance have agreed with their neighboring Bissau-Guinean vis-à-vis of Sanka and Cambajù on a joint exploitation of water and grazing resources.[51] It is in this sense also that weekly markets across the border have been revitalized. New markets are being negotiated among constituencies across the border to alleviate the criminalizing effects of wariness and banditry on cross-border trade and livelihoods.[52] Though they tend to rule over these initiatives, state governments support them by serving as guarantors and fundraisers. Even though it has not yet expanded to the northern borderlands with the Gambia, the Economic Community of West African States (ECOWAS) cross-border program reflects this governmental pretense.

Some Limitations and Challenges of Cross-Border Linkages

Though capable and efficient, cross-border peace and security linkages are restricted by serious limitations, at least by the sole fact that forces sustaining violence and predation may supersede them in the longer term. Through their *actor, structure* and *regime* dimensions, linkage politics reflect the same causal elements of the civil war whose cumulative manifestation is the prevalence of uneven state-making processes.[53]

Authoritarian incentives in favor of local councillors trigger the promptness of traditional authorities to league with modern legitimacies in sponsoring, coordinating and implementing decisions pertaining to sensitization, trade, security and social integration. However, while recognizing the legitimacy of administrative authorities and local councillors, traditional powers reject the involvement of "some actors" in illicit trade and corrupt deals. Their perception of some rules as arbitrary also often prevents from building cross-border reciprocal relationships. Concerning anticrime security, reciprocal agency is even more limited. For example, in the commune of Salikegne in Senegal, policemen are often blamed for refusing intervention of Bissau-Guinean border police and soldiers in cases of theft and crime, yet they often claim the right to pursue criminals on the other side of the boundary. Inversely, in the domain of forestry, Bissau-Guinean agents are always designated as environmental transgressors against reciprocities as they systematically ask for bribes.

The institutional or *structural dimension* of cross-border linkage politics is also a challenge. Undeniably, many institutions or structures for dialogue, consensus building and decision-making and enactment have successfully brought actors to cooperate across borders.[54] However, not only are these structures most of the time informally negotiated and established, but their functioning is also relativized by the lack of financial means, regularity and coherence. Indicative of uneven and rudimentary decentralization policies, this reflects the infrastructural and technocratic weaknesses of local governments and public services, often paralyzed by patrimonialism and reticular participation.[55]

Limitations also concern the *regime dimension* of institutions and covenants in borderlands as complex *hybrid* spaces where governance processes are shaped by both traditional and modern influences, especially as heterogeneity is stressed by political differences. Decentralized institutions are divided into three different cultures. As a consequence, modern rules and traditional ways of settling litigious cases often clash. As preeminent markers of governance and politics in trans-local areas, patrimonialism and informalism strongly influence the making and implementation of rules and norms, thus preventing regulations from effectively addressing common challenges. Obviously, modern state institutions are not yet shaped by populations who confess their difficulty to turn the wheels of justice and get through the administrative procedures for the security of their fellows, property or herd. Because populations most of the time keep silent about cases of armed robbery and physical assaults, border security forces are actually rarely successful to deal with these plagues. As an avoidance strategy, indifference is part of the challenges of cross-border peace and security building, especially as state regulations are not yet effective in the borderlands.

Conclusion

In this chapter, I have tried to look at the Casamance war from a renewed perspective, which is the borderland. Through this I attempted to get closer to its everyday dynamics. This perspective has enabled me to supplement the classical geopolitical perspective that describes this conflict as a mere secession or a peripheral conflict. Instead, to an important extent, the micro-level state–society and community interactions in the borderland reflect the macro-level regional politics in both Senegal and Guinea-Bissau. The interaction between these two scales of the Casamance conflict generates certain territorial effects, which in many respects reproduce the "civilian" character of this war. This is revealed in the trans-boundary character of borderland security dilemmas, the reproduction of which maintains the conflict in hibernation. Moreover, patterns of statehood are still found operating in the conflict in this micro-level analysis. The border effect of war prolongation still appears in the continued *marginalization* of the Casamance and its communities. As a matter of fact, despite the existence of local attempts to handle borderland insecurity dilemmas, grievances are still dormant, recurring and reproduced under the action of both political defection and armed violence inscribed at the same time in the survival strategies of some groups and individuals. In other words, despite efforts for borderland peace and security, chances are that violence against civilians and civil peace would prevail for some more time.

These initiatives indicate that the repercussions of a hibernation of the Casamance conflict are more importantly and more structurally experienced by borderland communities than at the level of the state. Both in Casamance and in Guinea-Bissau, prospects of peace are even gloomier as borderland communities are not yet accessing the official regime of the peace-building process, which is for the time being limited to the regional capital cities of Bissau and Ziguinchor. Even though local grassroots initiatives have been relatively efficient in maintaining a precarious stability and addressing daily challenges stemming from the protraction of the civil war, they are yet to be appropriated through coherent institutional processes and structures. This does not come as a surprise knowing that, in the context of the Casamance, borderland areas are marginalized and violent frontiers where the structural weaknesses of the modern state are very well manifested in the ineffectiveness of the institutions and the policies of decentralization. At the least, as exemplified in cross-border linkage politics, decentralization has just resulted in the engulfment of societal power structures without their genuine integration.

The close link between any solution to the Casamance conflict and the situation in Guinea-Bissau calls for a prior consideration of the issues of local borderland politics. Besides being more informative about the territorial triggers of the hibernation of the conflict, this borderland perspective even suggests two policy directions at least. From bilateral attempts, governments could strive toward a regional approach, as it is clear that Senegal would be further trapped in a lonely ride despite the ambiguous and discrete support of France. Neither can it expect any significant involvement from the ghost government of Guinea-Bissau. For these reasons, the negotiations that have been recalled and pushed on with no advancement have to be regionalized or perhaps internationalized. This implies crossing borders and linking borderland local initiatives to (inter)national initiatives. In a nutshell, borderlands have to be acknowledged as relevant passages to continental regions. To the extent that this should happen, emphasizing the bridging functions of borders calls for a greater scrutiny of how this should happen.

Acknowledgments

The author is grateful to the anonymous reviewers and to Timothy Raeymaekers (University of Zurich, Switzerland) and Mamadou Seydou Kane (Gaston Berger University, Senegal) for their useful comments and most valuable criticism on the earlier drafts of this chapter.

Notes

1. On this definitional controversy, see the special issue of the *Journal of Ethnopolitics and Minority Issues in Europe*, no. 8 (2009).
2. The Casamance conflict has not been an exception to such a paradigmatic prism all over the 29 years. See O. Faye, "La crise casamançaise et les relations du Sénégal avec la Gambie et la Guinée-Bissau (1980–1992)," in *Sénégal, trajectoires d'un Etat*, ed. M.-C. Diop (Dakar: CODESRIA, 1994), 190–212; J.-C. Marut, "Guinée-Bissau et Casamance: Stabilisation et instabilité," *Rapport WRITENET*, no. 15, 2000 (Dakar: UNHCR, 2001).
3. B. Sonko, "Le conflit en Casamance: Une guerre civile oubliée?," *Bulletin du CODESRIA* no. 3 & 4 (2004): 35–38.
4. S. Fanchette, "La Haute Casamance à l'heure de la régionalisation. Enjeux fonciers et territoriaux," in *La société sénégalaise entre le local et le global*, ed. M.-C. Diop (Paris: Karthala, 2002), 322–337; O. Faye, "La crise casamançaise et les relations du Sénégal avec la Gambie et la Guinée-Bissau (1980–1992)," in *Sénégal, trajectoires d'un Etat*, ed. M.-C. Diop (Dakar: CODESRIA, 1994), 190–191.
5. B. Sonko, "Le conflit en Casamance: Une guerre civile oubliée?," *Bulletin du CODESRIA*, no. 3 & 4 (2004): 36; J.-C. Marut, "Les représentations territoriales comme enjeux de pouvoir: La différence casamançaise." (Paper presented at the conference "Le territoire; lien ou frontière?," Paris, October 2–4, 1995), 6–7; Faye, "La crise casamançaise et les relations du Sénégal", 194–195.
6. O. Faye, "La crise casamançaise et les relations du Sénégal avec la Gambie et la Guinée-Bissau (1980–1992)," in *Sénégal, trajectoires d'un Etat*, ed. M.-C. Diop (Dakar: CODESRIA, 1994), 194.
7. A textbook of geography used in the primary school was the means for manipulation by the government about the natural and administrative limits of the

Casamance region. It is by I. D. Thiam, S. Mangane and S. Sow, *Géographie du Sénégal* (Dakar: NEA-EDICEF, 1989).

8. J.-C. Marut, "Guinée-Bissau et Casamance: Stabilisation et instabilité," *Rapport WRITENET*, no. 15, 2000 (Dakar: UNHCR, 2001), 7.

9. J.-C. Marut, "Guinée-Bissau et Casamance: Stabilisation et instabilité," *Rapport WRITENET*, no. 15, 2000 (Dakar: UNHCR, 2001), 7; F. A. Renner, "Ethnic affinity: Partition and political integration in Senegambia," in *Partitioned Africans. Ethnic relations across Africa's international boundaries 1884–1984*, ed. Anthony I. Asiwaju (Nigeria: University of Lagos Press, 1984): 75–78.

10. D. Darbon, *L'Administration et le paysan en Casamance* (Paris: Pedone, 1988).

11. J.-C. Marut, "Guinée-Bissau et Casamance: Stabilisation et instabilité," *Rapport WRITENET*, no. 15, 2000 (Dakar: UNHCR, 2001), 2–7; B. Sonko, "Le conflit en Casamance: Une guerre civile oubliée?," *Bulletin du CODESRIA*, no. 3 & 4, 2004: 35.

12. J.-C. Marut, "Les représentations territoriales comme enjeux de pouvoir: La différence casamançaise." (Paper presented at the conference "Le territoire; lien ou frontière?," Paris, October 2–4, 1995).

13. O. Faye, "La crise casamançaise et les relations du Sénégal avec la Gambie et la Guinée-Bissau (1980–1992)," in *Sénégal, trajectoires d'un Etat*, ed. M.-C. Diop (Dakar: CODESRIA, 1994), 198–199.

14. President Bacai Sanhá is showing health problems while former convicted general Buba Na Tchuto is lobbying for power within the military in which he can still maneuver, as exemplified by his acquittal from his charges of coup plotting in 2008. He has been reinstated as head of naval army even though restrained by his listing in the international anticrime prevention. See Integrated Regional Information Networks (IRIN), "Senegal: Rebels act on kidnap threats in Casamance." <http://www.unhcr.org/refworld/category,COI,IRIN,,SEN,47ea1fce1c,0.html> (March 20, 2008).

15. Serving to embolden military officers, the country's resumed drug industry as of the first semester of this year is estimated at USD1 billion. See S. Di Lorenzo, *Drugs return to Guinea Bissau, destabilizing it.* <http://www.google.com/hostednews/ap/article/ALeqM5gJesugYieOra7PfjTwVraPl9gg_wD9G53AO80> (June 15, 2010).

16. P. Ferreira, "Guinea Bissau: Between conflict and democracy," *African Security Review* 13, no. 4 (2004): 45–56.

17. See on the role of Brigadier Mané in the civil war in Guinea-Bissau: International Crisis Group, "Guinea Bissau: Beyond the rule of the gun," *Africa Briefing* no. 61, June 25, 2009. <http://se1.isn.ch/serviceengine/Files/ISN/102604/ipublicationdocument_singledocument/E30A686B-3A9D-4510-A602-A2638D94F257/en/b61_guinea_bissau.pdf> (June 26, 2009). And on the project of the revival of precolonial Gabu territorial state, see: O. Faye, "La crise casamançaise et les relations du Sénégal avec la Gambie et la Guinée-Bissau (1980–1992)," in *Sénégal, trajectoires d'un Etat*, ed. M.-C. Diop (Dakar: CODESRIA, 1994).

18. When the men of César Atoute Badiate and those of Salif Sadio were clashing at the Gambian borders around Kanilai and the Sama Forest between 2002 and 2005, only the former were arrested and delivered to Senegal while Salif Sadio and his men were protected and allowed free motion in Gambia.

19. This is facilitated by the facts that in certain places rebels do not have bases but are mixed up with people, who shield them from military action from loyalist Bissau-Guineans and Senegalese troops.

20. When in destitution or military disadvantage, for instance between 1998 and 2007, when the MFDC was counting on armed supplies from Gambia and high-ranked officers in Guinea-Bissau. See on those regional aspects: V. Foucher, "Pas d'alternance en Casamance? Le nouveau pouvoir sénégalais face à la revendication casamançaise," *Politique Africaine* 91 (2003): 106; J.-C. Marut, "Après avoir perdu l'Est, la Guinée Bissau perd t-elle aussi le Nord?," *Lusotopies* 1996: 81–92; J.-C. Marut, *Guinée-Bissau, Casamance et Gambie: Une zone à risques* (Institut d'Etudes de Sécurité de l'Union Européenne, December 2008); and T. Lehtinen, "The military–civilian crisis in Guinea Bissau," 2000: 121–131. www.conflicttransform.net/Guinea.pdf.

21. See on these "regional connections" that give the civil war a transnational dimension: A. Tandia, "The transnational actors and dimensions of the Casamance conflict" (Paper presented at the Africa Europe Group of Interdisciplinary Studies Summer School, Cortona, Italy, July 7–13, 2010).

22. V. Foucher, "Pas d'alternance en Casamance? Le nouveau pouvoir sénégalais face à la revendication casamançaise," *Politique Africaine* 91 (2003): 102–103.

23. The setup, display and failure of management options and strategies over the Casamance conflict have been analyzed with brilliant scholarly detailed scrutiny by Jean-Claude Marut, *Le conflit de Casamance: Ce que disent les armes* (Paris: Karthala, 2010). As concerns the Guinea-Bissau post–civil war and stabilization transition, see the concise and recent articles by Paolo Gorjão, "Guinea-Bissau: The inescapable feeling of 'déjà vu'," *Policy Brief,* Portuguese Institute of International Relations and Security, 2010: 1–8; and M. Telatin, "Questioning the European Union security sector reform in Guinea-Bissau," *Portuguese Journal of International Affairs* 2 (2009): 27–35.

24. T. Raeymaekers, "The power of protection: Governance and transborder trade on the Congo–Ugandan frontier," (PhD Thesis, Ghent University, 2007). <http://biblio.ugent.be/input/download?func=downloadFile&fileOId=492973>.

25. M. Diouf, "Privatisation des Etats africains: Commentaires d'un historien," *Politique Africaine* 73, 1999: 18.

26. P. Le Billon, *Geopolitics of resource wars: Resource dependence, governance and violence* (London: Frank Cass, 2005).

27. V. Foucher, "Pas d'alternance en Casamance? Le nouveau pouvoir sénégalais face à la revendication casamançaise," *Politique Africaine* 91 (2003): 101–119; A. Tandia, "The transnational actors and dimensions of the Casamance conflict" (Paper presented at the Africa Europe Group of Interdisciplinary Studies Summer School, Cortona, Italy, July 7–13, 2010).

28. J.-C. Marut, *Guinée-Bissau, Casamance et Gambie: Une zone à risques* (Institut d'Etudes de Sécurité de l'Union Européenne, December 2008), 2–5; T. Lehtinen, "The military–civilian crisis in Guinea Bissau," 2000: 121–131. <www.conflicttransform.net/Guinea.pdf>.

29. These gangs are of two types: one is the organized armed groups connected with international networks collaborating with mercenaries from Liberia and Sierra Leone. These gangs are part of the armed wing of the MFDC. The other comprises youngsters of neighboring villages, called the "dregs of the borderlands", who do not hesitate to attack their own neighbors under the burden of survival in a context where schooling or employment is a luxury.

30. S. Fanchette, "La Haute Casamance à l'heure de la régionalisation. Enjeux fonciers et territoriaux," in *La société sénégalaise entre le local et le global*, ed. M.-C. Diop (Paris: Karthala, 2002), 337–346. See also previous papers by A. Tandia, "Diplomatie locale et sécurité transfrontalière: Quelle pertinence pour la gouvernance sécuritaire régionale de la CEDEAO?," *Governance institute session, security governance in Africa*, (Dakar: CODESRIA, 2007) and "Cross-border trade and cross-border cooperation on the militarized borders of western Senegambia: Comparing configurations on the borderlands of Senegal, the Gambia and Guinea Bissau" (Paper presented at the African Borderlands Research Network Conference, Basel, Switzerland, September 8–11, 2010).

31. Major of the Commune of Salikegne (70 km from Kolda), May 10, 2010.

32. One can ask whether this reference to Jola ethnic group as being the substance of the insurgency is not an evidence of the inconsistency of the identitary basis of present-day MFDC with the ethnic and cultural diversity of the Casamance.

33. L. Sindjoun, *Sociologie des relations internationales africaines* (Paris: Karthala, 2002), 73.

34. L. E. Guarnizo and M. P. Smith, *Transnationalism from below* (New Brunswick: Transaction Publishers, 2006), 26.

35. From a historical perspective, borders are also expressions and products of histories constructed by way of strong sociocultural ties among ethnic groups that live astride them. See P. Nugent and A. I. Asiwaju, *African boundaries: Barriers, conduits and opportunities* (London: Pinter-Center of African Studies, 1996).

36. See S. Vertovec, "Conceiving and researching transnationalism," *Ethnic and Racial Studies* 22, no. 2 (1999): 447–462.

37. As I have underlined in the last section of this chapter, decentralization is not a sound basis for this trans-boundary collective action. See A. Tandia, "Borders and borderland identity in western Senegambia: A comparative perspective of cross-border governance in the neighbourhoods of Senegal, Gambia and Guinea Bissau," *African Nebula* 2 (2010): 19–42.

38. The local discourse patterns disclose the legitimating representation of what Sindjoun, *Sociologie des relations* (2002), calls a "communitarian transnationalism", which professes the transcending of the juridical boundaries by means of an ethic of tolerance that functions as the code of social relations. Given that any identity has a territorial expression, this localizing rhetoric of the

extraterritorial collective action expresses a conception of the border space as a symbolic and material resource that can support a collective action beneficial to one and the same community. See A. Tandia, "Borders and borderland identity in western Senegambia: A comparative perspective of cross-border governance in the neighbourhoods of Senegal, Gambia and Guinea Bissau," *African Nebula* 2 (2010): 33; L. E. Guarnizo and M. P. Smith, *Transnationalism from below* (New Brunswick: Transaction Publishers, 2006).

39. This may also explain why these community attempts are more likely to succeed than NGO programs. One can even ask why NGOs find it hard to surf on this identitary weakness of insurgency.

40. All customary chiefs and imams of different major localities affected by trans-boundary criminality and the conflict are invited to take part in the different meetings of the interstate committees in Bissau or Ziguinchor. However, this does not seem to be a systematic way of photographing and relieving affected localities.

41. One hardly finds initiatives like these in the borders between Gambia and the Casamance, though a form of cross-border cooperation is working since 1982 on the northern borders with Senegal. See A. Tandia, "Diplomatie locale et sécurité transfrontalière: Quelle pertinence pour la gouvernance sécuritaire régionale de la CEDEAO?," *Governance institute session, security governance in Africa* (Dakar: CODESRIA, 2007).

42. This has led to lesser frequentation of many road paths including the main road (the Nationale 6) linking Kolda to Ziguinchor, therefore enclosing furthermore localities like Salikegne, Medina El Hadj, Niangha and Tanaff, which leads to widespread banditry.

43. One week before our arrival in Salikegne, a shopkeeper named Ousmane Dabo had been the victim of armed gangs who faced the sole officer of the Salikegne border police station, while the borderline is stretched along 70 km. Some inhabitants we have interviewed feel that this insecurity is due to the enclavement of their locality which they silently blame on the MFDC because of the war it has been waging against the Senegalese government. This feeling is on behalf of the inhabitants tantamount to an increasing antipathy towards the insurgency.

44. Apart from southwestern Casamance, most mine-polluted places are areas around Tankanto Escale, Medina El Hadj in Kolda, and Tanaff, Niangha, Simbandi Brassou, Simbandi Balanta up to Samine, where the bases of the MFDC are located and have been mined twice, by the PAIGC African Party for the Independence of Guinea and Cape Verde (Partido Africano da independencia da Guiné e Cabo Verde) first and then by the MFDC.

45. They actually mean the effects of a history of violence characteristic of the borderlands, whose effects (community violence and tensions) have been fueled by cross-national economic hardships and poverty in the homelands.

46. See See S. Vertovec, "Conceiving and researching transnationalism," *Ethnic and Racial Studies* 22, no. 2 (1999): 447–462.

47. The organ that has been given the mandate for that, the Comité de Gestion et de Résolution des Conflits, gathers Bissau-Guineans and Senegalese. It is chaired by the *sous-préfet* of Cuntima in Guinea-Bissau.
48. The MJPI was the pioneer of two big festivals in Salikegne and Cambaju, which were attended in 2003 by the then Bissau-Guinea President Coumba Yala.
49. The MJPI holds its own radio station in the Communauté rurale of Dioulacolon. This radio called Endam FM (*Endam* means brotherhood in Mandinka) was created in 2006 and funded by the German cooperation agency GTZ-Procas. It covers six local councils in Senegal and some places of Guinea-Bissau (Kontouboel, Mansona and Dioumbembem) and is part of a network of 12 stations scattered on the borderlands of the three countries.
50. This has been more successful in places like Sanka and Tonia Taba with the support of GTZ-Procas.
51. New dikes have been built around the Léba Valley surrounded by Medina El Hadj, Tankanto Escale and Salikegne to foster rice growing and cattle breeding.
52. The markets of Sama and Bantama in Guinea-Bissau and in front of the Communauté rurale of Niangha, and that of Wensaco in Senegal have died. Only the *loumos* of Tonia Taba and Cambaju in Guinea Bissau are still surviving the Casamance conflict.
53. See G. Hyden, "Governance and the study of politics." in *Governance and politics in Africa*, ed. G. Hyden and M. Bratton (London: Lynne Rienner, 1995), 1–26.
54. These are the trans-frontier conflict management committees, peace forums, committees of forestry management, periodical meetings of chambers of commerce and vigilante groups.
55. See G. Bundo, "Logiques de Gestion Publique dans la Décentralisation Sénégalaise: Participation Factionnelle et Ubiquité Réticulaire." *Bulletin de l'APAD 15,* 1998, <http://apad.revues.org/document555.html?format=print> (August 27, 2007).

References

Bundo, G. "Logiques de Gestion Publique dans la Décentralisation Sénégalaise: Participation Factionnelle et Ubiquité Réticulaire." *Bulletin de l'APAD* 15: 1998. <http://apad.revues.org/document555.html?format=print>.
Darbon, D. *L'Administration et le paysan en Casamance*. Paris: Pedone, 1988.
Diouf, M. "Privatisation des Etats africains: Commentaires d'un historien." *Politique Africaine* 73 (1999): 16–23.
Di Lorenzo, S. *Drugs return to Guinea Bissau, destabilizing it.* (June 15, 2010). <http://www.google.com/hostednews/ap/article/ALeqM5gJesugYieOra7PfjTwVra Pl9gg_wD9G53AO80>.
Fanchette, S. "La Haute Casamance à l'heure de la régionalisation. Enjeux fonciers et territoriaux." In *La société sénégalaise entre le local et le global*, edited by M.-C. Diop. Paris: Karthala, 2002: 322–337.

Faye, O. "La crise casamançaise et les relations du Sénégal avec la Gambie et la Guinée-Bissau (1980–1992)." In *Sénégal, trajectoires d'un Etat*, edited by M.-C. Diop. Dakar: CODESRIA, 1994: 190–212.

Ferreira, P. M. "Guinea Bissau: Between conflict and democracy." *African Security Review* 13, no. 4 (2004): 45–56.

Foucher, V. "Pas d'alternance en Casamance? Le nouveau pouvoir sénégalais face à la revendication casamançaise." *Politique Africaine* 91 (2003): 101–119.

Gorjão, P. "Guinea-Bissau: The inescapable feeling of 'déjà vu'." *IPRIS Policy Brief* 2 (2010): 1–8.

Guarnizo, L. E. and M. P. Smith. *Transnationalism from below*. New Brunswick: Transaction Publishers, 2006.

Hyden, G. "Governance and the study of politics". In *Governance and politics in Africa*, edited by G. Hyden and M. Bratton. London: Lynne Rienner, 1995: 1–26.

Integrated Regional Information Networks. "Senegal: Rebels act on kidnap threats in Casamance." March 20, 2008. <http://www.unhcr.org/refworld/category,COI,IRIN,,SEN,47ea1fce1c,0.html.>

International Crisis Group. "Guinea Bissau: Beyond the rule of the gun." *Africa Briefing* 61, 25 June 2009. <http://se1.isn.ch/serviceengine/Files/ISN/102604/ipublicationdocument_singledocument/E30A686B-3A9D-4510-A602-A2638D94F257/en/b61_guinea_bissau.pdf>.

Marut, J.-C. "Les représentations territoriales comme enjeux de pouvoir: La différence casamançaise." Paper presented at the conference "Le territoire; lien ou frontière?" Paris, October 2–4, 1995. <http://horizon.documentation.ird.fr/exl-doc/pleins_textes/divers08-09/010014865-33.pdf>.

Marut, J.-C. "Guinée-Bissau et Casamance: Stabilisation et instabilité." *Rapport WRITENET,* no. 15/2000, UNHCR, 2001.

Marut, J.-C. *Le conflit de Casamance: Ce que disent les armes*. Paris: Karthala, 2010.

Marut, J.-C. "Après avoir perdu l'Est, la Guinée Bissau perd-t-elle aussi le Nord?" *Lusotopies*, 1996: 81–92. <http://www.lusotopie.sciencespobordeaux.fr/marut96.pdf>.

Marut, J.-C. "Guinée-Bissau, Casamance et Gambie: une zone à risques." Institut d'Etudes de Sécurité de l'Union Européenne, December 2008. <http://www.iss.europa.eu/uploads/media/Guinee-Bissau_Casamance_Gambie.pdf>.

Journal of Ethnopolitics and Minority Issues in Europe, no. 8 (1) 2009. <http://www.doaj.org/doaj>.

Le Billon, P. *Geopolitics of resource wars: Resource dependence, governance and violence*. London: Frank Cass, 2005.

Lehtinen, T. "The military–civilian crisis in Guinea Bissau." 2000: 121–131. <www.conflicttransform.net/Guinea.pdf>.

Nugent, P. and A. I. Asiwaju. *African boundaries: Barriers, conduits and opportunities*. New York: Pinter-Center of African Studies, 1996.

Raeymaekers, T. "The power of protection: Governance and transborder trade on the Congo–Ugandan frontier." Ph.D, Ghent University, 2007.

Renner, F. A. "Ethnic affinity: Partition and political integration in Senegambia." In *Partitioned Africans. Ethnic relations across Africa's international boundaries 1884–1984*, edited by A. I. Asiwaju. London: University of Lagos and Hurst & Company, 1984: 71–86.

Sindjoun, L. *Sociologie des relations internationales africaines*. Paris: Karthala, 2002.

Sonko, B. "Le conflit en Casamance: Une guerre civile oubliée?" *Bulletin du CODESRIA* 3, no. 4 (2004): 35–38.

Tandia, A. "Borders and borderland identity in western Senegambia: A comparative perspective of cross-border governance in the neighbourhoods of Senegal, Gambia and Guinea Bissau." *African Nebula* 2 (2010): 19–42.

Tandia, A. "Cross-border trade and cross-border cooperation on the militarized borders of western Senegambia: Comparing configurations on the borderlands of Senegal, the Gambia and Guinea Bissau." Paper presented at the African Borderlands Research Network Conference, Basel, Switzerland, September 8–11, 2010.

Tandia, A. "The transnational actors and dimensions of the Casamance conflict." Paper presented at the Africa Europe Group of Interdisciplinary Studies Summer School, Cortona, Italy, July 7–13, 2010.

Tandia, A. "Diplomatie locale et sécurité transfrontalière: Quelle pertinence pour la gouvernance sécuritaire régionale de la CEDEAO?" Governance Institute Session, *Security governance in Africa*, Dakar: CODESRIA, 2007.

Telatin, M. "Questioning the European Union security sector reform in Guinea-Bissau." *Portuguese Journal of International Affairs* 2 (2009): 27–35.

Thiam, I. D., S. Mangane and S. Sow. *Géographie du Sénégal*. Dakar: NEA-EDICEF, 1989.

Vertovec, S. "Conceiving and researching transnationalism." *Ethnic and Racial Studies* 22, no. 2 (1999): 447–462.

Epilogue: The View from the Border

Jonathan Goodhand

Introduction

This volume started by inviting the reader to imagine standing somewhere on the Khyber Pass, in order to observe the dynamic realities of everyday life and practices at the Afghan–Pakistan frontier. A very different vantage point for looking at the borderland could also be invoked; imagine sitting behind a computer screen in the Creech Air Force Base in Nevada in the United States, operating one of the many drones flying over the borderlands every day, engaged in the surveillance and pacification of this "unruly" space. Another vantage point might be a USAID desk officer sitting in an office in Kabul or Islamabad in high-security compounds behind high walls and razor wire, planning to funnel large injections of aid funding into the borderlands with the same goal of stabilizing this "ungoverned" territory. Although this constitutes an extreme case, it is perhaps illustrative of how detached policy-making and intervention in the twenty-first century have become from the reality of life in the frontier zones. Efforts to map and "know" the borderlands from a distance, and the standard tropes of redefining frontier regions as "rogue", "failing" or "fragile" states, arguably make them more unknowable and illegible to policy-makers.[1]

The contributions to this volume start from a very different premise; they are based upon extended and grounded research within selected African and Asian borderlands, and consequently highlight the need to pay attention to borderlands *in their own right* as a subject of analysis and as an important issue to be considered in the policy worlds of development and peace-building. Borderlands are interesting points of study in themselves, and they also provide a productive entry point for asking broader questions about the nature of the state, violent conflict and peace-building. The chapters provide a fine-grained analysis of the dynamics of conflict, development and state-building and state crisis in borderland regions. By starting from, and focusing on, the margins, these chapters have sought to demonstrate how borderlanders deal with states and the complex conflicts, negotiations, bargains and settlements that take place between central states and borderland leaders and populations.

In this epilogue I aim to return to some of the key themes introduced in the first chapter and which reoccur in subsequent contributions, in order to draw out their theoretical and practical implications. Although the borderlands literature has produced important theoretical and empirical insights, their impacts on the world of policy and practice, particularly in the fields of peace-building and development, have been rather limited. I will briefly explore why this may be the case and then attempt to map out how a borderlands perspective challenges policy-makers and practitioners to see and do things differently. I will focus on the volume's three cross-cutting themes—"violence, security and the border"; "states, sovereignty and identity"; "borders, war economies and peace economies"—in order to draw out some of the issues and questions raised in the chapters that have significant implications for policy. The aim of this chapter is rather diagnostic than prescriptive, but it is hoped to identify fruitful areas of future research, along with some of the policy implications of a borderland perspective.

Policy Narratives and Borderland Blindness

I would argue that there is a deep-seated (and sometimes willful) blindness among policy-makers to questions of space and borders. As Willem van Schendel[2] notes, the social sciences came into being at the same time as the European states emerged, and social scientists have largely stood in awe of the state. This "methodological territorialism", a state-centered and stasis-centered view of the world, is deeply insinuated into the spatial logic of the social sciences. It is also, I would argue, embedded in the worldviews and organizing principles of the aid and peace-building industry—manifest in the way the world is divided up into contiguous spatial units, the division into country teams and programs, the location of offices in capital cities, the aggregation of statistics and analysis at the national level and so forth. The point is not that policy-makers are necessarily blind to boundaries, but that they tend to "see like a state". And in so doing they take some (state-delineated) boundaries as natural and given, while ignoring and often inadvertently stepping on others.

First, policies and interventions are underpinned by a Cartesian image of space as a static, bounded block, linked to notions of territorial coherence and integrity. Space is understood as "a realm of stasis, as a pre-given, unchanging territorial platform upon which social action occurs".[3] Following this logic of abstract space, territorial control is located at the center and radiates outward toward the peripheries—there is an assumed hierarchy of space in which areas at the edge of sovereign space are necessarily marginal. Thus, state power is diffused outward from the center to periphery, penetrating and enclosing the unruly frontiers.

Second, this (usually implicit) conceptualization of space is tied to notions of absolute and indivisible sovereignty, and the state as the sole provider and guarantor of law, order and security.[4] Domestic sovereignty requires a source of authority (kingship, nation, people in government) that operates exclusively and effectively within the territory of the state.[5]

Third, societal institutions on the margins are viewed as a blank slate, waiting to be "written over" or pacified and made legible through processes of territorialization and the naturalization of national space. State simplifications such as mapping and censuses make society more legible and therefore governable. Old societal boundaries wither away with the drawing and inscription of hard territorial boundaries. And associated with the delineation are binary distinctions between state and non-state, legal and illegal, political and economic, formal and informal, citizen and noncitizen.

Fourth, central to state-building is the emergence of a Lockean contract; state legitimacy is based upon the ability to provide public goods including security, welfare, social protection and so forth. States, which diverge from this Lockean model and are unable to protect their populations, police their borders and consequently export "public bads" such as terrorism, insecurity, contraband and drugs, are somehow deficient and are labeled as "failing" or "fragile", thus requiring ameliorative measures in the form of exogenous state-building or even regime change. This is based on an assumption that sovereignty is a largely realized phenomenon in the West, but absent or unrealized elsewhere.

Fifth, borderlands are viewed as potentially dangerous and disconnected. They suffer from pathologies of the margins, which are the results of a failure to integrate into the state or an inability to engage with or profit from neoliberal development. The discourse of danger has a long history, marking a divide between the settled and nomadic ways of life, the civilized world and the barbarians.

Seeing like a (Non-)State; Looking beyond and below the State

The contributors to this volume all call into question the above narratives, though the authors come from different disciplinary backgrounds and deploy differing research methods. All have sought to look "beyond" and "below" the state in order to capture the everyday practices, dynamics and processes of border zones. The contributors have aimed at developing an ethnographic sensibility to capture the everyday dimensions of borders and the social practices of borderlanders. They take us away from a school atlas view of the world and instead reveal a messier (and far more interesting) reality, where boundaries are routinely transgressed and hybrids abound. They show the complexities of power, sovereignty and territory and the dynamic processes of deterritorialization and reterritorialization, de-bordering and re-bordering. Rather than seeing territory as bounded space, they highlight the historically produced, relational and dynamic dimensions of territory.

The chapters call into question simplistic teleological reflexes about frontiers, state-building and borderlands. They overturn the Turnerian narrative of frontiers as empty spaces or pre-state zones of transition that are swallowed up and disappear as borders are drawn and inscribed, and states penetrate and control unruly peripheries. This narrative assumes a natural, automatic and irreversible progression from frontier to borderland. Rather than assuming that frontiers will wither away or be swallowed up, as a single political authority establishes their hegemony over a region, the contributions to this volume reveal a rather different story. They show first that frontier dynamics live on in borderland regions—traces of the frontier may remain hardwired into the infrastructure and institutions of the borderland: for example, Pakistan's FATA (Chapter 1), whose regulatory regime retains many of its colonial frontier characteristics. Second, they provide powerful illustrations of how borderlands may revert to their pre-state origins as open frontiers, particularly in times of protracted conflict (see, for example, Chapter 8). In such regions, the state far from being a static, unchanging power container is contingent, contested and changing. In fact, borderlands may be more resilient and adaptive than the state, and borderland biographies[6] reveal surprising continuities in political and social arrangements at the border.

Therefore, borderlands have their own unique dynamics as state legibility and control may be less stable and marked than at the center. The chapters challenge an assumed dichotomy between the center and periphery by looking at questions of space in more dynamic and relational terms. What occurs in the margins may play a pivotal role in shaping developments at the center. For example, Chapter 4 demonstrates how militarized resistance at the periphery by the KNU and other ethnonationalist groups contributed in turn to the militarization of the Burmese state. Borderlands also play a role in shaping metropolitan centers on the other side of the border—for the political and military elites of Kampala for instance, the porous DRC border opens up a frontier zone of demographic expansion and resource extraction. Notions of center and periphery may also radically shift. As Wolfgang Zeller shows (Chapter 8), economically speaking the frontier region of "Sugango" (Uganda–Congo–Sudan triangle) is where the "action is"—it is where processes of accumulation, redistribution and investment are occurring, contributing to "actually existing" development on the putative margins.

Although the volume does not set out to be strictly comparativist, nor does it attempt to develop typologies or classifications of borderlands,[7] there are clearly interesting comparisons to be drawn from the different Asian and African borderlands. These borderlands stand at the interfaces of different "governable spaces",[8] and this interface produces different forms of rules and regulation, which may work against or stand in direct confrontation with each other. The emergence, inscription and defense of a line creates its own set of dynamics as people, institutions and structures adapt and change. The borderlands vary in different ways in terms of their origins, characteristics and effects:

- First, borderlands vary in terms of their structural characteristics including terrain, demography and resources, which influences the extent to which they constitute promising or unpromising sites for state-building.
- Second, these structural features in turn play a role in shaping the political relationship between the metropolitan power center and borderland elites—this is reflected in the level of state presence and control in terms of infrastructure, institutions and coercive capacity, which are in turn manifestations of the kinds of political settlements and social contracts involving the state and borderlanders. This may vary along a continuum ranging from violent pacification to perpetual standoff, to complex interdependencies. The state may have a very uneven presence across its various borderlands involving different kinds of encounter, contact and "contract".[9]
- Third, the level of state interest in borderland, the capacity of borderlanders to resist state encroachments and the dynamics of the border itself influence the "breadth" of the borderland—which essentially marks the fuzzy frontier between state and borderland, where the border effect recedes and the state effect becomes preeminent (very wide border in the case of Chapter 8) compared to a narrowing borderland in the case of Chapter 4, with both the Burmese and Thai states seeking to extend their control over the border areas by turning battlefields into marketplaces.
- Fourth, the permeability or hardness of the border, reflected in the institutions around the border, including policing and customs control, shows that while borderlands are tied together by horizontal flows and networks, they are also vertically separated by power relations and institutions. And a great deal of violence and coercion may go into maintaining borders.

- Fifth, the impulse to securitize a border is influenced by the "depth" of the border, thus the level of difference between the two sides—the US–Mexico border, for example, having much greater depth than the US–Canada border—and the strategic importance of the border to the center. The extent to which this level of difference is perceived as a source of threat and instability has consequences for the militarization of borders—by both the state and borderlanders.
- Sixth, the level of international and regional engagement in the borderland—compare, for example, the Indian case (where borderland instability is treated as a purely domestic problem) with internationally supported peace-building in the Ferghana Valley—reflects the state's capacity to resist external meddling in their borderlands.

Keeping in mind these broad comparisons, we turn now to three major themes in this volume.

War and Violence in the Borderlands

Frontiers and borderlands have histories of violence. The borderlands of Europe, as Tatiana Zhurzhenko notes, are "victim intensive places, with their historical memories shaped by collective traumas, former hostilities and shared guilt".[10] Historically, the main episodes of boundary formation have followed major wars and the breakup of empires. Boundary delineation may be legitimized through legal texts, but it is underpinned and maintained through raw power—in other words, demarcation through domination.[11] The violence associated with Indian partition follows a familiar pattern, whereby "vivisectionist violence"[12] unmixes populations and inscribes sharply defined boundaries between groups.

The liberal view of state-building tends to erase violence from the story— yet it is frequently at the borders where state-building projects of territorialization meet spaces of resistance, and the coercive face of the state is exposed. In "unruly" borderlands, the state deploys despotic rather than infrastructural power,[13] or in the terminology of Charles Tilly, state-building follows a coercion-intensive rather than a capital-intensive path.[14] Borderscapes contain physical reminders of this overreliance on, or over-accumulation of, coercive power in the form of barracks, watchtowers, walls and barriers, checkpoints, barbed wire and army camps. In the borderlands, the Leviathan is often a stranger, with the army, the police force and government officials being appointed by and coming from the center. Infrastructure including roads and settlement patterns may be shaped according to the logic of security and militarization. Writing about roads in the Andes, Fiona Wilson tellingly notes that for borderlanders, far from representing symbols of development and progress, they are known as places of ambush and assault. Roads located on "the fringes of the state are themselves war zones, a reminder of the fragility of sovereignty and the emptiness of the state's claim to sovereignty".[15]

However, the Leviathan is not necessarily unfamiliar to borderlanders. The metropolis may be both absent but forcefully present. As Ariel Ahram[16] notes, states are not necessarily monopolists and many do not claim or indeed try to secure a monopoly over the means of coercion. They rule through brokering arrangements, franchising out the means of violence to militias, bandits and men of violence on the periphery. Repertoires of violence shift accordingly, between targeted and indiscriminate killing, between ethnic cleansing and policing.

The case studies in this book show differences in the coercive power and presence of the state in border zones. The Indian (Chapter 7) and Burmese (Chapter 4) cases show the state at its most potent, relative at least to many of the African examples. Whereas the Indian state has a direct presence in the borderlands, and the means of coercion have largely been monopolized and institutionalized, in the Burmese case, the KNU remains a threat to the state's monopoly of violence, albeit a declining one, which is dealt with through a combination of peace agreements and a brutal counterinsurgency campaign.

The KNU are one of several examples of how violence needs a degree of organization, and quasi-state structures can emerge in the borderlands, which develop sustainable forms of financing and resource mobilization. People who travel from the borderland to the capital may have to pass through different "orders of violence" established by the state, militias and guerrillas.[17] These orders, and associated boundaries, may be more or less stable. It is at the interfaces between competing regulatory regimes where authority is contested and uncertain, and where the highest levels of indiscriminate violence are likely to be experienced[18]—for example, the gray zones between "cleared" (government-controlled) and "uncleared" (LTTE-controlled) territory saw the highest levels of predatory violence during Sri Lanka's war.[19]

Finally, the cases problematize and complexify the notion of a clear boundary between "war" and "peace". Borderlands within war zones may become interconnected neuralgia points in a wider regionalized conflict system.[20] But they can also be surprisingly stable—orders of violence are not just destructive, but also constitutive—they may normalize and institutionalize political figurations,[21] bringing about new forms of order and development. Conversely, borderlands in peace zones may be extremely violent, unpredictable and warlike—Ciudad Juárez on the Mexican–US border being a potent example, which has a homicide rate that exceeds the level of killing in many of today's war zones. In such settings, one can observe interconnections between different forms of violence, which blur the boundaries between criminal and political, individual and collective violence, indeed between war and peace.[22] Finally, international intervention in borderlands is another important element of the story of violence and insecurity—whether one is talking about militarized interventions in Afghanistan or rather ham-fisted efforts to "build peace" in the Ferghana Valley (Chapter 6), which have unpredictable and unsettling effects.

States, Sovereignty and Identity

The nation-state ideal not only involves monopolizing the means of violence, but also includes the standardization of political and administrative governance—what James Scott refers to as "state simplifications"—and the pursuit of policies of cultural homogenization within a clearly bordered territory.[23] Territoriality can be understood as an ideological practice and discourse that transforms national spaces and histories, cultures, economies and resources into bounded space. Citizens undergo processes of territorial socialization[24] in the form of stories, narratives, myths and legends, films, ceremonies and memorials, which aim to produce national imaginaries and a sense of allegiance to the state—to the extent that the state becomes important enough for people to be willing to kill and die for.

Central to the production of a national identity or in-group solidarity is the creation of dangerous out-groups. Minorities unsettle the nationalist myth of an ethnic homeland. Nation-states, in the words of Arjun Appadurai, "extrude blood"—they engage in acts of exclusion, cleansing and purification.[25] While the fit between nation, state and territory is never absolute, certain groups within the nation may be granted full citizenship—for example, the titular nationalities in Christine Bichsel's Central Asian case—the Kyrgyz, Uzbeks and Tajiks—while others receive only partial rights and entitlements (Chapter 6). This system of inclusion and exclusion is characterized by Joel Migdal as "segmented sovereignty",[26] which means in practice that different groups have differential levels of access to rights, services and protection, and as the Ethiopian (Chapter 2) and Indian (Chapter 7) cases show, non-favored or excluded groups in frontier regions may live in a permanent state of exception.

If nation-states are "imagined communities",[27] it is commonly assumed that nationalist narratives and iconography emerge from the center, in their most intense and "pure" forms—and in their journey from the center to the margins of the state, they become diluted and hybridized as they cross diverse social terrains. And yet it may be at the borders of the state where the nation is experienced most intimately in the daily dramas of chauvinism that monitor identity and citizenship. The nationalist political imagination depends on the constant invocation of border threats and dangers to the territorial integrity of the nation—and history suggests that these threats may not merely be "imagined", given that ethnonational border conflicts have more than tripled the number of states in the last 60 years.[28] Border regions are frequently rich in iconography, symbols and meanings that invoke allegiance to the state. Borderization can therefore be understood less as the product of identity differences than as the *producer* of such differences.[29] It is at the margins of state authority where extremism frequently flourishes. Historically, people from border areas have been strongly represented in nationalist movements, perhaps because the loyalty of borderland elites is likely to be scrutinized most closely by the central state. And so it is frequently at the borders where plays for legitimacy may be at their most intense and contested.

But states' monopolies over the production of symbols and narratives are always contested. There are countervailing narratives and processes of (re)territorial socialization.[30] Borderlands challenge the naturalization of the state and the taken-for-granted "fit" between state, nation and territory. As already noted, borderlands frequently retain or acquire many of the features of imperial frontier zones with mixed populations, hybrid identities and institutions. Frontier cities are particularly potent and interesting examples of this phenomenon. According to Liam O'Dowd,[31] frontier cities were often more culturally diverse than their hinterlands as a result of their role as nodes in the political, administrative and trading networks of empires. Their continued strategic importance has made them a fulcrum for subsequent nation-state-building efforts, but their diversity and hybridity undermine and unsettle the state's efforts at simplification and homogenization.

As Chapter 2 on the Ethiopian borderlands shows, central states have to deal with multiple peripheries, and may behave very differently in different border areas. Catherine Boone[32] and Paul Nugent[33] similarly argue that processes of state formation and consolidation in African states are highly uneven. States are not necessarily monopolistic and they do not always aim to pacify their borderlands. Sovereignty is more diffuse and layered than the Weberian ideal suggests. Some borderlands may be safely left alone as they constitute no threat and have little to offer the central state; they may be too sparsely populated, have too few resources and be too remote for the state to profitably administer.

The same state can therefore negotiate or impose very different "social contracts" on its different borderlands depending upon a range of factors including the power and reach of the state, the (in)security of the border region, its political mobilization, its resource endowment and so forth—this is very evident in the Indian (Chapter 7) and Burmese (Chapter 4) cases, where the state projects its power very dissimilarly in different borderland regions. What causes some borderlands to shift from being marginal and neglected (or powerful and advanced) to becoming unruly and militarized? The chapters show that a range of context-specific, historically contingent factors come into play. But sudden changes in the rules of the game and shifts in the power balance between center and periphery are clearly crucial. For example, powerful minorities such as the Karen in Burma (and the Tamils in Sri Lanka), who lost their privileged access to jobs and education enjoyed during the colonial period when a new national regime came into power, reacted through defensive mobilization, first politically and then militarily.

Finally, although many of the chapters deal with unruly borderlands, not all are war zones. To see borderlands only as non-state or antistate spaces of resistance is an oversimplification. They may also be zones of collaboration and collusion. For example, Peter Sahlins[34] shows, in his classic history of the emergence of national identity on the periphery of France and Spain, how a sense of nationhood on the margins occurred long before the infrastructure of the nation was built from the center—before national road networks, railroads and markets were constructed, and before compulsory primary schooling and military service were introduced. And hence the nation appeared on the periphery before it was built by the center. Nugent[35] tells a similar story in relation to the Ghana–Togo borderlands, arguing that a sense of Ghanaian identity has grown inward from the geographical margins at least as much as it has been disseminated from the center. His account shows how borderlanders, far from resisting the state and the imposition of a border, tilted new arrangements to their advantage. The story is a complex one, in which the state is forced to work with the grain of society, and consequently the structures of the state were remolded to accommodate the predilections of border populations who could not be coerced into compliance.

Borders, War Economies and Peace Economies

As noted at the beginning of this chapter, there is a dominant, state-based narrative about unruly borderlands as ungoverned spaces, which exhibit pathologies of the margins—they are political vacuums, and into this vacuum move warlords, terrorists, mafiosi and smugglers, creating zones of criminality and underdevelopment. Borderlands are dangerous and disconnected, their problems being rooted in a failure to modernize and integrate into a world of states and global capital. The chapters in this volume eschew the language of deficiency, distortion and breakdown, showing that far from being disconnected, borderlands are highly integrated into, and animated by, processes associated with globalization and transnationalism. They are structured by the dominant rhythm of world society,[36] often unmediated by state actors and institutions.

The global is traceable within local practices of violence and accumulation. Chapters 8 and 4 highlight the brutal processes of primitive accumulation associated with frontier zones: processes of enclosure and accumulation through dispossession.[37] These spaces of violence and danger are also high-risk, high-opportunity environments; a constant field of opportunity for mediators, traders and other "go-betweens" of all kinds. Borderlands provide a facility for retreat and a place of accumulation. Gatekeeper incomes can be made, and arbitrage economies and flourishing marketplaces emerge, living off the risk premiums and price differentials associated with cross-border agency and institutions.

Commercio-military alliances are forged, which frequently include state structures and actors. At certain moments, such borderland economies provide opportunities for the state to negotiate its way back into the borderlands, as has occurred in Burma, for example. As Kevin Woods shows, the military state has reinserted itself in the borderlands through a conglomeration of actors, such as state land agency workers, surveyors, regional military officers, local pro-government militia leaders as well as state-like actors, such as businessmen, ethnic elite leaders and nongovernmental organizations (NGOs).[38] But conversely borderland political economies may also provide borderland elites, and politico-military structures with the resources and autonomy to keep the state at bay, as occurred at different phases of the Burmese and Afghan conflicts. Chapter 5 demonstrates that border towns may play a central and catalytical role in the development of borderland economies. They become boomtowns and centers of entrepreneurship, production, markets, capital accumulation, investment and taxation or tribute. In many contexts, "twin" frontier towns expand upon each side of the border as traders have sought to exploit the advantages of both sides of the line.[39] Protracted fighting in the capital city and outward migration may further increase the relative size and importance of frontier towns. For weak and poor states with a low fiscal capacity, cross-border trade and customs may represent one of the most important potential sources of state revenue, and hence asserting its presence at border crossings and in frontier towns is key.

Economic activities in the borderlands are constantly adapting to (and seeking to evade) multiple forms of (international, national and local) regulation, whether we are talking about the effect of the North American Free Trade Agreement (NAFTA) on the US–Mexico border, the Afghan Transit Trade Agreement on the Afghan–Pakistani borderlands, the impacts of the Kimberley Process on the mining and trafficking of conflict diamonds in Sierra Leone or the more localized forms of taxation and tribute demanded by local politico-military elites. The Burmese government's strategy of turning battlefields into marketplaces has involved creating what Woods describes as policed resource extraction enclaves in ceasefire zones, which represents a form of counterinsurgency border development characterized by processes of "militarized territorialisation financed by different levels of the Chinese state and overseen by local military officers and regional military commanders".[40] Regulation, however, rarely achieves what policy-makers intended it to—for example, counter-narcotics policies and the militarization of borders have the effect of increasing the risk premium for traffickers and those who protect the drugs trade in Afghanistan.

Conclusions

There is a tendency in border studies to emphasize the spatial over the historical.[41] Yet the chapters show that processes of territorialization and deterritorialization cannot be abstracted from their historical context. Taking history seriously exposes the limitations of a teleological perspective on state formation, borderlands and frontiers. Thinking historically may also help us to probe further on the differences between Asian and African borderlands— an obvious one being that African states are generally younger than their Asian counterparts. Another interesting point of comparison would be to more systematically compare borderlands along a continuum of weak/fragile states to strong/developmental states.

The cases also invite us to ask broader questions that go beyond the state— how Asian and African borders are related to wider global processes and to better understand how parallel border dynamics are going on in different parts of the world, including processes of enclosure and opening, securitization, sealing and hardening alongside permeability and liberalizing, even in the same location, but more direct comparisons between "First World" and "Third World" borders will expose these power asymmetries at a global level. This also forces us to complexify notions of center and periphery; "globalisation makes borderlanders of us all, as it pokes through sovereignty, leaps over boundaries, implants peripherarians in the center and centralities in the peripheries".[42]

The case studies show that all borderlands are different, but perhaps one common feature is the crucial role of borderland brokers, who mediate simultaneously between the center and periphery and across the border. Brokerage is defined as a structural position or role in which an actor makes transactions and resource flows possible between two other social sites.[43] The hybridity of borderland institutions and practices creates opportunities for brokerage—this has a long history, as Karen Barkey notes, with frontiers always being populated by "interstitial men who belong to both sets of elites".[44] In borderland zones, states that are able to capture the brokerage functions between elites can use such a structural advantage to separate, integrate, reward and control groups.[45] But borderland brokers also aim to occupy this pivotal, meso-level position, linking the center to the periphery. By standing guard over the synapses of the state, connecting the national to the local levels,[46] these brokers mediate a complex interplay between central authorities, military, landowners, commercial interests and the peasantry. They are simultaneously both part of the connective tissue and point of friction between state and borderlands—they seek to manage problems, but never to fully resolve them, otherwise they would no longer have a role.

A borderland perspective reinforces what historical accounts of state formation tell us about the violence inherent in such processes—the brutal politics of sovereignty playing themselves out in many of today's borderlands are not anomalies or aberrations, diversions from the liberal, Lockean norm. To an extent, they *are* the norm historically speaking, and "unruly" borderlands are not automatic signifiers of state breakdown. In the long run, they may be part of a process of state consolidation, following less a smooth, linear, evolutionary trajectory, than one of "punctuated equilibrium" or sudden ruptures followed by the emergence of new political settlements and institutional arrangements.[47] This leads to rather unsettling questions about whether or not violence, wars and ethnic cleansing are necessary conditions for emergence of progressive political orders and stable, legitimate national borders.[48]

Notes

1. D. Gregory, "War and peace," *Transactions of the Institute of British Geographers* 35 (2010): 154–186.
2. W. van Schendel, "Spaces of engagement. How borderlands, illegal flows, and territorial states interlock," in *Illicit flows and criminal things*, ed. W. van Schendel and I. Abraham (Bloomington, IN: Indiana University Press, 2005).
3. N. Brenner, "Beyond state-centrism? Space, territoriality, and geographical scale in globalization studies," *Theory and Society* 28, no. 1 (1999): 41.
4. J. Bakonyi and B. Bliesemann de Guevara, "The mosaic of violence—An introduction," *Civil Wars* 11, no. 4 (2009): 297–413.
5. J. Agnew, "Sovereignty regimes: Territoriality and state authority in contemporary world politics," *Annals of the Association of American Geographers* 95, no. 2 (2005): 437–461.
6. N. Megoran, "B/ordering and biopolitics in Central Asia," in *A companion to border studies*, ed. T. M. Wilson and H. Donnan (Chichesterc: Wiley-Blackwell, 2012), 473–491.

7. See, for example, W. Zartman, *Understanding life in the borderlands. Boundaries in depth and motion* (Athens, GA: University of Georgia Press, 2010).

8. B. Korf, M. Engeler and T. Hagmann, "The geography of warscape," *Third World Quarterly* 31, no. 3 (2010): 385–399.

9. P. Nugent, "States and social contracts in Africa," *New Left Review* 63 (2010): 35–68; C. Boone, *Political topographies of the African state: Territorial authority and institutional choice* (Cambridge: Cambridge University Press, 2003).

10. T. Zhurzhenko, "Borders and memory," in *The Ashgate research companion to border studies,* ed. D. Wastl-Walter (London: Ashgate, 2011), 74.

11. J. Agnew, "Sovereignty regimes: Territoriality and state authority in contemporary world politics," *Annals of the Association of American Geographers* 95, no. 2 (2005): 437–461.

12. A. Appadurai, *Fear of small numbers. An essay on the geography of anger* (Durham, NC: Duke University Press, 2006).

13. M. Mann, "The autonomous power of the state: Its origins, mechanisms and results," *European Journal of Sociology* 25 (1984): 185–213.

14. C. Tilly, *Coercion, capital and European states, AD 1990–1992* (Cambridge: Blackwell, 1990).

15. F. Wilson, "Towards a political economy of roads: Experiences from Peru," *Development and Change* 35, no. 3 (2004): 525–546.

16. A. I. Ahram, "Learning to live with militias: Toward a critical policy on state frailty," *Journal of Intervention and Statebuilding* 5, no. 2 (2011): 175–192.

17. J. Bakonyi and B. Bliesemann de Guevara, "The mosaic of violence—An introduction," *Civil Wars* 11, no. 4 (2009): 408.

18. S. Kalyvas, *The logic of violence in civil war* (Cambridge: Cambridge University Press, 2006).

19. B. Korf, M. Engeler and T. Hagmann, "The geography of warscape," *Third World Quarterly* 31, no. 3 (2010): 385–399.

20. M. Pugh and N. Cooper with J. Goodhand, *War economies in a regional context. Challenges of transformation* (Boulder, CO: Lynne Rienner, 2004).

21. J. Bakonyi and B. Bliesemann de Guevara, "The mosaic of violence—An introduction," *Civil Wars* 11, no. 4 (2009): 397–413.

22. P. Bourgeois, "The continuum of violence in war and peace: Post–Cold War lessons from El Salvador," in *Violence in war and peace: An anthology,* ed. N. Scheper-Hughes and P. Bourgeois (Oxford: Blackwell, 2004), 425–434.

23. L. O'Dowd, "Contested states, frontiers and cities," in *A companion to border studies,* ed. T. Wilson and H. Donnan (Chichester: Wiley-Blackwell, 2012), 161.

24. D. Newman and A. Passi, "Fences and neighbours in the post-modern world: Boundary narratives in political geography," *Progress in Human Geography* 22, no. 2 (1998): 186–207.

25. A. Appadurai, *Fear of small numbers. An essay on the geography of anger* (Durham, NC: Duke University Press, 2006).

26. J. Migdal, "Statebuilding and the non-nation-state," *Journal of International Affairs* 58, no. 1 (2004): 17–46.

27. B. Anderson, *Imagined communities: Reflections on the origin and spread of nationalism* (New York and London: Verso, 1991).
28. L. O'Dowd, "Contested states, frontiers and cities," in *A companion to border studies*, ed. T. Wilson and H. Donnan (Chichester: Wiley-Blackwell, 2012), 159.
29. A. Grimson, "Nations, nationalism and 'borderization' in the Southern Cone," in *A companion to border studies,* ed. T. Wilson and H. Donnan (Chichester: Wiley-Blackwell, 2012), 194–213.
30. J. Bakonyi and B. Bliesemann de Guevara, "The mosaic of violence—An introduction," *Civil Wars* 11, no. 4 (2009): 404
31. L. O'Dowd, "Contested states, frontiers and cities," in *A companion to border studies*, ed. T. Wilson and H. Donnan (Chichester: Wiley-Blackwell, 2012), 158–176.
32. C. Boone, *Political topographies of the African state: Territorial authority and institutional choice* (Cambridge: Cambridge University Press, 2003).
33. P. Nugent, "States and social contracts in Africa," *New Left Review* 63 (2010): 35–68.
34. P. Sahlins, "The nation in the village: Statebuilding and communal struggles in the Catalan borderland during the eighteenth and nineteenth centuries," *Journal of Modern History* 60 (1988): 234–263.
35. P. Nugent, *Smugglers, secessionists & loyal citizens on the Ghana–Toga frontier: The life of the borderlands since 1914* (Ohio: Ohio University Press, 2002).
36. J. Bakonyi and B. Bliesemann de Guevara, "The mosaic of violence—An introduction," *Civil Wars* 11, no. 4 (2009): 409.
37. D. Harvey, *The new imperialism: Accumulation by dispossession* (Oxford: Oxford University Press, 2009).
38. Kevin Woods, "Ceasefire capitalism: Military–private partnerships, resource concessions and military-state building in the Burma–China borderlands," *Journal of Peasant Studies* 38, no 4 (2011): 747–770. Theo Ballve tells a similar story about the role of narco-paramilitaries in the Colombian borderlands, arguing that they have played a role in extending the territorial reach of the state, by "straddling the crucial synapses or junctures linking regional elites and state-mediated networks of power" (p. 5): T. Ballve, "Territory by dispossession: Decentralisation, statehood, and the narco land-grab in Colombia," Paper presented at the International Conference on Global Land Grabbing, April 6–8, 2011 http://www.ids.ac.uk/files/dmfile/TeoBallv.pdf.
39. P. Nugent, "Border towns and cities in comparative perspective," in *A companion to border studies,* ed. T. Wilson and H. Donnan (Chichester: Wiley-Blackwell, 2012), 557–572.
40. K. Woods, "Ceasefire capitalism: Military–private partnerships, resource concessions and military-state building in the Burma–China borderlands," *Journal of Peasant Studies* 38, no 4 (2011): 749.
41. L. O'Dowd, "Contested states, frontiers and cities," in *A companion to border studies*, ed. T. Wilson and H. Donnan (Chichester: Wiley-Blackwell, 2012), 172.
42. W. Zartman, *Understanding life in the borderlands. Boundaries in depth and motion* (Athens, GA: University of Georgia Press, 2010), 249.

262 • Jonathan Goodhand

43. K. Barkey, *Empire of difference. The Ottomans in comparative perspective* (Cambridge: Cambridge University Press, 2008).
44. K. Barkey, *Empire of difference. The Ottomans in comparative perspective* (Cambridge: Cambridge University Press, 2008),.39.
45. K. Barkey, *Empire of difference. The Ottomans in comparative perspective* (Cambridge: Cambridge University Press, 2008), 10.
46. E. Wolf, "Aspects of group relations in a complex society," *American Anthropologist* 58, no. 6 (1956): 1065–1078.
47. C. Cramer and J. Goodhand, "Try again, fail again: War, the state and the 'post conflict' challenge in Afghanistan," *Development and Change* 33, no. 5 (2002): 885–909.
48. C. Cramer, *Civil war is not a stupid thing. Accounting for violence in developing countries* (London: Hurst & Company, 2006); L. O'Dowd, "Contested states, frontiers and cities," in *A companion to border studies*, ed. T. Wilson and H. Donnan (Chichester: Wiley-Blackwell, 2012).

References

Agnew, J. "Sovereignty regimes: Territoriality and state authority in contemporary world politics." *Annals of the Association of American Geographers* 95, no. 2 (2005): 437–461.
Ahram, A. I. "Learning to live with militias: Toward a critical policy on state frailty." *Journal of Intervention and Statebuilding* 5, no. 2 (2011): 175–192.
Anderson, B. *Imagined communities: Reflections on the origin and spread of nationalism.* New York and London: Verso, 1991.
Appadurai, A. *Fear of small numbers. An essay on the geography of anger.* Durham, NC: Duke University Press, 2006.
Bakonyi, J. and B. Bliesemann de Guevara. "The mosaic of violence—An introduction." *Civil Wars* 11, no. 4 (2009): 397–413.
Ballve, T. "Territory by dispossession: Decentralisation, statehood, and the narco land-grab in Colombia." Paper presented at the International Conference on Global Land Grabbing, April 6–8, 2011. <http://www.ids.ac.uk/files/dmfile/TeoBallv.pdf>.
Barkey, K. *Empire of difference. The Ottomans in comparative perspective.* Cambridge: Cambridge University Press, 2008.
Boone, C. *Political topographies of the African state: Territorial authority and institutional choice.* Cambridge: Cambridge University Press, 2003.
Bourgeois, P. "The continuum of violence in war and peace: Post–Cold War lessons from El Salvador." In *Violence in war and peace: An anthology*, edited by N. Scheper-Hughes and P. Bourgeois. Oxford: Blackwell, 2004: 425–434.
Brenner, N. "Beyond state-centrism? Space, territoriality, and geographical scale in globalization studies." *Theory and Society* 28, no. 1 (1999): 39–78.
Cramer, C. and J. Goodhand, "Try again, fail again: War, the state and the 'post conflict' challenge in Afghanistan," *Development and Change* 33, no. 5 (2002): 885–909.

Cramer, C. *Civil war is not a stupid thing. Accounting for violence in developing countries.* London: Hurst & Company, 2006.

Gregory, D. "War and peace." *Transactions of the Institute of British Geographers* 35 (2010): 154–186.

Grimson, A. "Nations, nationalism and 'borderization' in the Southern Cone." In *A companion to border studies,* edited by T. Wilson and H. Donnan. Chichester: Wiley-Blackwell, 2012: 194–213.

Harvey, D. *The new imperialism: Accumulation by dispossession.* Oxford: Oxford University Press, 2009.

Kalyvas, S. *The logic of violence in civil war.* Cambridge: Cambridge University Press, 2006.

Korf, B., M. Engeler and T. Hagmann. "The geography of warscape." *Third World Quarterly* 31, no. 3 (2010): 385–399.

Mann, M. "The autonomous power of the state: Its origins, mechanisms and results." *European Journal of Sociology* 25 (1984): 185–213.

Megoran, N. "B/ordering and biopolitics in Central Asia." In *A companion to border studies,* edited by T. M. Wilson and H. Donnan. Chichester: Wiley-Blackwell, 2012: 473–491.

Migdal, J. "Statebuilding and the non-nation-state." *Journal of International Affairs* 58, no. 1 (2004): 17–46.

Newman, D. and A. Passi, "Fences and neighbours in the post-modern world: Boundary narratives in political geography." *Progress in Human Geography* 22, no. 2 (1998): 186–207.

Nugent, P. *Smugglers, secessionists & loyal citizens on the Ghana–Toga frontier: The life of the borderlands since 1914.* Ohio: Ohio University Press, 2002.

Nugent, P. "States and social contracts in Africa." *New Left Review* 63 (2010): 35–68.

Nugent, P. "Border towns and cities in comparative perspective." In *A companion to border studies,* edited by T. Wilson and H. Donnan. Chichester: Wiley-Blackwell, 2012: 557–572.

O'Dowd, L. "Contested states, frontiers and cities." In *A companion to border studies,* edited by T. Wilson and H. Donnan. Chichester: Wiley-Blackwell, 2012: 158–176.

Pugh, M. and N. Cooper with J. Goodhand. *War economies in a regional context. Challenges of transformation.* Boulder, CO: Lynne Rienner, 2004.

Sahlins, P. "The nation in the village: Statebuilding and communal struggles in the Catalan borderland during the eighteenth and nineteenth centuries." *Journal of Modern History* 60 (1988): 234–263.

Tilly, C. *Coercion, capital and European states, AD 1990–1992.* Cambridge: Blackwell, 1990.

Van Schendel, W. "Spaces of engagement. How borderlands, illegal flows, and territorial states interlock." In *illicit flows and criminal things,* edited by W. van Schendel and I. Abraham. Bloomington, IN: Indiana University Press, 2005: 38–68.

Wilson, F. "Towards a political economy of roads: Experiences from Peru." *Development and Change* 35, no. 3 (2004): 525–546.

Wolf, E. "Aspects of group relations in a complex society," *American Anthropologist* 58, no. 6 (1956): 1065–1078.

Zartman, W. *Understanding life in the borderlands. Boundaries in depth and motion.* Athens, GA: University of Georgia Press, 2010.

Zhurzhenko, T. "Borders and memory." In *The Ashgate research companion to border studies,* edited by D. Wastl-Walter. London: Ashgate, 2011: 63–84.

Notes on Contributors

Christine Bichsel is a senior researcher in the Department of Geosciences at the University of Fribourg, Switzerland. Her research interests are Political Geography, Historical Geography, Peace and Conflict Research and Development Studies.

Sylvia Brown's research interests cover youths in armed opposition groups, Asian borderlands, civil war and prolonged intrastate conflict, NGOs and international development, forced migration and refugees. She has recently completed a PhD in Development Studies from the School of Oriental and African Studies, University of London and is working as a consultant in the UK.

Karen Büscher is Assistant Professor and postdoctoral researcher at the Conflict Research Group, Ghent University. Her research focuses on dynamics of urbanism and urban transformation in a context of protracted violent conflict in the eastern Congolese borderland. Specific fields of interest are border towns, conflict urbanism and urban governance.

Martin Doevenspeck is a professor in Political Geography at the University of Bayreuth, Germany. His research focuses on mobility, territoriality, conflict and risk in West and Central Africa.

Dereje Feyissa (PhD, Halle) has been a research Fellow at Osaka University, the Max Planck Institute for Social Anthropology and the University of Bayreuth. Currently Dereje is an Associate Professor at the College of Law and Governance at Addis Ababa University. Dereje is the author of the book *Playing Different Games: The Paradox of Anywaa and Nuer Identification Strategies in the Gambella Region* (Berghahn, 2011) and coeditor of *Borders and Borderlands as Resources in the Horn of Africa* (James Currey, 2010). Besides, Dereje has authored numerous articles in peer-reviewed journals and edited volumes on local institutions of conflict resolution, ethnicity and conflict as well as Islam in contemporary Ethiopia.

Jonathan Goodhand is a Professor in Conflict and Development Studies at the School of Oriental and African Studies. He has conducted research and published on the political economy of aid, conflict and peace-building in South and Central Asia.

Tobias Hagmann (PhD, University of Lausanne) is associate professor in international development at Roskilde University in Denmark. He researches the political sociology of postcolonial states, the causes and consequences of violent conflict and natural resource management in the global South. Tobias is the coeditor of *Reconfiguring Ethiopia: The Politics of Authoritarian Reform* (Palgrave, 2013), *Contested Power in Ethiopia: Traditional Authorities and Multi-Party Elections* (Brill, 2012) and *Negotiating Statehood: Dynamics of Power and Domination in Africa* (Wiley-Blackwell, 2011).

Markus Virgil Hoehne, PhD, is postdoctoral researcher at the Max Planck Institute for Social Anthropology in Halle/Saale, Germany. His research interests include transitional justice, conflict, peace, state formation, borders/borderlands, identification and transnationalism. He has published widely on Somaliland, Somalia and the Horn of Africa. He is the coeditor of *Borders and Borderlands as Resources in the Horn of Africa* (James Currey, 2010).

Benedikt Korf teaches Political Geography at the University of Zurich, Switzerland. His research is concerned with the geographies of violence, thus the question of the making and unmaking of social and political (dis)order in the face of violence, coercion and political contestation, in South Asia and the Horn of Africa.

Gillian Mathys is a PhD student at Ghent University funded by the Research Council—Flanders. She is currently writing a thesis on borders and mobility in the Lake Kivu region from a historical perspective.

Timothy Raeymaekers (MA, MSc, PhD) has a long interest in the social transformations brought about by protracted armed conflict. His research in Central Africa and Europe involve the analysis of economies in war and economies of war, as well as the involvement of cross-border trade, population displacement and borderland dynamics in the transformation of regional political order in Africa's Great Lakes region. He is coeditor of *Conflict and social transformation in Eastern Democratic Republic of Congo* (Academia Press, with Koen Vlassenroot). He works at the University of Zurich, where he teaches conflict analysis and political geography.

Bert Suykens is a postdoctoral researcher with the Conflict Research Group, Ghent University. He holds a PhD in Political Science. His research focuses on the intersection of violence and governance in South Asia. He currently studies the role of non-state violent actors in everyday governance in Bangladesh, but has also done extensive fieldwork in central and northeast India.

Aboubakr Tandia is a PhD candidate in Political Science at the Gaston Berger University of Saint-Louis in Senegal. He cross-fertilizes religious studies, border studies and peace and conflict studies in western Senegambia and West Africa from a political history perspective of borderlands. His PhD thesis is precisely on religion, modernity and peace-building in independent Senegal.

Wolfgang Zeller (MSc, University of Helsinki) is the Coordinator of the African Borderlands Research Network and a Teaching Fellow at the Centre of African Studies at the University of Edinburgh. He has conducted fieldwork and published on smuggling, policing, traditional authorities and border boomtowns in the Namibia–Zambia borderland, as well as the border triangle of Uganda, DRC and South Sudan. He is the editor of a forthcoming volume in the Palgrave Series in African Borderland Studies titled *Secessionism in Africa*.

Index

Note: The letter 'n' followed by the locators refer to notes in the text.

Ballve, Theo, 261n37
banditry, 231–3, 235, 243n44
Bank of Uganda, 208
Barakat, S., 88
Barkey, Karen, 258–9
Barre, Mohamed Siyad, 57
Barth, Fredrik, 62
Barua, Anil, 178, 180
Baruah, Sanjib, 172
Bassila region, 41
Baud, Michael, 8, 19, 61, 76n11
3B axis (Banjul, Bignona and Bissau),
    222–3
Bayart, Jean-François, 19
Beatty, L., 97
Belgium, 122–3
Benin: agricultural colonization in, 41,
    44–5; forest reserves in, 42; frontier
    migrants in, 41–3; Kopytoff *vs.*
    Turner frontier logic and, 41–7;
    local and government power in,
    42–3; maps of, 41
Benin-Nigeria border, 41, 131,
    134
Berbera, Somalia, 37
Berlin conferences, 74, 122
Biagui, Jean Marie, 229
Bibia: boom and development in, 195,
    206, 207–11; border checkpoints,
    207–8; clean drinking water in,
    210; currency traders in, 209–10,
    212; as IDP camp, 206–7;
    information access and daily life in,
    210–11; as no-mans-land, 43–6,
    195–6; security and violence in,
    195, 196–7, 209, 210–11, 213;
    smuggling activities in, 208–9; *See
    also* Ugandan-South Sudanese
    border
Bichsel, Christine, 13, 16–17, 145, 254,
    265
Birere: administrative districts in, 125;
    ambiguity of space of in, 130, 134;
    citizenship and double nationality
    in, 130–4, 138n66; ethnic groups
    in, 125–6; *handicapés de Birere,*

128–9; as in-between space, 16,
    120–1, 125–33, 129, 134;
    infrastructure and public services
    in, 126; languages spoken in, 130,
    132; navigating different identities
    in, 129–34; population of, 125–6;
    poverty and crime in, 125–6; as
    socioeconomic space, 119, 126–7;
    as zones of opportunity, 126; *See
    also* Goma-Gisenyi border
Bissau-Guinean military. *See*
    Casamance region conflict;
    Guinea-Bissau
Blanchard, J-M., 90
Bobbit, Philip, 105
Boone, Catherine, 255
Boosaaso, Somalia, 37
border checkpoints, 124, 126, 128,
    207–8
border cities, 121–2
border concept: ambiguity of space and,
    7–8, 64, 130, 134, 146, 197, 201,
    211, 213; arbitrary borders, 56–8,
    60; borderland concept *vs.,* 56; as
    important and necessary, 30, 55–6,
    60–2, 90; margins and peripheries,
    4–5; margins of the state concept
    and, 194; as sociocultural places,
    30, 242n35; transnationalism and
    social relations, 234, 242n38;
    variations in defining, 30; where
    the state ends and, 4–5
borderland concept: analysis methods
    used, 19–20; border concept *vs.,*
    56; defining, 56, 194; "fragmented
    borderlands," 120, 133; frontier
    zones *vs.,* 9–13; as in-between
    places, 16, 120–1, 125–33, 129,
    134; as "meaning of nations," 168;
    as peripheral and marginalized
    spaces, 58–9, 74; spatialities of,
    10–13; worldviews of, 249–50
borderland economies. *See* borders as
    opportunity structures; transborder
    trade

Goma-Gisenyi border—*continued*
marginalization of Rwandophones,
132–3, 138n66; navigating
differences in Makoro, 127–9;
navigating different identities on,
129–33; RCD-Goma rebel
movement and, 123–4, 125,
139n77; settlement in neutral
zones, 124–5, 127; as source of
income and opportunity, 121, 134;
tax systems in, 124, 127–9;
transborder smuggling and crime,
121, 127–9, 137n55; transborder
trade, 123–4, 126–9; as twin cities,
3, 121, 124, 135n14; urbanization
and border city formation, 121–2
Gomez, Carlos, 226, 227
Gomez, Lewis, 228
Goodhand, Jonathan, 14, 247, 265
Goudiaby, Lansana, 229
Goudiaby, Mamadou, 229
governance. *See* borderland governance
Grande Barrière, 124, 126
Great Britain. *See* British colonization
GTZ Barken, 155–6, 158
GTZ-Procas, 244nn49–50
Guantanamo Bay, 60, 167
guerrilla movements. *See* rebel and
guerrilla movements
Guinea, 59
Guinea-Bissau: Casamance ethnic
groups and Gambian-Senegalese
border, 222–3, 238–9; civil war in,
223; conflict with Senegal, 235,
238–9; drug trafficking and trade
in, 240n15; liberation war in, 231,
232, 235; state failure of, 223–30;
Tonia Taba, 244n50, 244n52; *See
also* Casamance region conflict
Gupta, Akhil, 176

Hagmann, Tobias, 11, 14, 29
Haileselassie, (Emperor), 57
Haller, Dieter, 148
handicapés de Birere, 128–9
Hansen, Niles, 194

Hansen, Thomas Blom, 13, 20
Hargeysa, Somaliland, 68–74
Hastings, Donnan, 7, 32, 148
Havu people, 125
Hecq–Bethe agreement, 122
Henry, Thierry (Lamarana Boubacar
Coly), 225
herrenloses Land concept, 10, 11, 14,
30–1, 45
Hibou, Béatrice, 19
hidden transcript of power relations
model, 63
Highway A104, 202, 203, 206, 207
Hindu newspaper, 180
Hirsch, Francine, 148
Hobbes, Thomas, 40, 45
Hoehne, Markus Virgil, 14, 16, 55, 129,
266
homeland nationalism, 234
Horn of Africa. *See* African borders and
borderlands
Horsman, Mathew, 7
Horstmann, A., 64, 90
Hunde people, 125
Hüsken, Thomas, 63
Hutu people, 123, 125, 132
hybrid boundaries, 250

ICU (Islamic Courts Union), 39
identity and citizenship:
deterritorialization of space and,
130; double nationality as asset,
130–3, 138n66; *enfants de Birere*
and navigating identity, 129–34;
for Ethiopian Somalis, 37–8; on
Ethiopian-Sudanese border, 66–8,
72–3; in Ferghana Valley, 17,
150–1, 156–9; firstcomer principle
and, 40, 42–4, 46, 65; on
Goma-Gysenyi border, 129–34,
130–4, 138n66; marginalization
and, 132–3, 223, 238;
Rwandophones, 132–3, 138n66;
shared border identities, 131; state
borders *vs.* social borders and,
62–3; states, sovereignty and

Person, Y., 41
Peshawar, Pakistan, 3, 4
Petite Barrière, 124, 126, 128
Pillai report, 171
political authority. *See* borderland
  governance; sovereignty and
  political authority; state-making
  and statehood
political frontiers, 31–3, 45; *See also*
  Kopytoff frontier; Turner frontier
political marginalization, 221
political vacuums, 195, 256
Poole, Deborah, 4, 194
PRDP (Peace, Recovery and
  Development Plan), 199
property rights. *See* land ownership and
  property rights
"protected villages," 197–8, 202–3
Puntland. *See* Somaliland-Puntland
  border

radio broadcasting, 236, 244nn49–50
Raeymaekers, Timothy, 3, 62, 74, 266
Rally for Congolese Democracy-Goma
  (RCD-Goma), 123–4, 125,
  139n77
RDD (Regional Dialogue and
  Development) Project, 151–2, 159
rebel and guerrilla movements: Al
  Shabaab, 72; Assam Rifles, 170;
  borderland war and violence, 20,
  252–4, 261n37; exceptionalism as
  cause for, 8–9; Lord's Resistance
  Army (LRA), 59, 197–204, 207,
  211; marginalization of
  borderlanders and, 59; Mouvement
  des Forces Démocratiques de la
  Casamance (MFDC), 221, 223–6,
  229–31, 235, 241n20, 242n29,
  242n32, 243nn43–45; Ogaden
  National Liberation Front
  (ONLF), 37, 40, 59; Oromo
  Liberation Front (OLF), 59; Rally
  for Congolese Democracy-Goma
  (RCD-Goma), 123–4, 125,
  139n77; Sudan People's Liberation

Army (SPLA), 193, 204; Uganda
  People's Defence Force (UPDF),
  198, 201, 203–5, 207, 209–11;
  União Nacional para a
  Independência Total de Angola
  (UNITA), 59; weapons and arms
  trafficking and, 59, 224, 228, 230;
  youth at war, 235
re-bordering processes, 60, 250
Red Cross, 104
refugee camps. *See* IDP camps
Regional Dialogue and Development
  (RDD) Project, 151–2, 159
regulatory pluralism, 43–4, 194–5,
  234–5
Rehabilitation of Social Infrastructure
  Project, 151
Rengma Reserved Forest, 170, 175–6
Reserved Forests, Assam-Nagaland,
  169–70, 172, 175–9, 184n21
Revolutionary United Front (RUF), 59
Richards, Paul, 17
Rieber, Alfred J., 31
Rose, Nikolas, 194
Rösler, Michael, 30, 61
RUF (Revolutionary United Front), 59
Russia, 31
Rwanda: citizenship and nationality in,
  130–4, 138n66; European
  colonization of, 3, 121–3, 128,
  132; genocide and refugee camps
  in, 123; Kitgum military training
  exercises and, 199; Nkunda
  rebellion and, 124, 133, 139n77;
  relations with DRC, 119–20, 123;
  See also Goma-Gisenyi border
Rwandophones, 132–3, 138n66

Sadio, Salif, 224, 229, 241n18
Sahlins, Peter, 256
Salehyan, I., 90, 102
Salikegne, Senegal, 236, 237, 238,
  243n48, 243nn42–43, 244n51
Samba, Bourama, 225
Sambou, Teuw, 225
Sanaag region, 69–71

of, 58; founding of Puntland, 69;
social and political processes in, 15,
37, 64, 68–74; state practices
shaped by borderlanders in, 68–74
Somali language, 37
Sonko, Madia, 229
Sool, Sanaag and Ayn (SSC), 70–1,
79n63
Soon region, 69–71, 73
South African-Zimbabwean border, 131,
134
Southeast Asian borderland conflicts,
88–91
South Sudan: Ethiopian-Sudanese
border, 15, 64–8, 72–4;
independence of, 194, 199; Nimule
bordertown, 206, 207, 210, 212;
risk of future conflicts in, 58; *See
also* Ethiopian-South Sudanese
border; Ugandan-Sudanese border
sovereignty and political authority:
African state borders *vs.* social
borders and, 62–3; borderland as
central to, 20–1; in Central Asia,
89–90; changing modes of
contestation in Burma and,
96–104; exceptionalism and order
on Assam-Nagaland border, 167–8,
181–2; Kitgum military training
exercises and, 199–200; KNU
liberated zones and contestation,
15, 91–3, 95–105; local agency
and borders, 43–4, 56, 60–4; local
and government power in Benin,
42–3; national-territorial
delimitation and, 148–51, 162n19;
notions of space and, 248–9;
peripheries and multiple
sovereignty, 46–7; shrinking
sovereignty and irrelevant African
borders, 60; social sovereignty,
19–20; on Somaliland-Puntland
border, 68–74; as state of
exception, 14, 48, 195–6; states,
sovereignty and identity, 254–6; on
Ugandan-Sudanese border, 196–7,

213; "unsettled sovereignty" and
territory, 168, 170, 182; *See also*
borderland governance; citizenship
Soviet Central Asia. *See* Ferghana Valley
Soviet Union: disintegration of, 94, 150;
Ferghana Valley borders and,
148–51; Georgia-Turkey border,
64; national-territorial delimitation
and border formation by, 148–51,
162n19
space as static, 248–9
Spain, 256
SPLA (Sudan People's Liberation Army),
193, 204
"spontaneous districts," 125
Sri Lanka, 253, 256
SSC (Sool, Sanaag and Ayn), 70–1,
79n63
state-making and statehood: African
borders and, 32, 55–6; on
Assam-Nagaland border, 175–7,
181–2; borderland war and
violence for, 252–4, 261n37;
changing nature of boundaries and,
3–4; cross-border linkages and
challenges to, 235–9, 243nn40–42;
effect on borderland resources,
9–10; on Ethiopian-South
Sudanese border, 65–6; "global
paradigm" and, 59–60; gradual
power of borderlands and, 73–4;
identity, sovereignty and states,
254–6; KNU's state-making in
Burma, 90, 92–4, 97–104; modern
statehood *vs.* premodern ideas
about, 32; myth of the state and,
4–5; nation-states, 6–7, 254–6;
overlapping boundaries and, 37–8;
pre- and postcolonial conceptions
of, 88–9; by providing
private-public goods, 176–82, 249;
resistance to by locals in Southeast
Asia, 89–90; role of public goods
and services in, 177; sedentary
agriculture and, 40; statehood
patterns in Casamance, 220, 238

Printed in the United States of America

JAMES EARL CARTER LIBRARY
GA. SOUTHWESTERN UNIVERSITY